Early Intervention
The Essential Readings

Essential Readings in Developmental Psychology

Series Editors: Alan Slater and Darwin Muir

University of Exeter and Queen's University, Kingston, Ontario

In this series of nine books, Alan Slater and Darwin Muir, together with a team of expert editors, bring together selections of readings illustrating important methodological, empirical, and theoretical issues in the area of developmental psychology. Volumes in the series and their editors are detailed below:

Adolescent Development	*Gerald Adams*
Children and the Law	*Ray Bull*
The Nature–Nurture Debate	*Stephen J. Ceci and Wendy M. Williams*
Childhood Social Development	*Wendy Craig*
Teaching and Learning	*Charles Desforges and Richard Fox*
Early Intervention	*Maurice A. Feldman*
Childhood Cognitive Development	*Kang Lee*
Infant Development	*Darwin Muir and Alan Slater*
Language Development	*Michael Tomasello and Elizabeth Bates*

Each of the books is introduced by the volume editor with a rationale behind the chosen papers. Each reading is then introduced and contextualized within the individual subject debate as well as within the wider context of developmental psychology. A selection of further reading is also assigned, making each volume an ideal teaching resource for both classroom and individual study settings.

Early Intervention
The Essential Readings

Edited by Maurice A. Feldman

Blackwell
Publishing

Editorial material and organization © 2004 by Blackwell Publishing Ltd

350 Main Street, Malden, MA 02148-5020, USA
108 Cowley Road, Oxford OX4 1JF, UK
550 Swanston Street, Carlton, Victoria 3053, Australia

The right of Maurice A. Feldman to be identified as the Author of the Editorial Material in this Work has been asserted in accordance with the UK Copyright, Designs, and Patents Act 1988.

First published 2004 by Blackwell Publishing Ltd

Library of Congress Cataloging-in-Publication Data

Early intervention: the essential readings/edited by Maurice A. Feldman.
p. cm. – (Essential readings in developmental psychology)
Includes bibliographical references and index.
ISBN 1-4051-1169-0 (hc) – ISBN 1-4051-1168-2 (pbk.)
1. Child psychopathology–Prevention.   2. Developmental disabilities–Prevention.   I. Feldman, Maurice A. (Maurice Abraham), 1949–II. Series.
RJ499.E227 2003
618.92'8905—dc21
2003004193

A catalogue record for this title is available from the British Library.

Set in 10^1/$_2$/13pt Photina
by Graphicraft Limited, Hong Kong
Printed and bound in the United Kingdom
by MPG Books, Bodmin, Cornwall

For further information on
Blackwell Publishing, visit our website:
http://www.blackwellpublishing.com

Contents

Figures

Tables

Introduction: What Is Early Intervention?

Early intervention (EI) comprises a set of supports, services, and experiences to prevent or minimize long-term problems as early as possible (Dunst and Trivette, 1997; Guralnick, 1997). Conceptually, early intervention can be offered at any age before or in the early stages of disabling conditions and circumstances (e.g., Moniz-Cook, Agar, Gibson, Win, and Wang, 1998), but the term typically is reserved for infants and young children (Odom and Kaiser, 1997). Typically children receiving EI are at risk for developmental, emotional, social, behavioral, and school problems because of biological (e.g., low birth weight) and/or environmental (e.g., poverty) factors. Indeed, considerable research and services are focused on these children and this book will reflect this emphasis.

Starting in the 1960s, a growing body of child development research suggested that early experience has long-lasting impact on human development, and that intervening early may prevent or reverse developmental problems in at-risk children. This research, together with court decisions (e.g., *Brown* vs. *The Board of Education*, 1954), and the Civil Rights and Normalization movements, influenced the United States Congress to establish various laws, policies, and funding mechanisms to mandate or encourage states and communities to provide infant and preschool services for vulnerable children (Ramey and Ramey, 1998). The Individuals with Disabilities Education Act (IDEA) established birth to three and preschool early intervention services across the US to serve children with established developmental disabilities (e.g., Down syndrome, cerebral palsy) and other at-risk conditions (e.g., low birth weight; children of parents with intellectual disabilities). Head Start and other legislation (see chapter 2) targeted preschool children of poverty and provide an array of supports to the families, including early childhood special education, family support, child health and safety promotion, and parent education. Head Start has recently been expanded to reach infants and toddlers with environmental risk status (Ramey and Ramey, 1998). Other countries also have developed extensive early intervention systems, particularly for children with established disabilities.

Most EI programs can be conceptualized within a three-level prevention framework (Simeonsson, 1991): (1) primary prevention – intervene with the general (universal) or an at-risk (targeted) population to prevent the anticipated problem from ever arising – i.e., reducing incidence; (2) secondary prevention – intervene with a high-risk population to undo current early signs and prevent more serious problems – reducing prevalence; and (3) tertiary prevention (treatment) – intervene with an affected population and undo current serious problems and prevent re-occurrence or long-term sequelea – i.e., reducing recidivism. Some EI researchers advocate for a health promotion rather than a prevention model on the grounds that the absence of a problem does not necessarily imply positive individual and family functioning and quality of life (Dunst, Trivette, and Thompson, 1994). The two models are not incompatible, but the health promotion approach encourages interventions that focus on increasing capacities that yield measurable improvements in self-confidence and control, psychological and physical health, and competence (Dunst et al., 1994, p. 54).

EI approaches and orientations are numerous, and several popular ones are represented in this book. Some programs are based on the premise that the child needs an extraordinary learning environment not typically provided in the family home and offer at-risk or affected children enriched center-based or in-home early childhood educational experiences (usually with additional family support and other services – e.g., chapters 3 and 6). Other programs capitalize on the crucial role of the parents and home environment in shaping future child outcomes. These programs offer several types of family-focused interventions including case management, family support, respite, home visiting, and/or parent education (e.g., chapters 7 to 11). The trend is toward comprehensive "two-generation" programs that address the needs of the entire family (chapter 11; St Pierre, Layzer, and Barnes, 1995) and studies of the impact of EI on other family members are becoming more prevalent (chapter 11).

The book is organized into six sections, starting with an excellent overview by Gurnalick and ending with a chapter on future directions. In between are essential papers describing recent early intervention and prevention results of different EI methods (e.g., specialized preschool; home visiting) across various childhood problems. I will provide brief introductions to each section and chapter. This volume should be of interest to students, researchers, and practitioners in the variety of disciplines involved in EI, including psychology, social work, family medicine, pediatrics, nursing, and education.

This reader covers current theory, research, and practice in EI with young children. In choosing the selections, I opted for recent work that I believe represent the current state-of-the-art of EI. Although it was attempting to include some classic papers, the EI field has reached a stage of maturity that is reflected in papers that are included here. For many years EI researchers and practitioners promised that EI would pay off and would yield meaningful, long-term, beneficial effects to the children, their families, and society. Researchers patiently and persistently have followed their participants as they grew up and several recent key studies (included herein) with long-term follow-up and rigorous evaluation designs fulfill that promise. When one considers how difficult it is to do this kind of field research, over many years of follow-up, one can admire and respect the resourcefulness and perseverance of the many dedicated researchers in this field.

References

Dunst, C. J. & Trivette, C. M. (1997). Early intervention with young at-risk children and their families. In R. Ammerman & M. Hersen (Eds), *Handbook of prevention and treatment with children and adolescents: Intervention in the real world* (pp. 157–180). New York: Wiley.

Dunst, C. J., Trivette, C. M., & Thompson, R. B. (1994). Supporting and strengthening family functioning: Toward a congruence between principles and practice. In C. J. Dunst and C. M. Trivette (Eds), *Supporting & strengthening families, Vol. 1: Methods, strategies and practices* (pp. 49–59). Cambridge, MA: Brookline Books.

Guralnick, M. J. (1997). Second generation research in the field of early intervention. In M. J. Guralnick (Ed.), *The effectiveness of early intervention* (pp. 3–20). Baltimore, MD: Brookes.

Moniz-Cook, E., Agar, S., Gibson, G., Win, T., & Wang, M. (1998). A preliminary study of the effects of early intervention with people with dementia and their families in a memory clinic. *Aging and Mental Health, 2,* 199–211.

Odom, S. L. & Kaiser, A. P. (1997). Prevention and early intervention during early childhood: Theoretical and empirical bases for practice In W. E. MacLean, Jr (Ed.), *Ellis' handbook of mental deficiency, psychological theory and research* (3rd edn), (pp. 137–172). Mahwah, NJ: Lawrence Erlbaum Associates.

Ramey, C. T. & Ramey, S. L. (1998). Early intervention and early experience. *American Psychologist, 53,* 109–120.

Simeonsson, R. J. (1991). Primary, secondary, and tertiary prevention in early intervention. *Journal of Early Intervention, 15,* 124–134.

St Pierre, R., Layzer, J., & Barnes, H. (1995). Two-generation programs: Design, cost, and shared-term effectiveness. *The Future of Children, 5,* 76–93.

Part I

A Model of Early Intervention

Introduction to Chapter 1

Guralnick provides a comprehensive overview of EI practices and results, focusing on cognitive development in children with established disabilities, or at biological and/or environmental risk. He attempts to unify disparate approaches and findings through a developmental perspective. The interactional model that he proposes is consistent with those of other influential child and family researchers (e.g., Belsky, 1984; Bronfenbrenner, 1986, 1992; Ramey and Ramey, 1998; Sameroff and Chandler, 1975). This model proposes that a variety of risk and protective factors related to social, family, parent, child, and support characteristics affect parent and child outcomes (see page 9 for a description of some of the more common risk variables). The model emphasizes how many of these variables, some seemingly not directly related to child development (e.g., social support), may affect parenting that in turn mediates child outcomes. There is considerable empirical support for this model. For example, Sameroff and Chandler (1975) reported that low birth weight infants from middle-class, well-supported families did better than similar medically at-risk low birth weight children from less resourced, low-income families. Likewise, Dunst, Trivette, and Cross (1986) showed that family social support buffered the effects of stress of having a child with disabilities or illness and led to better child outcomes.

Guralnick demonstrates how the model can integrate current findings and practices and identify gaps in our knowledge. He also provides a review of research examining the short- and long-term impact of EI and he acknowledges the need for more well-controlled follow-up studies. Recent studies published after Guralnick's review (some of which are reprinted in this volume), are beginning to provide the needed evidence of long-term effects across a variety of important outcomes (chapters 3, 8, 9, 11).

As you read through the remaining chapters, you should try to relate the empirical studies and reviews to Guralnick's model. Consider: (1) how the early intervention program eliminated or compensated for risk factors (which ones and how many?); (2) to what extent did the program modify parenting practices, or provide stimulating experiences directly to the child independent of the parent; and (3) timing, duration, and intensity of the program.

References

Belsky, J. (1984). The determinants of parenting: A process model. *Child Development*, 55, 83–96.

Bronfenbrenner, U. (1986). Ecology of the family as a context for human development. *Developmental Psychology*, 22, 723–742.

Bronfenbrenner, U. (1992). Ecological systems theory. In R. Vasta, (Ed.), *Six theories of child development: revised formulations and current issues* (pp. 187–249). London: Jessica Kingsley.

Dunst, C. J., Trivette, C. M. & Cross, A. (1986). Mediating influences of social support: Personal, family and child outcomes. *American Journal of Mental Deficiency*. 90, 403–417.

Ramey, C. T. & Ramey, S. L. (1998). Early intervention and early experience *American Psychologist* 53, 109–120.

Sameroff, A. J. & Chandler, M. J. (1975). Reproductive risk and the continuum of caretaking causality. In F. D. Horowitz, M. Hetherington, S. Scarr-Salapatek, & G. Siegel, (Eds), *Review of child development research*. Vol. 4 (pp. 187–243). Chicago: University of Chicago Press.

ONE

Effectiveness of Early Intervention for Vulnerable Children: A Developmental Perspective

Michael J. Guralnick

In the past twenty-five years, the extraordinary vulnerability of young children at risk for developmental problems due to environmental and biological factors as well as of those children with established developmental disabilities has been recognized. Poverty, prematurity and low birth weight, parenting difficulties, abuse and neglect, prenatal exposure to illicit drugs or alcohol, continuing exposures to toxic substances during early childhood, and hazards found in hostile environments constitute well-known risk factors that can significantly compromise young children's health and development (Breslau et al., 1994; Guralnick, 1997b; Hack et al., 1994; Sameroff, Seifer, Barocas, Zax, and Greenspan, 1987). There exist as well substantial numbers of young children who manifest established developmental disabilities arising from an array of conditions, including genetic disorders and congenital infections (Lipkin, 1996). Prevalence estimates for children with established disabilities range widely in accordance with a child's chronological age and the ascertainment method (Yeargin-Allsopp, Murphy, Oakley, Sikes, and the Metropolitan Atlantic Developmental Disabilities Study Staff, 1992).

Guralnick, M. J. (1998). Effectiveness of early intervention for vulnerable children: A developmental perspective. *American Journal on Mental Retardation, 102,* 319–345. Copyright American Association on Mental Retardation.

Overall, in systematic surveys, investigators have found that approximately 800,000 children through age 5 years, a conservative estimate, manifest significant disabilities (2.2% of all children birth to 2 years of age and 5.2% of all 3- to 5-year-olds meet eligibility criteria to receive services under current federal legislation for early intervention [P.L. 99–457, 1986; now IDEA, 1997, see Bowe, 1995]).

The co-occurrence of multiple problems is now well-documented both for children at biological or environmental risk and for those with established disabilities. As discussed later, multiple risk factors, in particular, pose major challenges for the field of early intervention.

Poverty, for example, often implies the existence of numerous other risk factors that serve to compromise a child's development to an extraordinary extent (Halpern, 1993). Moreover, children referred to as "doubly vulnerable" (i.e., those at both biological and environmental risk) are not only increasing in number but are especially susceptible to significant developmental problems (Bradley et al., 1994; McGauhey, Starfield, Alexander, and Ensminger, 1991; Ross, Lipper, and Auld, 1990). The power of this combination of conditions is most evident in the difficulty in finding protective factors that can prevent adverse outcomes (Bradley et al., 1994; McGauhey et al., 1991).

Children with established developmental disabilities are also susceptible to multiple problems. Many disabilities co-occur, such that children with cognitive delays often must contend with motor impairments, language problems, sensory difficulties, or epilepsy (Boyle, Decouflé, and Yeargin-Allsopp, 1994). Moreover, these same young children with established disabilities are "doubly vulnerable" in another sense, as they increasingly find themselves experiencing stressors associated with poverty and related environmental risks. Bowe (1995) estimated that 35% of families with children birth to 5 years of age having significant disabilities fall below the Census Bureau's threshold for low income.

The strong advocacy movement on behalf of these vulnerable children (Turnbull and Turnbull, 1978), the emergence of developmentally and neurobiologically based theories and data suggesting the unusual potential of intervening during the first few years of life (e.g., Clarke-Stewart, 1988; Futterweit and Ruff, 1993), and a growing legislative agenda in support of children at risk and those with established disabilities (Florian, 1995; Hutchins, 1994; Ireys and Nelson, 1992; Richmond and Ayoub, 1993; Smith and McKenna, 1994; Zigler and Valentine, 1979), have resulted in the establishment of a complex array of early intervention programs, both preventive and ameliorative in nature, in virtually every major community in the United States (Guralnick, 1997b). Yet despite these accomplishments, a number of serious challenges to the viability of this system of early intervention programs has emerged in recent years. To some extent, these concerns are rooted in observations that the "system" of early intervention programs has evolved in a seemingly haphazard and fragmented manner. For children participating in formal developmental/educational programs, curricula and services differ radically, and it is difficult to find common theoretical ground even for children with similar risk or disability profiles (Bailey and Wolery, 1992; Bryant and Graham, 1993; Goodman and Pollak, 1993; Stayton and Karnes, 1994). The informal system of supports (e.g., respite care, parent groups, counseling) appears even more fragmented, as directories must be published and frequently reissued to guide families through the array of options, and coordination of services among health, education, and social services is always difficult (Benn, 1993). From this panoramic perspective, it is easy to understand how critics can argue that no truly coherent early intervention framework exists, thereby limiting prospects for meaningful benefits for children and families.

Equally damaging is the now intense professional debate surrounding claims of the effectiveness of early intervention. Fueled by the ascendance of more biologically oriented models of development, especially in relation to cognitive functioning (Herrnstein and Murray, 1994; Scarr, 1992), positions have been put forward suggesting that no long-term benefits of early intervention can be found; a conclusion that frequently finds receptive audiences at professional and political levels. Indeed, although I have argued later in this paper that this reading of the literature is not accurate either for children at risk or for those with established disabilities, sufficient data are nevertheless available to raise legitimate concerns regarding the long-term effectiveness of early intervention programs (Gibson and Harris, 1988; Spitz, 1986). Given the scrutiny with which all levels of government currently are examining the services they provide in this era of financial austerity, an analysis and framework that places this debate on the effectiveness of early intervention in perspective can have important conceptual, service, and public policy implications.

In this paper, I have attempted to demonstrate that a reliable and comprehensible pattern of early intervention effectiveness does exist and that this pattern is similar for children at risk and for those with established disabilities. Specifically, by placing early intervention services firmly within contemporary developmental theory, a rational basis for a seemingly haphazard array of services can be established, the mechanisms through which early intervention programs operate can be understood, and conflicting findings with respect to effectiveness, particularly in terms of long-term effectiveness, can be reconciled.

It is important to note that in this examination of the effectiveness of early intervention, I have focused exclusively on the domain of cognition. More specifically, the focus is on psychometrically defined intelligence (Neisser et al., 1996). Although other outcome domains are certainly critical for early intervention (Guralnick, 1990; Zigler and Trickett, 1978), standardized measures of cognitive development have been most widely applied across risk and disability samples, thereby increasing prospects for identifying consistent patterns of early intervention effectiveness. In addition, the primary studies evaluating effectiveness included in the analyses that follow were required to meet the following criteria: (a) were published since 1986 (i.e., post P.L. 99–457) or, if earlier, was part of a long-term evaluation of effectiveness; (b) investigator(s) employed a randomized, prospective, longitudinal design with appropriate control groups receiving traditional care (but not only contrasted with alternative interventions); (c) contained no significant methodological flaws; (d) investigator(s) intervened and/or followed children for at least a 3-year period; and (e) at minimum, investigator(s) evaluated the effects of early intervention during the first 5 years of life. Occasionally, to illustrate important points or because they presented a compelling pattern of outcomes, I included (a) studies not meeting all criteria (especially methodological issues) or (b) those in which meta-analyses were reported.

Short-term Effects of Early Intervention

Analyses of the course of intellectual development for children at risk and those with established disabilities in the absence of early intervention have revealed the existence of a ubiquitous pattern, namely, a general decline in children's intellectual development occurs across the first 5 years of life (see Guralnick, 1988). Declines for children at risk have ranged widely (from .50 to 1.5 standard deviations [SDs]) based on control group data from studies meeting criteria for inclusion in this review. For children with established disabilities, despite starting at a far lower level than children at risk, the order of magnitude of the decline is approximately .5 to .75 *SDs* (approximately 8 to 12 IQ points).

There now exists unequivocal evidence that the declines in intellectual development that occur in the absence of systematic early intervention can be substantially reduced by interventions implemented and evaluated *during the first 5 years of life*. For children with established disabilities, studies in which investigators employed prospective, longitudinal, randomized designs with appropriate control groups are, unfortunately, extremely rare (see Guralnick and Bricker, 1987). The widespread availability of services today only allows investigators to compare alternative intervention techniques. However, a meta-analysis of pre-P.L. 99–457 studies conducted by Shonkoff and Hauser-Cram (1987) focused on children birth to 3 years of age revealed that participation of children in early intervention programs yields an average effect size of .62 *SD* for measures of cognitive development. For children with Down syndrome, the etiological group receiving the most attention from researchers, there exists general agreement that immediate effects of similar magnitude in response to early intervention are obtained (Gibson and Harris, 1988; Guralnick and Bricker, 1987). Support for these short-term effects can be found as well in longitudinal studies of children with Down syndrome enrolled during the first year of life in comprehensive early intervention programs and continuing their participation for 3 to 5 years. Reports from Wales (Woods, Corney, and Pryce, 1984), Israel (Sharav and Shlomo, 1986), Australia (Berry, Gunn, and Andrews, 1984), and the United States (Schnell, 1984) reveal consistent findings indicating that, although control groups were not included, the decline in intellectual development that occurs after the first 12 to 18 months for children with Down syndrome can be prevented almost entirely. Of course, children with Down syndrome continue to exhibit mild to moderate developmental delays, but preventing the further decline in intellectual development that typically occurs during the first few years of life is an important accomplishment (effect sizes .5 to .75 *SD*).

Precisely the same short-term effects of early intervention are found for children at biological risk. For example, the decline in intellectual development was reduced substantially for premature, low-birthweight children who participated in 3 years of early intervention as part of the

Infant Health and Development Program (1990). An effect size of .83 was obtained for the heavier birthweight group (2001 g to 2500 g) and .41 for the lower birthweight group (< 2001 g). Two features of this study are notable. First, this large multisite randomized trial included samples that were highly heterogeneous with regard to family character-istics, although most families represented lower income groups. Second, the interventions were both comprehensive and intensive, containing center-based and home-visiting components as well as parent groups. Interestingly, a far less intensive intervention that occurred in the Ver-mont study (only 11 one-hour sessions, 7 just prior to hospital discharge followed by 4 home visits) for generally intact middle-class families in a rural setting yielded even more powerful short-term effects, evident when the children were both 3 and 4 years of age (Rauh, Achenbach, Nurcombe, Howell, and Teti, 1988). Why low intensity interventions are capable of producing such impressive effects remains an important question, which is addressed in a subsequent section of this paper.

Based on numerous studies for children at environmental risk, gen-eral agreement also exists that early intervention produces substantial short-term effects. Despite legitimate concerns regarding the quality of some of the experimental designs, these outcomes appear consistently for diverse types of interventions (Barnett, 1995; Bryant and Maxwell, 1997). Of importance, these advantages are observed in well-designed randomized trials as well. Specifically, in the Abecedarian Project (Ramey and Campbell, 1984) children at high environmental risk were enrolled in infancy, with experimental group subjects receiving early intervention services in an intervention-oriented daycare program for the first 5 years of life. Although declines in development were evident for both experimental and control groups, the rate of decline was con-siderably less for children receiving the intervention, with significant differences in intellectual development between the two groups appear-ing at 2 years of age. Of note, by age 4, approximately 18% of the control children received an IQ below 70, whereas this was the case for less than 3% of the children participating in the intervention. Although children of mothers with more limited resources, as reflected by maternal IQ below 70, benefitted most (Martin, Ramey, and Ramey, 1990), the overall effect size for children at 4 years of age was .82 SD. A replication of this intensive intervention that included a systematic parent com-ponent produced similar results (Wasik, Ramey, Bryant, and Sparling, 1990).

Summary

Taken together, contemporary comprehensive early intervention programs for children at risk and for those with established disabilities reveal a consistent pattern of effectiveness as these programs are able to reduce the decline in intellectual development that occurs in the absence of intervention. The magnitude of these effects is of potential developmental significance, with effect sizes averaging .50 to .75 SDs, depending on the group's risk or disability status. The outcomes described to this point are short-term, however, evident only during the course of the program, soon after the program has ended, or later on, but still during the first 5 years of life.

That declines in cognitive development are evident for control group children receiving traditional community care, particularly for more contemporary post-P.L. 99–457 samples, is somewhat surprising. A reasonable expectation is that control group families would be able to take advantage of existing early intervention service systems themselves. After all, in most of the studies noted above, traditional care provided to control group families included referrals to appropriate community services. Apparently, in view of the fact that declines still occur, such early intervention services may be difficult to access and coordinate, and families may well require considerable guidance to take full advantage of the complex system of services and supports that are available (see Palfrey, Singer, Walker, and Butler, 1987). This may be especially true of families living under poverty conditions (e.g., Bradley et al., 1994; Burchinal, Roberts, Nabors, and Bryant, 1996; Ramey and Campbell, 1984; Resnick, Eyler, Nelson, Eitzman, and Bucciarelli, 1987; Wasik et al., 1990). However, when families in control groups are able to access some components available in the early intervention system, such as quality daycare, the relative effectiveness of early intervention compared to the experimental group is attenuated (Neser, Molteno, and Knight, 1989; Wasik et al., 1990).

Understanding why early intervention is able to produce these short-term effects constitutes a question of vital importance to the entire early intervention enterprise. A thorough knowledge of the "mechanisms" through which delays in cognitive development occur initially and how early intervention programs can prevent or mitigate those delays provides guidance for innovative interventions, establishes a basis for understanding how control groups might benefit from access to contemporary community-based early intervention systems, and may even provide a framework for designing early intervention services that maximize long-term benefits. In the analysis presented next, these mechanisms are placed firmly within a developmental framework.

A Developmental Framework for Early Intervention

Experiential factors governing the course of child developmental outcomes, including a young child's cognitive development, can be divided into three sets of family patterns of interaction: (a) the quality of parent-child transactions, (b) family-orchestrated child experiences, and (c) health and safety provided by the family (Guralnick, 1997b) (see figure 1.1). Constructs derived from these three proximal patterns of interaction have well-established correlates with child developmental outcomes and well-developed measurement systems. For parent–child transactions, the dimensions and characteristics of family interaction patterns that appear to support optimal development include responding contingently, establishing reciprocity, providing affectively warm and nonintrusive interactions, appropriately structuring and scaffolding the environment, being discourse-based, and ensuring developmentally sensitive patterns of caregiver–child interactions (e.g., Baumrind, 1993; Clarke-Stewart, 1988; Dumas and LaFreniere, 1993; Hart and Risley, 1995; Lewis and Goldberg, 1969; Pratt, Kerig, Cowan, and Cowan, 1988; Wachs, 1992; Wachs and Gruen, 1982).

The second family pattern of interaction governing child developmental outcomes consists of children's experiences with the social and physical environment that are orchestrated by family members, primarily parents. Major dimensions include the variety and developmental appropriateness of toys and materials provided, the general stimulation value of the environment, and the frequency and nature of contacts with other adults and children that occur through parent-based friendship and family networks or alternative care arrangements. Many, though not all, of these dimensions of family-orchestrated child experiences are strongly correlated with child outcomes. Some of the dimensions captured in the HOME Inventory (Elardo, Bradley, and Caldwell, 1977) are most well-known, and sets of measures related to parental arranging of child experiences are now available (e.g., Ladd, Profilet, and Hart, 1992). Moreover, especially as children approach the preschool

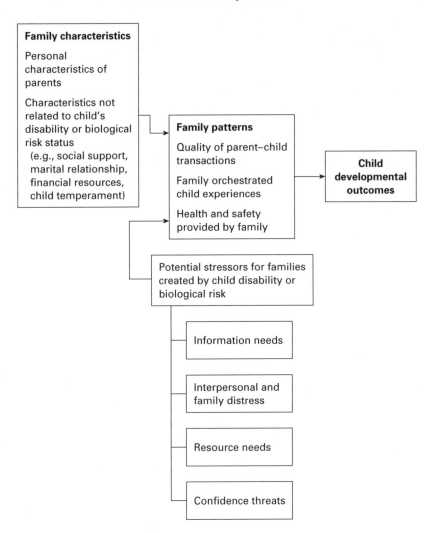

Figure 1.1 Factors influencing developmental outcomes for children. Figure taken from "Second-generation research in the field of early intervention" (p. 7) by M. J. Guralnick. In M. J. Guralnick (Ed.), *The Effectiveness of Early Intervention, 1997*, Baltimore: Brookes. Copyright 1997 by Brookes. Reprinted with permission

years, arranging for special developmental, educational, or recreational activities in response to their child's interests, talents, or even special needs becomes increasingly important in maximizing child development outcomes. Particularly for children with special needs, parents may elect to enroll their child in a developmentally oriented center-based program or in a highly specialized, therapeutic intervention. As discussed later, under certain conditions, various features of center-based interventions appear to make important independent contributions to child development. Finally, parents are directly responsible for ensuring the general health of and establishing a safe environment for their child (e.g., obtaining immunizations, providing adequate nutrition, protecting child from violence). Many of these dimensions operate in complex ways to alter child developmental outcomes, such as nutrition (Gorman, 1995). Others, such as protection from violence or witnessing violence, are not easily altered but are nevertheless likely to have a considerable impact on child developmental outcomes (Osofsky, 1995; Taylor, Zuckerman, Harik, and Groves, 1994).

These three general proximal patterns of family interaction that jointly or independently substantially influence child developmental outcomes are themselves products of an array of *family characteristics*, including parental attitudes and beliefs, maternal mental health status, coping styles, and existing supports and resources. As is generally the case, when these family characteristics are within normative levels, child development proceeds in an expected manner (see figure 1.1). From an alternative perspective, available evidence indicates that adverse family characteristics can stress or perturb the three patterns of family interaction that lead to optimal child developmental outcomes. Examples of such characteristics are maternal mental illness, particularly depression (Cicchetti and Toth, 1995), limited intellectual abilities of parents (Feldman, Case, Towns, and Betel, 1985), and inappropriate intergenerational and culturally transmitted beliefs and attitudes with respect to child-rearing (Crowell and Feldman, 1988; S. Miller, 1988; Murphey, 1992).

Similarly, other characteristics of the family (also not related to a child's disability or biological risk status) can also jeopardize the family's ability to establish optimal interaction patterns. These include the absence of adequate social supports (Cochran and Brassard, 1979; Melson, Ladd, and Hsu, 1993), stressful marital relationships (Emery and Kitzmann, 1995), and limited financial resources (Duncan, Brooks-

Gunn, and Klebanov, 1994; McLoyd, 1990). Moreover, individual child characteristics, such as a difficult temperament can, under certain circumstances, create nonoptimal family interaction patterns, particularly parent–child transactions (Lee and Bates, 1985; Sameroff, 1993).

Family environmental risk and stressors

The extent to which these (more distal) family characteristics are inconsistent with (more proximal) optimal family patterns of interacting can be said to constitute an important cluster of environmental risk factors in relation to children's development. Whether a child is considered to be "at risk" due to apparently adverse family characteristics depends on the definition of risk selected and the purpose for identifying risk status. Multiple risk indices can be extremely valuable, as it appears that it is the compounding of risk factors that governs the impact on children's cognitive development (Sameroff et al., 1987). Of course, chronic poverty alone may be sufficient to justify a child as being at risk, as this circumstance creates significant levels of stress, often adversely affecting other family characteristics that influence family patterns of interaction (Duncan et al., 1994; Huston, McLoyd, and Garcia Coll, 1994; Parker, Greer, and Zuckerman, 1988). Nevertheless, poverty does not have an overriding effect (Sameroff et al., 1987), suggesting that specific adverse family characteristics aggregate to create *stressors* sufficient to alter family interaction patterns and, ultimately, child developmental outcomes. Proximal family interaction measures, such as the quality of parent–child transactions, are often included in indices of environmental risk as well as measures related to the more distal family characteristic measures (e.g., Sameroff et al., 1987). As conceptualized here, environmental risk can be thought of as consisting of two separate components: (a) dimensions related to family characteristics and (b) family patterns of interaction. This second cluster of risk factors is considered causal in the model illustrated in figure 1.1 (see also Yoshikawa, 1994) but in reality can only constitute statements of elevated probabilities for adverse child development. Although the association between those proximal risk factors (family interaction patterns) and child development is well established, the connection is far from certain due to imperfect or incomplete measures or constructs, poorly understood interactions or unidentified risk factors, and protective factors within the individual child (Werner, 1995). Finally, the model in figure 1.1 reflects only unidirectional relationships and is, therefore, an oversimplification of the processes involved. However, the model does capture the important experiential dimensions affecting child development and serves as a useful device for explanatory purposes.

Child disability, biological risk, and stressors

Children born at biological risk or those with established disabilities create potential *additional* stressors with which families must contend. The lower portion of figure 1.1 identifies four categories of potential stressors: (a) information needs, (b) interpersonal and family distress, (c) resource needs, and (d) confidence threats. As suggested by the figure, similar to circumstances of high family or environmental risk, I argue here that these stressors exert their influence on child developmental outcomes by interfering with one or more of the three critical family interaction patterns.

First, families face a "crisis of information" with respect to their child's current and anticipated health and development. For example, for families of premature low-birthweight children, the newborn period in particular evokes numerous questions about highly technical medical procedures and the impact of those procedures on their child's health and well-being (Meyer et al., 1995). For children at biological risk and those with established disabilities, numerous issues continue to emerge over time, as families struggle with building a relationship and understanding their child's developmental and behavioral patterns and needs. As a consequence, discussions with professionals with respect to sleep–wake cycles, unusual lags in specific developmental domains, problems in establishing affective bonds or joint attention, and difficulties recognizing and interpreting their child's cues are frequently among the issues addressed that are vital in helping families gain information needed to support them in their parenting role (Donahue and Pearl, 1995; Guralnick and Bricker, 1987; Shonkoff, Hauser-Cram, Krauss, and Upshur, 1992). Correspondingly, information needs regarding the implications of a specific diagnosis with respect to their child's developmental or behavioral expectations persist across the early childhood years, often precipitated anew by transition points (hospital to home,

home care to day care, entry into an early intervention program, preschool to kindergarten). Finally, for many families, numerous questions arise as to the nature and effectiveness of therapeutic services and how to gain access to the most expert clinicians and programs available (see Sontag and Schacht, 1994).

The importance and stressful nature of these information needs and their impact on family interaction patterns should not be underestimated. For example, combined with other types of stressors (e.g., family distress), families of children with established disabilities often find it difficult to form those parent–child transactions that promote secure attachments. Indeed, the absence of secure attachments (with corresponding difficulties in maternal sensitivity) has been observed for an unusually large proportion of children with Down syndrome (Vaughn et al., 1994; see also Atkinson et al., 1995).

Considerable interpersonal and family distress also is often a consequence of a child's biological risk or established disability. This intensely emotional and personal experience can take its toll on parental well-being and marital harmony, often involving stressful reassessments of the parents' own lives and expectations for their child and the family as a whole (Beckman and Pokorni, 1988; Hodapp, Dykens, Evans, and Merighi, 1992; Margalit, Raviv, and Ankonina, 1992; E. Miller, Gordon, Daniele, and Diller, 1992; Waisbren, 1980). Of importance is the fact that this distress does not appear to be time-limited. Following an initial process of adaptation, the family faces additional distress that recurs at various developmental stages and transition points (Wikler, 1986). To be sure, many families adapt well to children with disabilities in their family (e.g., Trute and Hauch, 1988), but recent evidence continues to suggest that it is not uncommon for parents to experience long-term difficulties even in resolving issues surrounding the diagnosis of a disability, a stressful circumstance that can affect important caregiving processes (Pianta, Marvin, Britner, and Borowitz, 1996). Moreover, families can easily fall prey to the forces of social isolation (Bailey and Winton, 1989; Lewis, Feiring, and Brooks-Gunn, 1987) or stigmatization (Goffman, 1963). In fact, distress can arise simply from the process of confronting and coping with problems related to their child's biological risk or disability status (Affleck and Tennen, 1993; Atkinson et al., 1995; Behr and Murphy, 1993).

For the third category of potential stressors (i.e., resource needs), children with a disability and those at significant biological risk typically create considerable stress on the usual routines of families and their ability to provide the type of caregiving that is necessary (Beckman, 1983; Bristol, 1987; Dyson, 1993). Moreover, the burden of locating and even coordinating services for the child often falls on families, creating additional demands on their time and additional needs for resources (Rubin and Quinn-Curran, 1985). In fact, financial responsibilities for their child's health care, respite care, and therapeutic services can mount rapidly, particularly for children with severe disabilities or those at high biological risk (Birenbaum, Guyot, and Cohen, 1990).

Finally, these and related stressors conspire to undermine parental confidence in their ability to solve current and future child-related problems. The long-term well-being of the child and family is associated with the family's ability to maintain a sense of mastery and control over decision-making and to do so with reasonable competence and confidence (see Affleck and Tennen, 1993).

Interactions among family characteristics, family patterns of interaction, and stressors

The developmental approach presented in this paper is based on concepts and constructs derived from a number of related approaches that have been focused on diverse populations, including children at risk, children with established disabilities, as well as children and families not experiencing any unusual risks or stressors. As a consequence, the claim that this developmental framework is applicable to children and families with such a wide range of characteristics should not be surprising. Related approaches include Belsky's parenting model (Belsky, 1984; Belsky, Robins, and Gamble, 1984), Sameroff's transactional model (Sameroff, 1993; Sameroff and Chandler, 1975), Ramey's biosocial model (Ramey et al., 1992), Dunst's social support model (Dunst, 1985), and Bronfenbrenner's (1979) ecological model.

Central to most of these models, and the approach adopted here, is that numerous factors can interact to either mitigate or exacerbate stressors associated with risk or disability. Indeed, disastrous effects can result for children who are "doubly vulnerable," that is, those at both biological and environmental risk (e.g., Bradley et al., 1994). Figure 1.1 reflects the possible potentiating effects of these risk factors on family interaction patterns and subsequent child developmental outcomes.

From a more positive perspective, family characteristics that represent low environmental risk may well be able to mitigate many of the potential stressors associated with a child at biological risk or with an established disability. Evidence that such mitigated patterns operate for children at risk and those with established disabilities is widely available (e.g., Bradley, Rock, Whiteside, Caldwell, and Brisby, 1991; Crnic, Greenberg, Ragozin, Robinson, and Basham, 1983; Dunst, Trivette, and Cross, 1986). Moreover, as Belsky (1984) pointed out, the array of family characteristics is a buffered system itself, such that a high level of social support, for example, can mitigate the effects of a difficult marital relationship and, therefore, protect against Significant interference with appropriate family patterns of interaction. Accordingly, this issue of the actual impact (stress) of a child's biological risk or disability on family patterns of interaction in the context of the larger ecology of family characteristics is likely to be of considerable significance in the design of a cost-effective and efficient early intervention system and is considered in a subsequent section of this paper.

The Early Intervention System

The argument put forward here is that the stressors created by risk and disability conditions operate through family interaction patterns to produce the declines in intellectual development noted earlier. I have argued further that early intervention programs are capable of altering either those nonoptimal family interaction patterns directly or by moderating the impact of stressors that influence those patterns (i.e., family characteristics). If this analysis is correct, at least for short-term outcomes, in order for early intervention programs to produce the effect sizes noted earlier (.5 to .75 *SD*), the components of the system must be designed in a manner that is responsive to the stressors that have been identified. As presented in figure 1.2, I suggest that this is precisely how the contemporary early intervention system is organized. Analyses of early intervention program components found in increasingly larger numbers of communities (and representing, to varying degrees, the service features of the research projects noted earlier) indicate that this system is comprised of three major features: (a) resource supports, (b) social supports, and (c) the provision of information and services. These early intervention system components

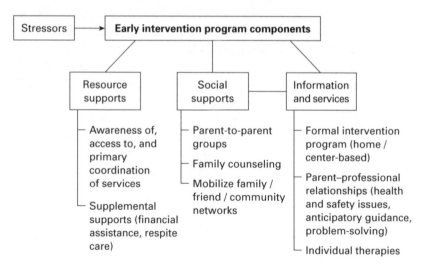

Figure 1.2 Components of early intervention programs as a response to stressors. Figure taken from "Second-generation research in the field of early intervention" (p. 9) by M. J. Guralnick. In M. J. Guralnick (Ed.), *The Effectiveness of Early Intervention, 1997*, Baltimore: Brookes. Copyright 1997 by Brookes. Reprinted with permission

are discussed next, first for children at biological risk and those with established disabilities and then for children at risk due to environmental factors.

Biological risk and established disability

Figure 1.2 summarizes the major components of early intervention programs as they are currently constituted. Organized into the major areas of resource supports, social supports, and information and services, these components appear to be closely attuned to the potential stressors facing families (see bottom portion of figure 1.1). Resource supports are perhaps most fundamental of all. Becoming aware of, accessing, and coordinating appropriate educational, health, and social services can be a formidable challenge for even the most adept of families. As a consequence, a service coordinator is often essential to assist eligible families. Fortunately, P.L. 99–457 mandates service coordination.

The provision of social supports for families has a long history, with leadership provided by numerous parent organizations (Santelli, Turnbull, Marquis, and Lerner, 1995). These remarkable support groups are a unique source of information and can be of enormous value in alleviating any interpersonal or family distress that may have arisen. These same groups are able to assist families to involve friends, extended family, and other community-based natural supports to establish a network that minimizes stressors (Cooley, 1994; Shonkoff, 1985). Attention to the cognitive coping styles of parents is important as well because these styles are associated with affective distress and the quality of parent–child transactions (Atkinson et al., 1995). If interpersonal and family distress become excessive, intensive family counseling must be considered.

Unquestionably, the most prominent and most expensive features of the early intervention system are the formal community-based intervention programs found in the third component of figure 1.2, the provision of information and services. Offered in the form of some combination of home- or center-based services, these programs tend to be comprehensive yet individualized to specific child and family needs. In this context, parents may be provided with techniques to facilitate parent–child interactions or with a framework to constructively interpret their child's behavior and development, and children may receive specific developmental or therapeutic interventions. To support this effort, interventionists have developed numerous formal curricula for both children at biological risk and those with established disabilities. Despite the diversity represented in these curricula (Bailey, 1997; Bruder, 1997), the structure and direction they provide appear to be important reasons for their effectiveness (Shonkoff and Hauser-Cram, 1987). It is also important to point out that, for the most part, these formal programs often constitute only a small portion of the overall early intervention system. On average, infants and toddlers with disabilities spend only 7 hours per month participating in formal, community-based early intervention programs (Shonkoff et al., 1992). The variability in the intensity of service provision is actually quite extensive, and in many research-based early intervention programs, the need for more direct child-focused services is emphasized (e.g., Infant Health and Development Program, 1990; Lovaas, 1987). As discussed shortly, although the number of service hours increases as the child reaches preschool age, the intensity of service provision remains one of the most critical issues in understanding early intervention effectiveness, particularly in connection with long-term outcomes.

A substantial proportion of families also seek advice and services outside of the formal early intervention program from primary care physicians, social service providers, occupational and physical therapists, and speech-language pathologists, among others (Shonkoff et al., 1992). The formation of relationships with knowledgeable professionals provides yet another vital and supportive component of the early intervention system. These parent–professional "partnerships" provide a context for discussion around expected developmental outcomes and the child's health and safety, provide anticipatory guidance, and establish a basis for independent assessments of the child's progress in relation to educational and therapeutic interventions.

Enrolling the child in formal early intervention programs and establishing relationships with other professionals are clearly *family-orchestrated activities* that are responsive to the child's special needs. As such, for children at risk and those with established disabilities, these activities constitute an important family pattern of interacting that can influence child developmental outcomes. It is the case that the family retains control over this entire process: gathering information, evaluating it, and making decisions as to the extent of their own or of their child's involvement in early intervention programs. Although parents may elect to relinquish that control to professionals at various times, the formation of collaborative parent–professional relationships appears to be an essential element of success. By centering assessment and interventions around family needs, professionals create a framework for expressing their views and successfully negotiating differences in perspectives and values (Bailey, 1987; Duwa, Wells, and Lalinde, 1993). In fact, unless early intervention services are attuned to the needs of families, they can be counterproductive (Affleck, Tennen, Rowe, Roscher, and Walker, 1989).

Finally, if the components of these early intervention systems are thoughtfully coordinated and integrated, the cumulative impact may well minimize any threats to the family's confidence in their ability to address the ongoing needs of their child. Parent–professional partnerships are particularly relevant in this regard. As Cooley (1994) has pointed out, "Professionals who foster cooperative partnerships with families are informally enhancing a family's self-confidence and feelings of mastery and control" (p. 18).

Summary

These major early intervention systems components (resource supports, social supports, provision of information and services) exist in increasingly larger numbers of communities and, if properly accessed, sequenced, and coordinated, appear capable of mitigating many of the stressors associated with a child's biological risk and disability status. In turn, reductions in the decline of intellectual development result to the degree described.

As presented in the model in figure1.1, these effects are mediated through a variety of interventions that appear to positively alter the three critical family interaction patterns identified (i.e., quality of parent–child transactions, family-orchestrated child experiences, and health and safety provided by family). The pattern of parent–child transactions in particular appears to be enhanced as a consequence of participation in the early intervention system (Guralnick, 1989; Mahoney and Powell, 1988; Resnick, Armstrong, and Carter, 1988; Seifer, Clark, and Sameroff, 1991; Spiker, Ferguson, and Brooks-Gunn, 1993). The variety of other supports and services that are provided continue to minimize stressors that can interfere with optimal family interaction patterns. Of note are the many recent reports suggesting that parents of children with disabilities experience more stress due to expected and inevitable child-related issues, but that for many families this stress does not appear to contribute to additional parent-related stress or to problems related to family functioning (Dyson, 1993; Gowen, Johnson-Martin, Goldman, and Appelbaum, 1989; Innocenti, Huh, and Boyce, 1992). This state-of-affairs may well be attributed to the supports and services available to families through the early intervention system.

Family or environmental risk

The stressors facing families at high environmental risk, in particular their magnitude, chronicity, and pervasiveness, pose special challenges for the early intervention system. The countless interpersonal problems found in many high-risk families, often compounded by drug or alcohol abuse, the transmission of intergenerational but nonptimal parenting patterns, and the day-to-day encounters in an often hostile environment, create circumstances in which family patterns of interaction are highly resistant to change. In general, the adverse conditions associated with poverty and high-risk status are difficult to counter and present a sobering assessment of the potential influence of preventive intervention programs for children at high risk due to environmental factors (Sameroff et al., 1987).

Despite these barriers, the program components illustrated in figure 1.2 appear to adequately characterize the early intervention system for children at environmental risk as well. To be sure, the specifics of these programs differ substantially from those of children at biological risk or those with established disabilities because the source of the stressors can be found primarily in family characteristics. Nevertheless, the early intervention system components of resource supports, social supports, and information and services apply. It is especially evident in these circumstances that successful programs must be comprehensive, seeking to address as many of the stressors (risk factors) as possible that can interfere with appropriate family interaction patterns (e.g., arrange support groups, provide mental health counseling, make emergency financial aid available, develop home programs, provide day care or preschool programs, ensure access to available social services). As noted previously, early interventions address both family characteristics and family interaction patterns. Yet, when accounting for the positive short-term effects of early intervention for children at high environmental risk, it appears that it is the family-orchestrated pattern of enrolling their child in intervention-oriented or quality day care that may be most significant (see Burchinal, Lee, and Ramey 1989; Wasik et al., 1990). Home-visiting programs do not alone seem to be effective (Scarr and McCartney, 1988; Wasik et al., 1990) because numerous other family interaction patterns are left unaltered. Far more intensive home visiting may be needed to yield short-term effects (Powell and Grantham-McGregor, 1989), but meaningfully influencing parent–child transactions for high environmental-risk groups within the context of early intervention programs remains a challenging problem. Enrollment in quality day care may be the key for these high-risk families, perhaps because of some combination of the unusual intensity of the intervention associated with day care and the highly specific child focus in the intervention-oriented day care program that may help compensate for other family characteristics and family interaction patterns that are difficult to alter. Whether lasting effects for children can be achieved in the absence of meaningful changes in family characteristics or many family interaction patterns remains to be determined.

Long-term Effectiveness of Early Intervention

Twenty-five years ago, families of vulnerable children confronted what was clearly a fractionated, uncoordinated set of services, often filled with low expectations for children and no meaningful system of social supports for families. Encouraged by many forces and culminating in the passage of P.L. 99–457 (1986), what is now in place in numerous communities is a system characterized by reasonable levels of coordination; knowledgeable professionals; and, in more and more communities, the existence of sophisticated, formal intervention programs. To be sure, most community programs do not represent the quality found in the research-based service programs that have been considered in this paper. Nevertheless, although far from ideal, sufficient resources and supports appear to be available to enable families who enter the early intervention system to benefit, at least in the short-term.

However, it has always been the expectation that the early intervention system would produce long-term effects, well worth the extensive resources put into place during the early years. The notions of attachment, sensitive periods, neural plasticity, and primacy of first learning have all been appealed to as the basis for this extraordinary investment (Anastasiow, 1990; Guralnick and Bennett, 1987; Rutter, 1980). Yet, critics of early intervention have argued that little evidence can be found for any long-term impact. By way of example, for children at environmental risk, it has long been acknowledged that any gains in cognitive development diminish quickly over time, often to the point that control and intervention groups are indistinguishable after a few years following the end of the program (Barnett, 1995). Modest (non-cognitive) long-term benefits for children participating in early intervention programs have been cited, such as less grade retention, fewer special education placements, and better school attendance (but see Locurto, 1991). Recent analyses have also strongly suggested that juvenile delinquency rates can be reduced through participation in comprehensive early intervention programs (Yoshikawa, 1994). Nevertheless, the absence of continued effects for cognitive development is of considerable concern.

Similar analyses of the long-term effects of early intervention for children with Down syndrome have not identified any advantages for children participating in early intervention programs (Gibson and Harris,

1988). Even for children with cerebral palsy who participated in a comprehensive early intervention program, once the program ended, gains in cognitive development disappeared within a few months (Palmer et al., 1988). Children at biological risk reveal a similar pattern. Despite the highly intensive 3-year intervention as part of the Infant Health and Development Program (1990), cognitive benefits for the entire sample did not last even 2 years after the program ended (Brooks-Gunn et al., 1994; McCarton et al., 1997).

   Despite the visibility accorded the failures to find long-term cognitive benefits of early intervention for the three primary groups of vulnerable children, as noted in the following discussion a broader perspective reveals that the negative findings are not nearly as consistent or pessimistic. What is needed is a framework that will guide our understanding of and establish reasonable expectations for both short- and long-term outcomes (Zigler and Styfco, 1994). In the following sections, I have attempted to demonstrate that the developmental model presented earlier can provide such a framework. To do so, however, requires understanding the relevance of the constructs of *intensity* and *specificity* in relation to early intervention.

Intensity of early intervention

By examining those studies (meeting criteria noted earlier) that have been able to produce long-term gains attributable to early intervention, it may be possible to identify critical elements and consider their fit within the developmental framework. Specifically, for children with established disabilities, data from an early intervention program conducted by Lovaas and his colleagues (Lovaas, 1987; McEachin, Smith, and Lovaas, 1993) for children with autism reveal substantial advantages in cognitive development for the intervention group, an advantage that has been maintained for participants at mean ages of 7 and 13 years. This early intervention program was unusual in terms of both the subject population (children with autism) and the intensity of the intervention. Children in the experimental (intervention) group received a minimum of 40 hours of intervention services per week in contrast to a maximum of 10 hours per week for the control group for at least 2 years. Because parents were trained to participated in the interventions, the actual intervention time extended to virtually all of the child's waking hours. Moreover, the intervention staff continued to work with children and families through kindergarten and for some, even first grade. For children progressing well, intervention was reduced to 10 hours per week during kindergarten, with only a minimal consultant relationship maintained for some families after the child began first grade. However, for those children not progressing well, the intensive intervention continued well into the elementary years. Nevertheless, the average time interval between the end of intervention and follow-up testing was 5 years in the intervention group, providing evidence for long-term impact.

Assuming the replicability of this study, including agreement on the diagnostic characteristics of the sample (Rutter, 1996), there are likely numerous reasons for its effectiveness. The intensity of the information and services, often provided on a one-to-one basis, and the related factor of the comprehensiveness of the program, which involved the child, family, and community, can be cited. Moreover, this level of intensity, provided over a relatively short-term period (2 years), was apparently sufficient to produce not only substantial increases in children's cognitive development but also likely established an entirely different set of future expectations (and confidence) for family, school, and community.

In fact, the importance of intensity in producing even short-term effects (while intervention is in place or shortly thereafter) was revealed in a re-analysis of the Infant Health and Development Program (1990) data for low birthweight, premature children (Ramey et al., 1992). An intensity measure was created by combining the actual participation of families and children in the various components of the intervention. Analyses revealed the existence of a rather dramatic association between level of participation (intensity) in the intervention and children's cognitive development. More specifically, for children who participated in the early intervention program to only a *limited extent*, approximately 20% had IQs of 85 or below, with the vast majority of children in this limited participation group (15%) obtaining scores below 70. In contrast, for those participating *extensively* in the intervention, only 8% of the children received IQs less than 85 and only 3%, less than 70. These outcomes were independent of the initial status and characteristics of children and families (e.g., birthweight, neonatal health, maternal education). Longer-term follow-up of these "Intensity" groups may prove to be instructive.

In addition to intensity based simply on interventions provided per unit of time (density), the Lovaas (1987) intervention for children with autism also was intensive due to its duration. Although beginning when children were approximately 3 years old, the intervention continued at various levels of involvement until children were well into kindergarten and first grade. Duration may indeed be a critical feature of early intervention for the following reasons. First, it simply increases total participation time, a factor associated with producing more substantial initial positive effects on cognitive development. Second, by its very nature, duration is associated with comprehensiveness; that is, more and different intervention components tend to be part of the early intervention program. Third, and perhaps most important, is the fact that for many families stressors continue to interfere with family interaction patterns over time and interventions extended in some form remain necessary.

Duration and stressors

Examining the last issue more closely, if stressors do continue to exert an adverse influence on families over time, then the effects of these stressors will be noticed as a decline in children's cognitive development that appears some time after the end of intervention. As noted, this is what generally happens. Stressors related to high (environmental) family risk are often characterized by chronic difficulties and by an unpredictability and instability that can easily create substantial stress over time. Similarly, for children with established disabilities or those at biological risk, stressors can arise as a consequence of unexpected problems (e.g., unanticipated atypical developmental patterns, the emergence of behavioral difficulties, lack of responsiveness to intervention). By providing early intervention across a more extended period, families have an opportunity to encounter a greater variety of problems and transition points and to rely on essential supports and services to assist in their resolution. This circumstance may not only minimize disturbances in family interaction patterns (see figure 1.1) but may also instill the level of family confidence and competence essential for accommodating to the inevitable stressors that lay ahead.

This analysis suggests that intensity defined as the level of intervention occurring within a specified time interval (*density*), intensity defined as occurring across a longer period of time (*duration*), and possibly intensity defined as containing more early intervention components (*comprehensiveness*) may well be essential for long-term effectiveness. Although it is difficult to separate out each of these three aspects of intensity, the importance of the intensity construct is perhaps most evident in studies of children at high risk due to environmental factors. Specifically, the recent follow-up of children who participated in the Abecedarian Project revealed that even by 12 years of age, children who participated in the intervention continued to outperform the control group on standardized tests of cognitive development (Campbell and Ramey, 1994). To be sure, some decline in intellectual development over the years occurred for the intervention group, but important long-term effects were nevertheless evident. Of considerable significance is the fact that the duration of the comprehensive intervention was 5 years (infancy through age 5). As noted earlier, less intensive interventions containing primarily parent–child interaction components do not appear to be effective for high environmental risk families, even in the short-term (Scarr and McCartney, 1988; Wasik et al., 1990). It is possible that the long-term success of the Abecedarian Project may be accounted for in part by children's higher initial cognitive development when entering school and the correspondingly increased positive effects on families (see Benasich, Brooks-Gunn, and Clewell, 1992).

Similarly, focusing on reading achievement, Reynolds (1994) reported that for children living in poverty, long-term positive effects can result if the intervention program extends from the early transition periods to third grade. In this natural group design, important school achievement gains were apparent 2 years following the end of a 5-year comprehensive intervention program beginning in preschool (one year preschool, one year kindergarten, 3 years primary grades). A briefer program during the early years was not nearly as effective (preschool plus kindergarten), but the absence of a pre-school component reduced the long-term benefits (even when equating for duration). Accordingly, for the group of children growing up under poverty conditions, both the duration and timing of the program appears to matter. Effectiveness may be improved when more transition points are influenced by the intervention. Whether the effects would be the same if the 5-year program was initiated from birth to 5, as in the Abecedarian Project, is not known. However, evidence from that project suggests that although duration is important, beginning intervention at some point during the first 5 years of life is also vital. Beginning intervention later (i.e., kindergarten through second grade) creates no long-term advantage in comparison to children receiving no intervention whatsoever (Campbell and Ramey, 1994). Clearly, attention must be given to both the timing and intensity of interventions to achieve positive long-term outcomes.

It is important to note that timing may be an especially critical issue for low-birthweight children. Als and her colleagues (Als et al., 1994; Buehler, Als, Duffy, McAnulty, and Liederman, 1995) have argued from a developmental neurobiological perspective and provided strong empirical evidence indicating that the provision of family-centered developmental care for children in neonatal intensive care units (NICU) is critical for optimizing children's long-term neurodevelopmental outcome and functioning. For low-birthweight children, perhaps a combination of NICU-based interventions and participation in subsequent intensive early intervention programs will prove to be most effective, especially for families at high environmental risk or for the very low-birthweight preterm infant. This issue of the linkage between intensity and specific characteristics of children and families is discussed next.

Specificity

Despite the importance of the intensity of early intervention as a factor producing long-term positive outcomes, the developmental framework presented earlier would not predict that intensive services would be needed under all risk and disability circumstances. In fact, the interactive nature of the model suggests that the effects of any one stressor or combination of stressors are likely to be moderated by the array of extant stressors associated with family characteristics and with a child's biological risk and disability status. This notion of *specificity* is central to an understanding of contemporary early intervention programs and has important policy implications for providing cost-effective services.

As cast within the developmental framework, the specificity construct can also help us understand why certain *low intensity* early intervention programs can have sustained effects. In particular, the follow-up of children in the Vermont study to age 9 years (Achenbach, Howell, Aoki, and Rauh, 1993) revealed that the low-birthweight children who received the 11 hours of intervention (combined hospital and home program) continued to be indistinguishable from a normal birthweight group, whereas the low-birthweight control group continued their gradual decline in cognitive development. This decline for the control group is a somewhat counter-intuitive finding given the low intensity of the program and the fact that the children in this study were from middle-class families and generally free of major health or congenital disorders. However, it appears that even for these low environmental-risk families, the rural nature of the setting and scarcity of professional resources made it difficult for families to access and coordinate the needed early intervention services and supports outlined in figure 1.2. As a consequence, it is reasonable to suppose that family patterns of interaction were adversely affected by the stressors associated with the child's biological risk, thereby accounting for the observed cognitive decline in the low-birthweight control group. In contrast, the intervention group children and families apparently responded well to the low intensity intervention, being provided with sufficient early intervention supports and services that not only mitigated the stressors initially but gave parents the confidence and competence to solve future problems without disturbing typical family patterns of interaction. Moreover, because of the relatively low environmental risk of these families, family interaction patterns were not perturbed by a constant source of additional stressors over time. Although some of the long-term success of this short duration program can be attributed specifically to interventions occurring directly in the NICU (see Als et al., 1994), positive changes in mothers' satisfaction with their roles as mothers and their self-confidence in carrying out parenting practices were also documented in the Vermont study (Rauh et al., 1988). For the intervention group, better quality parenting also was associated with better child cognitive outcomes during the first 4 years of life (Rauh et al., 1988). Even during the first year, for children at high biological risk, the quality of parent–child interactions is improved through early intervention and is strongly associated with child cognitive development (Resnick et al., 1988).

Importance of interactions

The pattern of findings for long-term effects related to intensity and specificity illustrates most clearly that early intervention programs can and should be uniquely tailored to the prevailing levels of family characteristics and stressors associated with a child's disability or risk status. For many children, early intervention may not be needed in its most intensive (and most expensive) forms where child-related stressors are either insufficient in magnitude or buffered by family characteristics that prevent interference with sound and developmentally appropriate family interaction patterns. A recent finding for children at biological risk illustrates this point. Although differences between children's cognitive development in the experimental and control groups at the end of the 3-year intervention period in the Infant Health and Development Program study was nearly 20 points for mothers with the lowest levels of education (high environmental risk), this program was ineffective for children with family characteristics indicating low environmental risks (Blair, Ramey, and Hardin, 1995). These family characteristics apparently enabled low-risk families either to adjust to stressors through their own internal resources or to seek out appropriate assistance in the community (Blair et al., 1995; Brooks-Gunn, Gross, Kraemer, Spiker, and Shapiro, 1992). Relatedly, to the extent that the intervention families were at lower environmental risk than were the control families in the Rauh et al. (1988) study (a methodological concern in that investigation), it is possible that differences in family characteristics rather than the low intensity intervention were responsible for the outcomes.

The argument offered here is not that early intervention was actually ineffective for the low risk families in the Infant Health and Development Program study, but simply unnecessary at that intensity level. In essence, these families took advantage of needed components of the prevailing early intervention system (see figure 1.2). In contrast, for children at high risk due to family characteristics, the combined biological and environmental risk conditions created an extensive array of stressors requiring a more intensive program. Accordingly, should the contemporary early intervention system be tampered with in any significant way, the prevention or reduction of substantial declines in children's intellectual development occurring across the first 5 years of life, even for relatively low risk groups, would no longer be realized (Guralnick, 1993).

Designing interventions

Taken together, the process of guiding interventions intelligently based on stressors has important implications for policy, research, and practice (Guralnick, 1988, 1991, 1997b). A far more sophisticated system can be put into place through matching the specifics of early intervention program components (e.g., intensity, type of curriculum) with child (e.g., type and severity of disability) and family character-istics (e.g., social supports, financial resources) and family interaction patterns (e.g., parent-child transactions). In this system, some families and children will require only surveillance or minimal supports, even for children with established disabilities; others will require highly intensive, long-term programs to produce important outcomes that are sustained beyond the early years. As a consequence, eligibility for early intervention programs (however defined) should not mean that the child and family has available the entire array of services; indi-vidual plans need to be far more discriminating. It is not just a cost issue but, in the absence of a more sophisticated system that matches needs and services, heavy burdens are needlessly placed on families and children.

Do we know enough to make this a reality? Only to some extent. Better risk indices and clinical instruments are needed consistent with the framework described in this paper to help identify stressors and their likely or actual effects on family interaction patterns. This is a complicated issue, reflecting the problematic nature of our measures and risk or stress indices and our ability to accurately and nonintrus-ively evaluate family characteristics and family patterns of interaction (see Shonkoff and Meisels, 1991). This includes developing sensitive assessments of needs for services and supports as perceived by families. Without such instruments and a coherent plan for their use, there is little hope of creating a meaningful match between family and child needs on the one hand and services and supports on the other.

Correspondingly, by focusing on specificity in what is best referred to as second generation research (Guralnick, 1993, 1997b), invest-igators will contribute studies that are more relevant to practice (i.e., addressing questions regarding for whom and under what conditions does early intervention really make sense?). Research results are now becoming available that relate child and family characteristics (including family interaction patterns), the program components of early intervention (e.g., intensity, type of curriculum), and goals or outcomes of early intervention (including longer-term effects). However, this task remains a formidable challenge for future investigators (Guralnick, 1997a).

Summary and Conclusions

Early intervention may well be the centerpiece in our nation's efforts on behalf of vulnerable children and their families. A coherent system of supports and services has emerged in the past 25 years in response to the needs of young children and families. On the basis of the analysis presented here, one can see that the early intervention system, if properly organized, is capable of preventing or minimizing the declines in cognitive development that typically occur in the absence of intervention during the first 5 years of a child's life. Moreover, the early intervention system produces its effects through the mechanisms of mitigating stressors generated by factors associated with family and child risk or child disability status that can adversely affect family interaction patterns and, hence, child development. It appears that the early intervention enterprise can be understood within a developmental model.

These short-term benefits of early intervention are highly reproducible, with effect sizes in the range of .5 to .75 *SD* consistently found for children at risk and for those with established disabilities. Achieving longer-term gains, however, may well require, in many instances, highly intensive interventions, particularly those that are of sufficient duration to extend over various transition points in the child's life. Similarly, we have seen that solving the specificity problem (i.e., understanding the relation between child and family factors, program factors that define the interventions, and types of outcomes desired) may well be the central task for the second generation of research in the field of early intervention. The importance of adjusting the intensity of early intervention as a consequence of the severity or type of a child's disability or degree of risk has served as an important example of the specificity concept, one that is highly relevant to the cost effectiveness of early intervention. Specificity also encourages further examination of the relative contributions of the various components of interventions, particularly the ability of early intervention to influence long-term parent-child interactions and related child development or child-focused features, such as the provision of quality educational or intervention-oriented daycare.

Translating and applying current and future research findings of experimental programs to practice in typical communities within the framework of the model and approach described in the present paper poses additional challenges. "Scaling-up" is always a complex issue; problems obtaining resources and maintaining quality are most difficult. As discussed, algorithms based on information from existing or newly developed clinical tools capable of evaluating family interaction patterns and taking into account prevailing stressors are critical to the process of determining the nature and intensity of supports and services likely to be optimally beneficial to children and families. The importance of having a framework for the development and application of these clinical tools and the decision-making process cannot be overemphasized.

In this paper I have focused on the effects of early intervention on children's cognitive development. Yet many of the same family characteristics and family interaction patterns that influence children's cognitive development are certain to influence other domains as well, such as children's social competence. Enhancing children's social competence, in particular, has been an expressed goal of early intervention for some time (Guralnick, 1990; Zigler and Trickett, 1978). In fact, the risk factors and associated stressors discussed in this paper for cognitive development have similar associations with important aspects of children's social competence (Patterson, Vaden, and Kupersmidt, 1991) and are likely to be enhanced by many of the same interventions appropriate for the cognitive domain (Guralnick and Neville, 1997). Although unique intervention approaches will certainly be required for each developmental outcome emphasized, the cross-domain features reflected in the developmental approach suggest that more widespread benefits of comprehensive early intervention are likely to result. To be sure, numerous other important issues remain as well, such as whether intervention during the sensorimotor period is essential for ensuring the long-term effectiveness of early intervention, what form interventions must take to produce benefits for children who have previously not responded to even the most intensive of interventions, or how parents experiencing unusual distress or even depression can be best supported by early intervention programs. Long-term, systematic examination of these and related issues, with the necessary degree of specificity within a developmental framework, are certain to yield information of relevance to all concerned with the wellbeing of vulnerable children and their families.

References

Achenbach, T. M., Howell, C. T., Aoki, M. F., & Rauh, V. A. (1993). Nine-year outcome of the Vermont Intervention Program for Low Birth Weight Infants. *Pediatrics, 91,* 45–55.

Affleck, G., & Tennen, H. (1993). Cognitive adaptation to adversity: Insights from parents of medically fragile infants. In A. P. Turnbull, J. M. Patterson, S. K. Behr, D. L. Murphy, J. G. Marquis, & M. J. Blue-Banning (Eds.), *Cognitive coping, families, and disability* (pp. 135–150). Baltimore: Brookes.

Affleck, G., Tennen, H., Rowe, J., Roscher, B., & Walker, L. (1989). Effects of formal support on mothers' adaptation to the hospital-to-home transition of high-risk infants: The benefits and costs of helping. *Child Development, 60,* 488–501.

Als, H., Lawhon, G., Duffy, F. H., McAnulty, G. B., Gibes-Grossman, R., & Blickman, J. G. (1994). Individualized developmental care for the very low-birth-weight preterm infant: Medical and neurofunctional effects. *Journal of the American Medical Association, 272,* 853–858.

Anastasiow, N. J. (1990). Implications of the neurobiological model for early intervention. In S. J. Meisels & J. P. Shonkoff (Eds.), *Handbook of early childhood intervention* (pp. 196–216). Cambridge: Cambridge University Press.

Atkinson, L., Chisholm, V., Dickens, S., Scott, B., Blackwell, J., Tam, F., & Goldberg, S. (1995). Cognitive coping, affective distress, and maternal sensitivity: Mothers of children with Down syndrome. *Developmental Psychology, 31,* 668–676.

Bailey, D. B. (1987). Collaborative goal-setting with families: Resolving differences in values and priorities for services. *Topics in Early Childhood Special Education, 7*(2), 59–71.

Bailey, D. B. (1997). Evaluating the effectiveness of curriculum alternatives for infants and preschoolers at high risk. In M. J. Guralnick (Ed.), *The effectiveness of early intervention* (pp. 227–247). Baltimore: Brookes.

Bailey, D. B., Jr., & Winton, P. J. (1989). Friendship and acquaintance among families in a mainstreamed day care center. *Education and Training in Mental Retardation, 24,* 107–113.

Bailey, D. B., & Wolery, M. (1992). *Teaching infants and preschoolers with disabilities* (2nd ed.). New York: MacMillan.

Barnett, W. S. (1995). Long-term effects of early childhood programs on cognitive and school outcomes. In R. E. Behrman (Ed.), *The future of children: Vol. 5. Long-term outcomes of early childhood programs* (pp. 25–50). Los Altos, CA: The Center for the Future of Children, The David and Lucile Packard Foundation.

Baumrind, D. (1993). The average expectable environment is not good enough: A response to Scarr. *Child Development, 64,* 1299–1317.

Beckman, P. J. (1983). The relationship between behavioral characteristics of children and social interaction in an integrated setting. *Journal of the Division for Early Childhood, 7*, 69–77.

Beckman, P. J., & Pokorni, J. L. (1988). A longitudinal study of families of preterm infants: Changes in stress and support over the first two years. *The Journal of Special Education, 2*, 56–65.

Behr, S. K., & Murphy, D. L. (1993). Research progress and promise: The role of perceptions in cognitive adaptation to disability. In A. P. Turnbull, J. M. Patterson, S. K. Behr, D. L. Murphy, J. G. Marquis, & M. J. Blue-Banning (Eds.), *Cognitive coping, families, and disability* (pp. 151–163). Baltimore: Brookes.

Belsky, J. (1984). The determinants of parenting: A process model. *Child Development, 55*, 83–96.

Belsky, J., Robins, E., & Gamble, W. (1984). The determinants of parental competence: Toward a contextual theory. In M. Lewis (Ed.), *Beyond the dyad* (pp. 251–279). New York: Plenum Press.

Benasich, A. A., Brooks-Gunn, J., & Clewell, B. C. (1992). How do mothers benefit from early intervention programs? *Journal of Applied Developmental Psychology, 13*, 311–362.

Benn, R. (1993). Conceptualizing eligibility for early intervention services. In D. M. Bryant & M. A. Graham (Eds.), *Implementing early intervention* (pp. 18–45). New York: The Guilford Press.

Berry, P., Gunn, V. P., & Andrews, R. J. (1984). Development of Down's syndrome children from birth to five years. In J. M. Berg (Ed.), *Perspectives and progress in mental retardation: Vol. 1. Social, psychological, and educational aspects* (pp. 167–177). Baltimore: University Park Press.

Birenbaum, A., Guyot, D., & Cohen, H. J. (1990). *Health care financing for severe developmental disabilities.* Washington, DC: American Association on Mental Retardation.

Blair, C. B., Ramey, C. T., & Hardin, J. M. (1995). Early intervention for low birth weight, premature infants. Participation and intellectual development. *American Journal on Mental Retardation, 99*, 542–554.

Bowe, F. G. (1995). Population estimates: Birth-to-5 children with disabilities. *The Journal of Special Education, 20*, 461–471.

Boyle, C. A., Decouflé, P., & Yeargin-Allsopp, M. (1994). Prevalence and health impact of developmental disabilities in US children. *Pediatrics, 93*, 399–403.

Bradley, R. H., Rock, S. L., Whiteside, L., Caldwell, B. M., & Brisby, J. (1991). Dimensions of parenting in families having children with disabilities. *Exceptionality, 2*, 41–61.

Bradley, R. H., Whiteside, L., Mundfrom, D. J., Casey, P. H., Kelleher, K. J., & Pope, S. K. (1994). Early indications of resilience and their relation to experiences in the home environments of low birthweight, premature children living in poverty. *Child Development, 65*, 346–360.

Breslau, N., DelDotto, J. E., Brown, G. G., Kumar, S., Ezhuthachan, S., Hufnagle, K. G., & Peterson, E. L. (1994). A gradient relationship between low birth weight and IQ at age 6 years. *Archives of Pediatric and Adolescent Medicine*, 148, 377–383.

Bristol, M. M. (1987). The home care of children with developmental disabilities: Empirical support for a model of successful family coping with stress. In S. Landesman & P. M. Vietze (Eds.), *Living environments and mental retardation* (pp. 401–422). Washington, DC: American Association on Mental Retardation.

Bronfenbrenner, U. (1979). *The ecology of human development*. Cambridge: Harvard University Press.

Brooks-Gunn, J., Gross, R. T., Kraemer, H. C., Spiker, D., & Shapiro, S. (1992). Enhancing the cognitive outcomes of low birth weight, premature infants: For whom is the intervention most effective? *Pediatrics*, 89, 1209–1215.

Brooks-Gunn, J., McCarton, C. M., Casey, P. H., McCormick, M. C., Bauer, C. R., Bernbaum, J. C., Tyson, J., Swanson, M., Bennett, F. C., Scott, D. T., Tonascia, J., & Meinert, C. L. (1994). Early intervention in low-birth-weight premature infants. *Journal of the American Medical Association*, 272, 1257–1262.

Bruder, M. B. (1997). The effectiveness of specific educational/developmental curricula for children with established disabilities. In M. J. Guralnick (Ed.), *The effectiveness of early intervention* (pp. 523–548). Baltimore: Brookes.

Bryant, D. M., & Graham, M. A. (1993). Models of service delivery. In D. M. Bryant & M. A. Graham (Eds.), *Implementing early intervention* (pp. 183–215). New York: Guilford Press.

Bryant, D. M., & Maxwell, K. (1997). The effectiveness of early intervention for disadvantaged children. In M. J. Guralnick (Ed.), *The effectiveness of early intervention* (pp. 23–46). Baltimore: Brookes.

Buehler, D. M., Als, H., Duffy, F. H., McAnulty, G. B., & Liederman, J. (1995). Effectiveness of individualized developmental care for low-risk preterm infants: Behavioral and electrophysiologic evidence. *Pediatrics*, 96, 923–932.

Burchinal, M., Lee, M. W., & Ramey, C. T. (1989). Type of day-care and pre-school intellectual development in disadvantaged children. *Child Development*, 60, 128–137.

Burchinal, M. R., Roberts, J. E., Nabors, L. A., & Bryant, D. M. (1996). Quality of center child care and infant cognitive and language development. *Child Development*, 67, 606–620.

Campbell, F. A., & Ramey, C. T. (1994). Effects of early intervention on intellectual and academic achievement: A follow-up study of children from low-income families. *Child Development*, 65, 684–698.

Cicchetti, D., & Toth, S. L. (1995). Developmental psychopathology and disorders of affect. In D. Cicchetti & D. J. Cohen (Eds.), *Developmental psychopathology: Vol. 2. Risk, disorder, and adaptation* (pp. 369–420). New York: Wiley.

Clarke-Stewart, K. A. (1988). Parents' effects on children's development: A decade of progress? *Journal of Applied Developmental Psychology, 9,* 41–84.

Cochran, M. M., & Brassard, J. A. (1979). Child development and personal social networks. *Child Development, 50,* 601–615.

Cooley, W. C. (1994). The ecology of support for caregiving families. Commentary. *Journal of Developmental and Behavioral Pediatrics, 15,* 117–119.

Crnic, K. A., Greenberg, M. T., Ragozin, A. S., Robinson, N. M., & Basham, R. B. (1983). Effects of stress and social support on mothers and premature and full-term infants. *Child Development, 54,* 209–217.

Crowell, J. A., & Feldman, S. S. (1988). Mothers' internal models of relationships and children's behavioral and developmental status: A study of mother-child interaction. *Child Development, 59,* 1273–1285.

Donahue, M. L., & Pearl, R. (1995). Conversational interactions of mothers and their preschool children who had been born preterm. *Journal of Speech and Hearing Research, 38,* 1117–1125.

Dumas, J. E., & LaFreniere, P. J. (1993). Mother-child relationships as sources of support or stress: A comparison of competent, average, aggressive, and anxious dyads. *Child Development, 64,* 1732–1754.

Duncan, G. J., Brooks-Gunn, J., & Klebanov, P. K. (1994). Economic deprivation and early childhood development. *Child Development, 65,* 296–318.

Dunst, C. J. (1985). Rethinking early intervention. *Analysis and Intervention in Developmental Disabilities, 5,* 165–201.

Dunst, C. J., Trivette, C. M., & Cross, A. H. (1986). Mediating influences of social support: Personal, family, and child outcomes. *American Journal of Mental Deficiency, 90,* 403–417.

Duwa, S. M., Wells, C., & Lalinde, P. (1993). Creating family-centered programs and policies. In D. M. Bryant & M. A. Graham (Eds.), *Implementing early intervention* (pp. 92–123). New York: Guilford.

Dyson, L. L. (1993). Response to the presence of a child with disabilities: Parental stress and family functioning over time. *American Journal on Mental Retardation, 98,* 207–218.

Elardo, R., Bradley, R., & Caldwell, B. (1977). A longitudinal study of the relations of infants' home environments to language development at age three. *Child Development, 48,* 595–603.

Emery, R. E., & Kitzmann, A. M. (1995). The child in the family: Disruptions in family functions. In D. Cicchetti & D. J. Cohen (Eds.), *Developmental psychopathology: Vol. 2. Risk, disorder, and adaptation* (pp. 3–31). New York: Wiley.

Feldman, M. A., Case, L., Towns, F., & Betel, J. (1985). Parent education project I: The development and nurturance of children of mentally retarded parents. *American Journal of Mental Deficiency, 90,* 253–258.

Florian, L. (1995). Part H early intervention program: Legislative history and intent of the law. *Topics in Early Childhood Special Education, 15,* 247–262.

Futterweit, L. R., & Ruff, H. A. (1993). Principles of development: Implications for early intervention. *Journal of Applied Developmental Psychology, 14,* 153–173.

Gibson, D., & Harris, A. (1988). Aggregated early intervention effects for Down's syndrome persons: Patterning and longevity of benefits. *Journal of Mental Deficiency Research, 32,* 1–17.

Goffman, E. (1963). *Stigma.* Englewood Cliffs, NJ: Prentice-Hall.

Goodman, J. F., & Pollak, E. (1993). An analysis of the core cognitive curriculum in early intervention programs. *Early Education and Development, 4,* 193–203.

Gorman, K. S. (1995). Malnutrition and cognitive development: Evidence from experimental/quasi-experimental studies among the mild-to-moderately malnourished. *Journal of Nutrition, 125,* 2239S–2244S.

Gowen, J. W., Johnson-Martin, N., Goldman, B. D., & Appelbaum, M. (1989). Feelings of depression and parenting competence of mothers of handicapped and nonhandicapped infants: A longitudinal study. *American Journal on Mental Retardation, 94,* 259–271.

Guralnick, M. J. (1988). Efficacy research in early childhood intervention programs. In S. L. Odom & M. B. Karnes (Eds.), *Early intervention for infants and children with handicaps: An empirical base* (pp. 75–88). Baltimore: Brookes.

Guralnick, M. J. (1989). Recent developments in early intervention efficacy research: Implications for family involvement in P.L. 99–457. *Topics in Early Childhood Special Education, 9*(3), 1–17.

Guralnick, M. J. (1990). Social competence and early intervention. *Journal of Early Intervention, 14,* 3–14.

Guralnick, M. J. (1991). The next decade of research on the effectiveness of early intervention. *Exceptional Children, 58,* 174–183.

Guralnick, M. J. (1993). Second generation research on the effectiveness of early intervention. *Early Education and Development, 4,* 366–378.

Garalnick, M. J. (Ed.). (1997a). *The effectiveness of early intervention.* Baltimore: Brookes.

Guralnick, M. J. (1997b). Second generation research in the field of early intervention. In M. J. Guralnick (Ed.), *The effectiveness of early intervention* (pp. 3–20). Baltimore: Brookes.

Guralnick, M. J., & Bennett, F. C. (Eds.). (1987). *The effectiveness of early intervention for at-risk and handicapped children.* New York: Academic Press.

Guralnick, M. J., & Bricker, D. (1987). The effectiveness of early intervention for children with cognitive and general developmental delays. In M. J. Guralnick & F. C. Bennett (Eds.), *The effectiveness of early intervention for at-risk and handicapped children* (pp. 115–173). New York: Academic Press.

Guralnick, M. J., & Neville, B. (1997). Designing early intervention programs to promote children's social competence. In M. J. Guralnick (Ed.), *The effectiveness of early intervention* (pp. 579–610). Baltimore: Brookes.

Hack, M., Taylor, H. G., Klein, N., Eiben, R., Schatschneider, C., & Mercuri-Minich, N. (1994). School-age outcomes in children with birth weights under 750g. *The New England Journal of Medicine, 331*, 753–759.

Halpern, R. (1993). Poverty and infant development. In C. H. Zeanah, Jr. (Ed.), *Handbook of infant mental health* (pp. 73–86). New York: Guilford.

Hart, B., & Risley, T. R. (1995). *Meaningful differences in the everyday experience of young American children*. Baltimore: Brookes.

Herrnstein, R. J., & Murray, C. (1994). *The bell curve: Intelligence and class structure in American life*. New York: Free Press.

Hodapp, R. M., Dykens, E. M., Evans, D. W., & Merighi, J. R. (1992). Maternal emotional reactions to young children with different types of handicaps. *Journal of Developmental and Behavioral Pediatrics, 13*, 118–123.

Huston, A. C., McLoyd, V. C., & Garcia Coll, C. G. (1994). Children and poverty: Issues in contemporary research. *Child Development, 65*, 275–282.

Hutchins, V. L. (1994). Maternal and Child Health Bureau: Roots. *Pediatrics, 94*, 695–699.

Individuals With Disabilities Education Act (IDEA) Amendments of 1997, PL 105–17, Title 20, U.S.C. 1400 *et seq.*

Infant Health and Development Program. (1990). Enhancing the outcomes of low-birth-weight, premature infants: A multisite, randomized trial. *Journal of the American Medical Association, 263*, 3035–3042.

Innocenti, M. S., Huh, K., & Boyce, G. C. (1992). Families of children with disabilities: Normative data and other considerations on parenting stress. *Topics in Early Childhood Special Education, 12*(3), 403–427.

Ireys, H. T., & Nelson, R. P. (1992). New federal policy for children with special health care needs: Implications for pediatricians. *Pediatrics, 90*, 321–327.

Ladd, G. W., Profiled, S. M., & Hart, C. H. (1992). Parents' management of children's peer relations: Facilitating and supervising children's activities in the peer culture. In R. D. Parke & G. W. Ladd (Eds.), *Family-peer relationships: Modes of linkage* (pp. 215–253). Hillsdale, NJ: Erlbaum.

Lee, C. L., & Bates, J. E. (1985). Mother-child interaction at age two years and perceived difficult temperament. *Child Development, 56*, 1314–1325.

Lewis, M., & Goldberg, S. (1969). Perceptual-cognitive development in infancy: A generalized expectancy model as a function of mother-infant interaction. *Merrill-Palmer Quarterly, 15*, 81–100.

Lewis, M., Feiring, C., & Brooks-Gunn, J. (1987). The social networks of children with and without handicaps: A developmental perspective. In S. Landesman & P. Vietze (Eds.), *Living environments and mental retardation* (pp. 377–400). Washington, DC: American Association on Mental Retardation.

Lipkin, P. H. (1996). Epidemiology of the developmental disabilities. In A. J. Capute & P. J. Accardo (Eds.), *Developmental disabilities in infancy and childhood: Vol. 1. Neurodevelopmental diagnosis and treatment* (2nd ed., pp. 137–156). Baltimore: Brookes.

Locurto, C. (1991). Beyond IQ in preschool programs? *Intelligence, 15,* 295–312.

Lovaas, O. I. (1987). Behavioral treatment and normal educational and intellectual functioning in young autistic children. *Journal of Consulting and Clinical Psychology, 55,* 3–9.

Mahoney, G., & Powell, A. (1988). Modifying parent-child interaction: Enhancing the development of handicapped children. *Journal of Special Education, 22,* 82–96.

Margalit, M., Raviv, A., & Ankonina, D. B. (1992). Coping and coherence among parents with disabled children. *Journal of Clinical Child Psychology, 21,* 202–209.

Martin, S. L., Ramey, C. T., & Ramey, S. (1990). The prevention of intellectual impairment in children of impoverished families: Findings of a randomized trial of educational day care. *American Journal of Public Health, 80,* 844–847.

McCarton, C. M., Brooks-Gunn, J., Wallace, I. F., Bauer, C. R., Bennett, F. C., Bernbaum, J. C., Broyles, S., Casey, P. H., McCormick, M. C., Scott, D. T., Tyson, J., Tonascia, J., & Meinert, C. L. (1997). Results at age 8 years of early intervention for low-birth-weight premature infants. The Infant Health and Development Program. *Journal of the American Medical Association, 277,* 126–132.

McEachin, J. J., Smith, T., & Lovaas, O. I. (1993). Long-term outcome for children with autism who received early intensive behavioral treatment. *American Journal on Mental Retardation, 97,* 359–372.

McGauhey, P. J., Starfield, B., Alexander, C., & Ensminger, M. E. (1991). Social environment and vulnerability of low birth weight children: A social-epidemiological perspective. *Pediatrics, 88,* 943–953.

McLoyd, V. C. (1990). The impact of economic hardship on black families and children: Psychological distress, parenting, and socioemotional development. *Child Development, 61,* 311–346.

Melson, G. F., Ladd, G. W., & Hsu, H-C. (1993). Maternal support networks, maternal cognitions, and young children's social and cognitive development. *Child Development, 64,* 1401–1417.

Meyer, E. C., Garcia Coll, C. T., Seifer, R., Ramos, A., Kilis, E., & Oh, W. (1995). Psychological distress in mothers of preterm infants. *Journal of Developmental and Behavioral Pediatrics, 16,* 412–417.

Miller, A. C., Gordon, R. M., Daniele, R. J., & Diller, L. (1992). Stress, appraisal, and coping in mothers of disabled and nondisabled children. *Journal of Pediatric Psychology, 17,* 587–605.

Miller, S. A. (1988). Parents' beliefs about children's cognitive development. *Child Development, 59,* 259–285.

Murphey, D. A. (1992). Constructing the child: Relations between parents' beliefs and child outcomes. *Developmental Review, 12,* 199–232.

Neisser, U., Boodoo, G., Bouchard, T. J., Jr., Boykin, A. W., Brody, N., Ceci, S. J., Halpern, D. F., Loehlin, J. C., Perloff, R., Sternberg, R. J., & Urbina, S. (1996). Intelligence: Knowns and unknowns. *American Psychologist, 51,* 77–101.

Neser, P. S. J., Molteno, C. D., & Knight, G. J. (1989). Evaluation of preschool children with Down's syndrome in Cape Town using the Griffiths Scale of Mental Development. *Child: Care, Health and Development, 15,* 217–225.

Osofsky, J. D. (1995). The effects of violence exposure on young children. *American Psychologist, 50,* 782–788.

Palfrey, J. S., Singer, J. D., Walker, D. K., & Butler, J. A. (1987). Early identification of children's special needs. A study in five metropolitan communities. *Journal of Pediatrics, 111,* 651–659.

Palmer, F. B., Shapiro, B. K., Wachtel, R. C., Allen, M. C., Hiller, J. E., Harryman, S. E., Mosher, B. S., Meinert, C. L., & Capute, A. J. (1988). The effects of physical therapy on cerebral palsy. *New England Journal of Medicine, 318,* 803–808.

Parker, S., Greer, S., & Zuckerman, B. (1988). Double jeopardy: The impact of poverty on early child development. *The Pediatric Clinics of North America, 35,* 1227–1240.

Patterson, C. J., Vaden, N. A., & Kupersmidt, J. B. (1991). Family background, recent life events and peer rejection during childhood. *Journal of Social and Personal Relationships, 8,* 347–361.

Pianta, R. C., Marvin, R. S., Britner, P. A., & Borowitz, K. C. (1996). Mothers' resolution of their children's diagnosis. Organized patterns of caregiving representations. *Journal of Infant Mental Health, 17,* 239–256.

Powell, C., & Grantham-McGregor, S. (1989). Home visiting of varying frequency and child development. *Pediatrics, 84,* 157–164.

Pratt, M. W., Kerig, P., Cowan, P. A., & Cowan, C. P. (1988). Mothers and fathers teaching 3-year-olds: Authoritative parenting and adult scaffolding of young children's learning. *Developmental Psychology, 24,* 832–839.

Public Law 99–457. The Education of the Handicapped Act Amendments (1986).

Ramey, C. T., Bryant, D. M., Wasik, B. H., Sparling, J. J., Fendt, K. H., & LaVange, L. M. (1992). Infant Health and Development Program for low birth weight, premature infants: Program elements, family participation, and child intelligence. *Pediatrics, 89,* 454–465.

Ramey, C. T., & Campbell, F. A. (1984). Preventive education for high-risk children: Cognitive consequences of the Carolina Abecedarian Project. *American Journal of Mental Deficiency, 88,* 515–523.

Rauh, V. A., Achenbach, T. M., Nurcombe, B., Howell, C. T., & Teti, D. M. (1988). Minimizing adverse effects of low birthweight: Four-year results of an early intervention program. *Child Development, 59,* 544–553.

Resnick, M. B., Armstrong, S., & Carter, R. L. (1988). Developmental intervention program for high-risk premature infants: Effects on development and parent-infant interactions. *Journal of Developmental and Behavioral Pediatrics,* *9,* 73–78.

Resnick, M. B., Eyler, F. D., Nelson, R. M., Eitzman, D. V., & Bucciarelli, R. L. (1987). Developmental intervention for low birth weight infants: Improved early developmental outcome. *Pediatrics, 80,* 68–74.

Reynolds, A. J. (1994). Effects of a preschool plus follow-on intervention for children at risk. *Developmental Psychology, 30,* 787–804.

Richmond, J., & Ayoub, C. C. (1993). Evolution of early intervention philosophy. In D. M. Bryant & M. A. Graham (Eds.), *Implementing early intervention* (pp. 1–17). New York: Guilford.

Ross, G., Lipper, E. G., & Auld, P. A. M. (1990). Social competence and behavior problems in premature children at school age. *Pediatrics, 86,* 391–397.

Rubin, S., & Quinn-Curran, N. (1985). Lost, then found: Parents' journey through the community service maze. In M. Seligman (Ed.), *The family with a handicapped child. Understanding and treatment* (pp. 63–94). New York: Grune & Stratton.

Rutter, M. (1980). The long-term effects of early experience. *Developmental Medicine and Child Neurology, 22,* 800–815.

Rutter, M. (1996). Autism research: Prospects and priorities. *Journal of Autism and Developmental Disorders, 26,* 257–275.

Sameroff, A. J. (1993). Models of development and developmental risk. In C. H. Zeanah, Jr. (Ed.), *Handbook of infant mental health* (pp. 3–13). New York: Guilford.

Sameroff, A. J., & Chandler, M. J. (1975). Reproductive risk and the continuum of caretaking casualty. In F. D. Horowitz, M. Hetherington, S. Scarr-Salapatek, and G. Siegel (Eds.), *Review of child development research* (Vol. 4, pp. 187–244). Chicago: University of Chicago Press.

Sameroff, A. J., Seifer, R., Barocas, R., Zax, M., & Greenspan, S. (1987). Intelligence quotient scores of 4-year-old children: Social-environmental risk factors. *Pediatrics, 79,* 343–350.

Santelli, B., Turnbull, A. P., Marquis, J. G., & Lerner, E. P. (1995). Parent to parent programs: A unique form of mutual support. *Infants and Young Children, 8*(2), 48–57.

Scarr, S. (1992). Developmental theories for the 1990s: Development and individual differences. *Child Development, 63,* 1–19.

Scarr, S., & McCartney, K. (1988). Far from home: An experimental evaluation of the mother-child home program in Bermuda. *Child Development, 59,* 531–543.

Schnell, R. (1984). Psychomotor development. In S. Peuschel (Ed.), *The young child with Down syndrome* (pp. 207–226). New York: Human Sciences.

Seifer, R., Clark, G. N., & Sameroff, A. J. (1991). Positive effects of interaction coaching on infants with developmental disabilities and their mothers. *American Journal on Mental Retardation, 96*, 1–11.

Sharav, T., & Shlomo, L. (1986). Stimulation of infants with Down syndrome: Long-term effects. *Mental Retardation, 24*, 81–86.

Shonkoff, J. P. (1985). Social support and vulnerability to stress: A pediatric perspective. *Pediatric Annals, 14*, 550–554.

Shonkoff, J. P., & Hauser-Cram, P. (1987). Early intervention for disabled infants and their families: A quantitative analysis. *Pediatrics, 80*, 650–658.

Shonkoff, J. P., Hauser-Cram, P., Krauss, M. W., & Upshur, C. C. (1992). Development of infants with disabilities and their families. *Monographs of the Society for Research in Child Development, 57*(6, Serial No. 230).

Shonkoff, J. P., & Meisels, S. M. (1991). Defining eligibility for services under P.L. 99–457. Implementation of P.L. 99–457, Part H. [Special issue]. *Journal of Early Intervention, 15*, 21–25.

Smith, B. J., & McKenna, P. (1994). Early intervention public policy: Past, present, and future. In L. J. Johnson, R. J. Gallagher, M. J. LaMontagne, J. B. Jordan, J. J. Gallagher, P. L. Hutinger, & M. B. Karnes (Eds.), *Meeting early intervention challenges* (pp. 251–264). Baltimore: Brookes.

Sontag, J. C., & Schacht, R. (1994). An ethnic comparison of parent participation and information needs in early intervention. *Exceptional Children, 60*, 422–433.

Spiker, D., Ferguson, J., & Brooks-Gunn, J. (1993). Enhancing maternal interactive behavior and child social competence in low birth weight, premature infants. *Child Development, 64*, 754–768.

Spitz, H. H. (1986). *The raising of intelligence: A selected history of attempts to raise retarded intelligence.* Hillsdale, NJ: Erlbaum.

Stayton, V. D., & Karnes, M. B. (1994). Model programs for infants and toddlers with disabilities and their families. In L. J. Johnson, R. J. Gallagher, M. J. LaMontagne, J. B. Jordan, J. J. Gallagher, P. L. Hutinger, & M. B. Karnes (Eds.), *Meeting early intervention challenges: Issues from birth to three* (2nd ed., pp. 33–58). Baltimore: Brookes.

Taylor, L., Zuckerman, B., Harik, V., & Groves, B. M. (1994). Witnessing violence by young children and their mothers. *Journal of Developmental and Behavioral Pediatrics, 15*, 120–123.

Trute, B., & Hauch, C. (1988). Building on family strength: A study of families with positive adjustment to the birth of a developmentally disabled child. *Journal of Marital and Family Therapy, 14*, 185–193.

Turnbull, A. P., & Turnbull, H. R. (1978). *Parents speak out: Views from the other side of the two-way mirror.* Columbus, OH: Merrill.

Vaughn, B. E., Goldberg, S., Atkinson, L., Marcovitch, S., MacGregor, D., & Seifer, R. (1994). Quality of toddler-mother attachment in children with

Down syndrome: Limits to interpretation of strange situation behavior. *Child Development, 65,* 95–108.

Wachs, T. D. (1992). *The nature of nurture.* Newbury Park, CA: Sage.

Wachs, T. D., & Gruen, G. E. (1982). *Early experience and human development.* New York: Plenum Press.

Waisbren, S. (1980). Parents' reactions after the birth of a developmentally disabled child. *American Journal of Mental Deficiency, 84,* 345–351.

Wasik, B. H., Ramey, C. T., Bryant, D. G., & Sparling, J. J. (1990). A longitudinal study of two early intervention strategies: Project CARE. *Child Development, 61,* 1682–1696.

Werner, E. E. (1995). Resilience in development. *Current Directions in Psychological Science, 4,* 81–85.

Wikler, L. M. (1986). Family stress theory and research on families of children with mental retardation. In J. J. Gallagher & P. M. Vietze (Eds.), *Families of handicapped Persons* (pp. 167–195). Baltimore: Brookes.

Woods, P. A., Corney, M. J., & Pryce, G. J. (1984). Developmental progress of preschool Down's syndrome children receiving a home-advisory service: An interim report. *Child: Care, Health and Development, 10,* 287–299.

Yeargin-Allsopp, M., Murphy C. C., Oakley, G. P., Sikes, R. K., & the Metropolitan Atlanta Developmental Disabilities Study Staff. (1992). A multiple-source method for studying the prevalence of developmental disabilities in children: The Metropolitan Atlanta Developmental Disabilities Study. *Pediatrics, 89,* 624–630.

Yoshikawa, H. (1994). Prevention as cumulative protection: Effects of early family support and education on chronic delinquency and its risks. *Psychological Bulletin, 115,* 28–54.

Zigler, E., & Styfco, S. J. (1994). Head Start: Criticisms in a constructive context. *American Psychologist, 49,* 127–132.

Zigler, E., & Trickett, P. K. (1978). IQ, social competence, and evaluation of early childhood intervention programs. *American Psychologist, 33,* 789–798.

Zigler, E., & Valentine, J. (Eds.). (1979). *Project Head Start: A legacy of the war on Poverty.* New York: The Free Press.

Early Out-of-home Programs: Primary Prevention of Cognitive Deficits and School Failure in At-risk Children

Introduction to Part II

Children growing up in poverty are at-risk for a variety of problems, including cognitive delay, school failure, and delinquency. Early intervention programs have been established for impoverished children that provide out-of-home experiences. The premise is to compensate for the presumed lack of stimulation at home and prepare the child for academic learning and the school routine. Although these programs are center-based, most of them also encourage parental involvement to increase the quality of the home environment. Chapter 2 describes the largest program – Head Start in the United States. Support for an out-of-home model comes from several early intervention projects that started over twenty years ago. Chapter 3 presents the long-term results of one of the most rigorously evaluated out-of-home programs – the Carolina Abecedarian Project, directed by Craig Ramey. Chapter 4 presents evidence that even regular daycare experience may benefit low-income children.

Introduction to Chapter 2

Edward Zigler is one of the leaders in early intervention and a founder of Head Start. In this chapter, he and Sally Styfco present the history and future directions of Head Start. Interestingly, despite its pervasiveness in the United States (and its serving as a model for preschool services for disadvantaged children in many other countries), the effectiveness of Head Start *per se* has not been clearly demonstrated. The strongest support for preschool intervention comes from experimental programs such as the Perry Preschool Project (Schweinhart, Barnes, and Weikart, 1993), Chicago Child-Parent Center (Reynolds and Temple, 1998), and the Carolina Abecedarian Project (chapter 3). Nonetheless, Head Start has survived seven administrations and is undergoing considerable expansion.

As the authors note, although Head Start started as an anti-poverty program, it became clear that a program of such limited scope would have little impact on ending poverty and institutionalized biases in the United States. Today, Head Start is seen as a way to prepare for success in school in children traditionally at risk for academic delay, school failure, and drop-out. Even academic achievement may be too far-reaching. As the authors point out, interventions targeted to preschool children only will have limited impact. They now recommend seamless programs focusing on the child and parents that start at or near birth (cf., Abecedarian Project), continue through the preschool years, and carry on for the first several primary grades. The authors highlight the importance of quality control in real-world implementation of model programs. Failure to maintain high standards and empirically supported methods is one of the major reasons why promising programs fail to replicate when they move from research to practice. Future evaluations will determine if the new long-term developmental outlook of Head Start can be universally implemented while maintaining best-practice standards, and results in more persistent benefits than existing short-term programs.

References

Reynolds, A. J. & Temple, J. A. (1998). Extended early childhood intervention and school achievement: Age thirteen findings from the Chicago Longitudinal Study. *Child Development*, 69, 231–246.

Schweinhart, L. J., Barnes, H. V., & Weikart, D. P. (1993). Significant benefits: The High/Scope Perry Preschool study through age 27. *Monographs of the High/Scope Educational Research Foundation, 10.* Ypsilanti, MI: High/Scope Press.

TWO

Applying the Findings of Developmental Psychology to Improve Early Childhood Intervention

Edward Zigler and Sally J. Styfco

Social scientists have long studied the effects of poverty on children's development. A translation of an 1870 survey by the Pedagogical Society of Berlin noted that "the conditions of the various parts of the city exercise different influences . . . in consequence of which the mental receptivity of children of different wards show a noticeable inequality" (in Bronfenbrenner and Crouter, 1983, p. 360). In roughly the century between that survey and the time Bronfenbrenner developed his ecological model, a lot of data were gathered to show how "different social addresses" affect children and their rearing (p. 361). During these years psychologists built an understanding of how addresses in poverty-stricken neighborhoods adversely impact the children living there. The scientist's job, however, was only to study the risks associated with poverty. Helping children to overcome these risks was a task assumed by church women and social reformers (Cahan, 1989).

Zigler, Edward, Styfco & Sally J. (1998). Applying the findings of developmental psychology to improve early childhood intervention. From Paris, Scott G., & Wellman, Henry M. (Eds). *Global prospects for education: Development, culture and schooling*, pp. 345–365. Washington DC, American Psychological Association. Copyright © 1998 by The American Psychological Association. Reprinted with permission.

A turning point came in 1969, when George Miller delivered his presidential address to the American Psychological Association. He admonished psychologists to "give psychology away" by providing intellectual leadership in solving the behavioral and social problems they worked so hard to understand (Miller, 1969, p. 1071). His message was acted upon by Harold Stevenson. In 1971, when Harold was president of the Society for Research in Child Development, he chose to forego the traditional presidential address and instead held a forum among policy makers and leading developmentalists. The discussion convinced many who attended that the two interests had much to offer one another (Zigler, 1996). A few years later, Harold headed the second in the network of Bush Centers in Child Development and Social Policy. His leadership and example over the years have encouraged many scholars and students to apply their science to developing programs and policies for the benefit of children.

Theirs was not always an easy course to take, because children's causes have not always been high on the national agenda. As a case in point, when the War on Poverty was launched in 1964, the effort targeted adults. Among the new antipoverty initiatives, only the Job Corps, an employment and training program for severely disadvantaged teenagers and young adults, and Head Start, a preschool intervention, considered the needs of children living in poverty. Interestingly, although most of the War's programmatic weapons have been dismantled, the Job Corps and Head Start remain.

Applied developmental psychology, a field that Harold helped stake, has devoted a great deal of attention to the Head Start model and has generated knowledge that can be used fruitfully throughout early care and education systems. For these reasons, Head Start will be the focus of this chapter.

Now Head Start has helped millions of children with economic disadvantages enter school healthier and better prepared to learn. Their parents have acquired better child-rearing skills, have become involved in their children's education, and many have gained job skills and a better quality of life. Social scientists involved in the Head Start experiment have learned a great deal about the needs of children affected by poverty and how to meet them. These accomplishments have earned the program a broad base of grass-roots support and the approbation of policy makers. A widespread hope is that if Head Start is made available to all preschoolers who live below the federal poverty level, they will not grow up to be poor.

But Head Start did not end poverty in the 1960s, nor can it conquer the crueler circumstances of poverty that have taken hold in the 1990s. The program instead showed that it is possible to enhance the educational outcomes of children who have economic disadvantages and to boost some aspects of their families' functioning. These are no small accomplishments. Updated and improved, Head Start has the potential to become even more effective and to serve as a model for new intervention efforts.

Surprisingly, after operating for over 30 years, graduating more than 15-million children, and progressing to an annual budget of over $3.5 billion, Head Start is still widely misunderstood and often confused with other types of intervention. Therefore, we will briefly describe the program before we offer our ideas for enhancing Head Start's services and leadership role.

Historical Overview of Head Start

Head Start opened in 1965, just months after its planners first convened to develop the idea of a program for impoverished preschoolers. The project began on a massive scale, serving over one-half million children in its first summer. It was actually a summer program, lasting 6–8 weeks before children entered kindergarten. It soon became a school-year program, which it essentially is today.

Head Start currently serves over 750,000 children in some 42,500 classrooms around the nation. The majority are 3- and 4-year-olds whose families have incomes below the poverty line. Nearly 13% are children with disabilities. Each Head Start center must focus on three major activities: child development services (physical and mental health, nutrition, preschool education); family and community partnerships (including parent involvement and social support services); and program design and management (to improve quality and accountability). Although these components must conform to a national set of performance standards, centers are encouraged to adapt their services to local needs and resources. Thus, Head Start is the prototype of comprehensive, two-generation, community-based service programs that scholars today endorse.

The wisdom of the Head Start approach took some time to be appreciated. One aspect of the program that was unheard of and highly controversial back in the 1960s was the central role accorded parents. They were invited to participate in their children's classrooms and were given the opportunity to attend classes of their own. They were also included in the planning and administration of their local centers. One reason for the decision to involve parents on so many levels was that Head Start originated in the War on Poverty's Community Action Programs, which were to provide "maximum feasible participation" by people of low incomes in programs designed to serve them. Another reason is that one member of the planning committee was Urie Bronfenbrenner, who was just beginning to develop his ecological approach to human development. Bronfenbrenner (1979) argued that there is a complex interrelationship among children, their families, and communities, so an intervention must touch all of these areas to be effective. This insight was astute, and far ahead of its time. Today, parent participation is considered crucial to the effectiveness of early intervention as well as to later schooling.

The basic goal of Head Start is, and always was, to prepare children for school (Zigler and Styfco, 1997). But instead of providing the academic skills and concepts that are the standard fare of nursery schools, Head Start takes a whole-child approach to school readiness. Children receive inoculations, physical and dental exams, and follow-up treatment if needed. They are served hot meals and nutritious snacks, while their parents are taught to provide healthy diets at home. The preschool education component is developmentally and culturally appropriate; it includes language and other school readiness skills as well as experiences to promote social and emotional development. Parents volunteer in the classrooms, attend classes of their own, and serve on the Parent Committee and the Policy Council (the governing bodies of Head Start centers and grantees). Family needs and goals are assessed and support services are provided through the program and links to community agencies. Head Start also initiates the development of community partnerships to enhance the availability and delivery of needed human services.

The reasoning behind these many services is that children who are healthy, have the academic and social skills they need, have parents who are involved in their education, and have familes whose basic needs are met will be more socially competent when they arrive at school.

The program's methods are thus quite complex, and its purpose somewhat modest.

The goal of Head Start was indeed too modest for the 1960s, a time
of over-optimism and "can do" attitudes. Just think about the fact that
we launched a *war* on poverty. Not a program to reduce poverty, nor
an antipoverty initiative, but a war. Americans were not used to losing
wars, and we fully expected to win this one. A sense of the times can be
gained from the speech President Johnson gave in the Rose Garden to
announce the opening of the Head Start summer program: "This program this year means that 30 million man-years – the combined lifespan
of these youngsters – will be spent productively and rewardingly, rather
than wasted in tax-supported institutions or in welfare supported
lethargy" (in Califano, 1997, p. 68). This certainly is a lot to ask of a
program that is so brief in the life of a child.

The exuberance of the sixties also invaded the social sciences community, where psychologists were enthralled with the possibility of
raising IQ scores. This was the time when parents were buying crib
mobile to give their infants superior minds and books about teaching
2-year olds to read. They themselves were reading media articles about
how to raise their children's IQs by 20 points and J. McVicker Hunt's
(1971 claims that IQ gains of 70 points were possible. Given society's
infatuation with intelligence, it is not surprising that IQ tests became
central in the evaluation of Head Start and other early interventions.
This enthusiasm ballooned when results showed that just about any
program – even the 6-week Head Start – raised children's IQs by 10
points or more. When these gains were found to fade out shortly after
children began school, the balloon burst. Arguments much like those
presented recently in *The Bell Curve* (Herrnstein and Murray, 1994)
were made, and pessimism set in that little could be done to help under-
privileged children do better in school. The Head Start "lovefest" came
to an end, and the program was nearly dismantled.

In hindsight, it is easy to see the emptiness of the promise inherent
in the inoculation model. The notion that psychologists could take
children who have lived their whole young lives in poverty, provide
them with a few weeks or months of intervention, and forever immunize
them against the ill effects of continuing economic disadvantage was
absurd. And as rebuttals to *The Bell Curve* are now making clear, IQ is
not the only feature responsible for a person's success in life (Gardner,
1995; Sternberg, Wagner, Williams, and Horvath, 1995). The Head

Start program's goal of helping children be more socially competent – improving their behavioral functioning instead of their IQs – is beginning to make sense.

The scientific literature now has given us insights into the true effects of intervention and has thereby shaped more realistic expectations. In brief, quality early intervention programs do help prepare children for school. Once there, they are better able to meet the expectancies of school by having better attendance, less grade retention, and fewer special class placements (Barnett, 1995; Consortium for Longitudinal Studies, 1983). Longitudinal studies of some programs also suggest the possibility of lowered juvenile delinquency and welfare dependency and better high-school graduation rates (Schweinhart, Barnes, and Weikart, 1993). These effects are not as exciting as turning children into geniuses, but they are certainly worthwhile outcomes.

Requirements for Program Success

In the thirty years since the Head Start program and the early intervention movement began, the field has matured tremendously and the theories have become increasingly sophisticated. There is now general agreement on the necessary elements of effective intervention and a sense of how they should be delivered (National Head Start Association, 1990; Price, Cowen, Lorion, and Ramos-McKay, 1988; Schorr, 1988; Zigler and Berman, 1983; Zigler and Styfco, 1993b). First, programs must be comprehensive in scope, attending to the needs of the whole child and supporting families in their roles. Second, programs must involve parents, who are the child's first and most influential teachers. Third, program services must be of high quality to produce desired outcomes. Finally, programs must last longer than the year or so before a child enters school. There is no inoculation against poverty. We must commit to a sustained effort that dovetails services throughout a child's developing years. The following discussion expands on these points.

The first lesson is the need for *comprehensive services*, that is services that address physical and mental health, age-appropriate learning experiences, and social support for the children and their families. Each area is important in its own right, but here we will focus on mental health and family-support services. There are many threats to the psychological well-being of poor children, many of whom have witnessed or have been victims of violence, have myriad unmet needs, and may have been abused or neglected by the adults who are supposed to nurture them. Unfortunately, practitioners in the field of mental health services have focused more on adults and older children than on the very young. This void was recently addressed by the American Orthopsychiatric Association's Task Force on Head Start and Mental Health (1994). Although the group focused on strengthening the mental health component in Head Start, their work is applicable to early childhood programs in general. Their efforts are an example of the applied science advocated by Harold Stevenson.

Family-support services are not that common in early childhood programs, but they should be. Many parents with low or limited incomes move from place to place frequently and become socially isolated. They do not have nearby relatives or friends to advise them about child rearing or help them solve problems. Assistance with basic needs such as housing, food, and medical and child care may be available in their communities, but they do not know how to access it. By linking families with the support services they need, early intervention personnel can help to strengthen the family and thus improve the child's rearing environment.

The second lesson from the early intervention literature is the need for *parent involvement*. It took psychologists a long time to step down from their professional pedestals and acknowledge that parents raise children, not teachers or those who design preschool programs. Parents can carry on the goals of the intervention long after the child graduates from the program. There is now some evidence from other types of intervention that there are diffusion effects to siblings (Seitz and Apfel, 1994), because the mothers became better socializers of all their children. If so, the benefits of parental involvement are more far-reaching than we ever imagined.

As for the third lesson, the need for *high quality services* is a given for any childhood program, but it must be stressed in programs that serve at-risk children. Simply put, good programs are better for children than bad ones. The early care and education literature clearly defines the characteristics of good programs (Bredekamp, 1987; Cost, Quality, and Child Outcomes Study Team, 1995). For example, the physical environment must be free of safety hazards; group sizes should not be too large; child-to-staff ratios should be high; teachers should be trained in early childhood development; and the program should be appropriate to the developmental level of each child. Such criteria have been found to relate to children's developmental outcomes (see Cost, Quality, and Child Outcomes Study Team, 1995; Peisner-Feinberg, 1995).

The imperative of quality was underscored during the recent Head Start expansion, when it became evident that not all centers were delivering good services (Chafel, 1992; Inspector General, 1993; Zigler and Styfco, 1994). Inconsistent quality in Head Start has actually existed from the very beginning. The program started off so big and so fast that quality controls were left behind. Funding levels that fell further and further behind inflation later eroded the ability of many centers to provide quality programs. It is important to stress this is not the case in all centers. Many Head Start programs are excellent (Brush, Gaidurgis, and Best, 1993; Sibley, VandeWiele, and Herrington, 1996). Yet there are some that are only mediocre, and a few that are not good at all. Congress and the Clinton administration have now taken steps to enhance quality throughout Head Start, an effort that will be discussed in the next section.

The final lesson, the need for programs that last longer, derives from what we now know about the importance of *developmental continuity*. We must never again be so naive to believe that a preschool education will guarantee all children success in school and later life. Child development does not begin and end at the age of four. Most of it occurs during prior and succeeding years. Head Start's planners were aware of this, at least they were aware that not much could be accomplished in 6 weeks. Head Start was therefore designed as a national laboratory for the development of further means of intervention. It immediately began to test models for serving very young children and to dovetail services into the early years of elementary school. Both efforts are now well enough developed to be integrated into the national Head Start program. Steps in this direction have already begun, and are described in the context of modernizing Head Start.

Toward a System of Preventive Intervention

Our vision of the Head Start of the future is actually a system of early care and education that spans the age range from birth to 8 years. It begins with Early Head Start, a program that has recently been mounted for families and children from the prenatal period through age 3. This is followed by preschool Head Start that is universally of high quality. Finally, there is a Head Start Transition to School program that continues appropriate services from kindergarten through third grade.

Infants and toddlers

Early Head Start grew out of the work of the Carnegie Task Force on Meeting the Needs of Very Young Children (1994) and a paper requested of us by the Clinton transition team (Zigler and Styfco, 1993a). The project was designed by the Advisory Committee on Services for Families with Infants and Toddlers (1994). Unlike the planners of the original Head Start, this committee had an established knowledge base and a wealth of expertise from which to draw. The culmination of this knowledge in Early Head Start represents the most promising chance we have had since 1965 for our society to attempt new ways to address the ills of poverty and the causes of school failure.

The general structure of the new program includes all the components that experience has proven necessary for good developmental outcomes. The content of these services will, of course, be adjusted to the special needs of infants and toddlers. Because parents are the child's first teachers and socializers, many aspects of the intervention are parent-focused. In response to recent policies to reduce welfare and send welfare recipients to work, the 0-to-3 programs are encouraged to make quality child care services available. A research and evaluation component is written into the program's design.

Early Head Start services are to be guided by national quality standards adapted to the needs of very young children. The standards cover qualifications of personnel, adult-to-child ratios, group sizes, and program features that promote sound development. These quality elements are absolutely necessary for at-risk children to have a chance at optimal development. Today too many young children are in care settings that are horrific, devoid of so many environmental nutrients that their development is being compromised (Cost, Quality, and Child Outcomes Study Team, 1995). For children whose futures are already threatened by poverty, such care only gives them a start on the road leading to their own socioeconomic failure. We hope the federal standards will do more than ensure quality in Early Head Start. They can set an example for the entire nation of how to improve the quality of care delivered to millions of children, including those who are not economically disadvantaged.

Preschoolers

The basic features and administration of the preschool Head Start program remain sound and are often used as the comparative standard for early childhood services (General Accounting Office, 1995). However, many Head Start centers have had difficulties meeting the needs of their children and families because of inadequate funding and changes in the population they serve. For example, teachers earn an average of $15,000 a year, and aides earn $9,500. It can be hard to attract and retain qualified staff with such low wages. Social services workers have caseloads that are far too high, averaging 91 families, and staff in charge of parent involvement are assigned to over 175 families (Verzaro-O'Brien, Powell, and Sakamoto, 1996). These large caseloads are particularly troublesome because Head Start now serves a high proportion of dysfunctional families with myriad needs. Parental involvement needs to be strengthened throughout Head Start, which is a challenge now that so many mothers work outside the home or are still children themselves. Finally, research, evaluation, and dissemination – so necessary to guiding Head Start's evolution – once diminished to the point where they consumed less than 1% of the budget.

Congress took steps to address quality problems in Head Start when it passed the Human Services Reauthorization Act of 1990 and subsequent legislation. The Act began the practice of reserving one quarter of Head Start's budget increases after inflation for quality improvements. Half of the set-aside money is used for raising salaries and benefits. Training and technical assistance are being expanded. Soon all classrooms must have at least one teacher with a Child Development Associate credential. Facilities and transportation are also being upgraded.

When rapid expansion threatened implementation of these improvements, Health and Human Services Secretary Donna Shalala appointed the Advisory Committee on Head Start Quality and Expansion (1993). Their ideas built upon the enhancements covered by the Reauthorization Act and also addressed evaluation, management, and administration.

Secretary Shalala and Administration on Children, Youth and Families (ACYF) Commissioner Olivia Golden also had the courage to do something that has rarely been done before: close bad centers. With the full support of President Clinton, they are standing behind their regional directors' efforts to deny Head Start grants to poor performers and give the money to grantees who can do a better job. Finally, four Research Centers on Head Start Quality have been funded recently to guide the development of more effective services. All these efforts, along with better monitoring, are bringing us closer to the time when every Head Start center will deliver the quality services that children deserve and that are necessary for positive developmental outcomes. The rate of improvement may have slowed with the minimal budget increase (and hence quality set-aside) Head Start received in fiscal year 96, but the program is now headed in the right direction.

One reason that policy makers have been supportive of expanding and improving Head Start is that they see it as a step toward achieving the national education goals. The first goal is that all children will enter school ready to learn, and Head Start has been demonstrably successful in this regard. Its accomplishments have inspired the growth of public school prekindergartens nationwide, but whether these will help to realize Goal One is uncertain. A survey by the Children's Defense Fund showed that 32 states now fund preschool programs (Adams and Sandfort, 1994). Like Head Start, most of the state programs are for children deemed at-risk of having problems in public school. However, many of these programs do not provide the quality and services that are absolutely necessary to produce benefits. In Texas, for example, teacher-to-child ratios in public preschools are greater than 1:20, more than twice the ratio recommended for Head Start (Mitchell, Seligson, and Marx, 1989). A study by the General Accounting Office (1995) showed that although some public preschools provide services that go beyond education, none approaches the level of services in Head Start. Only 35%, for instance, offer any type of health services. Even Head Start's educational component generally surpasses the state preschools in that it is more appropriate to the developmental needs of young children. In sum, despite the criticisms of quality in Head Start, the program has been found superior to many public as well as private preschools (Layzer, Goodson, and Moss, 1993). To achieve the national education goals, the Head Start model should be followed more closely by public schools that are serving at-risk preschoolers.

Transition to school

The third component of an early intervention system applies to children beginning elementary school. In the early years of Head Start, studies showed that the preschool graduates began school with better academic skills than comparison children who did not attend (Datta, 1997). This initial advantage soon appeared to fade, however, leaving critics to argue whether Head Start or the public-school system was to blame. Later research showed that Head Start and similar programs do have lasting benefits in the areas of social and academic adjustment (Barnett, 1995; Consortium, 1983), but that sustained improvement in academic performance is better achieved when preschool services are followed by coordinated programming in elementary school. The Head Start Transition Project, conceptualized by Senator Edward Kennedy (1993) and mounted by ACYF, is such an effort.

This program begins at the time of transition from the preschool to the elementary school environment and lasts through third grade. Comprehensive services are continued for these 4 years, giving children more protection against common health and social problems that can interfere with learning. Also continued are Head Start's individualized and developmentally appropriate programs. Preschool and elementary school educators are required to coordinate their curricula and pedagogies, making the two school experiences less fragmented for young learners. Parental involvement is assured because, as in Head Start, each Transition Project grantee must have a plan for including parents in the design, management, and operation of the program.

The Transition Project clearly contains all the elements known to make intervention effective. Further, there is a small but very convincing body of evidence (reviewed by Zigler and Styfco, 1993b; see also Reynolds, 1996) that supports the project's premise that continuous intervention for an adequate length of time can help children who live in poverty succeed in school. Expansion of the Transition Project to serve all Head Start graduates would seem to be the next logical step. This will take money, however, money that can be found by redirecting the massive. Title I education program. Title I receives over $7 billion annually – almost twice as much as Head Start – but it has had only minor impact on the achievement levels of children in low income families (Arroyo and Zigler, 1993; U.S. Department of Education, 1996).

The reason is that the program contains none of the elements that are necessary for successful intervention: It is remedial rather than preventive, services are academic rather than comprehensive, and parent involvement and developmental continuity are minimal. To improve its benefits and cost-effectiveness, we have developed a proposal for Title to adopt the model of the Transition Project and become the school-age version of Head Start (Zigler and Styfco, 1993b).

As Head Start expands to serve all eligible children, Title I programs can continue their interventions in grammar school. Coordinated curricula and continued parent involvement and comprehensive services can then be firmly placed in schools that serve populations of students whose parents are below the poverty level. The merger will also help shape a coherent federal policy about how to help children with economic disadvantages succeed in school. With some 11 federal agencies and 20 offices funding over 90 programs for at-risk children (General Accounting Office, 1994), the need for such a policy is clear.

The three-stage intervention system described here would constitute ameaningful effort to enable children and families to overcome the negative effects of poverty. A parent–child program would begin prenatally and continue through age 3. Quality preschool services would then be provided, overlapping with the start of elementary school to ensure a smooth transition between the two learning environments. To keep the momentum toward success going in the long process of public education, dovetailed services would continue from kindergarten through third grade. Each phase of the intervention would provide health care and nutrition, developmentally appropriate social and educational experiences, parent involvement, and family support. Our current knowledge strongly suggests that such a system would be successful.

Some Limits of Intervention

Though efforts are being planned to improve, expand, and extend Head Start services, there are several issues that need to be contemplated. One is the frequently heard plea that Head Start become a full-time, all-year program to provide child care for working parents. This idea is gaining more attention now that federal and state policies are phasing out welfare entitlements. Wartime excepted, national support of child care has, in fact, always been linked to welfare reform. But Head Start is not a child-care program. It is a comprehensive, two-generation intervention. A small percentage of centers do provide child care as part of their mission to meet the needs of participating families. In an ideal world with unlimited finances, all Head Start centers could offer child care. But finances are limited, and lawmakers must be careful to preserve the Head Start model as it exists and not overextend it.

Linkages between Head Start and community child-care services are being tried in some places (Koppel, 1995; Poersch and Blank, 1996). Such collaborations have the advantage of ensuring the quality of care by holding it to Head Start's performance standards. They help Head Start to meet family needs and allow participants the opportunity to interact with children from other socioeconomic groups. Another plus is that they permit Head Start to concentrate on its primary mission.

Another issue to ponder as Head Start is renovated and increasing funds are spent on it and other early childhood programs concerns our expectations. The nationwide preschool movement and the massive Head Start expansion have occurred amidst a clamor of exaggerated claims. Many people seem to believe that preschool programs will improve IQ, high-school graduation rates, and the nation's productivity. These programs are also supposed to lower rates of delinquency, teenage pregnancy, and welfare use. Some of these outcomes were actually reported for the Perry Preschool, which was a small project run in the 1960s that provided quality preschool education and some parent involvement activities (Schweinhart et al., 1993). Although the Perry graduates did better than they would otherwise have done, the absolute level of their functioning remains quite low. The reality is that no program offered to young children for a brief portion of their lives can solve deep-rooted problems such as underachievement and poverty.

So what can early intervention accomplish? Head Start and similar programs have had some success in preparing children for school. If society wants to do more, it must mount a comprehensive prevention system that involves the child, family, and community and lasts long enough to make a difference. Such a system could conceivably prevent more than school failure. The risks associated with poor school performance include child factors, such as ability and motivation; family factors, such as parenting skills and economic status; and community factors, such as the quality of education and health services. These factors also coincide with a model developed by Yoshikawa (1994) to describe the risks associated with juvenile delinquency. If intervention can alleviate some of the risks that make a child likely to fail, it might also lessen the likelihood that a child will turn to crime. A number of workers have now discussed early childhood intervention as a possible tool in delinquency prevention (Farrington, 1994; Watson, 1995; Wilson, 1987; Yoshikawa, 1995; Zigler and Hall, 1987; Zigler and Styfco, in press; Zigler, Taussig, and Black, 1992). A great deal of research is needed to examine this possibility, of course, but the hypothesis is certainly promising.

Conclusion

The ideas presented here about the future of early childhood intervention derive from an extensive literature and broad knowledge base. They are built on the findings of sound empirical work and will depend on the same to realize their potential. Developmentalists have accomplished much, but there is still much to accomplish. We are indebted to Harold Stevenson for showing us how to do good research and how to put it to good use.

References

Adams, G., & Sandfort, J. (1994). *First steps, promising futures. State prekindergarten initiatives in the early 1990s.* Washington. DC: Children's Defense Fund.

Advisory Committee on Head Start Quality and Expansion. (1993). *Creating a 21st century Head Start.* Washington, DC: U.S. Department of Health and Human Services.

Advisory Committee on Services for Families with Infants and Toddlers. (1994). *Statement of the Advisory Committee on Services for Families with Infants and Toddlers.* Washington, DC: U.S. Department of Health and Human Services.

Arroyo, C. G., & Zigler, E. (1993). America's Title I/Chapter 1 programs: Why the promise has not been met. In E. Zigler & S. J. Styfco (Eds.), *Head Start and beyond: A national plan for extended childhood intervention* (pp. 73–95). New Haven, CT: Yale University Press.

Barnett, W. S. (1995). Long-term effects of early childhood programs on cognitive and school outcomes. *Future of Children,* 5(3), 25–50.

Bredekamp, S. (Ed.). (1987). *Accreditation criteria and procedures.* Washington DC: National Association for the Education of Young Children.

Bronfenbrenner, U. (1979). *The ecology of human development.* Cambridge MA: Harvard University Press.

Bronfenbrenner, U., & Crouter, A. C. (1983). The evolution of environment models in developmental research. In P. H. Mussen (Series Ed.) & Kessen (Vol. Ed.), *Handbook of child psychology: Vol. 1. History, theory, and methods* (4th ed., pp. 357–414). New York: Wiley.

Brush, L., Gaidurgis, A., & Best, C. (1993). *Indices of Head Start program quality.* Report prepared for the Administration on Children, Youth and Families, Head Start Bureau. Washington, DC: Pelavin Associates.

Cahan, E. (1989). *Past caring: A history of U.S. preschool care and education for the poor, 1820–1965.* New York: National Center for Children in Poverty.

Califano, J. A., Jr. (1997). Head Start, a retrospective view: The foundation Section 1: Leadership within the Johnson administration. In E. Zigler & J. Valentine (Eds.), *Project Head Start: A legacy of the War on Poverty* (2nd ed., pp. 43–72). Alexandria, VA: National Head Start Association.

Carnegie Task Force on Meeting the Needs of Young Children. (1994). *Starting points: Meeting the needs of our youngest children.* New York: Carnegie Corporation.

Chafel, J. A. (1992). Funding Head Start: What are the issues? *American Journal of Orthopsychiatry, 62,* 9–21.

Consortium for Longitudinal Studies. (Ed.). (1983). *As the twig is bent: Lasting effects of preschool programs.* Hillsdale, NJ: Erlbaum.

Cost, Quality, & Child Outcomes Study Team. (1995). *Cost, quality, and child outcomes in child care centers, Public report* (2nd ed.). Denver: University of Colorado at Denver, Economics Department.

Datta, L. (1997). Another spring and other hopes: Some findings from national evaluations of Project Head Start. In E. Zigler & J. Valentine (Eds.), *Project Head Start: A legacy of the War on Poverty* (2nd ed., pp. 405–432). Alexandria, VA: National Head Start Association.

Farrington, D. P. (1994, April). *Delinquency prevention in the first few years of life.* Plenary address, Fourth European Conference on Law and Psychology, Barcelona, Spain.

Gardner, H. (1995). Cracking open the IQ box. In S. Fraser (Ed.), *The bell curve wars: Race, intelligence, and the future of America* (pp. 23–35). New York: Basic Books.

General Accounting Office. (1994, October). *Early childhood programs. Multiple programs and overlapping target groups* (GAO/HEHS-95-4FS). Washington, DC: Author.

General Accounting Office. (1995, March). *Early childhood centers. Services to prepare children for school often limited* (GAO/HEHS-95-21). Washington, DC: Author.

Herrnstein, R. J., & Murray, C. (1994). *The bell curve. Intelligence and class structure in American life.* New York: Free Press.

Hunt, J. McV. (1971). Parent and child centers: Their basis in the behavioral and educational sciences. *American Journal of Orthopsychiatry, 41,* 13–38.

Inspector General (Office of). (1993). *Evaluating Head Start expansion through performance indicators* (Rep. No. OEI-09-91-00762). Washington, DC: U.S. Department of Health and Human Services.

Kennedy, E. M. (1993). The Head Start Transition Project: Head Start goes to elementary school. In. E. Zigler & S. J. Styfco (Eds.), *Head Start and beyond: A national plan for extended childhood intervention* (pp. 97–109). New Haven, CT: Yale University Prees.

Koppel, S. G. (1995). *Head Start and child care: Partners not competitors.* Lumberville, PA: Support Services for Child Care Professionals.

Layzer, J. I., Goodson, B. D., & Moss, M. (1993). *Life in preschool: Vol. 1. An observational study of early childhood programs for disadvantaged four-year-olds.* Final report (Contract No. EALC 890980, U.S. Dept. of Education). Cambridge, MA: ABT Associates.

Miller, G. A. (1969). Psychology as a means of promoting human welfare. *American Psychologist, 24,* 1063–1075.

Mitchell, A., Seligson, M., & Marx, F. (1989). *Early childhood programs and the public schools.* Dover, MA: Auburn House.

National Head Start Association. (1990). *Head Start: The nation's pride, a nation's challenge.* Report of the Silver Ribbon Panel. Alexandria, VA: Author.

Peisner-Feinberg, E. (1995). Child care quality and children's developmental outcomes. In *Cost, quality, and child outcomes in child care centers. Public report* (2nd ed., pp. 305–310). Denver: University of Colorado at Denver, Economics Department.

Poersch, N. O., & Blank, H. (1996). *Working together for children: Head Start and child care partnerships.* Washington, DC: Children's Defense Fund.

Price, R. H., Cowen, E., Lorion, R. P., & Ramos-McKay, J. (Eds.). (1988). *Fourteen ounces of prevention: A casebook for practitioners.* Washington, DC: American Psychological Association.

Reynolds, A. J. (1996). *Chicago Child-Parent Centers: A longitudinal study of extended early childhood intervention.* New York: Foundation for Child Development.

Schorr, L. B. (1988). *Within our reach: Breaking the cycle of disadvantage.* New York: Doubleday.

Schweinhart, L. J., Barnes, H. V., & Weikart, D. P. (1993). *Significant benefits: The High/Scope Perry Preschool study through age 27. Monographs of the High/Scope Educational Research Foundation, 10.* Ypsilanti, MI: High/Scope Press.

Seitz, V., & Apfel, N. H. (1994). Parent-focused intervention: Diffusion effects on siblings. *Child Development, 65,* 677–683.

Sibley, A., VandeWiele, L., & Herrington, S. (1996). *Quality initiative, year one report. Georgia Head Start.* Atlanta, GA: Quality Assist.

Sternberg, R. J., Wagner, R. K., Williams, W. M., & Horvath, J. A. (1995). Testing common sense. *American Psychologist, 50,* 912–927.

Task Force on Head Start and Mental Health. (1994, April). *Strengthening mental health in Head Start: Pathways to quality improvement.* New York: American Orthopsychiatric Association.

U. S. Department of Education. (1996). *Mapping out the national assessment of Title I: The interim report.* Washington, DC: Author.

Verzaro-O'Brien, M., Powell, G., & Sakamoto, L. (1996). *Investing in quality revisited. The impact of the Head Start Expansion and Improvement Act of 1990 after five years of investment.* Alexandria, VA: National Head Start Association.

Watson, J. (1995). Crime and juvenile delinquency prevention policy: Time for early childhood intervention. *Georgetown Journal on Fighting Poverty, 2,* 245–270.

Wilson, J. Q. (1987). Strategic opportunities for delinquency prevention. In J. Q. Wilson & G. C. Loury (Eds.), *From children to citizens: Vol. 3. Families, schools, and delinquency prevention* (pp. 291–312). New York: Springer-Verlag.

Yoshikawa, H. (1994). Prevention as cumulative protection: Effects of early family support and education on chronic delinquency and its risks. *Psychological Bulletin, 115,* 28–54.

Yoshikawa, H. (1995). Long-term effects of early childhood programs on social outcomes and delinquency. *Future of Children, 5*(3), 51–75.

Zigler, E. (1996). *Child development and social policy.* Unpublished manuscript, Yale University, New Haven, CT.

Zigler, E., & Berman, W. (1983). Discerning the future of early childhood intervention. *American Psychologist, 38,* 894–906.

Zigler, E., & Hall, N. (1987). Preventing juvenile delinquency. In E. Aronowitz & R. Sussman (Eds.), *Issues in community mental health: Youth.* Canton, MA: Prodist.

Zigler, E., & Styfco, S. J. (1993a). An earlier Head Start: Planning an intervention program for economically disadvantaged families and children ages zero to three. *Zero to Three, 14*(2), 25–28.

Zigler, E., & Styfco, S. J. (1993b). Strength in unity: Consolidating federal education programs for young children. In E. Zigler & S. J. Styfco (Eds.), *Head Start and beyond: A national plan for extended childhood intervention* (pp. 111–145). New Haven, CT: Yale University Press.

Zigler, E., & Styfco, S. J. (1994). Head Start: Criticisms in a constructive context. *American Psychologist, 49,* 127–132.

Zigler, E., & Styfco, S. J. (in press). Can early childhood intervention prevent delinquency? A real possibility. In *Constructive and destructive behavior:*

Implications for family, school, and society. A Festschrift in honor of Seymour and Norma Feshbach.

Zigler, E., & Styfco, S. J. (1997). A "Head Start" in what pursuit? IQ vs. social competence as the objective of early intervention. In B. Devlin, S. E. Fienberg, D. Resnick, & K. Roeder (Eds.), *IQ, race, and public policy: An analysis of* The Bell Curve (pp. 283–314). New York: Springer-Verlag.

Zigler, E., Taussig, C., & Black, K. (1992). Early childhood intervention: A promising preventative for juvenile delinquency. *American Psychologist, 47,* 997–1006.

Introduction to Chapter 3

The Abecedarian Project was one of the first randomized clinical trials of a comprehensive EI program and is a forerunner of the current Two-Generation programs for low-income families. This chapter provides a summary of previous and most recent findings of this project. Although a variety of in-home and parent services were included, the hallmark of this intervention was the child's enrolment in an intensive, specialized, out-of-home full-day preschool (and a subsequent supplemental K-2 home visiting teacher program). A curriculum designed on learning principles was provided to keep the child from falling behind in cognitive development and school performance. The results indicated that Ramey and his colleagues achieved this goal for the first 15 years of the child's life. Although the Carolina Abecedarian families primarily lived in rural communities, other comparable out-of-home early enrichment programs for inner-city, low-income, academically at-risk children have reported remarkably similar findings in nonrandomized trials (Garber, 1988; Reynolds and Temple, 1998).

"Biosocial Developmental Contextualisin" served as the conceptual model for the Abecedarian project and is similar to the model proposed by Guralnick in chapter 1. Ramey and Ramey (1998, pp. 115–118) elucidated six basic principles of effective EI that were incorporated into the Abecedarian Project:

1 Programs should begin as early as possible and continue past preschool (Abecedarian children started as early as 6 weeks of age and some continued to receive additional educational supports until second grade).
2 Programs should be intense (Abecedarian children attended preschool all day, 5 days a week, 11 months a year).
3 Programs should provide direct educational experiences to the child (the Abecedarian children were taught by specially trained teachers following a manualized curriculum based on empirically validated learning principles).
4 Programs should provide comprehensive and flexible services (the Abecedarian families received a variety of supports, as needed).
5 Programs should recognize individual differences in response to interventions (those Abecedarian children whose mothers had

lower IQs had greatest need for, and benefited the most from, the intervention).

6 Programs should provide or arrange for ongoing supports in the early grades to maintain the child's preschool gains (the follow-up results suggest that those supports the children continued to receive post-Abecedarian involvement likely contributed to the maintenance of the gains, with the children who received specialized support until grade 2 doing the best).

Inbedded in the Biosocial Developmental Contextualism model are six "Psychosocial Developmental Priming Mechanisms" that children should experience to maintain typical cognitive development (Ramey and Ramey, 1998, p. 113):

1 encouragement of exploration and curiosity;
2 tutoring new developmental skills;
3 reinforcement of new skills;
4 practice and extension of skills;
5 avoidance of discouragement and punishment;
6 ongoing language stimulation.

When, for whatever reasons, the home environment does not provide these experiences to maintain typical development in impoverished children, then the type of out-of-home preschool experience provided in the Abecedarian Project and other programs (Garber, 1988; Reynolds and Temple, 1998) appears to be able to compensate for this lack of stimulation.

References

Garber, H. L. (1988). *The Milwaukee Project: Preventing mental retardation in children at risk*. Washington, DC: American Association on Mental Retardation.

Ramey, C. T. & Ramey, S. L. (1998). Early intervention and early experience. *American Psychologist*, 53, 109–120.

Reynolds, A. J. & Temple, J. A. (1998). Extended early childhood intervention and school achievement: Age thirteen findings from the Chicago Longitudinal Study. *Child Development*, 69, 231–246.

THREE

Persistent Effects of Early Childhood Education on High-Risk Children and Their Mothers

Craig T. Ramey, Frances A. Campbell,
Margaret Burchinal, Martie L.
Skinner, David M. Gardner, and
Sharon L. Ramey

Intergenerational poverty is pernicious. Impairments in cognitive development, school performance, and social competence are all associated with growing up poor (Duncan and Brooks-Gunn, 1997; Duncan, Brooks-Gunn, and Klebanov, 1994; Huston, 1992; McLloyd, 1998; Ramey, MacPhee, and Yeates, 1982). Currently, approximately 23% of children spend some or all of their childhood in poverty (Hernandez, 1997, p. 18).

Over the past four decades, educators, psychologists, social workers, and physicians have designed multidisciplinary intervention programs to benefit children from high-risk families. These programs can be conceptualized as applied developmental science probes into factors associated with the malleability of developmental processes and outcomes

Ramey, R. T., Campbell, F. A., Burchinal, M., Skinner, M. L., Gardner, D. M., and Ramey, S. L. (2000). Persistent effects of early childhood education on high-risk children and their mothers. *Applied Developmental Science, 4,* 2–14. Includes use of tables 1–4 and figures 1–9. Copyright Lawrence Erlbaum Associates Inc., Hillsdale, NJ.

(Ramey and Finkelstein, 1981; Ramey et al., 1982; Ramey and Ramey, 1998). A number of scientifically rigorous early childhood programs in which participants were randomly assigned to treatment and control groups have reported initially positive effects on the cognitive development of poor children (e.g., Bryant and Maxwell, 1997; and Ramey and Ramey, 1998; for reviews). However, only a few investigators of true experiments have conducted systematic, long-term, follow-ups of their samples into adolescence or beyond (e.g., Campbell and Ramey, 1995; Gray, Ramsey, and Klaus, 1982; Lazar, Darlington, Murray, Royce, and Snipper, 1982; Schweinhart, Barnes, Weikart, Barnett, and Epstein, 1993). Such long-term follow-up is important because it conditions practical expectations for the developmental outcomes associated with various early intervention procedures and thus is directly relevant to educational, welfare, and health policies.

It is the purpose of this article to report practical, long-term effects of the Abecedarian Project. The Abecedarian Project was a two-phase, comparative, early childhood education, pediatric healthcare, and family support program that began in early infancy. Three educational treatment conditions have been compared to an educational control condition. Child participants have now been followed systematically until 15 years of age.

Method

Recruitment

The Abecedarian Project was initially conceptualized as a randomized controlled trial of the efficacy of early intervention for children born to low-income, multirisk families. Local prenatal clinics and the department of social services were screened for eligible participants using the 13-factor Risk Index in table 3.1. Families who expressed interest (99%) were then visited by study personnel to conduct a formal assessment of the family's eligibility for inclusion in the project. The condition of random assignment to early childhood treatment or comparison groups was explained during the enrollment process. Ninety-three percent of eligible families chose to participate. Entry characteristics of the preschool treatment and control participants are presented in table 3.2.

Table 3.1 High-risk index

Factor	Weight
Mother's educational level (last grade completed)	
6	8
7	7
8	6
9	3
10	2
11	1
12	0
Father's educational level (last grade completed)	
6	8
7	7
8	6
9	3
10	2
11	1
12	0
Family income ($ per year)	
1,000	8
1,001–2,000	7
2,001–3,000	6
3,001–4,000	5
4,001–5,000	4
5,001–6,000	0
Father absent for reasons other than health or death	3
Absence of maternal relatives in local area	3
Siblings of school age one or more grades behind age-appropiate level or with equivalently low scores on school-administered achievement tests	3
Payments received from welfare agencies within past 3 years	3
Record of father's work indicates unstable or unskilled and semiskilled labor	3
Records of mother's or father's IQ indicate scores of 90 or below	3
Records of sibling's IQ indicates scores of 90 or below	3
Relevant social agencies in the community indicate the family is in need of assistance	3
One or more members of the family has sought counseling or professional help in the past 3 years	1
Special circumstances not included in any of the above that are likely contributors to cultural of social disadvantage	1

Note: Criterion for inclusion in high-risk sample was a score of more than 11.

Table 3.2   Entry level demographic data for preschool-treated and
control families

	Group					
	Experimental[a]		*Control*[b]		*Total*[c]	
Variables	M	SD	M	SD	M	SD
Mean maternal age (years)	19.56	3.88	20.28	5.77	19.92	4.90
Mean maternal education (years)	10.45	1.75	9.98	1.91	10.22	1.84
Mean maternal full scale IQ	85.49	12.43	84.18	10.78	84.84	11.61
Percentage intact family	23		26		24	
Percentage African American	96		100		98	

Notes: [a]N = 55. [b]N = 54. [c]N = 109.

Participants

Four cohorts of infants, born between 1972 and 1977, were enrolled in
the study. Newborns had to appear healthy and free from biological
conditions associated with developmental disabilities. The enrolled
sample included 111 children, 57 randomly assigned to the preschool
treatment group and 54 to the pre-school control group (two families
had two children each enrolled in the project).

The families were predominantly African American (98%) although
ethnicity was not a selection criterion. At birth, 76% of the children
lived in single parent or multigenerational households. Mothers' ages
ranged from 13 to 44 years, with an average age of slightly less than
20 years. Mean maternal education when the focal child was born was
approximately 10th grade in both groups. Average maternal IQ as
assessed by clinical examination was approximately 85.

Of the 57 children (from 55 families) originally assigned to the preschool treatment group, 48 remained in the study through the 8-year
experimental period (84% retention); of the 54 preschool control group
children, 42 remained (78% retention). Analysis of the key demographic
factors for the 19 families lost to attrition showed no significant differences from those retained, with the exception that 71% of the lost
participants were girls.

Table 3.3 Summary of Abecedarian preschool treatment and control conditions

Preschool treatment[a]	Control treatment[b]
Nutritional supplements	Nutritional supplements
Family support social services	Family support social services
Pediatric care and referral	Pediatric care and referral
Early childhood education	
6 weeks to 5 years of age	
Good teacher–child ratios and a	
year-round program that met or	
exceeded NAEYC standards	
Developmentally appropriate practices	
Hours of operation: 7:30 a.m. to 5:30 p.m.	
Partners for Learning curriculum plus other	
documented approaches	
Preservice and inservice training	
Individualized learning experiences in	
natural preschool atmosphere	
Emphasis on language, cognition, social,	
emotional, and physical development	
Promotion and support for parent involvement	
Daily transportation	

Note: NAEYC = *National Association for the Education of Young Children.* [a]N = 57. [b]N = 54.

Experimental Phase I: Abecedarian Preschool Program

The Abecedarian preschool treatment and control conditions are summarized in table 3.3. Study particulars have been reported in detail in previous publications (Ramey, Bryant, Campbell, Sparling, and Wasik, 1988; Ramey, Campbell, and Blair, 1998; Ramey and Haskins, 1981; Ramey et al., 1982; Ramey, McGinness, Cross, Collier, and Barrie-Blackley, 1981; Ramey, Sparling, and Wasik, 1981). Therefore, the treatment and control conditions will be summarized only briefly here.

Conceptual framework

In general, the Abecedarian preschool program was a comprehensive education, healthcare and family support program that provided an individualized approach to at-risk children and their families, drawing as needed on a pool of available services. The preschool intervention program's conceptual framework derived from developmental systems theory (Bertalanffy, 1975), which articulates the role of a stimulus-rich, positive, responsive social environment in facilitating instrumental and conceptual learning (Ramey and Finkelstein, 1981). Pragmatic features of conversational language were given a strong emphasis (Ramey, McGinness et al., 1981; Vygotsky, 1978). Ramey and Ramey (1998) summarized these orientations into a general developmental conceptual framework called Biosocial Developmental Contextualism that emphasizes the quality and quantity of adult–child transactions as one major pathway undergirding early brain and behavioral development. Biosocial Developmental Contextualism also explicitly acknowledges the importance of developmental genetics and neurobiology, health conditions, and sociological norms and practices as major influences on individual development. For these and other reasons, health care, good nutrition, and family support services were an integral part of the program. Services were provided based on continuous assessments of family needs and the daily status and behavior of children.

Program goal

The primary goal of the preschool phase (Phase I) was to enhance school readiness and, thus, to establish a better base for a successful transition into elementary school. It is important to note that the Abecedarian Project was located in a generally affluent college town where the vast majority of families were well educated. Thus, there were relatively few families in the local population who would be considered socioeconomically at risk. Those who did fit this category tended to be of African American descent. The community leaders had a generally progressive stance toward disadvantaged families and therefore provided funds for many public and private services for those in need. In the year in which the project began, for example, there were 33 separate agencies in the town devoted, in whole or in part, to meeting the needs of poor and multirisk families. Those services are presumed to have improved the performance of the control group children over what would have occurred in a poorer, less resourceful community. Moreover, the Abecedarian Project provided additional services to both treated and control group participants, including referrals of control children for follow-up treatment in cases where study assessments indicated poor cognitive performance of clinical significance. It is thus reasonable to view the research design as a conservative test of the power of educationally oriented, systematic, early intervention with an emphasis on early childhood education to affect the life course of children from intergenerationally poor and multirisk families.

Preschool intervention effects

To place the Abecedarian K-2 Educational Support Program and the long-term follow-up in life-course context, we briefly summarize findings from the preschool period into six key points. For each point, pertinent references containing additional details are noted.

(1) *Preschool intervention reduced the incidence of delayed cognitive development during the preschool years.*

Effect Sizes. Developmental delay, on average, was first detected in the control group in the 2nd year of life and persisted throughout the preschool years (Ramey and Campbell, 1984). Figure 3.1 (created from data reported by Ramey [1992] and Ramey and Campbell [1984]) depicts the average z scores from 3 to 54 months after amalgamating the data of treated and control participants at each age, standardizing the combined distribution and then calculating the mean z scores for the treatment and control groups separately.

The graph depicts data from the Bayley Mental Development Index, the Stanford-Binet IQ and the McCarthy Scales of General Cognitive Development at appropriate age points in months. The number at each z score is the treatment or control group mean IQ score or equivalent. ($M = 100$, $SD = 15$ in the standardization samples of these tests). Below each age point on the X axis is the effect size estimates based on IQ scores using the following formula:

$$\frac{M \text{ treatment group} - M \text{ control group}}{SD \text{ of control group}}$$

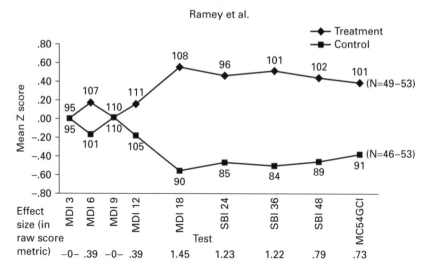

Figure 3.1　Mean Z scores and mean standardized scores for high-risk preschool treatment and control children in the Abecedarian Project at nine preschool measurement occasions

Effect sizes greater than .25 are generally considered by educators to have practical significance (Cohen, 1977). Our calculations reveal that the effect size differences at 3 months were nonexistent. Over the first 18 months of age the differences became larger and consistently favored the performance of the preschool treated group over the control group. The average effect size of preschool treatment between 18 months and 4¹/₂ years was 1.08, a remarkably large average effect size in the early intervention literature.

Practical Significance. To learn the extent to which the High-Risk Index successfully identified children at risk for developmental retardation during the preschool period, Ramey and Campbell (1984) reported the percentages of children who obtained a Stanford–Binet IQ of 85 or less at various occasions during the preschool years. For example, at 48 months approximately 40% of control group children scored in this range compared to less than 5% of the preschool intervention group.

(2) The most vulnerable children benefitted the most from the preschool program. We estimated the effects of the preschool treatment on intellectual development from 6 through 54 months of age (Martin, Ramey, and

Ramey, 1990). The IQs of preschool treatment group children ranged from 8 to 20 points higher than those of control children when maternal mental retardation and home environment, both important factors in the occurrence of developmental delay, were statistically accounted for via multiple-regression analyses. The children who benefitted the most had mothers with IQs below 70.

(3) *Some preschool control group children benefitted from other preschool programs.* Burchinal, Lee, and Ramey (1989) reported analyses that demonstrated the positive association between attendance at other preschool programs and cognitive performance during the prekindergarten years.

(4) *Preschool intervention increased children's cognitive resilience to nonoptimal biological and behavioral conditions.* The Abecedarian Preschool Treatment significantly ameliorated the effects of some biological and behavioral risk factors including low Apgar scores (Brietmayer and Ramey, 1986), difficult temperament (Ramey et al., 1982), and fetal undernourishment (Zeskind and Ramey, 1978, 1981). The primary mechanism for this increased resilience was through improving children's cognitive development by enhancing their responsiveness to their early social environments (Burchinal, Campbell, Bryant, Wasik, and Ramey, 1997).

(5) *The Abecedarian Preschool Program did not harm the mother–child attachment process or mother–child interactions.* Home observations using Caldwell and Bradley's Home Observation for Measurement of the Environment instrument (Caldwell and Bradley, 1984) revealed no measurable negative effect on the socioemotional climate of the home associated with the preschool treatment program (Ramey, Mills, Campbell, and O'Brien, 1975). This finding is buttressed by similar conclusions from the recent report from the National Institute for Child Health and Human Development (NICHD) longitudinal study of day care (NICHD Early Child Care Research Network, 1997). Direct observations of mother–child interactions under laboratory conditions revealed that mothers and children tended toward more involvement as a dyad if the child was enrolled in the preschool (Farran and Ramey, 1980). It is noteworthy that this finding has recently been confirmed with a much larger sample in the Infant Health and Development Program,

an educational intervention for low-birth-weight children whose treatment represented a slight modification of the Abecedarian Preschool Program (Spiker, Ferguson, and Brooks-Gunn, 1993).

(6) *Teen mothers of children receiving the center-based preschool program had an increased likelihood of completing high school and obtaining postsecondary training.* By the time their children entered kindergarten, 46% of teen mothers in the preschool treatment group had graduated from high school and obtained postsecondary training compared to only 13% in the control group (Campbell, Breitmayer, and Ramey, 1986).

Phase II: Abecedarian K-2 Educational Support Program

Research design

Given the positive preschool effects on children and their mothers, at kindergarten entry we were faced with a dilemma. Should we simply follow these children's progress in school to see how they fared or should we provide an educational support program to aid their transitions into school? Because there were no directly relevant data from previous randomized controlled trials to guide us, we decided to do both, and to do so within the two-stage randomized design presented in figure 3.2.

We made this decision although we realized that subdividing a relatively small group of children and families had the disadvantage of reducing the statistical power to detect group differences. On balance, however, we decided that the potential scientific benefits outweighed the risks associated with reduced statistical power. The new design necessitated a revision of our basic statistical approach (a two-group comparison). We now proposed the additional hypothesis that cognitive and academic achievement benefits should be proportional to the duration of the intervention as tested by linear trend analyses of variances (for continuously distributed outcome variables), across the four groups. We then complemented that analysis with a preschool versus no preschool contrast.

At school entry, each cohort of children was rank ordered by 48-month Binet IQs from highest to lowest within both the preschool treatment and control groups. One member of each consecutive pair

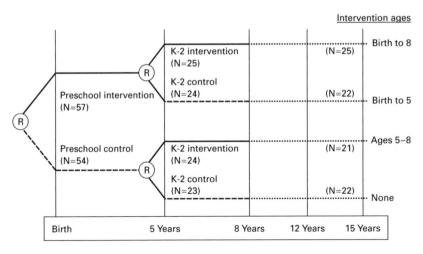

Figure 3.2 Design of Abecedarian Project

within each group was then assigned randomly to the Abecedarian K-2 Educational Support Program.

This design provided the opportunity to examine and compare the long-term effects of (a) early and continuing intervention, (b) early intervention only, and (c) late intervention only, relative to performance of participants in a continuous control group.

We turn now to a brief description of the K-2 Educational Support Program.

Abecedarian K-2 Educational Support Program: Conceptual Framework

The K-2 Program was consistent with the hypothesis that supplementary intervention programs potentially can influence children via modifications in their social environments and learning experiences. It was based largely on the view that parent involvement in schoolwork is an important factor in public school success. The support program was therefore designed to influence the child's home learning support, to individualize school experiences during the academic year in a developmentally appropriate fashion, and to provide additional learning support over the summer – a period during which high-risk children typically lose ground academically (Entwistle and Alexander, 1998). Thus, school-age treated children were offered educational support both in school and at home for the first 3 years they attended public school. Classroom teachers were given continuing consultation and technical assistance to ensure that children's school experiences were developmentally appropriate and parents were shown how to enhance schoolwork by engaging in specific supplemental educational activities at home.

These educational support services were provided by master teachers with extensive, successful backgrounds in primary education, and successful experience in working with at-risk children and families. Known as Home–School Resource Teachers (HSTs), these professionals had graduate degrees in education.

We hypothesized that regular visits by a professional educator who knew the challenges and joys of classroom teaching and had specific knowledge about the child's classroom activities and performance, would help high-risk parents feel more comfortable in helping their children successfully negotiate school routines and meet academic demands. These parents, many of whom had had great difficulty in school themselves, would benefit from an HST who could answer their questions, discuss their concerns, and demonstrate specific learning materials and procedures. At times, the HSTs encouraged schools to refer children for available special services, and helped parents to be actively involved in the referral process and educational therapies provided.

The activities by the HSTs were conceptualized as supplements to the school's regular educational program. No part of the K-2 program was intended to preclude the child's regular school participation or to supplant any services the schools had to offer. It should be noted that the public schools in the university town where the study was conducted were generally well regarded and consistently performed near or at the top of public schools throughout the state on measures of student performance. Further, although at-risk students made up only a very small portion of the student body, a high level of resources was devoted to their education and general welfare. Analogous to the stringency of comparing preschool program outcomes for children and parents in a resource-rich community, the many school-based programs for children at risk makes the comparison of school-age treatment and control group differences a stringent one in relation to what might have been obtained in less resourceful systems. The availability of many learning supports (reading groups, pull-out special education programs, self-contained classes) probably undergirded and raised the school performance of the control group children relative to what would have been obtained in less resourceful school districts.

Typically, an HST worked each year with 12 children, their families, and their classroom teachers. She became an advocate for the family within the school and community systems and for the school within the family.

Learning activities

Individualized learning activities based on the objectives established with the classroom teacher were a major component of the K-2 program. A task–analysis approach defined the component skills necessary to achieve each objective. The sequencing of tasks into manageable steps, characteristic of the task–analysis approach, was used. The activities were calibrated to be challenging but within the child's range of success.

In a typical year, approximately 60 different learning activities were designed for each child. A log of these activities was maintained by the HST to document the curriculum. The primary emphasis for these activities was on basic skills in reading and mathematics. Many were original games created by HSTs. In addition, ready-made activities to give practice in handwriting, phonics, and math concepts and facts were also used. The caregiver was asked to use the activities with the child on a regular basis. On subsequent visits, parents always were asked for feedback on the materials, including how much time they had spent doing them during the previous 2 weeks. Parents were asked to document their use of these activities on a special calendar provided by the HST.

The learning materials were generally popular with parents; most reported high levels of success and satisfaction in using them. On average, parents reported that they worked with their child about 15 minutes a day. Parents especially liked the specificity of the activities because, as one parent said, "they took the guess work out of what to do."

Other family services

Family life and adult issues were also discussed with HSTs at the parents' initiation. Many mothers said that they derived social support from their home visitors, and came to reveal to them personal concerns and problems and to seek advice or help. Parents were referred as necessary to community agencies for social services, housing, medical care, adult education, or employment.

Summer program

In addition to the Abecedarian K-2 school-year program, children were provided with summer camp experiences. While they offered many traditional camp activities, such as arts and crafts, music, games, and sports, these camps also had a "hidden curriculum" in that they featured academic skills in a playful context. Camps were 8 weeks in duration, were based in an elementary school, and made extensive use of community parks, pools, and recreation centers. The camps were staffed by the HSTs and supplemented by paid and volunteer students and adults. Table 3.4 contains a brief summary of the Abecedarian K-2 Transition Program.

Overall, teachers were positive about the K-2 program and the parents participated enthusiastically and frequently in the home activities. At the project's end, all parents reported that they had found it a very positive experience and would have liked to continue to participate if the program had lasted longer.

Table 3.4   Summary of Abecedarian K-2 Educational Support Program

Individualized focus on academically related activities in school and at home
Emphasis on reading, and mathematics, and writing
Master Home/School Resource Teachers with 12 children and families
    per year
Development of an individualized and documented supplemental curriculum
    for each child
Explicit attention and action relevant to family circumstances, as needed
Summer camps with academically relevant experiences

Long-term Results: Academic Achievement, Intellectual Outcomes, and School Progress

Treatment endpoint, age 8

Academic outcomes during the primary grades represent a direct and practical test of the efficacy of the K-2 Educational Support Program as well as an initial test of the persistence of the preschool effects in the case of no additional K-2 program. Achievement in reading and mathematics was considered most important because these two basic subjects are crucial to success in the early elementary grades and they had been the primary focus of the K-2 Educational Support Program. Moreover, they are the skills to which teachers, school administrators, and the public pay particular attention. In this article we have presented age-referenced standard scores ($M = 100$, $SD = 15$) on reading and math derived from the Woodcock–Johnson Psychoeducational Battery (Woodcock and Johnson, 1977) individually administered to children at school by project personnel.

We also have reported group administered achievement tests given by the school staff to elementary school children. The Woodcock–Johnson test results are consistent with those from the school administered tests, as reported by Horacek, Ramey, Campbell, Hoffmann, and Fletcher (1987). As noted before, we hypothesized a linear trend with academic performance increasing as a positive function of the duration of intervention. The age 8 standard score results for reading and mathematics performance are presented in Figure 3.3. They conform perfectly to the expected pattern for both reading and math, but more dramatically for reading than for math.

Effect sizes for the three treatment conditions at age 8 were calculated relative to the mean and standard deviation for participants in the control condition. In figure 3.3 the effect sizes for reading achievement at age 8 vary from .28 to 1.04 for the treatment conditions and are consistent with our hypothesis about duration of program, that is, the longer the program the larger the effect. The most effective treatment condition was the Preschool Plus K-2 Program, followed by the Preschool Only, and then the K-2 Program Only, relative to controls. A similar pattern of findings was obtained for mathematics achievement with somewhat more modest effects (i.e., effect sizes ranging from

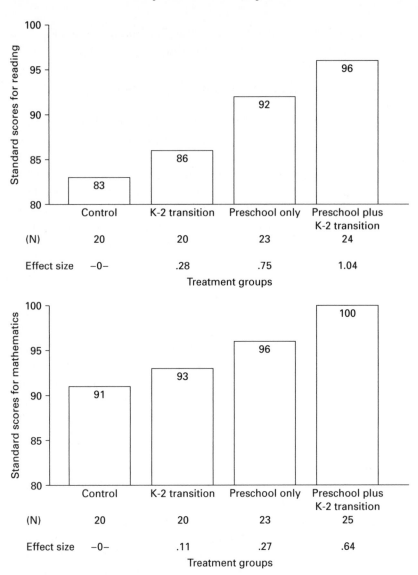

Figure 3.3   Abecedarian Project Woodcock–Johnson age-referenced reading and mathematics standard scores at age 8. Effect sizes for the top graph are relative to the control condition and are calculated as $\dfrac{M_T - M_C}{SD_C}$. T = treatment condition; C = control condition

.11 to .64). Overall, the K-2 Educational Support Program, by itself, was marginally significant for reading (*ES* = .28) but not practically significant for mathematics (*ES* = .11).

Academic achievement at age 12

It was only possible to provide the Educational Support Program for the first 3 years in school. Thereafter, the Abecedarian Project conducted two follow-up studies. When the children were 12 years of age we repeated the earlier assessments of cognitive and academic achievements. Woodcock–Johnson results are presented in figure 3.4. At age 12 the treatment effect sizes across the three groups range from .23 to .86 for reading and from .24 to .63 for math. For reading, the pattern is strikingly consistent with what was obtained at age 8 with the Preschool Plus K-2 Support condition producing the largest effects followed by the Preschool Only condition followed by the K-2 Program Only. For math the pattern was similar with the exception that the two preschool conditions were very similar.

Academic achievement at age 15

A subsequent follow-up was conducted 3 years later when child participants had completed 10 years in school and were turning 15 years old. This probe permitted us to assess progress in middle adolescence, just prior to the age when school attendance is no longer mandated in the local school district.

When the follow-up study was conducted at age 15 we again observed the same pattern of scores for reading and mathematics as was seen at age 12 (Figure 3.5). The effect sizes varied from .14 to .87 in proportion to duration of treatment for reading and from .09 to .65 for mathematics. Again, there was a strong effect both for the Preschool Plus K-2 Educational Support Program and for the Preschool Only condition. By this age, however, the K-2 Program, by itself, proved to be of no practical lasting benefit. Thus, there is clear evidence for a practical and persistent effect of intensive early intervention and especially so for reading when it was supplemented by the K-2 Transition Program.

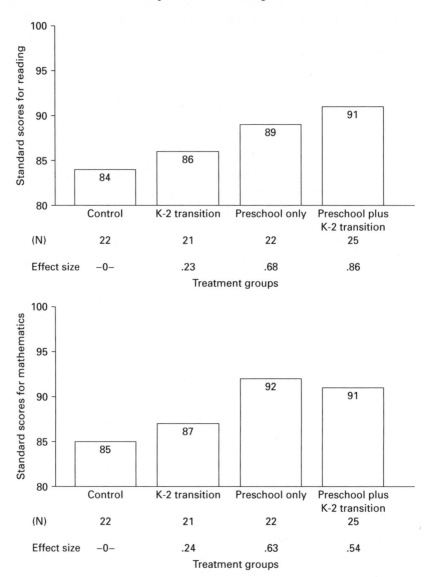

Figure 3.4 Abecedarian Project Woodcock–Johnson age-referenced reading and mathematics standard scores at age 12. Effect sizes for the top graph are relative to the control condition and are calculated as $\dfrac{M_T - M_C}{SD_C}$. T = treatment condition; C = control condition.

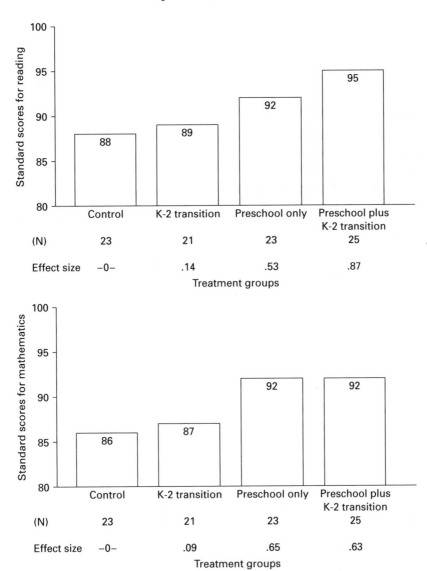

Figure 3.5 Abecedarian Project Woodcock–Johnson age-referenced reading and mathematics standard scores at age 15. Effect sizes for the top graph are relative to the control condition and are calculated as $\frac{M_T - M_C}{SD_C}$. T = treatment condition; C = control condition

Long-term intellectual outcomes

Figure 3.6 presents the mean z scores on age-appropriate Wechsler Scales of Intelligence from age 5 to age 15 for each of the four groups. The right side of the figure also lists the mean age 15 standardized Wechsler Intelligence Scale for Children–Revised IQ scores. Repeated measures analyses of variances for the z scores revealed a main effect for the preschool condition only. The z score effect sizes for the preschool treatment groups average .39 and show no significant time trends over the 10-year period covered.

Following up the finding that children of very low IQ mothers benefitted most from early treatment, we examined the effect size of preschool treatment on child IQ at age 15. Among the 12 individuals for whom follow-up data were available (6 treatment and 6 controls) the effect of preschool treatment on child IQ continued to be substantial – 10 IQ points (91 vs. 81 respectively) for an effect size of .76.

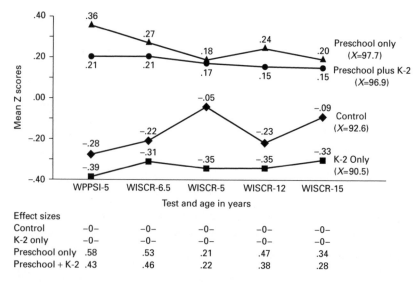

Figure 3.6 Z scores and effect sizes in intellectual performance as a function of treatment condition in the Abecedarian Project

Retention in grade up to age 15

One important real-world measure of a student's scholastic progress is retention in grade. Independently of whether this is an effective remedial practice, it clearly indicates that the school faculty was dubious about the child's readiness for a more advanced curriculum. At age 15, information about grade retention was extracted from school records.

The findings here are quite striking. Only the preschool program had an effect on grade retention – reducing it from 55% overall to 30% overall. The K-2 Program by itself had no measurable effect.

Special education placement to age 15

Figure 3.7 shows the percentage of individuals in each treatment group who had never been assigned to special services over the 10 years they attended school. The figures indicate that students in the preschool control condition were more likely to be placed, but the expected linear trend showing fewer placements as years of treatment increased, is not seen. The special education data need to be interpreted, we think, in light of the role of the HSTs who were Special Educators and who therefore sought out special education services whenever they were thought

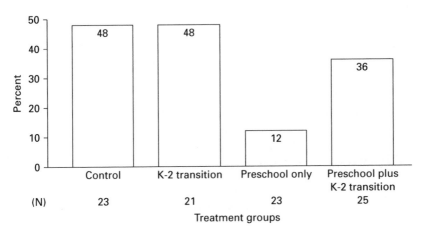

Figure 3.7 Abecedarian Project: percentage of treatment group participants assigned to special services, grades K-9

to be potentially useful. During the primary years, the increased developmental surveillance afforded by the K-2 program may have inflated the rate above what would have occurred in the natural ecology. The most unbiased estimates of a preschool effect can probably be obtained in the Preschool Only versus control comparison. In that comparison 12% of the Preschool Only group was placed in special education versus 48% of the control group.

Maternal outcomes

For parents, the most likely important aspect of family support afforded by the Abecedarian early childhood program was 5 years of free, full-time, educational childcare and accompanying services. Thus, a major question was the significance of this service in the lives of the mothers who received it. We examined the effects of preschool treatment on maternal educational change and employment. The biological mother was the custodian of record for all child participants at study entry. Subsequent examination of gains in maternal education was necessarily confined to those cases where data for the same individual were again available.

Figure 3.8 shows the percentage of all mothers in the preschool treatment and control groups who reported having attained education beyond high school at the time of their child's birth, and at three later points: after 4, 8, and 15 years. The figure also contains this information for the subsample of mothers who were teens (aged 17 or younger) when the target child was born. The younger mothers whose children had preschool intervention were significantly more likely to have post high school educational attainment by the time their children were age 15 (80%) than comparable control mothers (28%).

Figure 3.9 shows the rates of employment for the entire sample and for the subsample of teen mothers within each full set, at age 15. The mothers most likely to be employed were teen mothers in the preschool treatment group (92%) and the least likely were teen mothers in the preschool control condition (66%).

Discussion

The Abecedarian Project children showed positive cognitive effects of participating in an early intervention program. These preschool effects

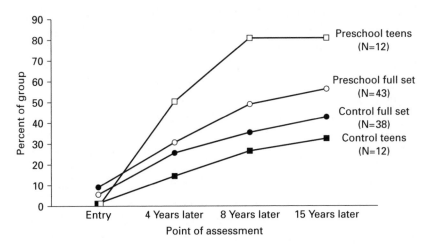

Figure 3.8   Percentage of total group and teen mother subgroup with post-high school education at study entry and three subsequent points by preschool treatment group

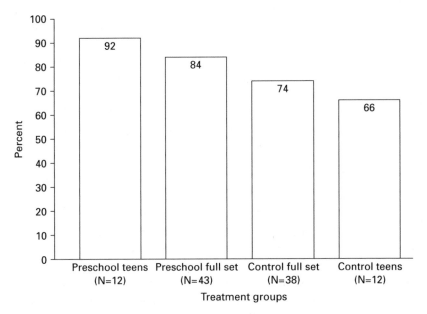

Figure 3.9   Percentage of full set of teen mothers employed when children were age 15

have now been replicated in Project CARE (Ramey, Bryant, Sparling, and Waski, 1985; Wasik, Ramey, Bryant, and Sparling, 1990) and the Infant Health and Development Program (1990; Ramey et al., 1992). In the Abecedarian Program, up to at least 10 years after intervention ended, children with preschool intervention significantly outscored those in the preschool control group on standardized measures of academic achievement and were less likely to be retained in grade or placed in special education. This was particularly true when the preschool intervention was followed up with the K-2 Educational Support Program. This finding is currently being pursued in a separate experiment on a much larger scale in the Head-Start-Public School Transition Demonstration Project (Ramey and Ramey, in press).

Mothers whose children received high-quality, full-time childcare during the preschool years in the Abecedarian Project made gains in their own educational attainment and employment relative to mothers in the preschool control group. Educational gains were particularly striking for women who were teenagers when their child was born. These findings have clear relevance to current debates about welfare reform.

It remains to be seen whether the practically significant and persistent academic gains made by the high-risk children who experienced preschool treatment ultimately lead to better social adjustment and greater degrees of self-sufficiency in adulthood. These issues are being pursued in follow-up work that is currently in progress.

In this era of education, health, and welfare reform the Abecedarian findings are germane to the public policy discussions. Specifically, if high-quality childcare is available, many poor women will avail themselves of the opportunity to become better prepared educationally. This effect is greatest for teen mothers who are having their first child. Such young women transform these educational gains into meaningful employment. This makes sense because providing childcare for a second or third child in a family does not change the mother's situation as much as providing that care for an only child or for all children. This, however, does not fully address the problem of unemployment of undereducated mothers. There must be good jobs for which poor women can train. In the Research Triangle area of North Carolina, during the conduct of this study, unemployment averaged less than 3%. Most mothers found jobs eventually, but there was a disturbing trend for younger women, who had not had the benefit of the preschool childcare program, to have the highest rate of unemployment as their children got older.

Early childhood programs alone probably cannot fully meet the needs of young children as they progress through school. These children appeared to enter school ready to learn, and those with preschool treatment had an academic advantage still apparent after 10 years in school. Their advantages, however, were enhanced by a specific and intensive school-age program that aided their transition into public school and provided them with specialized support for early school learning. This finding is particularly important in recognition of the town in which the study was conducted, a moderate-sized college town located in the burgeoning Research Triangle. Throughout the time that the study has been conducted the economy in that area, which includes Raleigh, Durham, and Chapel Hill, has been one of the most rapidly expanding and robust in the country with very low rates of unemployment. The school system was strong and the proportion of disadvantaged children was below 10%. A strong social ethic to help disadvantaged children and families was accompanied by strong in-school programs for disadvantaged children. Many high-quality family support programs, both public and private, operated in the local community. Thus, it is particularly noteworthy that, in addition to these services, the high-risk children nonetheless needed further educational assistance, as reflected by the higher rates of academic failure and special education placement in the educationally untreated Abecedarian control group. When such assistance was provided to the treated group in the form of a high-quality preschool, especially when an additional K-2 Educational Support Program was added, high-risk children performed near the national average in reading, even after 10 years in school. Positive effects were also seen in mathematics performance.

We are currently concentrating on two main questions in our continuing research program within the Abecedarian Project. First, to what extent do these academic advantages and disadvantages relate to early adulthood educational, social, and economic competence? And, second, what are the mediating and moderating factors linked to differential outcomes? It is our hope that this research program will help to show effective and practical ways to alter the life course of children and families who begin life in high-risk circumstances.

References

Bertalanffy, L. V. (1975). *Perspectives on general system theory.* New York: Braziller.

Breitmayer, B. J., & Ramey, C. T. (1986). Biological nonoptimality and quality of postnatal environment as codeterminants of intellectual development. *Child Development, 57,* 1151–1165.

Bryant, D., & Maxwell, K. (1997). The effectiveness of early intervention for disadvantaged children. In M. Guralnick (Ed.), *The effectiveness of early intervention* (pp. 23–46). Baltimore: Brookes.

Burchinal, M. R., Campbell, F. A., Bryant, D. M., Wasik, B. H., & Ramey, C. T. (1997). Early intervention and mediating processes in cognitive performance of children of low-income African American families. *Child Development, 68,* 935–954.

Burchinal, M. R., Lee, M., & Ramey, C. T. (1989). Type of day care and preschool intellectual development in disadvantaged children. *Child Development, 60,* 128–137.

Caldwell, B., & Bradley, R. (1984). *Home Observation for Measurement of the Environment.* Little Rock, AR: University of Arkansas at Little Rock.

Campbell, F. A., Breitmayer, B. J., & Ramey, C. T. (1986). Disadvantaged teenage mothers and their children: Consequences of educational day care. *Family Relations, 35,* 63–68.

Campbell, F. A., & Ramey, C. T. (1995). Cognitive and school outcomes for high risk African American students at middle adolescence: Positive effects of early intervention. *American Educational Research Journal, 32,* 743–772.

Cohen, J. (1977). *Statistical power analysis for the behavioral sciences* (Rev. ed.). New York: Academic.

Duncan, G. J., & Brooks-Gunn, J. (1997). Income effects across the life span: Integration and interpretation. In G. J. Duncan & J. Brooks-Gunn (Eds.), *Consequences of growing up poor* (pp. 596–610). New York: Russell Sage Foundation.

Duncan, G. J., Brooks-Gunn, J., & Klebanov, P. K. (1994). Economic deprivation and early childhood development *Child Development, 65,* 296–318.

Entwistle, D. R., & Alexander, K. L. (1998). Facilitating the transition to first grade: The nature of transition and research on factors affecting it. *The Elementary School Journal, 98,* 351–364.

Farran, D. C., & Ramey, C. T. (1980). Social class differences in dyadic involvement during infancy. *Child Development, 51,* 254–257.

Gray, S. W., Ramsey, B. K., & Klaus, R. A. (1982). *From 3 to 20. The Early Training Project.* Baltimore: University Park Press.

Hernandez, D. J. (1997). Poverty Trends. In G. Duncan & J. Brooks-Gunn (Eds.), *Consequences of Growing Up Poor* (pp. 18–34). New York: Russell Sage Foundation.

Horacek, H. J., Ramey, C. T., Campbell, F. A., Hoffmann, K. P., & Fletcher, R. H. (1987). Predicting school failure and assessing early intervention with high-risk children. *American Academy of Child and Adolescent Psychiatry, 26,* 758–763.

Huston, A. (Ed.). (1992). *Children in poverty.* New York: Cambridge University Press.

Infant Health and Development Program. (1990). Enhancing the outcomes of low-birth-weight, premature infants. *Journal of the American Medical Association, 263,* 3035–3042.

Lazar, I., Darlington, R., Murray, H., Royce, J., & Snipper, A. (1982). Lasting effects of early education: A report from the Consortium for Longitudinal Studies. *Monographs of the Society for Research in Child Development, 47* (2–3, Serial No. 195).

Martin, S. L., Ramey, C. T., & Ramey, S. L. (1990). The prevention of intellectual impairment in children of impoverished families: Findings of a randomized trial of educational day care. *American Journal of Public Health, 80,* 844–847.

McLloyd, V. C. (1998). Socioeconomic disadvantage and child development. *American Psychologist, 53,* 185–204.

NICHD Early Child Care Research Network (1997). Poverty and patterns of child care. In G. J. Duncan & J. Brooks-Gunn (Eds.), *Consequences of growing up poor* (pp. 100–130). New York: Russell Sage Foundation.

Ramey, C. T. (1992). High-risk children and IQ: Altering intergenerational patterns. *Intelligence, 16,* 239–256.

Ramey, C. T., Bryant, D. M., Campbell, F. A., Sparling, J. J., & Wasik, B. H. (1988). Early intervention for high-risk children: The Carolina Early Intervention Program. In H. R. Price, F. L. Cowen, R. P. Lorion, & J. Ramos–McKay (Eds.), *14 ounces of prevention* (pp. 32–43). Washington, DC: American Psychological Association.

Ramey, C. T., Bryant, D. M., Sparling, J. J., & Wasik, B. H. (1985). Educational interventions to enhance intellectual development: Comprehensive day care versus family education. In S. Harel & N. Anastasiow (Eds.). *The "at-risk" infant: Psychological, social, and medical aspects* (pp. 75–85). Baltimore: Brookes.

Ramey, C. T., Bryant, D. M., Wasik, B. H., Sparling, J. J., Fendt, K. H., & LaVange, L. M. (1992). Infant Health and Development Program for low birth weight, premature infants: Program elements, family participation, and child intelligence. *Pediatrics, 89,* 454–465.

Ramey, C. T., & Campbell, F. A. (1984). Preventive education for high-risk children: Cognitive consequences of the Carolina abecedarian project. *American Journal of Mental Deficiency, 88,* 515–523.

Ramey, C. T., Campbell, F. A., & Blair, C. (1998). Enhancing the life-course for high-risk children: Results from the Abecedarian Project. In J. Crane (Ed.), *Social programs that really work* (pp. 163–183). New York: Sage.

Ramey, C. T., & Finkelstein, N. W. (1981). Psychosocial mental retardation: A biological and social coalescence. In M. Begab, H. Garber, & H. C. Haywood (Eds.), *Psychological influences in retarded performance* (pp. 65–92). Baltimore: University Park Press.

Ramey, C. T., & Haskins, R. (1981). The causes and treatment of school failure: Insights from the Carolina Abecedarian Project. In M. Begab, H. Garber, & H. C. Haywood (Eds.), *Causes and prevention of retarded development in psychosocially disadvantaged children* (pp. 89–112). Baltimore: University Park Press.

Ramey, C. T., MacPhee, D., & Yeates, K. O. (1982). Preventing developmental retardation: A general systems model. In J. M. Joffee & L. A. Bond (Eds.), *Facilitating infant and early childhood development* (pp. 343–401). Hanover, NH: University Press of New England.

Ramey, C. T., McGinness, G., Cross, L., Collier, A., & Barrie-Blackley, S. (1981). The Abecedarian approach to social competence: Cognitive and linguistic intervention for disadvantaged preschoolers. In K. Borman (Ed.), *The social life of children in a changing society* (pp. 145–174). Hillsdale, NJ: Lawrence Erlbaum Associates, Inc.

Ramey, C. T., Mills, P. J., Campbell, F. A., & O'Brien, C. (1975). Infants home environments: A comparison of high-risk families and families from the general population. *American Journal of Mental Retardation, 80,* 40–42.

Ramey, C. T., & Ramey, S. L. (1998). Prevention of intellectual disabilities: Early interventions to improve cognitive development. *Preventive Medicine, 27,* 13–9.

Ramey, C. T., & Ramey, S. L. (in press). *The transition to school for "at-risk" children: A conceptual framework and related research.* Commissioned paper for the Synthesis Conference on the Transition to Kindergarten, National Center for Early Development and Learning, Charlottesville, VA.

Ramey, C. T., Sparling, J. J., & Wasik, B. (1981). Creating social environments to facilitate language development. In R. Schiefelbusch & D. Bricker (Eds.), *Early language intervention* (pp. 444–476). Baltimore: University Park Press.

Schweinhart, L. J., Barnes, H. V., Weikart, D. P., Barnett, W. S., & Epstein, A. S. (1993). *Significant benefits: The High Scope Perry Preschool project through age 27.* Ypsilanti, MI: The High Scope Press.

Spiker, D., Ferguson, J., & Brooks-Grunn, J. (1993). Enhancing maternal interactive behavior and child social competence in low birth weight, premature infants. *Child Development, 64,* 754–768.

Vygotsky, L. A. (1978). *Mind in society: The development of higher psychological processes:* Cambridge, MA: Harvard University Press.

Wasik, B. H., Ramey, C. T., Bryant, D. M., & Sparling, J. J. (1990). A longitudinal study of two early intervention strategies: Project CARE. *Child Development, 61,* 1682–1696.

Woodcock, R. W., & Johnson, M. B. (1977). *Woodcock–Johnson Psycho-Educational Battery: Part 2: Tests of academic achievement*. Boston: Teaching Resources Corporation.

Zeskind, P. S., & Ramey, C. T. (1978). Fetal malnutrition: An experimental study of its consequences on infant development in two caregiving environments. *Child Development, 49*, 1155–1162

Zeskind, P. S., & Ramey, C. T. (1981). Preventing intellectual and interactional sequelae of fetal malnutrition: A longitudinal, transactional, and synergistic approach to development. *Child Development, 52*, 213–218.

Introduction to Chapter 4

Can quality daycare boost development and serve as a low(er)-cost and readily available form of early intervention? Although the debate of whether daycare is an acceptable replacement for parental nurturance continues to rage (see citations on page 106), it may provide beneficial and diverse learning experiences that certain children would not receive at home. Suggestive evidence comes from the Abecedarian project (chapter 3) in which low-income children in the control group who were enrolled by their parents in quality daycares had higher IQs than control children who did not attend daycare (Ramey and Ramey, 1992; see also Wasik, Ramey, Bryant, and Sparling, 1990).

In this chapter, Caughy et al. relied on the extensive database compiled by the US National Longitudinal Survey of Youth to test the hypothesis that quality daycare would serve as a protective factor for low-income children. As seen in figure 4.1, the researchers found a small, but appreciable effect of accumulating years of daycare, especially in reading recognition. Children from higher-income families did not benefit. Note that the researchers did not measure IQ but, rather, academic achievement, so it is not known to what extent the daycare experience influenced intelligence. The daycare results appear modest and it is likely that children at risk for cognitive delay and academic failure would show greater gains in an intensive EI program (e.g., Abecedarian) or in a comprehensive Head Start-type intervention. These programs are not universally available to all at-risk children and ubiquitous daycares may fill the gap. Low-income parents who wish to give their children the opportunity to experience the possible beneficial daycare effect observed in this study should note that only quality daycares were associated with the positive results obtained.

References

Ramey, C. T., and Ramey, S. L. (1992). Effective early intervention. *Mental Retardation, 30*, 337–345.

Wasik, B. H., Ramey, C. T., Bryant, D. G., and Sparling, J. J. (1990). A longitudinal study of two early intervention programs: Project CARE. Child *Development, 61*, 1682–1696.

FOUR

Day-Care Participation as a Protective Factor in the Cognitive Development of Low-income Children

Margaret O'Brien Caughy, Janet A. DiPietro, and Donna M. Strobino

Developmental risk research focuses on identifying factors related to poor outcome in children and understanding the processes by which these factors operate. Much risk research has centered around the influence of biologic conditions such as prenatal exposure to teratogenic or infectious agents, preterm birth, or perinatal complications on later cognitive, social, and emotional development. In spite of the emphasis on the effects of adverse biologic conditions, the overwhelming impact of adverse *environmental* conditions on child development has been a recurrent finding (see Kopp and Krakow, 1983, for a review). Children who are raised in poverty are at "double jeopardy" for poor developmental outcome (Parker, Greer, and Zuckerman, 1988). Children in poverty are not only more likely to be exposed to potential risk factors such as preterm birth, poor health, teratogens, and family stress but also are more likely to experience more serious consequences as a result of such exposure than are children raised in middle-class and higher-income

Caughy, M. O., DiPietro, J., and Strobino, M. (1994). Day care participation as a protective factor in the cognitive development of low income children. *Child Development, 65*, 457–471. Includes use of tables 1–2, and figures 1–2. Copyright 1994 the Society for Research in Child Development Inc.

families (Bellinger, 1989; Cohen, Parmelee, Beckwith, and Sigman, 1986; Escalona, 1982; Hanshaw et al., 1976; Ricciuti and Scarr, 1990; Werner, Simonian, Bierman, and French, 1968; Wilson, 1985).

In contrast to an emphasis on studying the factors that increase the risk of poor developmental outcome, there is an emerging interest in identifying those characteristics of the child and/or his environment which are related to a *reduced* risk of poor outcome (Werner, 1990). The presence of such "protective factors" is related to successful adaptation in the presence of known risk factors such as an impoverished home environment. The identification of protective factors is important to the development of intervention strategies for disadvantaged children.

Participation in day-care during infancy is an environmental factor which has been implicated to affect development. The effect of day-care participation on specific characteristics of socioemotional development, such as attachment, aggressivity, and compliance, is currently the subject of much research and controversy (Barglow, Vaughn, and Moliter, 1987; Belsky and Rovine, 1988; Chase-Lansdale and Owen, 1987; Clarke-Stewart, 1988; Field, 1991; Jacobsen and Wille, 1984; Lamb, 1990; Richters and Zahn-Waxler, 1988; Rubenstein, Howes, and Boyle, 1981; Schwartz, 1983; Schwarz, Strickland, and Krolick, 1974).

This study, however, focuses on the relation between day-care participation and cognitive development. Specifically, this study examines how one particular aspect of cognitive functioning, academic readiness, is affected by participation in routine child care during the first 3 years of life. Existing knowledge about the impact of day-care on the cognitive functioning of disadvantaged children has come primarily from studies of center-based programs, designed specifically to foster cognitive development. Based on models of early enrichment, these programs were designed to supplement the impoverished home environment of low-income children by providing social and intellectual experiences to promote optimal cognitive development (Ramey and Baker-Ward, 1982). Results of these intervention efforts are encouraging. Disadvantaged children who participate in developmental day-care centers have improved cognitive functioning when compared with low-income children who do not (Burchinal, Lee, and Ramey, 1989; Darlington, Royce, Snipper, Murray, and Lazar, 1982; Ramey, Bryant, Sparling, and Wasik, 1985; Ramey, Bryant, and Suarez, 1985; Ramey, Yeates, and Short, 1984).

Developmental day-care is a costly intervention. For example, one of the most successful of these centers, the Carolina Early Intervention

Program (Ramey, 1988), requires full-time participation from 3 months of age in a high-quality, developmentally appropriate infant and early childhood curriculum. The majority of low-income day-care children are not enrolled in centers of this kind. The impact of participation in day-care that is not specifically designed as an intervention program is less well documented. Improved cognitive development for low- and middle-income children participating in "average" Swedish day-care during the first several years of life has been reported (Andersson, 1989, 1992). The relevance of these findings to typical day-care settings in the United States is unknown. However, improved cognitive development of low-income children participating in community-based day-care in the United States has also been reported (Burchinal et al., 1989). In that study, children attending community-based day-care had cognitive scores intermediary to those participating in a university-based center and to those with minimal day-care experience.

The most generalizable studies concerning typical day-care settings in this country have used data from the National Longitudinal Survey of Youth, based on a national probability sample. Baydar and Brooks-Gunn (1991) reported a negative impact of day-care participation during the first year of life on the Peabody Picture Vocabulary Test (PPVT) for 3- and 4-year-olds. Desai, Chase-Lansdale, and Michael (1989) also found negative effects for nonmaternal care during infancy on cognitive functioning during preschool, but only for boys from high-income families.

Desai et al. (1989) propose a model in which the impact of day-care participation varies with family income. The impact of nonparental care on child development is dependent on the opportunities for learning provided by nonparental care as compared to those that the home can provide. Parenting style and family environment are factors that mediate the relation between socioeconomic status and child development. Higher SES parents may provide better learning environments than those which are provided by nonparental care. In contrast, the opportunities for learning provided by nonparental care for low SES children may be as good as or better than those which are provided by their own homes. If so, participation in day-care during early childhood may serve to promote the development of low-income children and serve as a protective factor against otherwise adverse environmental conditions.

The use of secondary analysis of a large national data set is a relatively new methodology for the study of developmental questions.

The advantages of secondary data analysis in developmental research have been recently discussed (Brooks-Gunn, Phelps, and Elder, 1991; Chase-Lansdale, Mott, Brooks-Gunn, and Phillips, 1991; Cherlin, 1991; Duncan, 1991; McCall and Appelbaum, 1991). Chase-Lansdale et al. (1991) suggest that "macro methodologies" such as large-scale surveys can identify patterns of associations and provide impetus for subsequent research to understand the processes which mediate the observed relations.

The National Longitudinal Survey of Youth (NLSY) is a national data set that has recently begun to be tapped by developmental researchers. The NLSY includes a national probability sample of over 12,000 young men and women between the ages of 14 and 21. The sample over-represents blacks, Hispanics, and economically disadvantaged whites to provide large enough numbers of these individuals to allow for the study of these high-risk groups. The original purpose of the NLSY was to analyze the labor market participation of this sample of young adults. The men and women in the sample were interviewed yearly, and follow-up of subjects exceeded 90% for each of the interview waves. In 1982, the NLSY received additional support to allow for data collection on the children of the women in the NLSY sample. In 1986, the NLSY completed in-home assessments of almost 5,000 children to measure social, behavioral, and cognitive functioning. Data were collected from a variety of sources, including maternal report, interviewer observation, and direct assessment of the child using rigorous quality control procedures. The NLSY continues to evaluate the children every 2 years, and in 1990 the total number of children assessed exceeded 8,000.

This study takes advantage of the NLSY's broad-based data to examine the relation between participation in day-care during the first 3 years of life and cognitive development of low-income children. As stated previously, cognitive development in this study is assessed using a measure of academic achievement or academic readiness. The following three hypotheses are proposed:

1. Participation in routine day-care early in life will be related to improved academic readiness. Although there is conflicting evidence in the literature, the balance of research appears to indicate that day-care participants perform better on tests of academic readiness.

2. Routine day-care participation will enhance the academic readiness for lower-income children, but the effect on higher-income children will either be negligible or adverse. That is, for lower-income children,

the environmental stimulation provided by day-care participation will supplement the resources in the low-income child's environment but may not compensate for benefits provided by maternal care of higher-income children.

3. Positive effects of day-care participation for low-income children will persist after confounding factors are controlled. Because this study is necessarily quasi-experimental in nature, selection bias in determining day-care participation may be present. Therefore, it is important to control for non-day-care factors which may influence results.

Method

Subjects

The sample for this study included all children who were 5 or 6 years of age at the time of the 1986 assessment. Nine hundred twenty-one children had a reported age between 60 and 83 months at the time of the 1986 assessment, and this sample included 52 sets of siblings. In order to maintain independence between observations, a coin flip was used to eliminate one sibling of each pair from the sample. In addition to the elimination of these 52 children, two children were excluded from the sample because of misreported year of birth. The year of birth was used to create variables which were linked to the age of the child. For this reason, it was essential that the year of birth be correct. Therefore, the primary sample for the analysis includes 867 5- and 6-year-old children who completed the 1986 assessment wave of the NLSY. The distributions of gender, race/ethnicity, family income, and family composition are displayed in table 4.1. As is characteristic of the NLSY, the children were born to a sample of relatively young mothers: the average age at birth was 19.9 years (SD = 2.04, range = 15–24).

Procedures

Yearly maternal interviews

As a part of the NLSY cohort, mothers were interviewed yearly beginning in 1979. Information routinely collected as part of this interview

Table 4.1   Characteristics of the study sample

Characteristic	n	(%)
Gender:		
Boys	464	53.5
Girls	403	46.5
Race/ethnicity:		
Nonblack/non-Hispanic	408	47.1
Black	296	34.1
Hispanic	163	18.8
Annual family income:		
<$15,000	470	54.2
$15,000–$29,000	318	36.7
$30,000+	72	8.3
No information	7	.8
Predominant family structure (first 3 years):		
Mother alone	109	12.6
Mother + spouse/partner[a]	615	70.9
Other[b]	120	13.8
Mixed[c]	21	2.4
No information	2	.2

Notes: [a]This category includes those families in which the mother and her spouse/partner lived with extended family. [b]"Other" family structure includes those families in which the mother lived with other adult relatives and/or nonrelatives. [c]"Mixed" family structure includes those children for whom there was no predominant family structure during the first 3 years.

included household composition, household income, respondent education, and respondent employment status. In the annual 1986 interview, mothers were questioned regarding child day-care participation. Data collected included whether or not the child was in day-care for each of the first 3 years of life, the number of different day-care arrangements the child attended per year, and the type of each day-care arrangement.

Child assessments

In 1986, home visits were conducted and a number of child and home assessment tools administered.

Training procedures

Interviewers were subject to fairly rigorous quality control procedures. Training included a $2\frac{1}{2}$-day seminar focused on interviewing, assessment administration, and data management policies and procedures. Reliability was based on submission of each interviewer's initial two cases with an audiocassette of the interviews. Cases were edited according to written specifications, and successful completion of the edit was required before the interviewer could continue. Failure of the case edit prompted additional training with subsequent case edit reliability or termination. In addition, callbacks were made to 15% of all cases to verify the date and duration of the interview and the accuracy of selected information collected during the interview. Once completed cases were received, data were coded and edited according to written procedures. Cases with missing or inconsistent data were referred to a special retrieval department for further processing.

Instruments

Assessment tools included an observation of the home environment and an assessment of academic readiness.

The quality of the home environment was assessed using a shortened version of the HOME scale (Bradley and Caldwell, 1979), the Home Observation for Measurement of the Environment – Short Form (HOME-SF). The HOME-SF included 26 yes/no items that were scored by either maternal report or interviewer observation. The items measured the degree to which the child's home environment provided emotional support and cognitive stimulation. The internal consistency of the HOME-SF was assessed. The Cronbach's alpha was .67 for 5-year-olds and .70 for 6-year-olds.

Academic readiness was assessed by the Peabody Individual Achievement Test (PIAT). The 1970 version of the PIAT was the most current version at the time of the 1986 NLSY child assessments and was, therefore, the version utilized. The PIAT battery is a wide-range, brief assessment of academic achievement consisting of five subtests: mathematics, reading recognition, reading comprehension, spelling, and general information. Each subtest consists of 84 questions except for the reading comprehension subtest, which consists of 66 questions. The questions are arranged in order of increasing difficulty, and test administration involves finding basal and ceiling levels for each child. Three subtests were administered to the children of the NLSY: mathematics, reading recognition, and reading comprehension. The PIAT is standardized to have a mean of 100 and a standard deviation of 15. However, Baker and Mott (1989) point out that the test was standardized over twenty years ago and that the mean may no longer be 100. Evidence supporting such an upward drift in the mean score was found in the NLSY data.

Standard scores for the PIAT mathematics, reading recognition, and reading comprehension subtests are included with the NLSY Merged Mother-Child Data. Of the 828 children in the sample who completed the math subtest, standardized scores are available for 825. Of the 815 children who completed the reading recognition subtest, standardized scores are available for 814. Of the 814 children who completed the reading comprehension subtest, however, standardized scores are available for only 378. Many of the children in the NLSY sample under 8 years old could not be assigned a normed score on the reading comprehension subtest because their scores were lower than the national PIAT sample used in the norming procedure (Baker and Mott, 1989). Because of these missing data, the reading comprehension subtest will not be used for our analyses.

Constructed variables

For this study, a number of variables were constructed from the annual NLSY interview of the mothers. These are:

1   *Average family income:* The Consumer Price Index was used to adjust the reported family income to 1986 dollars. The family incomes reported for each of the first 5 years of life were averaged.
2   *Maternal education:* The number of completed years of education as of May 1, 1986.
3   *Day-care participation:* As part of the NLSY data base, three binary variables represent whether or not the child was enrolled in day-care during the first 3 years of life. These variables were used to create two additional variables reflecting the pattern of day-care participation: the total number of years during the first 3 years of life that the child participated in day-care, and the year day-care participation began. In addition to this information,

the predominant day-care arrangement was reported for each of the first 3 years of life and was categorized as in the child's own home, in another home, or day-care center/school. It should be noted that information regarding Head Start participation was also collected at the time of the 1986 assessment. Because Head Start participation did not commence before the child's third birthday, there is no overlap between day-care participation and participation in Head Start

Analysis strategy

The first set of analyses tested the effect of day-care participation and its interaction with family income on cognitive outcome using analysis of variance (ANOVA). In the second set of analyses, multiple linear regression was used to investigate the relation between patterning of day-care participation and outcome, controlling for confounding variables. The patterns analyzed include total number of years of day-care during the first 3 years of life, the year of initiation of day-care participation, and the predominant type of day-care arrangement.

Results

Day-care participation: analysis of variance

The effect of day-care participation in the first 3 years (day-care each year vs. no day care) by family income on performance on the PIAT mathematics and reading recognition subscales was analyzed by two 2×3 ANOVAs. For this categorical analysis, family income was divided into three income groups: less than $15,000 per year, $15,000–$29,999, and $30,000 or more per year. These income groups were chosen to roughly correspond to the income levels currently required for subsidized day-care. Means and F values for the tests of main effects for day-care participation are presented in table 4.2. Day-care participation in the first year of life was not associated with either PIAT subscale, while day-care participation in the third year was associated with significantly better performance on both the mathematics and reading recognition subscales. In addition, the results of these analyses are presented by family income category, and the F values for the day-care

Table 4.2 Mean PIAT scores by day-care participation during each year of life and family income

| | | | | | Income category | | | | | |
| | | Overall | | <$15,000 | | $15,000–$29,999 | | $30,000+ | | Overall | Daycare × income |
Year of life		n	Mean	n	Mean	n	Mean	n	Mean	F	F
Mathematics											
1	No day-care	568	97.7	337	95.8	180	99.8	33	105.6	.62	1.41
	Day-care	231	99.3	87	97.6	105	101.0	34	97.6	—	—
2	No day-care	504	97.5	311	95.7	151	99.5	29	101.03	1.53	1.09
	Day-care	290	99.6	107	98.0	137	101.1	37	98.11	—	—
3	No day-care	454	96.8	279	95.1	137	99.2	27	101.1	5.98[a]	1.76
	Day-care	332	100.0	132	98.6	150	101.0	39	98.2	—	—
Reading recognition											
1	No day-care	559	104.9	337	103.1	180	106.4	33	114.8	2.21	8.50[a]
	Day-care	232	107.1	87	107.0	105	107.6	34	105.5	—	—
2	No day-care	496	104.4	311	102.6	151	106.5	29	113.5	7.69[a]	7.88[a]
	Day-care	288	107.8	107	108.3	137	107.3	37	107.6	—	—
3	No day-care	449	103.9	279	102.4	137	105.5	27	113.7	13.17[b]	6.28[b]
	Day-care	328	107.9	132	107.7	150	108.0	39	107.8	—	—

Notes: [a] $p < .01$. [b] $p < .001$.

× income interactions are included. The interaction between day-care participation and income in performance on the reading recognition subscale was significant for participation during each of the first 3 years of life. The interaction was not significant for the mathematics subscale.

T tests were conducted to compare reading recognition performance within each of the three income groups, for nine total tests. Children in the lower-income group who attended day-care in the first, second, or third years had significantly higher scores than lower-income children who did not attend day-care (first year: $t(428) = -2.88$, $p < .01$; second year: $t(421) = -4.51$, $p < .001$; third year: $t(415) = -4.48$, $p < .001$). For middle-income children, reading recognition performance was only related to day-care participation for participation during the third year, with those attending day-care having higher scores than those who did not attend, $t(292) = -1.99$, $p < .05$. For children in the upper-income group, reading recognition scores were related to day-care attendance in the first year, $t(65) = 2.98$, $p < .01$, but not to attendance during the second or third years. Upper-income children who attended day-care during the first year had significantly lower reading recognition scores than did upper-income children who did not attend day-care.

Day-care patterning: multiple linear regression

The relations among day-care participation and PIAT performance may be confounded by differences in day-care utilization across sociodemographic characteristics. Chi-square tests were used to assess how the three day-care measures varied by two of these variables measured in the NLSY, family structure and race/ethnicity. The type of day-care differed significantly by race/ethnicity, with black children most likely to attend a center or school and Hispanic children least likely to attend a center or school, $\chi^2(4) = 12.48$, $p < .05$. No other differences in day-care utilization by family structure or race/ethnicity were detected.

Empirically and conceptually, maternal education and characteristics of the home environment are factors which may mediate any observed relations among these measures. Maternal education and the HOME-SF scale are both significantly and positively correlated with family income, $r(852) = .27$, $p < .01$, and $r(831) = .30$, $p < .01$, respectively, and with the measures of day-care participation and patterning (all r's significant at $p < .01$). In order to control for the influence of these confounding variables, multiple linear regression was used. A total of six regressions were conducted to test for the effects of the three day-care pattern measures (i.e., number of years in day-care, timing of day-care initiation, and type of day-care) on each of the two PIAT subscales. Family income, maternal education, race/ethnic group, school enrollment status, and the total score on the HOME-SF were entered first into each regression. Race/ethnicity was included in all regressions along with family income to account for the sampling design of the NLSY as recommended by Korn and Graubard (1991). School enrollment status, a binary variable representing whether or not the child was enrolled in school, was included in all regressions to account for the bias associated with differences in school experience. In the first set of regressions, the number of years in day-care in the first 3 years was entered on this step. In the second, three dummy variables representing the year of day-care initiation were entered on this step (the reference group was children who had not attended any day-care). In the third, the predominant type of day-care during years 2 and 3 were combined and entered as three dummy variables. Day-care type during the first year was not included based on the nonsignificant findings in table 4.2. Finally, the interaction between day-care and family income was tested on the third step of each regression by entering the product(s) of family income by day-care variable(s).

Results of these regressions revealed no significant main effects or income × day-care interactions for the mathematics sub-scale for any day-care measure when confounding factors were controlled. For reading recognition, however, there were significant and marginal main effects for both type of day-care and total years in day-care, respectively, and all day-care × income interactions were at least marginally significant.

One hypothesis to explain why day-care participation is more beneficial for low-income children would be that day-care provides an environment which is as good as or better than that which is available in their own homes (Desai et al., 1989). This hypothesis assumes that lower income implies a lower quality of home environment. However, because the quality of the home environment was assessed in this study, this hypothesis can be tested more directly by testing the interaction between the three measures of day-care participation and the HOME-SF. Although the HOME-SF is significantly correlated with income, $r(831) = .30$, $p < .01$, the magnitude of the association is modest. In

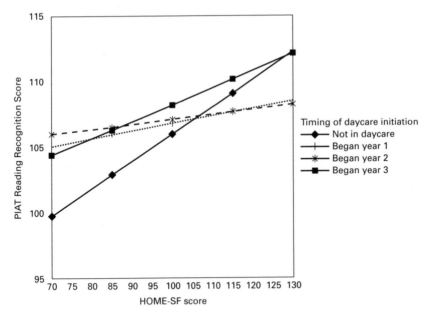

Figure 4.1 PIAT Reading Recognition scores by year of day-care initiation and HOME-SF total score

order to compare the influence of income versus the home environment, the three sets of regressions described above were repeated with a different interaction variable, HOME × day-care, entered on the final step. Although no day-care × income interactions were significant, a significant interaction between day-care and the HOME-SF emerged for mathematics.

For reading recognition, timing of day-care initiation demonstrates a significant interaction with the quality of the home environment for those children who started day-care before their second birthday. This effect is plotted in figure 4.1. Children from impoverished environments who started attending day-care before their first birthday had higher reading recognition scores than children from comparable home environments who did not attend day-care at all.

For mathematics, there is a significant interaction between the quality of the home environment and the type of day-care arrangement. This effect is depicted in figure 4.2. For children from more impoverished environments, day-care attendance in a center or school is related

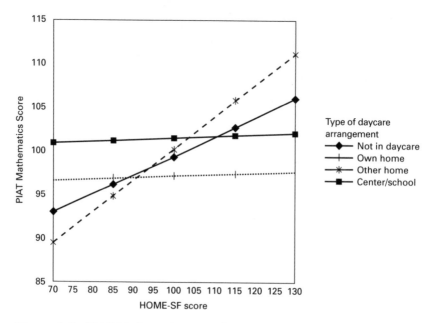

Figure 4.2 PIAT Mathematics scores by type of day-care arrangement and HOME-SF total score

to the best performance on the PIAT mathematics subtest followed by nonmaternal care in the child's home, no day-care at all, and, finally, nonmaternal care in another home. For children from homes rated at the higher end of the HOME-SF scale, however, the relation between type of day-care and mathematics performance was the opposite, with children attending day-care in another home scoring the highest followed by children not in day-care, children attending a center or school, and children receiving nonmaternal care in their own home.

Discussion

The results of this study indicate that day-care participation during the first 3 years of life is positively related to the subsequent development of mathematics and reading skills for children from impoverished environments. This relation is strongest for reading skills if participation commences before the child's second birthday. For mathematics skills, it appears that center-based care in particular exerts a protective effect over the developmental liabilities of an impoverished environment. These findings support other reports of the benefits of day-care for the cognitive development of disadvantaged children (Burchinal et al., 1989; Darlington et al., 1982; Ramey, Bryant, and Suarez, 1985). However, these studies focused on the effects of *good-quality* day-care, either in the form of university-based day-care programs or high-quality community-based programs. The impact of enrollment in ordinary day-care, that is, in a setting which did not include special enrichment activities, has not been a primary focus of previous research.

Some of these findings conflict with other reports on the impact of day-care on cognitive development. Baydar and Brooks-Gunn (1991) analyzed the Peabody Picture Vocabulary Test (PPVT) scores of the 3–4-year-old cohort of the NLSY. Children who entered day-care during the first year of life had lower PPVT scores than children who did not attend day-care during the first year. The regression coefficients for entry during the second and third years were positive but not significant. In addition, the interaction between maternal employment and poverty status during the first year was not significant. Interactions between economic status and nonmaternal care during the second and third years of life were not reported. Desai et al. (1989) also studied the impact of non-maternal care during infancy on cognitive development. In their analysis of the impact of maternal employment patterns on the intellectual ability of the 4-year-old cohort of the NLSY, nonmaternal care during the first year had a negative impact on the cognitive abilities of boys from high-income families. The effect of nonmaternal care was not significant for girls or for children of either gender from low-income families.

There are a number of possible reasons for the differences between the Baydar and Brooks-Gunn findings, the Desai et al. findings, and the findings of this study. Although Baydar and Brooks-Gunn and Desai et al. also used the NLSY, both used a younger cohort of children (i.e., 4-year-olds) than the cohort that was used for this study and a different outcome measure (i.e., the PPVT, an assessment of receptive language ability). However, the present study also detected some adverse effects of day-care attendance. In particular, initiation of day-care before the second birthday was negatively associated with reading recognition performance, and participation in day-care that was center-based or in the child's own home was negatively associated with mathematics performance of children from homes at the upper end of the HOME-SF.

Two alternative hypotheses could be advanced to explain why an inverse association of day-care participation and child functioning by family income was detected. On the one hand, the environment provided by day-care may be more optimal than that which is provided by the home environment of low-income children. Desai et al. (1989) proposed that, in order to foster development, the quality of nonmaternal care must match or exceed that which would be provided by the child's own family. This may explain why day-care was beneficial for low-income children and not beneficial for higher-income children. On the other hand, the day-care available to children from lower-income families may have been of higher quality than that of middle-class families in the sample because of their participation in subsidized day-care programs. Because the sample in this study is primarily from middle- and lower-income families, the inverse association between day-care and child outcome as a function of family income may instead reflect an inverse relation between family income and the quality of day-care purchased.

This explanation of the inverse association between family income and day-care participation assumes that the quality of the home environment varies monotonically with family income. However, the correlation between the HOME-SF and family income was modest, at best. Family income can influence the quality of the home environment directly by influencing the resources available to the family for the purchase of books, toys, and other tangible items that are assessed as part of the HOME-SF. However, the HOME-SF measures more intangible aspects of the home environment by assessing, for example, maternal responsiveness and affection toward the child. Such socioemotional characteristics of the home are less likely to vary monotonically with family income.

As a measure of environmental impoverishment, the HOME-SF allowed us to test more directly for the interaction between day-care participation and environmental conditions. If the Desai et al. hypothesis is to be supported, we would expect to find an interaction between day-care participation and the HOME-SF. On the other hand, if the interaction between day-care and family income actually reflects an inverse relation between family income and the quality of day-care purchased for middle and lower SES families (see Hayes, Logan, and Zaslow, 1990, for a summary), we would not expect the interaction between day-care participation and the HOME-SF to be significant. Analyses revealed a significant interaction between timing of day-care initiation and the HOME-SF for reading and between type of day-care arrangement and the HOME-SF for mathematics. It is notable that the interaction with the timing of day-care initiation was significant regardless of whether the initiation variable was interacted with family income or with the HOME-SF. Regardless of which interaction variable was used, results supported the assertion that children from low-income, more impoverished environments had better reading recognition performance if they began attending daycare before their first birthday.

The fact that beneficial effects of typical day-care in the first 3 years of life have not been previously reported in the developmental literature may be the result of the small sample sizes ordinarily used in developmental studies. Although significant, the effects of day-care detected (both positive and negative) were small and added only minimal additional amounts of unique variance to the regression models. However, the procedures used in this study, in which the environmental confounds of income, maternal education, and HOME scale were entered into the equations first, provide a conservative estimate of the independent effects of day-care. It is notable that given the impact of these confounding variables on development, day-care patterning continues to contribute additional unique variance, however small, to cognitive outcome.

In addition, the possibility of selection bias cannot be dismissed. Research indicates that dry-care utilization varies with family demographic characteristics (Hofferth and Kisker, 1992). Analyses of these data revealed that the timing of day-care initiation differed with family structure and income and that the type of day-care arrangement chosen differed by race/ethnicity. However, inclusion of these factors in the analyses as control variables did not change the findings. Although demographic characteristics were controlled in the regressions, it is possible that mothers who enroll their children in day-care differ on nonmeasured characteristics (e.g., motivational) that are important to cognitive development. The most obvious intrinsic confound in all day-care research involves maternal employment status. However, because effects on outcome differed based on type of day-care arrangement, there is reason to believe that the day-care findings, at least for mathematics, cannot be attributed to maternal factors alone.

There are clear advantages and disadvantages to using the NLSY and other large data bases in addressing developmental issues. The large sample size and concomitant statistical power allow the exploration of higher-order, interactive relations. Unlike many developmental studies which rely on convenience samples, national probability samples such as this one permit greater generalizability. The ability to investigate ordinary day-care arrangements on a national basis provides important information in this area. Although there is variability in the quality and accuracy of data collected by large projects, the NLSY features data collection procedures which were well controlled and represent multiple sources.

On the negative side, the NLSY utilized a sampling frame which included young adults and oversampled for minorities and disadvantaged groups. As a result, the sample used for this study was a sample of children of relatively poor young mothers, thereby limiting generalizability of the findings. In addition, projects of this scope are limited in the depth of information which can be collected in any domain. In this study, both the dependent and independent measures are compromised by lack of depth. The PIAT, limited to two subscales, is at best a narrow assessment of cognitive development. The PIAT is more accurately described as a measure of academic achievement rather than a measure of cognitive development. Academic achievement is affected not only by cognitive development but also by instructional experience. This may explain why our results indicated a positive impact of day-care participation whereas other researchers have not reported similar benefits using other measures of cognitive status.

Although we have detected differential effects of type of day-care arrangement on outcome, more detail concerning specific features and quality of day-care is necessary to adequately investigate these relations. The day-care variables used in this study were limited to maternal recall of participation during the first 3 years for those children who were 5–6 years old in 1986. Maternal recall of day-care participation may or may not have been accurate. In addition, for these data, the NLSY does not include information regarding the number of hours per week spent in day-care or the staffing patterns and qualifications of day-care providers. Such information would be useful for investigating the effects of variations in day-care quality and patterns of use on child outcome. However, these data were collected as part of the NLSY for a younger cohort of children. The NLSY is continuing to assess children in the sample at 2-year intervals, providing an opportunity to investigate these issues as this younger cohort ages.

Although these analyses have detected a significant association between day-care and development, it is not possible to determine the mechanisms through which these processes operate other than in a rudimentary manner. For example, how does early initiation of day-care participation affect subsequent reading skills? How does the type of day-care arrangement differentially affect the development of mathematics skills? We can speculate about possible mechanisms for these relations. Initiation of day-care participation before the first birthday may provide a child from a low-income family with significant additional exposure to language. This may be of critical importance for the emergence of language skills over the second year of life. Alternatively, children who begin day-care before their first birthday may be more likely to continue attending day-care until they enter school. Therefore, the effect of early initiation on language skills may represent a cumulative effect of day-care participation rather than a "critical period" effect. Day-care attendance at a center or school may foster the development of mathematics ability in children from impoverished environments because these settings are more likely to incorporate structured activities to stimulate the development of number skills. On the other hand, more indirect processes involving behavior and attention may be operating. Findings from large-scale studies can function as an impetus to more developmentally oriented, primary data collection research.

Given these limitations, the findings from this study still provide evidence of better cognitive development for children from impoverished environments participating in non-university-based day-care. An early advantage in reading and mathematics skills may provide a child with an important boost in the early school years. However, somewhere in the middle to upper range of environmental quality, children either experience no beneficial effect or an adverse effect from day-care participation on mathematics and reading skills. The relation between day-care and income supports principles of the transactional nature of the relation between the child and its environment in the developmental process (Sameroff and Chandler, 1975).

There is current movement at the federal and local levels to recognize the contribution of the early years of a child's life on later development and achievement. Our findings concerning the benefits of day-care for low-income children have policy implications. It suggests that subsidy of programs which provide affordable day-care to low-income families may have the dual benefit of promoting employment and of fostering child development. Further research will be needed to determine the qualities and characteristics of day-care which mediate these relations. Legislation is being passed and funding is being provided to develop programs which can improve the outcome of children in our society. The burden is on researchers to increase understanding of the protective factors that enhance child development under conditions of risk and to assist each child in our society in achieving his or her potential.

References

Andersson, B. E. (1989). Effects of public day-care: A longitudinal study. *Child Development, 60*, 857–866.

Andersson, B. E. (1992). Effects of day-care on cognitive and socioemotional competence of thirteen-year-old Swedish school children. *Child Development, 63*, 20–36.

Baker, P. C., & Mott, F. L. (1989). *NLSY Child Handbook 1989: A guide and resource document for the National Longitudinal Survey of Youth 1986 Child Data.* Columbus, OH: Center for Human Resource Research.

Barglow, P., Vaughn, B. E., & Moliter, N. (1987). Effects of maternal absence due to employment on the quality of infant-mother attachment in a low-risk sample. *Child Development, 58*, 945–954.

Baydar, N., & Brooks-Gunn, J. (1991). Effects of maternal employment and child-care arrangements on preschoolers' cognitive and behavioral outcomes: Evidence from the Children of the National Longitudinal Survey of Youth. *Developmental Psychology, 27*, 932–945.

Bellinger, D. (1989). Prenatal/early postnatal exposure to lead and risk of developmental impairment. *Birth Defects: Original Article Series, 25*, 73–97.

Belsky, J., & Rovine, M. J. (1988). Nonmaternal care in the first year of life and the security of the infant-parent attachment. *Child Development, 59*, 157–167.

Bradley, R. H., & Caldwell, B. M. (1979). Home observation for measurement of the environment: A revision of the preschool scale. *American Journal of Mental Deficiency, 84*, 235–244.

Brooks-Gunn, J., Phelps, E., & Elder, G. H. (1991). Studying lives through time: Secondary data analyses in developmental psychology. *Developmental Psychology, 27*, 899–910.

Burchinal, M., Lee, M., & Ramey, C. (1989). Type of day-care and preschool intellectual development in disadvantaged children. *Child Development, 60*, 128–137.

Chase-Lansdale, P. L., Mott, F. L., Brooks-Gunn, J., & Phillips, D. A. (1991). Children of the National Longitudinal Survey of Youth: A unique research opportunity. *Developmental Psychology, 27,* 918–931.

Chase-Lansdale, P. L., & Owen, M. T. (1987). Maternal employment in a family context: Effects on infant-mother and infant-father attachments. *Child Development, 58,* 1505–1512.

Cherlin, A. (1991). On analyzing other people's data. *Developmental Psychology, 27,* 946–948.

Clarke-Stewart, K. A. (1988). "The 'effects' of infant day care reconsidered" reconsidered: Risks for parents, children and researchers. *Early Childhood Research Quarterly, 3,* 293–318.

Cohen, S. E., Parmelee, A. H., Beckwith, L., & Sigman, M. (1986). Cognitive development in preterm infants: Birth to 8 years. *Developmental and Behavioral Pediatrics, 7,* 102–110.

Darlington, R. B., Royce, J. M., Snipper, A. S., Murray, H. W., & Lazar, I. (1980). Preschool programs and later school competence of children from low-income families. *Science, 208,* 202–204.

Desai, S., Chase-Lansdale, P. L., & Michael, R. T. (1989). Mother or market? Effects of maternal employment on the intellectual ability of 4-year-old children. *Demography, 26,* 545–561.

Duncan, G. J. (1991). Made in heaven: Secondary data analysis and interdisciplinary collaborators. *Developmental Psychology, 27,* 949–951.

Escalona, S. K. (1982). Babies at double hazard: Early development of infants at biologic and social risk. *Pediatrics, 70,* 670–676.

Field, T. (1991). Quality infant day-care and grade school behavior and performance. *Child Development, 62,* 863–870.

Hanshaw, J. B., Scheiner, A. P., Moxley, A. W., Gaev, L., Abel, V., & Scheiner, B. (1976). School failure and deafness after "silent" congenital cytomegalovirus infection. *New England Journal of Medicine, 295,* 468–470.

Hayes, C. D., Logan, J. L., & Zaslow, M. J. (Eds.). (1990). *Who cares for America's children?* Washington, DC: National Academy Press.

Hofferth, S., & Kisker, E. (1992). The changing demographics of family day care in the United States. In D. Peters & A. Pence, (Eds.), *Family day care: Current research for informed public policy.* New York: Teachers College Press.

Jacobsen, J. L., & Wille, D. E. (1984). Influence of attachment and separation experience on separation distress at 18 months. *Developmental Psychology, 20,* 477–484.

Kopp, C. B., & Krakow, J. B. (1983). The developmentalist and the study of biological risk: A view of the past with an eye toward the future. *Child Development, 54,* 1086–1108.

Korn, E. L., & Graubard, B. I. (1991). Epidemiologic studies utilizing surveys: Accounting for sampling design. *American Journal of Public Health, 81,* 1166–1173.

Lamb, M. (1990). Do we really know how day-care affects children? *Journal of Applied Developmental Psychology, 11,* 351–379.

McCall, R. B., & Appelbaum, M. I. (1991). Some issues of conducting second-ary analyses. *Developmental Psychology, 27,* 911–917.

Parker, S., Greer, S., & Zuckerman, B. (1988). Double jeopardy: The impact of poverty on early child development. *Pediatric Clinics of North America, 35,* 1227–1240.

Ramey, C. T. (1988). Early intervention for high-risk children: The Carolina early intervention program. In R. Price, E. Cowan, R. Lorion, & J. Ramos-McKay (Eds.), *Fourteen ounces of prevention.* Washington, DC: American Psychological Association.

Ramey, C. T., & Baker-Ward, L. (1982). Psychosocial retardation and the early experience paradigm. In D. Bricker (Ed.), *Intervention with at risk and handicapped infants.* Baltimore: University Park Press.

Ramey, C. T., Bryant, D. M., Sparling, J. J., & Wasik, B. H. (1985). Project CARE: A comparison of two early intervention strategies to prevent retarded development. In R. Fewell (Ed.), *Topics in early childhood special education.* Austin, TX: PRO-ED.

Ramey, C. T., Bryant, D. M., & Suarez, T. (1985). Preschool compensatory educa-tion and the modifiability of intelligence: A critical review. In D. K. Detterman (Ed.), *Current topics in human intelligence.* Norwood, NJ: Ablex.

Ramey, C. T., Yeates, K. O., & Short, E. J. (1984). The plasticity of intellectual development: Insights from preventive intervention. *Child Development, 55,* 1913–1925.

Ricciuti, A. E., & Scarr, S. (1990). Interaction of early biological and family risk factors in predicting cognitive development. *Journal of Applied Developmental Psychology, 11,* 1–12.

Richters, J. E., & Zahn-Waxler, C. (1988). The infant day-care controversy: Current status and future directions. *Early Childhood Research Quarterly, 3,* 319–336.

Rubenstein, J. L., Howes, C., & Boyle, P. (1981). A two-year follow-up of infants in community-based day care. *Journal of Child Psychology and Psychiatry, 22,* 209–218.

Sameroff, A. J., & Chandler, M. J. (1975). Reproductive risk and the continuum of caretaking casualty. In F. D. Horowitz, E. M. Hetherington, & S. Scarr-Salapatek (Eds.), *Review of child development research* (Vol. 4). Chicago: University of Chicago Press.

Schwartz, P. (1983). Length of day-care attendance and attachment behavior in eighteen-month-old infants. *Child Development, 54,* 1073–1078.

Schwarz, J. C., Strickland, R. G., & Krolick, G. (1974). Infant day care: Behavioral effects at preschool age. *Developmental Psychology, 10,* 502–506.

Werner, E. E. (1990). Protective factors and individual resilience. In S. Meisels & J. Shonkoff (Eds.), *Handbook of early childhood intervention.* New York: Cambridge University Press.

Werner, E., Simonian, K., Bierman, J. M., & French, F. E. (1968). Cumulative effect of perinatal complications and deprived environment on physical, intellectual and social development of preschool children. *Pediatrics, 39,* 490–505.

Wilson, R. S. (1985). Risk and resilience in early mental development. *Developmental Psychology, 21,* 795–805.

Secondary and Tertiary Prevention Programs for Children with Established Disabilities

Introduction to Part III

One to 3 percent of children have conditions associated with developmental delay and many government- and charitable-funded EI services have been created for these children and their families. Some conditions have known or suspected genetic origins (e.g., Down syndrome, Fragile X syndrome, Autistic Spectrum Disorders) while others result from infections, toxicity, or unknown reasons during pregnancy (e.g., congential rubella, fetal alcohol syndrome, spina bifida, and cerebral palsy). Developmental problems also may be related to perinatal conditions (e.g., prematurity, low birth weight, anoxia) or early experience and exposure (e.g., acquired brain injury, meningitis, lead ingestion).

When disorders can be detected at birth (e.g., Down syndrome, low birth weight), primary and secondary prevention models can be applied in an attempt to prevent or minimize the impact of the disorder before the symptoms become serious (e.g., learning problems associated with low birth weight, see chapter 5). Several disorders, however, do not manifest in an obvious way until symptoms require treatment (e.g., Autistic Spectrum Disorders, Fragile X syndrome, global developmental delay, hearing impairment). For these conditions, a tertiary model is relevant.

Many services are available for families of children with established disabilities. Initially, case coordination services are offered that provide parents with basic information about the condition and local service availability. Depending on family and child needs and preferences, referrals are made to follow-up assessment and intervention services, such as developmental pediatricians; infant development; occupational, behavior, and speech-language therapists; specialized preschool; respite care; family counseling; and parent and sibling support groups. In many countries these families also are entitled to extra monetary and/or tax benefits to partially offset the additional costs of caring for a child with disabilities. As illustrated in chapters 5 and 6, although great advances have been made, for the most part, existing programs are unable to totally undo the developmental and related problems in most children with established disabilities.

Even though elimination of the developmental problems of these children remains elusive, it is now universally agreed that persons with established disabilities have the fundamental right to be fully integrated in their communities. Unlike in the past, when children with disabilities routinely were shunted into institutions for the remainder of their lives, since the 1970s, most children with disabilities grow up in their family homes, attend integrated daycares, go to neighborhood schools (although still sometimes in segregated classes), and participate in a full range of community activities with their typically developing peers. Thus, most EI programs provide an array of supports to promote social inclusion and prepare the child for an integrated school experience. Despite the ubiquitous belief that inclusion facilitates development, research studies comparing integrated to segregated settings have found no or little additional benefit of inclusion for children with established disabilities (Buysee and Bailey, 1993). However, this overall finding can be viewed in a positive light: inclusion is, at the very least, not harmful to children with disabilities (nor to typically developing children). Together, the chapters in this part illustrate just some of the many early intervention approaches for children with or at-risk for developmental disabilities. New breakthroughs in genetics, early detection, prevention, and treatments will continue to improve the quality of the lives of children with established disabilities and their families.

Reference

Buysee, V., & Bailey, D. B. (1993). Behavioral and developmental outcomes in young children with disabilities in integrated and segregated settings: A review of comparative studies. *Journal of Special Education*, 26, 434–461.

Introduction to Chapter 5

The first part of this chapter provides a segue from the previous section on low-income children. The remainder of the chapter focuses on low birth weight, a biological condition related to poverty (but not exclusively) and often resulting in varying degrees of cognitive and behavioral problems. The authors describe the Infant Health and Development Program (IHDP), an ambitious randomized clinical trial of EI for low birth weight children from birth to 3 years of age conducted across the US. The IHDP consisted of several facets including family support, case coordination, information, and specialized preschool. Both short- and long-term results are provided (up to 5 years after program termination) with reasonably low attrition rates. Analyses clearly reveal that the program benefited low birth-weight children weighing more than 2,001g at birth more than the lighter children (birth weight <2,001g). The differences between program and nonprogram participants are also more pronounced at the younger than older ages and for families with lower parental education. Importantly, the program improved the quality of parent–child interactions assumed to mediate child development (see chapter 1) and, not surprisingly, the evidence suggests that families who more fully participated did better.

While the 8-year-old IQ findings are statistically significant between the intervention and control groups, the actual differences may not be clinically significant. In other words, are the heavier 8-year-old program participants with a mean IQ of 96.5 more cognitively competent and actually perform better in school than the control children with a mean IQ of 92.1? The diminishing intervention effects over the 5-year follow-up led the authors to conclude that perhaps interventions for low birth-weight children should last longer than 3 years (see chapter 3) and more intensive support may be needed for children with birth weights below 2,000g.

FIVE

The Effectiveness of Early Intervention: Examining Risk Factors and Pathways to Enhanced Development

Lisa J. Berlin, Jeanne Brooks-Gunn,
Cecelia McCarton, and
Marie C. McCormick

Early Human Development: Vulnerability and Opportunity

Early human development is at once a time of great vulnerability and great opportunity. The first 3 years of human life comprise a longer period of immaturity and dependence than is experienced by any other species. At the same time, this period is characterized by rapid and dramatic physical and mental developments. These developments, in turn, are increasingly being viewed as the principal building blocks of adult cognitive and emotional functioning. Evidence of the current, widespread interest in understanding and enhancing early development include the Carnegie Corporation's reports *Starting Points*[1] and *Years*

Berlin, L. J., Brooks-Gunn., McCarton, C., & McCormick, M. C. (1998). The effectiveness of early intervention: Examining risk factors and pathways to enhanced development. *Preventive Medicine, 27*, 238–245. Includes use of table 1 and figures 1 & 3. Copyright 1998 American Health Foundation and Academic Press.

of Promise,[2] the cover feature of a recent *Time*,[3] and the recent White House conferences on early development and learning and child care. A theme common to each of these endeavors is the importance of early experiences – especially supportive relationships and intellectual stimulation – for later development.

The current interest in early development originated in part from a series of early intervention programs implemented in the 1960s as part of the Johnson administration's "war on poverty." Many of these programs drew on the writings of contemporary scholars emphasizing the power of early experiences for shaping individual development.[4,5] According to this perspective, early development lays the groundwork for cognitive and perhaps emotional development. Although individuals can change over the life course, once a trajectory is initiated, changes are difficult to implement and even harder to sustain. During the 1970s and 1980s, developmentalists questioned whether this focus on the first few years of life was too rigid, suggesting instead that limited or injurious early experiences do not necessarily doom people to a lifetime of limited competence. Instead, later life changes can and do occur.[6] The current perspective on early development and intervention takes an even more nuanced approach. This approach eschews determinism but at the same time presumes that altering the life trajectories of people who have not had supportive early experiences is more difficult than providing these experiences in the first place.[7]

Recent findings from some of our work on the effects of income poverty further illustrate this perspective. Specifically, income poverty, as has long been assumed, has negative consequences for children.[8] These negative consequences span the life course from birth (e.g., low birth weight) through toddlerhood and the pre-school years (e.g., cognitive test scores) to adolescence (e.g., high school completion, literacy, and teenage childbearing). The effects of poverty have been documented above and beyond the effects of other demographic and social indicators, including single parenthood, parental education, parental occupation, neighborhood poverty/affluence, and ethnicity.[9,10] To build on and add to this knowledge, members of our research team have recently drawn on data for 1,300 youths from the nationally representative Panel Survey of Income Dynamics.[11] Specifically, we have examined the question of whether the *timing* of income poverty affects high school graduation and entrance into postsecondary school education. We investigated three developmental periods: early childhood (1 to 5 years), middle childhood (6 to 10 years), and early adolescence (11 to 15 years). Only income poverty during the early childhood period was associated with high school graduation rates.[12]

The Promise of Early Intervention

Early intervention programs aim to counter the effects of poverty and other frequently coexisting risk factors such as low birth weight, low parental education, and family stress. Program goals and activities include enhancing home safety and health, strengthening children's skills, providing parents with various types of information and/or social and emotional support, strengthening parents' coping abilities and child-rearing skills, and instructing parents in providing their children emotional support and intellectual stimulation.[13,14,15] Contemporary exemplars include home visiting programs such as the Memphis New Mothers' Project,[16] the Home Instruction Program for Preschool Youngsters,[17] and Parents as Teachers.[18] Center-based early intervention programs include the Abecedarian Project,[19] the Infant Health and Development Program,[20,21,22] and the Chicago Child Parent Center and Expansion Program.[23] In the past decade these approaches have been augmented by what have been termed "two-generation" programs[24,25] such as the Teenage Parent Demonstration Program,[26,27] New Chance,[28] the Comprehensive Child Development Program,[29] and the recently initiated Early Head Start Program.[30] Many of these programs will be profiled in a forthcoming report commissioned by the U.S. Departments of Education and Health and Human Services titled, "Young Children's Education, Health, and Development: Profile and Synthesis".[31]

As the Profile and Synthesis report will illustrate, to date, many evaluations of early intervention have focused principally on outcomes related to children's cognitive development and have neglected outcomes centering on children's socioemotional development. Similarly, although parents are generally viewed as playing a pivotal role in early intervention programs, relatively little attention has been paid to parenting beliefs and behaviors as either outcomes or mediating pathways.[32] Finally, the Profile and Synthesis report will emphasize the importance of researchers looking beyond intervention group differences to examine the extent to which early intervention effects are more pronounced for some children and families than others and to examine the *processes* underlying children's and families' participation in early intervention programs. In the subsequent sections of this article we will summarize findings from the Infant Health and Development Program that help address these outstanding issues.

The Infant Health and Development Program

Background

The Infant Health and Development Program (IHDP) served a particularly vulnerable group of infants – low-birth-weight, premature infants. Low-birth-weight premature infants are disproportionately likely to face a host of difficulties, including major neurosensory handicapping conditions, neurodevelopmental deficits, cognitive delays, academic failures, and social and psychological problems.[33,34,35,36,37] Currently ongoing, the IHDP evaluation is a longitudinal, eight-site randomized trial of the effectiveness of early child development and family support services for approximately 1,000 low-birth-weight premature infants from birth to age 3. The IHDP's large, heterogeneous sample and the availability of a randomly assigned comparison group make the IHDP data a singularly rich source of information on early intervention and on early development, on the whole.

Eligible low-birth-weight premature infants were those who weighed 2,500g or less at birth, who were 37 or fewer weeks postconceptional age between January 1985 and October 1985, and who were born in one of the eight participating medical institutions.[38] Shortly after hospital discharge, eligible infants were stratified by two birth-weight groups, lighter (<2,001g) and heavier (2,001–2,500g), and then randomized into either the intervention or the follow-up only group. Two-thirds of the sample came from the lighter group and one-third of the sample came from the heavier group. In addition, one-third of the infants within each birth-weight group were randomly assigned to the intervention group, and two-thirds were assigned to the follow up group. Of the 1,302 eligible participants, 985 were successfully randomized and have since constituted the principal sample. The sample is racially and socioeconomically diverse, with 52% African-American families, 37% European-American families, 11% Hispanic-American families, and a broad range of family incomes represented.

The intervention program

The IHDP intervention program began immediately following hospital discharge and continued until 3 years corrected age. All infants received a pediatric follow-up of medical and developmental assessments and were referred for other services as needed. The intervention infants received three types of additional services: (a) *home visits* designed to provide the family with health and child development information and family support were conducted on a weekly basis during the first year and on a biweekly basis during the infants' second and third years, (b) *child development centers* provided the intervention children with an enriched extrafamilial education from 12 months for approximately 20 h per week, and (c) *parent groups* designed to provide child-rearing information and social support met at the child development centers every other month from the time the centers opened until the end of the program.

Assessment schedule

Regular assessments began when infants were 40 weeks (postconceptionally) and continued through 36 months. Over the first 3 years of the study, both intervention and follow-up group participants were assessed at regular clinic visits conducted when infants were 40 weeks (postconception) and at 4, 8, 12, 18, 24, 30, and 36 months. During each visit, growth measurements were taken, general demographic information was collected, and mothers were interviewed about their children's health. Cognitive assessments were made yearly until the end of the intervention (i.e., at 12, 24, and 36 months). Socioemotional assessments were made at 24, 30, and 36 months. Assessment of both intervention and follow-up groups continued after the intervention had terminated, with roughly 90% of the participants retained for follow-ups when children turned 5 and 8.

The Effectiveness of the Infant Health and Development Program for Children and Their Parents

In this section we present data on the IHDP's effects on children's cognitive and socioemotional development and on parenting, on processes underlying the children's and families' participation in the intervention, and on sustained intervention effects.

Intervention effects on young children's cognitive development

Significant intervention effects emerged for children's cognitive development, according to the Bayley Scales of Infant Development at 24 and 36 but not at 12 months (the Bayley Scales and all other cognitive tests have a mean of 100 and a standard deviation of 15 or 16, based on normative samples).[39] At 24 months, intervention group children scored 9.75 points (about 60% of a standard deviation) higher than follow-up group children. This effect persisted even after controlling for children's 12-month Bayley scores. Similarly, at 36 months, intervention children scored 9.31 points (60% of a standard deviation) higher than follow-up children on the Stanford–Binet Intelligence Scale (see figure 5.1).[40]

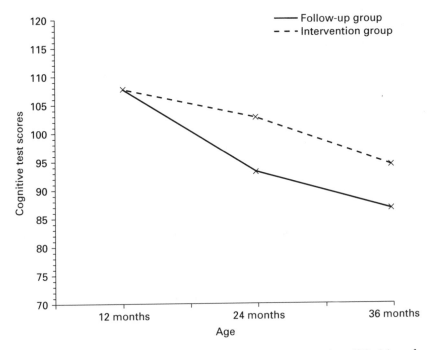

Figure 5.1 Children's cognitive development group over time (12, 24, and 36 months). Redrawn from note 40

Table 5.1   Differences between low-birth-weight premature children in the Infant Health and Development Program intervention and follow-up only groups at ages 3 (end of intervention), 5, and 8 (cognitive test scores)

	Intervention	*Follow-up*	*Difference*
IQ scores			
Heavier birth weight			
(2,001–2,500g)			
Age 3 IQ score	97.9	83.6	14.3***
Age 5 IQ score	95.4	91.7	3.7*
Age 8 IQ score	96.5	92.1	4.4**
Lighter birth weight			
(2,000g or less)			
Age 3 IQ score	91.5	84.4	7.1***
Age 5 IQ score	89.8	91.3	−1.5
Age 8 IQ score	88.3	89.5	−1.2
PPVT-R scores			
Heavier birth weight			
(2,001–2,500g)			
Age 3 PPVT	92.7	83.3	9.4***
Age 5 PPVT	84.5	78.5	6.0**
Age 8 PPVT	92.4	85.7	6.7**
Lighter birth weight			
(2,000g or less)			
Age 3 PPVT	89.2	84.4	4.8***
Age 5 PPVT	80.9	80.3	0.6
Age 8 PPVT	81.6	84.4	−2.8

Notes: IQ, intelligence test scores. Multiple linear regression models and population marginal means with covariates fixed at their average value in the total sample were used to adjust means and mean differences for site, sex, race/ethnicity, maternal education, maternal age, and Neonatal Health Index. *** $P < 0.001$. ** $P < 0.01$. * $P < 0.05$

Sources: refs 21, 22.

Finally, at 36 months, children in the intervention group also received higher scores than follow-up children on the Peabody Picture Vocabulary Test, revised version.[21,41]

As was mentioned earlier, it is important to examine the extent to which intervention effects are more pronounced for some children and families than others. In the IHDP, intervention effects consistently interacted with birth weight. Specifically, as described above, infants were stratified into two birth-weight groups, lighter (<2,001g) and heavier (2,001 to 2,500g). Intervention effects consistently favored the heavier infants. At both 24 and 36 months, there were greater intervention effects on children's cognitive development for children in the heavier birth-weight group.[20,21] At 36 months, within the heavier group, intervention children scored 14.3 points higher on the Stanford–Binet IQ test than follow-up children; in the lighter group, intervention children scored 7.1 points higher on the Stanford–Binet than follow-up children. At 36 months, intervention–control group differences on receptive vocabulary were also more pronounced for the heavier than for the lighter low-birth-weight children (see Table 5.1).[20,21]

Intervention effects also interacted with family characteristics – especially maternal education. Intervention effects have consistently favored children of less educated mothers. Specifically, children whose mothers' education was confined to high school or less were more likely to benefit from the intervention than children whose mothers had attended college.[42]

Another view into the role of both child and family characteristics in moderating the effects of the intervention has come from a study focusing on the intersection of the intervention with (a) families' multiple risk factors (13 factors including birth weight, maternal education, and maternal mental health) and (b) family poverty. The intervention was equally effective in enhancing children's cognitive development for children with few and many risk factors. There were, however, different intervention effects in poor versus nonpoor families: in poor families, the intervention was more effective for those children with fewer than five risk factors; there was no such effect for nonpoor families (see figure 5.2). These findings imply that when there was an extreme accumulation of risk, the usefulness and/or effectiveness of the intervention may have declined.

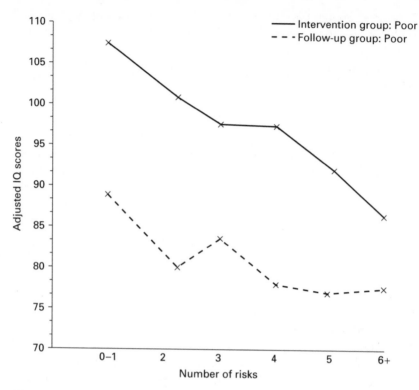

Figure 5.2   Adjusted IQ scores by risk groups and poverty status. Redrawn from note 44

Intervention effects on children's socioemotional development

In addition to intervention effects on children's cognitive development, intervention effects emerged for children's socioemotional development. At 24 and 36 months, mothers of intervention children reported their children to have fewer behavior problems than mothers of follow-up children, according to an adapted version of the Richman-Graham Behavior Checklist (BCL)[43,44] (at 24 and 36 months) and the Child Behavior Checklist for Ages 2–3 (CBCL)[45,46] (at 36 months). At 36 months, when behavior problems were measured with the CBCL, this effect persisted even after controlling for children's 24-month BCL scores (although this effect did not persist for 36-month behavior problems measured with the BCL).[40] Similarly to the ways in which child and family characteristics interacted with intervention effects on children's cognitive development, the intervention effect for children's mother-reported behavior problems at 36 months was more pronounced for children in the heavier group than for children in the lighter group, and more pronounced for children of less educated than more educated mothers.[20]

Intervention effects also emerged for children's behaviors observed during a mother–child problem-solving assessment at 30 months. Intervention children scored higher than follow-up children on task persistence and enthusiasm and on an overall rating of competence and involvement; intervention children also spent less time "off task" than follow-up children.[47]

Intervention effects on parents and parenting

Parents play key roles in most early intervention programs. In the IHDP, the intervention was associated not only with enhanced child cognitive and socioemotional development but also with changes in parents and in parenting. We consider each of these changes in turn.

With regard to changes in parents, when infants were 12 months of age, intervention mothers reported fewer symptoms of depression than follow-up mothers.[48] Additionally, at 36 months, the intervention mothers were marginally more likely to be employed and averaged a significantly greater number of months of employment over the 3 years of the intervention than the follow-up mothers.[49]

With regard to changes in parenting, intervention effects were observed across four domains: (a) intellectual stimulation in the home environment, (b) warmth in the home environment, (c) the quality of mothers' assistance to their children during problem-solving, and (d) mothers' disciplinary practices with their sons. Specifically, at 36 months, intervention families' homes were found to provide more opportunities for learning and to be emotionally "warmer" than follow-up families' homes, as assessed by an adapted subscale of the Home Observation Measurement of the Environment (HOME).[50,51] Moreover, at 30 months, in the mother–child problem-solving assessment, intervention mothers provided higher quality assistance to their children than follow-up mothers; intervention children and their mothers also received higher scores than follow-up dyads on "mutuality" (extent to which the inter-action appeared mutually satisfying). Finally, for boys only, there were intervention effects on mothers' disciplinary practices: at 36 months, intervention mothers were less likely to hit and harshly scold their sons than follow-up mothers.[52]

Thus, one route to the enhanced development seen in the intervention children may have been a more supportive home and/or a more emotionally available and supportive mother. The intervention appeared to foster the positive aspects of the child–mother relationship (e.g., the provision of intellectually stimulating materials at home, mutually satisfying problem-solving interactions) as well as to curtail negative processes within the child–mother relationships such as mothers' harsh disciplinary practices (at least for their sons). Further analyses are required to test the mediating effects of these factors.

Processes underlying intervention effects: mothers' and children's "active" participation

Further information on the processes underlying the effects of the IHDP intervention has come from a few inquiries illustrating connec-tions between several aspects of mothers' and children's participation in the intervention and children's cognitive development. These aspects of participation include quantity of services received (e.g., number of home visits completed)[19] and "rate" of program delivery – proportion of home-visit and center-based intervention activities that mothers and children actually completed.[53] More important than either of these dimensions, however, appears to be the extent to which both mothers and children were *active* participants in the intervention: within the intervention group, the mothers and children who participated most actively in the intervention also evinced higher HOME ratings and higher child IQ scores.[54] Although the fact that these analyses were confined to the intervention group may have permitted selection effects, it is notable that these findings held above and beyond a series of covariates including child birth weight, maternal education, and family poverty.

Sustained intervention effects: the 5- and 8-year follow-ups

The 5- and 8-year follow-up inquiries indicated that initial successes of the IHDP intervention were sustained into early childhood for the heavier but not the lighter low-birth-weight children. Specifically, at age 5, heavier intervention children had higher full-scale IQ scores and higher verbal IQ scores than the follow-up children. At 5, the heavier low-birth-weight children in the intervention group also received higher scores on the PPVT-R assessment of receptive language and marginally lower scores ($P < 0.07$) on mother-reported behavior problems than the heavier low-birth-weight children in the follow-up group.[21] Similar findings emerged from the 8-year follow-up: heavier low birth-weight children in the intervention group had higher full-scale IQ scores, higher verbal IQ scores, higher performance IQ scores, higher mathematics achievement scores, and higher receptive language scores than the children in the follow-up group (see table 5.1).[22]

The long-term findings for the heavier birth-weight children are similar to those reported by high-quality early intervention programs for poor children[55,56] (these programs did not specifically target low-birth-weight children, although it is likely that low-birth-weight children were overrepresented among their participants). For example, in the Abecedarian Project, a 7-point difference between treatment and control groups was seen at the end of the 5-year intervention. Several years later, the difference favoring the intervention group was 4 points on full-scale IQ (similar to the 3.7-point IHDP 5-year difference just reported) and 6 points on verbal IQ (the same as the IHDP 5-year difference on PPVT just reported).[19]

Conclusions and policy implications

Findings from early intervention programs speak to both the effectiveness of early intervention and the complexity of early development. Although the IHDP is but one of many contemporary early intervention programs and is limited to low-birth-weight infants, it is a uniquely rich source of data. At the same time, it is notable that some of the same types of findings have emerged from several other smaller-scale early intervention programs.[31,55,56]

Analyses of intervention effects have demonstrated the Infant Health and Development Program's considerable effectiveness in enhancing young children's early cognitive and socioemotional development, especially at 24 and 36 months, when intervention children were receiving both home- and center-based intervention services. Intervention effects consistently favored the heavier-born infants and the children of less educated mothers. The 5- and 8-year follow-ups conducted after the intervention was terminated illustrate that intervention effects on children's cognitive development were sustained for infants born at heavier birth weights.

The decrease in the size of the intervention effects 2 and 5 years after the termination of intervention services suggests that intervention programs may increase their effectiveness by delivering more extensive and/ or longer-lasting services.[57,58] Moreover, the fact that the effects of the intervention were not sustained into early childhood for the children weighing 2000g or less at birth suggests that practitioners may need to consider a different set of services for the lighter, more biologically vulnerable infants. Similarly, the cumulative risk data imply that different services for extremely vulnerable (multiproblem) families may be required. Researchers must now address the interrelated questions of (a) how and how much longer to extend services and (b) given an increase in overall service duration, how early to begin service delivery (e.g., is it necessary to begin service delivery immediately after birth?).

The intervention also influenced mothers' parenting and the child–mother relationship. The process analyses also revealed links between the quality of mothers' and children's participation in the intervention activities and both child and family outcomes including child IQ and the quality of the home environment. Further research should turn to such questions as (a) the extent to which these changes actually mediated the effects of the intervention on children's cognitive and socioemotional development and (b) the existence of causal pathways (e.g., from active participation in the intervention to a more intellectually supportive home environment to child IQ). In the meantime, both practitioners and researchers might fruitfully regard participants' active engagement in intervention activities as a treatment goal in and of itself.

In conclusion, the data we have shared illustrate the value of early intervention. Effective interventions, however, increasingly require striking a fine balance among the characteristics of the participants, the characteristics of the services, and service use (especially participants' active involvement). Policy-makers, moreover, cannot expect early interventions to inoculate vulnerable infants to future difficulties. Rather, as a nation we must support multifaceted early intervention programs and evaluations that will, in turn, continue to shed light on enhancing development throughout the life span.

References

1   Carnegie. *Task Forces on Meeting the Needs of Young Children*. Starting points: meeting the needs of our youngest children. New York: Carnegie Corporation of New York 1994, Apr.

2   Carnegie. *Task Force on Learning in the Primary Grades*. Years of promise: a comprehensive learning strategy for America's children. New York: Carnegie Corporation of New York, 1996 Sep.

3   Nash J. M. Fertile minds. *Time* 1997;49–62.

4   Bloom B. S. *Stability and change in human characteristics*. New York: Wiley, 1961.

5   Hunt J. M. *Environment and experience*. New York: Roland Press, 1961.

6   Brim O. G. Jr, Kagan, J. *Constancy and change in human development*. Cambridge (MA): Harvard Univ. Press, 1980.

7   Brooks-Gunn J., Furstenburg F. F. Jr. Continuity and change in the context of poverty: adolescent mothers and their children. In: Gallagher J. J., Ramey C. T., editors. *The malleability of children*. Baltimore: Brookes Publ., 1987.

8   Brooks-Gunn J., Duncan G. *Growing up poor*. New York: Sage, 1997.

9   Duncan G., Brooks-Gunn J. Income effects across the life span: integration and interpretation. In: Duncan G., Brooks-Gunn J., editors. *Consequences of growing up poor*. New York: Sage, 1997.

10   Brooks-Gunn J., Duncan G. The effects of poverty on children. *Future Child* 1997;7:55–71.

11   Hill M. *The panel study of income dynamics*, Vol 2, Sage series guide to major social science data bases. Newbury Park (CA): Sage, 1992.

12   Duncan G., Yeung W., Brooks-Gunn J., Smith J. How much does childhood poverty affect the life chances of children? *Am Soc Rev*. In press.

13   Benasich A. A., Brooks-Gunn J., Clewell B. C. How do mothers benefit from early intervention programs? *J Appl Dev Psychol* 1992;13:311–62.

14   Guralnick M. *The effectiveness of early intervention*. Baltimore: Brookes Publ., 1997.

15   Meisels S. J., Shonkoff J. R. *Handbook of early childhood intervention*. New York: Cambridge Univ. Press, 1990.

16 Kitzman H., Olds D. L., Henderson C. R., Hanks C., Cole R., Tatelbaum R., McConnochie K. M., et al. Effect of prenatal and infancy home visitation by nurses on pregnancy outcomes, childhood injuries, and repeated child-bearing. *J Am Med Assoc* 1997;278:644–52.

17 Westheimer M. Ready or not: one home based response to the readiness dilemma. Submitted for publication.

18 Pfannestiel J. C., Seltzer D. A. Evaluation of an early parent education program. *Early Child Res Q.* 4:1–18.

19 Ramey C., Campbell F. Poverty, early childhood education, and academic competence: the Abecedarian Experiment. In: Huston A., editor, *Children in poverty*. Cambridge (MA): Cambridge Univ. Press, 1991.

20 The Infant Health and Development Program. Enhancing the outcomes of low-birth-weight, premature infants: a multisite, randomized trial. *J Am Med Assoc* 1990;263:3035–42.

21 Brooks-Gunn J., McCarton C. M., Casey P. H., McCormick M. C., Bauer C. R., Bernbaum J. C., et al. Early intervention in low-birth-weight premature infants. *J Am Med Assoc* 1994;272:1257–62.

22 McCarton C., Brooks-Gunn J., Wallace I., Bauer C., Bennett F., Bernbaum J., et al. Results at 8 years of intervention for low-birth-weight premature infants: the Infant Health and Development Program. *J Am Med Assoc* 1997;227:126–32.

23 Reynolds A. Effects of a preschool plus follow-on intervention for children at risk. *Dev Psychol* 1994;30:787–804.

24 Smith S. *Two generation programs for families in poverty: a new intervention strategy*. Norwood (NJ): Ablex Publ., 1995.

25 Smith S. Two generation programs: a new intervention strategy and directions for the future. In: Chase-Landsdale P. L., Brooks-Gunn J., editors. *Escape from poverty: what makes a difference for children?* New York: Cambridge Univ. Pres, 1995.

26 Aber J. L., Brooks-Gunn J., Maynard R. Effects of welfare reform on teenage parents and their children. *Future Child* 1995;5:53–71.

27 Brooks-Gunn J., Berlin L. J., Aber J. L., Carcagno G. Moving from welfare to work: what about the family? Submitted for publication.

28 Quint J. C., Polit D. F., Bos H., Cave G. *New chance: interim findings on a comprehensive program for disadvantaged young mothers and their children*. New York: Manpower Demonstration Res Corp, 1994.

29 Smith A. N., Lopez M. *Comprehensive child development program: a national family support demonstration*. U.S. Department of Health and Human Services, 1994.

30 U.S. Department of Health and Human Services. *Statement of the advisory committee on services for families with infants and toddlers*. Washington: U.S. Gov. Printing Office, 1994.

31 Brooks-Gunn J., Berlin L. J., Fuligni A. S. Young children's education, health, and development: profile and synthesis. Manuscript in preparation.

32 Brooks-Gunn J. Children and families in communities: risk and intervention in the Bronfenbrenner tradition. In: Moen P., Elder G. H., Lusher K., editors. *Examining lives in context: perspectives on the ecology of human development*. Washington: Am. Psychol. Assoc., 1996;467–519. [For further discussion of this issue].

33 Field T. M. Interaction patterns of pre-term and term infants. In: Field T. M., Sostek A. M., Goldberg S., Shuman H. H., editors. *Infants born at risk*. New York: Spectrum, 1979.

34 Hoy E. A., Bill J. M., Sykes D. H. Very low birthweight: a long-term developmental impairment? *Int J Behav Dev* 1988;11:37–67.

35 Klein N., Hack M., Gallagher J., Fanaroff A. V. Preschool performance of children with normal intelligence who were very low-birthweight infants. *Pediatrics* 1985;75:532–7.

36 McCormick M. C. Long-term follow-up of infants discharged from neonatal intensive care units. *J Am Med Assoc* 1989;261:24–31.

37 McCormick M. C., Brooks-Gunn J., Workman-Daniels K., Turner J., Peckham G. The health and developmental status of very low birth weight children at school age. *J Am Med Assoc* 1992;267:2204–8.

38 University of Arkansas for Medical Sciences, Little Rock, AR; Albert Einstein College of Medicine of Yeshiva University, Bronx, NY, Harvard Medical School, Boston, MA; University of Miami School of Medicine, Miami, FL; University of Pennsylvania, Philadelphia, PA; University of Texas Health Science Center at Dallas, TX; University of Washington School of Medicine, Seattle, WA; Yale University School of Medicine, New Haven, CT.

39 Bayley N. *Bayley scales of infant development*. New York: Psychological Corp., 1993.

40 Brooks-Gunn J., Klebanov P. K., Liaw F., Spiker D. Enhancing the development of low birth weight, premature infants: changes in cognition and behavior over the first three years. *Child Dev* 1993;64:736–53.

41 Dunn L. M., Dunn L. M. *Peabody picture vocabulary test – revised*. Circle Pines (MN): American Guidance Service, 1981.

42 Brooks-Gunn J., Gross R. T., Kraemer H.C., Spiker D., Shapiro S. Enhancing the cognitive outcomes of low-birth-weight, premature infants: for whom is the intervention most effective? *Pediatrics* 1992;89:1209–15.

43 Richman N., Graham P. J. A behavioral screening questionnaire for use with three-year-old children. *J Child Psychol Psychiatry* 1971;12:5–33.

44 Richman N., Stevenson J., Graham P. J. Prevalence of behavior problems in three-year-old children: an epidemiological study in a London borough. *J Child Psychol Psychiatry* 1975;16:277–88.

45   Achenbach T. M., Edelbrock A., Howell C. T. Empirically based assessment of the behavioral/emotional problems of 2- and 3-year-old children. *J Abnorm Child Psychol* 1987;15;629–50.

46   McConaughty S. H., Achenbach T. M. *Practical guide for the child behavior checklist and related materials*. Burlington (VT): Univ. of Vermont. Department of Psychiatry, 1988.

47   Spiker D., Ferguson J., Brooks-Gunn J. Enhancing maternal interactive behavior and child social competence in low birth weight, premature infants. *Child Dev* 1993;64:754–68.

48   Klebanov P. K., Brooks-Gunn J., McCormick M. C. Maternal social and emotional health in context of early intervention: the Infant Health and Development Program, 1995. [Unpublished]

49   Brooks-Gunn, J., McCormick, M. C., Shapiro, S., Benasich A. A., Black, G. W.: The effects of early intervention on maternal employment, public assistance, and health insurance: The Infant Health and Development Program. *Am J Public Health* 1994;84:924–931.

50   Bradley R. H., Caldwell, B. M. Home observation for measurement of the environment: a validation study of screening efficiency. *Am J Ment Defic* 1977;81:417–20.

51   Brooks-Gunn J., Klebanov P. K., Liaw F. The learning, physical, and emotional environment of the home on the context of poverty: the Infant Health and Development Program. *Child Youth Serv Rev* 1994;17:251–76.

52   Smith J. R., Brooks-Gunn J. Correlates and consequences of harsh discipline for young children. *Arch Pediatr Adolesc Med* 1997;151:777–86.

53   Sparling J., Lewis I., Ramey C. T., Wasik B. H., Bryant D. M. LaVange L. M. Partners: a curriculum to help premature, low-birth-weight infants get off to a good start. *Top Early Child Spec Educ* 1991;11:36–55.

54   Liaw F., Meisels S. J., Brooks-Gunn J. The effects of experience of early intervention on low birth weight, premature children: the Infant Health and Development Program. *Early Child Res Q* 1995;10:405–31.

55   Barnett W. S. Long-term effects of early childhood programs on social outcomes and school outcomes. *Future Child* 1995;5:25–50.

56   Yoshikawa H. Long-term effects of early childhood programs on social outcomes and delinquency. *Future Child* 1995;5:51–75.

57   Lee V., Brooks-Gunn J., Schnur E., Liaw F. R. Are Head Start effects sustained? A longitudinal comparison of disadvantaged children attending Head Start, no preschool, and other preschool programs. *Child Dev* 1990;61:495–507.

58   Zigler E., Styfco S. J. *Head Start and beyond: a national plan for extended childhood intervention*. New Haven (CT) Yale Univ. Press, 1993.

Introduction to Chapter 6

In 1987, Ivar Lovaas published a landmark study showing considerable gains (some say "miraculous") in 19 preschool children with autism who received early intensive behavioral intervention. At age 7, the EIBI group showed significantly improved development and fewer autistic features than two comparison groups with nine of the treated children appeared to completely recover – no autistic behaviors and developmental delay. A follow-up study (McEachin, Smith, and Lovaas, 1993) reported that the gains were maintained in all the children and the nine children noted above remained indistinguishable from typically developing peers.

Over the years, Lovaas' study has been the subject of much controversy. Among other concerns (see this chapter, p. 155), the most serious issue raised was the fact that the study was not a randomized trial. Instead of randomly assigning children to EIBI (40 hours of one-to-one instruction per week for two years) or a less intensive treatment (10 hours per week), he filled up his treatment group first and the subsequently referred children formed the control group. Although Lovaas and his associates argued that the children in the two groups did not differ initially on potentially confounding variables, a matched study simply does not control for potential between-group baseline differences and biases as well as does random assignment.

Although other early intervention studies have been published showing positive benefits of behavioral intervention strategies similar to those used by Lovaas (Smith, 1999), until Smith, Groen, and Wynn (2000), there had yet to be a published randomized trial.

In this study, Smith et al. (2000) deviated from the original Lovaas (1987) study is several significant ways. First, children were randomly assigned to conditions. Second, the comparison condition was a (presumably) less intensive treatment provided by trained parents as opposed to trained early childhood educators. Third, Smith et al.'s children were not exclusively autistic, but also included children diagnosed with a related milder condition – pervasive developmental disorder (not otherwise specified) (PDD-NOS). Finally, Smith et al. provided on average only 20 hours of treatment (one-half the intensity of Lovaas' treatment).

Overall, Smith et al. found that EIBI produced substantial improvements in the children as compared to those in the parent training group. What is striking about Smith et al.'s overall findings, as compared to

Lovaas (1987) and McEachin et al. (1993), is that Smith et al. provided about half the treatment (20 versus 40 hours) and got half the effects in terms of the proportion of children who appeared to "lose" their autistic features and developmental delay. These findings suggest an EIBI dose effect, but systematic parametric studies would be needed to test this hypothesis. From a practice standpoint, increasing numbers of young children diagnosed with autism and PDD-NOS are receiving state- (or insurer) funded EIBI, but often funding is limited to 20 hours or less per week. If Smith et al.'s results are confirmed, then the current situation may be shortsighted because it may not produce optimal results. Full funding may yield substantial and sustained benefits, not just to the child and his/her family, but also to the state (Feldman, 1998). Jacobson, Mulick and Green (1998) have estimated that providing 40 hours a week for 2 to 3 years to a preschool child with autism would save millions of dollars over the life of the person in terms of reduced need for specialized educational, health, social, and other support services typically utilized by persons with autism. Although more clinical trials with larger samples still are needed, evidence is beginning to accumulate that EIBI may be effective in reducing autistic features and developmental delay in many young children (and perhaps, eliminating them in some of the children). More research is needed to determine which children benefit the most and what are the essential ingredients that maximize efficacy for the greatest number of children.

References

Feldman, M. A. (1998). Cost–benefit of effective interventions (editorial). *Journal on Developmental Disabilities, 6*(1), i–vi.

Jacobson, J. W., Mulick J. A., and Green, G. (1998). Cost–benefit estimates for early intensive behavioral intervention for young children with autism-general model and single state case. *Behavioral Interventions, 13,* 201–226.

Lovaas, O. I. (1987). Behavioral treatment and normal educational and intellectual functioning in young autistic children. *Journal of Consulting Clinical Psychology, 55,* 3–9.

McEachin, J. J., Smith, T., and Lovaas, O. I. (1993). Long-term outcome for children with autism who received early intensive behavioral treatment. *American Journal on Mental Retardation, 97,* 359–372.

Smith, T. (1999). Outcome of early intervention for children with autism. *Clinical Psychology: Science and Practice, 6,* 33–49.

SIX

Randomized Trial of Intensive Early Intervention for Children with Pervasive Developmental Disorder

Tristram Smith, Annette D. Groen, and Jacqueline W. Wynn

After years of debating whether or not early intervention helps children with developmental delays (Weinberg, 1989), researchers have largely come to agree on a middle ground: Early intervention is beneficial for many children, but gains tend to be limited (e.g., Scarr and Arnett, 1987). For example, many researchers in the area of early intervention for children with developmental disabilities have shown that such intervention prevents declines in intellectual development and may reduce family stress (e.g., Guralnick, 1998), though children continue to display substantial delays.

Nevertheless, there have been reports of larger improvements. Of particular interest, in peer-reviewed studies, seven independent groups of investigators have described dramatic gains with early intervention for children with autism (reviewed by Smith, 1999). In all studies, interventions were based on applied behavior analytic research and theory

Smith, T., Groen, A. D., & Wynn, J. W. (2000). Randomized clinical trial on intensive intervention for children with persuasive developmental disorder. *American Journal on Mental Retardation, 105*, 269–285. Includes use of tables 1–4. Copyright American Association on Mental Retardation.

(Green, 1996) and were intensive (15 to 40 hours per week). Reported gains have included average increases of approximately 20 points in IQ (Harris, Handleman, Gordon, Kristoff, and Fuentes, 1991; Lovaas, 1987; Sheinkopf and Siegal, 1998) and other standardized test scores (Anderson, Avery, DiPietro, Edwards, and Christian, 1987; Birnbrauer and Leach, 1993; Hoyson, Jamison, and Strain, 1984; McEachin, Smith, and Lovaas, 1993), as well as less restrictive school placements (Fenske, Zalenski, Krantz, and McClannahan, 1985; Lovaas, 1987).

Such results may not only enhance the outlook for children with autism but also raise optimism about the extent to which children with other developmental disorders may benefit from early intervention (Guralnick, 1998). However, the validity of the results has been a topic of intense debate. A study by Lovaas and colleagues (Lovaas, 1987; McEachin, Smith, and Lovaas, 1993) has garnered particular attention. Lovaas evaluated three groups of children with autism who were under 4 years old at intake. The experimental group ($n = 19$) received intensive treatment, which consisted of 40 hours per week of one-to-one, in-home, applied behavior analytic intervention for 2 or more years. One control group ($n = 19$) received minimal treatment (10 hours per week or less); a second control group ($n = 21$) was treated at other agencies and had no contact with Lovaas's clinic. Though the three groups did not appear to differ at intake, the intensively treated children substantially outperformed the children in control groups at age 7. Their mean IQ was 83 compared to 52 and 58, respectively. Also, 9 of 19 received passing grades without special assistance in classes for typically developing children compared to only 1 of 40 in the control groups. Moreover, at a follow-up conducted when the children averaged 12 years of age, the intensively treated children maintained their gains and also functioned more satisfactorily than did minimally treated children on measures of adaptive behavior and personality (McEachin et al., 1993).

McEachin et al. (1993) identified a number of strengths of this study, including (a) experimental and control groups that did not differ on 19 of 20 intake variables, (b) intake and follow-up evaluations conducted by blind examiners independent of the study, (c) reliance on treatment approaches developed from extensive research on reducing maladaptive behaviors and enhancing skills in children with autism (cf. Newsom and Rincover, 1989), (d) use of a detailed treatment manual (Lovaas et al., 1981) and associated videotapes to standardize the interventions that children received, and (e) follow-ups to assess maintenance of treatment gains conducted many years after termination of treatment. However, others identified many possible flaws, notably the following (Gresham and MacMillan, 1997; Schopler, Short, and Mesibov, 1989): First, assignment to groups was based on whether or not therapists were available to provide intensive treatment rather than on a more arbitrary procedure, such as the use of a random numbers table. Thus, assignment could have been biased. Second, because children were referred to outside examiners, they received a variety of different tests rather than a uniform assessment protocol. Hence, assessment results may have been unreliable. Third, selection criteria such as IQ cut-offs may have been unduly restrictive, yielding a sample with an unusually favorable prognosis. Fourth, the large amount of treatment and the level of expertise required for proper implementation may have been too much for other professionals to duplicate, too stressful for most children and families to tolerate, and too costly for funding agencies to support. Lovaas and colleagues concurred with the first two of these criticisms, though doubting the importance of the second. They disputed the other criticisms but emphasized the need for replication to confirm the results (Lovaas, Smith, and McEachin, 1989; Smith and Lovaas, 1997; Smith, McEachin, and Lovaas, 1993).

Anderson et al. (1987), Birnbrauer and Leach (1993), and Sheinkopf and Siegal (1998) conducted partial replications of the study by Lovaas and colleagues. Children in these studies received fewer hours of treatment (18 to 25 hours per week vs. 40 hours) from less experienced personnel than in the Lovaas study. All studies showed substantial average increases in nonverbal IQ (22 to 29 points), but gains in other areas were smaller than those reported by Lovaas (1987).

The present study was designed to extend this literature. Children received early intervention based on the same treatment manual used by Lovaas (1987), implemented by personnel who met the qualifications specified in that study and were independent of Lovaas (1987). However, because of concerns about cost of service delivery and stress on children and families, intervention was made less intensive than that in the Lovaas study, as described later in the *Treatment* section. To address criticisms of previous research and increase methodological rigor, we conducted a fully randomized clinical trial with uniform, comprehensive assessment protocols for all participants. To evaluate treatment efficacy for a wider range of children, we studied not only children with autism but also children with pervasive developmental disorder not otherwise specified (NOS). Because such children are often viewed as having "mild autism" (Towbin, 1997), they were hypothesized to be appropriate candidates for the intervention we provided.

Method

Participants

All referrals to the UCLA Young Autism Project between 1989 and 1992 who met the following criteria were enrolled in the study: (a) chronological age (CA) between 18 and 42 months at the time of referral, (b) residence within a one-hour drive of the research/treatment site (the UCLA Young Autism Project), (c) IQ ratio between 35 and 75, (d) diagnosis of autism or pervasive developmental disorder NOS, and (e) absence of major medical problems other than autism or mental retardation (e.g., cerebral palsy, blindness or deafness, known genetic disorders such as Down syndrome, or neurological conditions such as uncontrolled seizure disorders). Twenty-eight children met these criteria and participated in the study, including 14 diagnosed with autism and 14 diagnosed with pervasive developmental disorder NOS. There were no dropouts among this group of children. However, one child's family declined participation at intake, and 8 other children were excluded (4 because they did not have a diagnosis of autism or pervasive developmental disorder NOS; 2 because they scored below the IQ cutoff; and 2 because they were in foster care, without a permanent residence in which to provide the home-based services offered to children in this study).

Diagnosis for all 28 participants was made independently of the study by licensed psychologists at the California State Regional Centers (a state agency that coordinates services for individuals with developmental disabilities). Nineteen participants had also received a second, independent diagnosis prior to entry into the study (8 from the UCLA Neuropsychiatric Institute; 3 from White Memorial Hospital; 3 from former clinic supervisors at the UCLA Young Autism Project who had become licensed, doctoral psychologists and were blind to the children's previous diagnostic history and independent of the study; 1 from the University of Southern California Medical Center; 1 from Children's Hospital; and 1 from Cedars-Sinai Hospital). The second diagnosis was identical to the Regional Center diagnosis for all participants except

Table 6.1 Background information by group

Characteristic	Intensive treatment (n = 15)	Parent training (n = 13)
Intake CA (in months)[a]	36.07 (6.00)	35.77 (5.37)
Follow-up CA (in months)[a]	94.07 (13.17)	92.23 (17.24)
Diagnosis[b]	7/8	7/6
Boy: girl ratio	12:3	11:2
Ethnicity		
White	7	7
Hispanic	4	2
Black	1	3
Asian	3	1
Single parent household (n)	4	4
Household income[c]	$40–50,000	$40–50,000
	(<$10,000 to	(<$10,000 to
	$75–100,000)	$75–100,000)
Years of schooling[c]		
Mother	12 (10–16+)	15 (12–16+)
Father	13–14 (<6–16+)	15 (12–16+)
Siblings[c]	1 (0–4)	1 (0–2)
Medical conditions[d]	1	1
Motor delays[e]	2	1

Notes: [a] Mean (*SD*). [b] Autism/pervasive developmental disorder NOS (not otherwise specified). [c] Median (range). [d] Defined as any prenatal, perinatal, or neurological condition that resulted in medical treatment or any other medical condition that resulted in hospitalization. Medical conditions in the intensive group: one child had a skull fracture at 4 months of age; in the parent training group, one child had tubercular meningitis at 15 months of age. [e] Defined as sitting independently after 8 months of age or walking independently after 16 months of age.

one, who was diagnosed with autism at the UCLA Neuropsychiatric Institute but pervasive developmental disorder NOS at the Regional Center (and, hence, was classified as having pervasive developmental disorder NOS for the purposes of this study).

Table 6.1 summarizes background information on all participants in the two groups (intensive treatment and parent training, described in "Treatment"), as reported by each child's primary caregiver on the Family Background Questionnaire (Siegal and Elliott, 1988). The groups appeared similar on all variables. Participants had diverse ethnic and socioeconomic backgrounds, consistent with the general population in the Los Angeles area. In addition, they resembled other populations of children with pervasive developmental disorder in terms of sex ratio (Smith, 1997) and frequency of medical conditions (Rutter, Bailey, Bolton, and LeCouteur, 1994).

Design

Children were assigned to intensive treatment or parent training based on the following matched-pair, random assignment procedure: Once intake assessments had been completed on 4 to 8 children, they were divided into two cohorts, those with a diagnosis of autism and those with a diagnosis of pervasive developmental disorder. Their first names and Bayley IQs were then given to an independent statistician, who had no other information about the children. The statistician paired the children in each cohort based on IQ (the two highest forming one pair, the next two forming another pair, etc.). Finally, using a random numbers table, he assigned one member of each pair to the intensive treatment group and the other to the parent training group. The unequal size of these groups resulted from a design change. We originally intended to study not only children with autism or pervasive developmental disorder NOS but also children who had mental retardaiton without pervasive developmental disorder. Hence, for subject assignment we divided the children into two cohorts: those with autism and those with other diagnoses. We then assigned them to groups as just described. Because our sample included only 4 children with mental retardation and no pervasive developmental disorder [1 assigned to intensive treatment and 3 to parent training], we could not draw reliable inferences about these children's responsivity to treatment and, hence, removed them from the study after they had completed their participation. Intake and follow-up data on the children were obtained and are available from the first author. The data do not alter the results of the significance testing presented later in the "Results" section.

Treatment

The authors, who had a combined total of 10 years experience at the UCLA Young Autism Project under Lovaas's supervision prior to the outset of the study, directed treatment. While the study was ongoing, we received no input from Lovaas except quarterly, one-hour consultations pertaining to the UCLA Young Autism Project administrative issues and, hence, we were essentially independent. In both intensive treatment and parent training, children received intervention based on Lovaas et al.'s (1981) manual. The treatment progressed gradually and systematically from relatively simple tasks, such as responding to basic requests made by an adult, to more complex skills, such as conversing and making friends with peers. The implementation of empirically supported teaching approaches developed by behavior analysts was emphasized (Newsom and Rincover, 1989).

Intensive treatment group

The goal of intensive treatment was to maximize children's intellectual, adaptive, and socioemotional functioning and, thereby, reduce their subsequent need for special education services. For our purposes in the present study, intensive treatment was defined as 30 hours per week of intervention for each child for 2 to 3 years. Children received treatment from teams of 4 to 6 student therapists working under our close supervision. Each child's primary caregiver was asked to conduct 5 hours per week of treatment, working alongside a student therapist, for the first 3 months of treatment.

At the outset of treatment, student therapists relied primarily on a one-to-one, discrete trial format, implemented in children's homes, so that they could provide highly individualized interventions that maximized children's successes. At this stage, the children were not yet attending school. Once they spoke in short phrases; cooperated with verbal requests from others; played appropriately with toys; and acquired self-care skills, such as-dressing and toileting (approximately one year after treatment onset, with large variation across children), the focus shifted to more naturalistic instruction in group settings, such as classrooms. They were entered into classrooms in the public schools for typically developing children. Student therapists served as aides to assist the children in adjusting to classrooms, and hours in one-to-one treatment gradually decreased as children progressed at school. If children did not master the aforementioned skills after 18 months of treatment, they were enrolled in special education classrooms, based on the Individualized Education Plan developed by school personnel. If requested by parents or school personnel, information on children's present level of performance and recommended educational goals was provided by staff from the UCLA Young Autism Project, but staff did not participate in decisions about classroom placement (see McEachin et al., 1993, and Smith, Donahoe, and Davis, in press, for additional details on transitioning to school and terminating services from the UCLA Young Autism Project).

The treatment in the present study was less intensive than that provided by Lovaas (1987) in four respects: First, the aim was to provide 30 rather than 40 hours per week of intervention, as done by Lovaas (1987). Second, treatment was phased out after 18 months for children who were progressing slowly (as defined in the preceding paragraph), rather than continuing for up to 10 years, as Lovaas (1987) did. Third, fewer requirements were placed on parents, who, in the Lovaas (1987) study, were asked to take a year off from their jobs to participate in their children's treatment. Finally, though contingent aversives were employed briefly with the first 4 children, they were then stopped for all children, whereas Lovaas (1987) employed this intervention more extensively.

Parent training group

The goal of parent training was to teach parents to use treatment approaches described in the Lovaas et al. (1981) manual and assist them in using these approaches to help their children acquire skills. The children's families received two sessions per week of parent training totaling 5 hours per week, in their homes for 3 to 9 months. Parent trainers had a minimum of one year of experience at the UCLA Young Autism Project, including 6 or more months instructing novice therapists. They received one hour per week of individual supervision from the first author, with additional supervision available as needed. The first author also met with the parents at the first training session, every 3 months thereafter, and at the termination of parent training. An emphasis was placed on collaboration between parents and parent trainers, with parents selecting goals for their children and parent trainers demonstrating ways to work toward these goals. In the first session of parent training, parents were asked to identify three skills they wanted their children to achieve. The first author and parent trainer then outlined a plan for helping the child acquire these skills, using the treatment approaches described by Lovaas et al. (1981). For example, if a parent indicated that a goal was for the child to acquire expressive language, the therapist described the sequence of steps presented by Lovaas et al. (1981) for achieving this goal (first obtaining cooperation with simple requests, followed by teaching imitation of nonverbal actions, increasing the child's rate of vocalizations, teaching imitation of sounds, chaining sounds together to form words, associating words with objects and events, and generalizing this vocabulary to everyday settings). In the next session, the parent trainer outlined the basic principles of discrimination learning, discrete trial formats, and functional analyses of maladaptive behaviors and assigned the chapters on these principles in Lovaas et al.'s (1981) manual. In subsequent sessions, the parent trainer worked for 2 to 3 minutes with the child on a particular treatment program (e.g., teaching imitation of nonverbal actions), requested that the parent work on the same program with therapist present, then demonstrated another program, and so on. At the end of each 2 to 3 minutes of teaching, the parent trainer and parent gave each other feedback on their work with the child. Between sessions, parents were asked to work an additional 5 hours per week implementing the teaching programs set up with the parent trainer. Throughout parent training, children in this group were enrolled in special education classes in the public schools for 10 to 15 hours per week, with no direct involvement from the UCLA Young Autism Project.

Treatment fidelity

To check how much intervention children in the intensive treatment group actually received, student therapists recorded start and stop times for each treatment session. Their lead therapist summed these hours and reported them in monthly summaries of children's progress. One child was kept at low levels of service (10 to 15 hours per week) throughout treatment because therapy procedures appeared ineffective for him (as shown by lack of progress on the Early Learning Measure, described in "Measures"). Monthly summaries indicated that the other 14 children received a mean of 24.52 hours per week (SD = 3.69, range = 18.40 to 30.79) during the first year, with gradual reductions thereafter. Across all children in this group, the mean number of total treatment hours was 2,137.88 (SD = 1,304.76, range = 1,141.5 to 5,451.75), and the mean length of treatment was 33.44 months (SD = 11.00, range = 18 to 63). These results indicated that children received fewer hours of treatment per week, and the number of months of treatment was more variable than had been planned.

To ensure treatment quality in both intensive treatment and parent training, we implemented the same procedures used by Lovaas (1987; McEachin et al., 1993) for selecting, training, and supervising student therapists. In addition, to be allowed to continue at the UCLA Young Autism Project beyond their first 3 months, student therapists needed to obtain a passing grade on a test of knowledge about the UCLA Young Autism Project treatment, achieve a satisfactory score in a standard behavior observation of their proficiency at discrete trials, and receive favorable ratings from their supervisors. To become supervisors (developing treatment plans for children and training novice student therapists under the direction of the authors), student therapists needed to accumulate a minimum of 1,500 hours of one-to-one treatment experience at the UCLA Young Autism Project, demonstrate mastery of research pertaining to applied behavior analytic treatment for children with pervasive developmental disorder, perform satisfactorily during a behavior observation of their skill at designing and implementing treatment plans, and obtain satisfactory ratings from other supervisors and from other children's parents (see Smith et al., in press, for more detail).

Measures

Most measures in the present study were standardized instruments designed to assess a broad range of skills for both typically and atypically developing children. Smith et al. (1993) recommended the use of such measures because they have more extensive psychometric data, cover more areas of functioning, and may have more clinical relevance than do measures specifically developed to assess functioning in children with pervasive developmental disorder (but see Mundy, 1993, for a different perspective). In addition to standardized instruments, however, the assessment also included one measure used in previous studies, namely, the type of classroom in which children were placed (Lovaas, 1987) and two measures developed specifically for evaluating treatment provided by the UCLA Young Autism Project (one assessing skill acquisition early in treatment and one assessing parental satisfaction with treatment).

Intellectual functioning

At intake and follow-up, the Stanford-Binet Intelligence Scale, which was designed for individuals with a mental age (MA) of 2 years and older (Thorndike, Hagen, and Sattler, 1986) was administered to participants. If they did not achieve a basal (as defined in the manual), examiners administered the Bayley Scales of Infant Development-Mental Development Index (Bayley, 1969), which is a test given to children with developmental levels of 0 to 30 months. Both the Stanford-Binet and Bayley have been extensively used and validated for children with pervasive developmental disorder (Newsom and Hovanitz, 1997). In addition, children completed the Merrill-Palmer Scale of Mental Tests (Stutsman, 1948), a commonly used instrument that primarily assesses visual-spatial skills in children with developmental levels of 1.5 to 6.5 years and that has been shown to predict the later functioning of children with pervasive developmental disorder (e.g., Lord and Schopler, 1989). Children who did not answer any items correctly on this test were assigned a score of 18 months (the lowest MA covered by the test). Children who did not reach a ceiling were assigned a score of 78 months (the highest MA covered by the test).

Language functioning

At intake and follow-up, children completed the Reynell Developmental Language Scales (Reynell, 1990), which is used to assess comprehension (receptive language) and expressive language in children ages 1 to 6 years. This instrument is commonly administered to assess children with pervasive developmental disorder (Sparrow et al., 1997), though its psychometric properties have not been studied with this population. Children who did not answer any items correctly were assigned a score of 12 months in the Comprehension domain and 15 months in the Expressive Language domain (the lowest developmental ages covered by these scales). Children who did not reach a ceiling were assigned a score of 72 months (the highest developmental age covered by these scales).

Adaptive functioning

At intake and follow-up, children's parents completed the survey form of the Vineland Adaptive Behavior Scales (Sparrow, Balla, and Cicchetti, 1984), which is an interview given to caregivers regarding the everyday functioning of children ages 0 to 18 years in the areas of communication, daily living skills, and socialization. The Vineland is widely regarded as the instrument of choice for assessing adaptive functioning in children with pervasive developmental disorder (Newsom and Horowitz, 1997).

Socioemotional functioning

At follow-up, children's primary caregivers completed the Achenbach Child Behavior Checklist and their teachers completed a parallel form of this checklist, the Teacher Report Form (Achenbach, 1991). The Child Behavior Checklist and Teacher Report Form both measure behavior problems in the areas of social withdrawal, somatization, anxiety/depression, social problems, thought problems, attention problems, delinquency, and aggression. These two instruments are the most extensively studied measures of socioemotional functioning in children, but their utility for assessing children with pervasive developmental disorder has not been investigated.

Academic achievement

Children completed the Wechsler Individualized Achievement Test (Wechsler, 1992). This instrument is a well-normed measure of academic skills from preschool to adulthood.

Class placement

At follow-up, children's report cards and/or individualized education plans (IEPs) were obtained in order to determine their class placement: *regular classroom* (defined as placement in a classroom for typically developing children without an IEP or special services such as assistance from an aide), *regular classroom with support* (defined as placement in a regular classroom with an IEP or special services), or *self-contained classroom*. Class placement may be influenced by factors other than the child's functioning (e.g., parent advocacy or school district policy) but provides a measure of "real world outcome" (Kazdin and Weisz, 1998, p. 29).

Progress in treatment

Children in the intensive treatment group completed the Early Learning Measure (available from the first author), which is a behavior observation instrument developed by Smith, Eikeseth, Buch, and Lovaas (1995) for assessing children's progress during the first 4 months of treatment. At intake, the examiner identified 40 instructions to which the child did not give the correct response, including 10 in each of the following four areas: receptive language (e.g., request to clap or wave), nonverbal imitation (e.g., imitating arms held up over the head), verbal imitation (e.g., imitating sounds of letters such as "ah" or "em"), and expressive language (e.g., stating "ball" when shown a ball). The instructions were re-administered at 1-month intervals during the first 4 months of treatment. Children's rate of acquisition of correct responses was used to predict outcome at follow-up. Leaf (1982) found that mastery of verbal imitation items in the first 3 months of treatment was strongly associated with outcome at age 7 years for 16 of the 19 intensively treated children studied by Lovaas (1987).

Parent evaluation

The Family Satisfaction Questionnaire (Smith, 1990), is a 20-item, written survey with questions on primary caregivers' appraisal of children's progress with treatment, quality of treatment, impact of treatment on the family, and relationship between the family and treatment staff. Respondents rated each item on a 7-point Likert scale. The psychometric properties of the Family Satisfaction Questionnaire have not yet been tested, apart from its correlations with other measures used in the present study (summarized in "Parent Ratings").

Data collection

Pretreatment evaluations occurred in the 3 months prior to treatment onset. Follow-up evaluations occurred at a CA of 7 to 8 years. Parents completed surveys without a staff member present and were assured that their responses would not be disclosed to treatment personnel. Standardized tests were administered by doctoral students in clinical psychology at UCLA. These examiners had completed approximately 20 hours of training from the first or third author on the particular tests used in the study (as described by Smith et al., in press) and were blind to children's group assignment and treatment history. At pretreatment, 10 children had completed the Bayley with an examiner at an outside agency in the preceding 3 months. Therefore, to check reliability, we compared Bayley scores obtained by the UCLA Young Autism Project and those from the outside agency. Four of the 10 children were deemed untestable by the outside examiner but testable by the study examiner, who reported IQs ranging from 37 to 46. The 6 remaining children obtained an average IQ of 60 from the outside examiner and 57 from the study examiner, with a significant Pearson correlation between examiners, $r(6) = .90$, $p < .05$. The difference in IQ between examiners was 4 to 9 points for individual children. Thus, the UCLA examiner often obtained an IQ when the outside examiner did not; when both examiners obtained scores, these scores were similar, providing some evidence of reliability.

Senior staff members at the UCLA Young Autism Project (postgraduate or graduate students with a minimum of 2 years treatment experience) administered the Early Learning Measure. They were not blind to the child's treatment history, having interacted infrequently with the child (once a week or less). However, all administrations were videotaped and scored by an independent rater who was blind to the child's treatment history, and interrater reliability was evaluated by having a second independent, blind rater score 50% of the videotapes (Cohen's $\kappa = .86$).

Results

Comparison between groups

To test for differences between the intensive treatment and parent training groups at intake, we conducted two-tailed pooled variance t tests on IQ, Merrill-Palmer score, total Reynell score (Comprehension plus Expressive Language), and Vineland composite score. Another set of t tests was performed for individual scale scores on the Reynell and Vineland. Each set of t tests was Dunn-Bonferroni corrected for a family-wise error of .10. This procedure was also applied to follow-up data for these measures, with the modification that tests were one-tailed.

Table 6.2 presents intake and follow-up data. At intake, the groups appear to have been closely matched on all variables, with no statistically significant between-group differences. As expected, children displayed major developmental delays. For example, no child achieved a basal on the Stanford-Binet. Moreover, 23 of 28 children (82%)

Table 6.2 Means and SDs of children's standardized test scores by group and time

| | Intensive treatment | | | | | | Parent training | | | | | |
| | Autism | | PDD NOS[e] | | Total | | Autism | | PDD NOS | | Total | |
Measure	Mean	SD	Mean	SD	Mean	SD	Mean	SD	Mean	SD	Mean	SD
IQ[a]												
Intake	51.00	13.94	50.13	9.11	50.53	11.18	50.71	14.24	50.67	14.79	50.69	13.88
Follow-up	55.29	24.09	76.25	20.69	66.49	24.08	52.57	22.83	47.13	17.89	49.67*	19.74
Merrill–Palmer[b]												
Intake	21.29	4.65	21.88	4.64	21.60	4.49	23.57	6.11	20.00	4.43	21.92	5.50
Follow-up	54.43	23.60	68.63	13.41	64.33	18.74	45.67	23.64	52.67	20.60	49.17*	21.43
Reynell[b] Comprehension												
Intake	15.14	4.91	12.00	0.00	13.47	3.60	14.86	4.88	12.33	0.82	13.69	3.73
Follow-up	39.00	26.00	46.25	19.98	42.87	22.29	32.14	19.04	34.20	15.66	33.00	16.86
Expressive												
Intake	15.29	0.76	15.00	0.00	15.13	0.52	17.00	3.46	15.50	1.2	16.31	2.69
Follow-up	40.57	25.13	48.00	23.05	44.53	23.48	32.14	20.93	41.00	22.3	36.23	21.19
Total (rec.+exp.)												
Intake	30.43	5.59	27.00	0.00	28.60	4.07	31.86	8.32	27.83	2.04	30.00	6.34
Follow-up	79.57	41.99	94.25	41.99	87.40	46.21	64.29	39.25	57.20	21.48	75.20	31.88

Table 6.2 (cont'd)

Measure	Intensive treatment						Parent training					
	Autism		PDD NOS[e]		Total		Autism		PDD NOS		Total	
	Mean	SD	Mean	SD	Mean	SD	Mean	SD	Mean	SD	Mean	SD
Vineland[c]												
Communication												
Intake	61.00	5.69	55.75	4.40	58.20	5.56	62.29	5.74	61.67	7.06	62.00	6.11
Follow-up	66.14	33.97	69.38	28.55	67.87	30.08	64.43	15.72	56.50	19.44	60.77	17.26
DLS[d]												
Intake	75.57	8.62	65.00**	4.11	69.93	8.37	68.43	8.66	73.17	14.59	70.62	11.50
Follow-up	65.57	30.85	63.88	22.49	62.33	25.76	64.71	15.89	61.00	19.47	63.00	16.97
Socialization												
Intake	66.00	8.17	59.25	6.40	62.40	7.82	69.14	3.76	69.17	12.98	69.15	8.75
Follow-up	66.57	28.50	66.13	23.06	66.33	24.78	67.00	15.33	71.12	19.88	68.92	16.94
Composite												
Intake	68.86	11.16	59.2	4.99	63.44	9.35	65.00	9.54	65.40	10.41	65.17	9.44
Follow-up	62.14	32.84	60.44	25.11	61.19	29.72	61.86	16.83	53.80	16.84	58.50	16.58

Notes: [a]Bayley scored as ratio IQ. Stanford-Binet as deviation IQ. [b]Developmental age (months). [c]Standard score (population $M[SD] = 100[15]$). [d]Developmental Language Scales. [e] Pervasive development delay not otherwise specified. * $p < 0.05$, Intensive Treatment > Parent Training. ** $p < 0.05$, PDD NOS > Autism.

appeared to be nonverbal; they demonstrated no receptive or expressive vocabulary and uttered no words on the Reynell (13 children assigned to intensive treatment and 10 assigned to parent training). Also, 14 (50%) obtained a raw score of 0 on the Merrill-Palmer (6 intensive and 7 parent training children). Vineland scores also tended to be far below the national average.

At follow-up, as shown in table 6.2, the intensive treatment group had a statistically significant advantage over the parent training group in IQ, visual-spatial skills (as measured by the Merrill-Palmer), but not language development or adaptive behavior in everyday settings (as indexed by the Vineland). The between-group differences on the Merrill-Palmer may have been underestimated because of ceiling effects. Eight intensively treated children achieved the highest possible Merrill-Palmer score, compared to 1 child in parent training. Also, 4 intensively treated children obtained the maximum scores in both Comprehension and Expressive Language on the Reynell; no child in parent training did so. (One child in parent training did reach the maximum in Expressive Language, but not Comprehension). However, floor effects appeared to apply about equally to the two groups. Four intensively treated and 5 parent training children did not achieve a basal on the Stanford-Binet; 1 intensively treated and 2 parent training children tested as nonverbal on the Reynell; and 1 intensively treated and 2 parent training children had substantially delayed visual-spatial skills, as evidenced by raw scores of 0 on the Merrill-Palmer. In addition, as indicated in table 6.2, there was little difference between groups in mean Vineland scores.

The intensively treated group also had higher WIAT scores than did the parent training group. The mean standard score was 75.71 ($SD = 21.31$) for the intensively treated group and 58.44 ($SD = 18.43$) for the parent training group. Table 6.3 presents results for the only other test given at follow-up, the Child Behavior Checklist. It can be seen from the table that there was little difference between groups in behavior problems, as reported by parents and teachers.

Comparison between children with autism and pervasive developmental disorder NOS

Within each group, children with autism were compared to those with pervasive developmental disorder NOS. The statistical procedures were

Table 6.3 Results of follow-up assessment by group on the child behavior checklist

| Measure | Intensive treatment | | | | Parent training | | | |
| | Parent | | Teacher | | Parent | | Teacher | |
	Mean	SD	Mean	SD	Mean	SD	Mean	SD
Child behavior checklist T score								
Withdrawal	59.33	10.26	61.89	7.04	60.17	7.81	55.00	4.40
Somatization	56.11	8.16	52.33	4.95	56.11	8.16	54.86	8.47
Anxiety/depression	52.22	5.24	54.22	5.26	59.67	11.59	54.57	4.08
Social problems	60.11	13.46	59.78	9.59	64.33	11.34	57.43	8.02
Thought problems	67.11	10.82	64.67	13.62	64.47	12.74	62.57	7.55
Attention problems	64.78	10.32	64.89	12.80	67.50	4.18	61.57	9.29
Delinquency	54.67	9.24	53.44	6.39	59.00	6.42	54.00	5.13
Aggression	56.11	9.10	60.00	10.81	59.67	10.41	55.71	5.53

the same as those used to compare intensive treatment to parent training, with the exception that all tests were two-tailed. Table 6.2 summarizes the data for children with autism and those with pervasive developmental disorder NOS in each of the two treatment groups. As shown, intake test scores of children with autism were similar to those of children with pervasive developmental disorder NOS in the intensive treatment group and in the parent training group. Differences between diagnostic categories in follow-up test scores also did not reach statistical significance. However, visual inspection of the results indicates that within the intensive training group, children with pervasive developmental disorder NOS tended to obtain higher scores than did children with autism. For example, children with pervasive developmental disorder NOS averaged 17 IQ points above those with autism. Given this finding and the low statistical power to detect differences between diagnostic categories (due to small cell sizes and large within-group variability), it is possible that important differences existed in the follow-up scores achieved by children with pervasive developmental disorder NOS and those achieved by children with autism.

Prediction of outcome in the intensive treatment group

Two of the 15 intensively treated children (1 with autism and 1 with pervasive developmental disorder NOS) met the criteria used by McEachin et al. (1993) for classifying children as "best outcome" (placement in regular classes without special services and IQ > 85). An additional 2 children in this group (1 with autism and 1 with pervasive developmental disorder NOS) met the placement criterion while scoring just below the IQ cutoff. These 4 children performed in the average range on all other tests, with the exception that clinically significant behavior problems were reported for 1 child on the Child Behavior Checklist by the parent (though not the teacher). By contrast, only 1 child in the parent training group scored in the average range on any test at follow-up (a child with pervasive developmental disorder NOS who scored 87 on the Stanford-Binet and 93 on the WIAT, but below 75 on all other tests, and who had a full-time, individual aide in a regular class).

Though Lovaas and Smith (1988) reported that best-outcome children tended to have higher intake IQs than did non-best-outcome children, this finding was not replicated in the present study. Of the 4 intensively treated children described in the preceding paragraph, 1 scored above the mean IQ at intake, 1 scored at the mean, and 2 scored below. More generally, the correlation between intake and follow-up IQ in the intensive treatment group was small and not statistically significant, Pearson $r(15) = .08$. Further, unprotected Pearson correlations indicated that intake IQ did not significantly correlate with any other outcome variable. In addition, unprotected Pearson correlations for each intake measure (including both demographic variables and standardized test scores) with each follow-up measure revealed only three statistically significant associations: intake Merrill-Palmer with follow-up Merrill-Palmer (.43), intake Reynell with follow-up Reynell (.36), and intake Reynell with follow-up Vineland (.48). Given the large number of correlations performed, even these statistically significant findings may have been spurious. Overall, then, intake data were poor predictors of follow-up scores.

Lovaas and Smith (1988) suggested that the Early Learning Measure would predict follow-up tests more strongly than would intake standardized tests. Specifically, they proposed that mastery of verbal imitation on the Early Learning Measure 3 months after treatment onset would predict who achieved average functioning at follow-up. Eight of the 15 intensively treated children (including all 4 children who scored in the average range on a majority of tests at follow-up) met this mastery criterion. Thus, the criterion identified the 4 children who achieved average functioning on most follow-up tests but also yielded false positives. Three of these 4 children also demonstrated mastery of expressive labels at 3 months, whereas no other child did so. Hence, mastery of expressive labels may also have been associated with outcome. However, the other two scales (Receptive Actions and Nonverbal Imitation) were not associated with outcome because almost all children (13 of 15) showed mastery 1 month after treatment onset.

Parent ratings

Table 6.4 summarizes parent ratings for each of the 20 items on the Family Satisfaction Questionnaire. As shown in the table, parents in both groups tended to report that children improved. On average, they described moderate gains. All parents expressed ongoing concern about

Table 6.4   Parent ratings of treatment by group

Rating	Intensive treatment		Parent training	
	Mean	SD	Mean	SD
Child's progress[a]				
Language/communication	2.41	0.67	2.50	0.84
Social skills	2.58	0.67	2.50	0.55
Play skills	2.42	1.00	2.33	0.82
Aggression/tantrums	2.25	1.22	2.17	1.17
Self-stimulatory/ritualistic behaviors	2.25	1.42	2.00	1.27
Self-help	1.92	0.67	2.00	1.27
Workload[b]				
For child	4.08	0.67	4.33	1.03
For parent	3.91	0.29	5.00	1.10
Stress during treatment[c]				
For child	4.33	0.66	3.83	1.84
For parent	3.08	1.68	4.60	1.34
Quality of treatment[d]				
Treatment methods	1.27	0.67	2.00	1.27
Therapist motivation and concern	1.75	0.87	1.20	0.45
Comparison with services from other agencies	1.75	1.06	2.80	1.10
Recommendation of treatment to others	1.58	1.73	1.20	0.45
Worth time/effort	1.25	0.62	1.20	0.45
Would enroll again	1.17	0.39	1.00	0.00
Overall opinion	1.17	0.39	1.00	0.00

Notes: There was no statistically significant between-group differences on any question. [a] 1 = no longer a problem, 4 = no change, 7 = much worse. [b] 1 = much too little, 4 = just right, 7 = too much. [c] 1 = greatly reduced, 4 = no effect, 7 = greatly increased. [d] 1 = very positive, 4 = neutral, 7 = very negative.

their children's communication skills, but some reported that other behaviors were no longer a problem: social skills (1 in intensive treatment), play and leisure skills (3 in intensive treatment, 1 in parent training), tantrums and aggression (4 in intensive treatment, 2 in parent training), self-stimulatory behaviors (4 in intensive treatment, 2 in parent training), self-help (3 in intensive treatment, 1 in parent training). No ratings indicated that children's behavior worsened, apart from one report of a slight worsening of aggression for a child in intensive treatment. Spearman correlations between parent ratings and follow-up IQ, Merrill-Palmer, Reynell, and Vineland were moderately high, with rs ranging from .24 to .67. However, correlations between parent ratings of a particular behavior and standardized tests designed to measure the same behavior tended to be no higher than correlations across behaviors. For example, the correlation coefficient for parent ratings of communication and post-treatment Reynell score was .47, but the coefficients between these ratings and IQ, Merrill-Palmer, and Vineland were .50, .67, and .62, respectively. Hence, parent ratings and follow-up test scores may have had convergent but not discriminant validity. This finding indicates that parent ratings were generally consistent with objective measures of children's progress but reflected children's overall improvement rather than improvement in a particular behavior (e.g., communication, social skills).

As also shown in table 6.4, parents in both groups tended to give very favorable ratings for quality of treatment, impact of treatment on the family, and relationship between the family and treatment staff. One parent in the parent training group reported that the treatment was stressful for her. However, there were no other negative ratings.

Discussion

Consistent with previous studies based on the treatment manual we used (McEachin et al., 1993), intensively treated children outperformed children in a parent training group at follow-up on measures of intelligence, visual-spatial ability, and academic achievement. Extending previous reports, results of the present study reveal that parents in both groups held highly positive views about the services their children received. Also, children with pervasive developmental disorder NOS benefited at least as much from intensive treatment as did children with autism. Despite these favorable outcomes, between-group differences in follow-up IQ were roughly half that reported by McEachin et al. (16 vs. 31 points) as was the proportion of children placed in regular classes without special services (27% vs. 47%). Further, in the present study, intensively treated children did not differ from children in the parent training group on standardized tests of behavior problems and adaptive functioning in everyday settings at follow-up, whereas McEachin et al. (1993) found substantial advantages for intensively treated children on these variables.

The present study retained features that were strengths of previous research (manualized treatments based on extensive research and supervised by experienced personnel, blind examiners, and long-term follow-up). We also incorporated improvements, particularly the use of a true experimental design and a comprehensive assessment battery that was uniform across children. Still, the study has limitations. The small sample size and heavy tailed, skewed distributions of scores precluded conducting some statistical procedures, such as factorial analyses of variance to examine diagnosis-by-treatment interactions, that might have helped in interpretation of the results, and it yielded low power to detect predictors of treatment response. The assessment instruments included only one measure of social skills (the Vineland Socialization Domain), a parent satisfaction questionnaire with untested psychometric properties, no measure of children's or parent's quality of life, and no measure of parent's participation in treatment. Also, the assessment measures used in the study consisted mostly of instruments developed for both typically and atypically developing children rather than ones specifically developed for children with developmental disabilities (e.g., the Achenbach Child Behavior Checklist instead of the Aberrant Behavior Checklist – Aman and Singh, 1986). The addition of measures designed for children with developmental disabilities might have been useful. Finally, the study lacked a standardized diagnostic instrument (and had no follow-up diagnostic assessment at all). A standardized instrument now exists for identifying young children with autism (Lord, 1995), though not for differentiating between autism and pervasive developmental disorder NOS (Myhr, 1998).

We are currently participating in multisite research projects aimed at overcoming these the limitations (Smith et al., in press). Nevertheless, we believe that the present study supports several conclusions. First, results confirm that some children with pervasive developmental disorder may make large gains with early intervention. Second, in view of the differences observed between groups at follow-up, intensive treatment may be more effective than is parent training, even when parent training incorporates many features recommended by professionals (e.g., individualized, collaborative services in the family home). Third, given that children with pervasive developmental disorder NOS obtained outcomes at least as positive as those obtained by children with autism, intensive early intervention may be especially beneficial for children with pervasive developmental disorder NOS. Fourth, because parents who varied greatly in socioeconomic status and other demographic variables consistently evaluated treatment favorably, a wide range of parents may experience the treatment as helpful rather than stressful, despite its high intensity. Fifth, in view of the positive ratings given by parents in both intensive and parent training groups, the differences between groups are likely to have arisen from specific aspects of the intervention rather than placebo factors (e.g., the credibility of intensive treatment or the warm relationships it fostered between families and staff). Finally, because the Early Learning Measure appeared to be more strongly associated with outcome than were any of the intake standardized tests, measures of children's skill acquisition early in treatment warrant further scrutiny as predictors of outcome.

Although some conclusions are supported by results of the study, new questions are also raised. First, considering that we used the same treatment manual as did Lovaas and colleagues (Lovaas, 1987; McEachin et al., 1993), why were our results less favorable? One possibility, of course, is that the treatment is really not as effective as Lovaas (1987) reported. Nevertheless, another possibility is that methodological differences between studies accounted for the differences. For example, despite the use of assessment procedures that yielded scores for children who might otherwise have been classified as untestable (see "Initial analyses"), intensively treated children had a lower intake IQ and level of language than those in Lovaas's investigation and most other published outcome studies (cf. Smith, 1999). As an illustration, the mean intake IQ of intensively treated children was 50 in the present study compared to 63 in Lovaas (1987). Neither IQ nor language strongly predicted follow-up scores in the present study, but they have been predictive in other studies (Smith, 1999) and, hence, may have been a factor in the relatively modest results reported here. Studies with large samples and without IQ cutoffs are needed to determine whether these intake variables are reliably associated with outcome in intensive early intervention.

Second, changes in the treatment may have undermined its effectiveness. For example, we directed treatment in the present study, whereas treatment in the Lovaas (1987) study was overseen by its originators (Lovaas et al., 1981). Because we had many years of training prior to the study and employed rigorous training and evaluation procedures to ensure the quality of therapy (Smith et al., in press), we expected that the change in treatment directors would not affect the results, but our results suggest the need for further research on this issue. Another change in the present study was that we reduced the intensity of inter- vention, as described in "Treatment". This change may have lowered treatment efficacy. For example, the intervention we provided was focused on skill-building in a one-to-one setting before generalizing to school and other everyday settings. Therefore, phasing out treatment for children who were progressing slowly may have prevented them from improving their performance on measures of everyday functioning, such as the Vineland and Child Behavior Checklist. Reducing parental involvement for intensively treated children may also have contributed to the lack of improvement on these measures. The relatively low num- ber of treatment hours, relative to Lovaas (1987), may have limited gains on all follow-up measures. Direct investigations of treatment intensity are needed to evaluate these possibilities.

Children received an average of 25 hours of treatment per week rather than the 30 hours that we intended to provide. Our impression is that this shortfall resulted from staff shortages, scheduling conflicts, and illnesses. Thus, the logistics of arranging for intensive treatment turned out to be more formidable than we had anticipated and may pose more of an obstacle to replication than we have previously acknowledged (e.g., Smith and Lovaas, 1997). Employing paid staff instead of students may ensure a steadier supply of therapists, and scheduling extra hours may compensate for missed sessions. Both would increase expenses, but the intervention may still be cost effective (Jacobson, Mulick, and Green, 1998).

A final, critical question is whether it is appropriate to provide inten- sive treatment to achieve the outcomes we have reported. We think the answer is plainly *yes* for the children who achieved average function- ing on most follow-up measures but less clear for the remaining chil- dren. The latter children increased their rate of skill acquisition when they entered treatment yet did not make gains in standardized test scores at follow-up. One possible reason for this finding is that the children may have made advances while in treatment but regressed afterward. Another is that the children may have reached a plateau in treatment that they would have eventually reached without treatment. Alternat- ively, they may have continued to acquire skills more rapidly than they would have without treatment, but their skill acquisition did not raise standardized test scores. Unfortunately, our data do not provide a basis for deciding among these possibilities (and there may be others). Each possibility, however, suggests that the treatment is potentially appropriate for children who do not achieve average functioning but needs substantial additions or modifications (e.g., identifying continuation services that enable children to maintain gains, determining when children reach a plateau and making a transition to another program at that time, and setting less ambitious goals for treatment).

Although the results were more mixed than in some previous studies, the present study substantiates the view that intensive early intervention can be a powerful intervention. Of particular importance may be the finding that children with pervasive developmental disorder NOS gained as much as or more than did children with autism. This finding suggests that intensive early intervention may be effective not only for autism but also for other pervasive developmental disorder.

References

Achenbach, T. M. (1991). *Integrative guide for the 1991 Child Behavior ChecklistL/ 4–18, YSR, and Teacher Report Form profiles.* Burlington: University of Vermont, Department of Psychiatry.

Aman, M. G., & Singh, N. N. (1986). *Aberrant Behavior Checklist: Manual.* E. Aurora, NY: Slosson.

Anderson, S. R., Avery, D. L., DiPietro, E. K., Edwards, G. L., & Christian, W. P. (1987). Intensive home-based intervention with autistic children. *Education and Treatment of Children, 10,* 352–366.

Bayley, N. (1969). *Bayley Scales of Infant Development.* New York: Psychological Corp.

Birnbrauer, J. S., & Leach, D. J. (1993). The Murdoch Early Intervention Program after two years. *Behaviour Change, 10,* 63–74.

Fenske, E. C., Zalenski, S., Krantz, P. J., & McClannahan, L. E. (1985). Age at intervention and treatment outcome for autistic children in a comprehensive intervention program. *Analysis and Intervention in Developmental Disabilities, 5,* 49–58.

Green, G. (1996). Early behavioral intervention for autism: What does research tell us? In C. Maurice (Ed.), *Behavioral intervention for young children with autism* (pp. 29–44). Austin, TX: Pro-Ed.

Gresham, F. M., & MacMillan, D. L. (1997). Autistic recovery? An analysis and critique of the empirical evidence on the Early Intervention Project. *Behavioral Disorders, 22,* 185–201.

Guralnick, M. J. (1998). Effectiveness of early intervention for vulnerable children: A developmental perspective. *American Journal on Mental Retardation,* *102,* 319–345.

Harris, S., Handleman, J., Gordon, R., Kristoff, B., & Fuentes, F. (1991). Changes in cognitive and language functioning of preschool children with autism. *Journal of Autism and Developmental Disabilities, 21,* 281–290.

Hoyson, M., Jamieson, B., & Strain, P. S. (1984). Individualized group instruction of normally developing and autistic-like children: A description and evaluation of the LEAP curriculum model. *Journal of the Division of Early Childhood, 8,* 157–181.

Jacobson, J. W., Mulick, J. A., & Green, G. (1998). Cost-benefit estimates for early intensive behavioral intervention for young children with autism: General models and single state case. *Behavioral Interventions, 13,* 201–226.

Leaf, R. B. (1982). Predicting outcome in the UCLA Autism Project. In O. I. Lovaas (Chair), *The UCLA Autism Project.* Symposium conducted at the annual meeting of the American Psychological Association, Washington, DC.

Lord, C. (1995). Follow-up of two-year-olds referred for possible autism. *Journal of Child Psychology and Psychiatry, 36,* 1365–1382.

Lovaas, O. I. (1987). Behavioral treatment and normal educational and intellectual functioning in young autistic children. *Journal of Consulting and Clinical Psychology, 55,* 3–9.

Lovaas, O. I., Ackerman, A. B., Alexander, D., Firestone, R., Perkins, J., & Young, D. (1981). *Teaching developmentally disabled children: The ME book.* Austin, TX: Pro-Ed.

Lovaas, O. I., & Smith, T. (1988). Intensive behavioral treatment for young autistic children. In B. B. Lahey & A. E. Kazdin (Eds.), *Advances in clinical child psychology* (Vol. 11, pp. 285–324). New York: Plenum.

Lovaas, O. I., Smith, T., & McEachin, J. J. (1989). Clarifying comments on the young autism study: Reply to Schopler, Short, and Mesibov. *Journal of Consulting and Clinical Psychology, 57,* 165–167.

McEachin, J. J., Smith, T., & Lovaas, O. I. (1993). Long-term outcome for children with autism who received early intensive behavioral treatment. *American Journal on Mental Retardation, 97,* 359–372.

Myhr, G. (1998). Autism and other pervasive developmental disorders: Exploring the dimensional view. *Canadian Journal of Psychiatry, 43,* 589–595.

Newsom, C., & Hovanitz, C. A. (1997). Autistic disorder. In E. J. Mash & L. G. Terdal (Eds.), *Assessment of childhood disorders* (3rd ed., pp. 408–452). New York: Guilford.

Newsom, C., & Rincover, A. (1989). Autism. In E. J. Mash & R. A. Barkley (Eds.), *Treatment of childhood disorders* (pp. 286–346). New York: Guilford.

Reynell, J. K. (1990). *Reynell Developmental Language Scales.* Los Angeles: Western Psychological Association.

Rutter, M., Bailey, A., Bolton, P., & LeCouteur, A. (1994). Autism and known medical conditions: Myth and substance. *Journal of Child Psychology and Psychiatry, 35*, 311–322.

Scarr, S., & Arnett, J. (1987). Malleability: Lessons from intervention and family studies. In J. J. Gallagher & C. T. Ramey (Eds.), *The malleability of children* (pp. 71–84). Baltimore: Brookes.

Schopler, E., Short, A., & Mesibov, G. B. (1989). Relation of behavioral treatment to "normal functioning": Comment on Lovaas. *Journal of Consulting and Clinical Psychology, 57*, 162–164.

Sheinkopf, S., & Siegal, B. (1998). Home-based behavioral treatment for young autistic children. *Journal of Autism and Developmental Disorders, 28*, 15–23.

Siegal, B., & Elliott, G. R. (1988). *Stanford Developmental History Questionnaire.* Stanford, CA: Author.

Smith, T. (1990). *Family Satisfaction Questionnaire.* Unpublished instrument. (Available from Dr. T. Smith, Department of Psychology, Washington State University, PO Box 644820, Pullman, WA 99164-4820)

Smith, T. (1997, June 23). Girls with pervasive developmental disorders. *Medscape Mental Health, 2*, 1–9.

Smith, T. (1999). Outcome of early intervention for children with autism. *Clinical Psychology: Science and Practice, 6*, 33–49.

Smith, T., Donahoe, P. A., & Davis, B. J. (in press). The UCLA treatment model. In J. S. Handleman & S. L. Harris (Eds.), *Preschool education programs for children with autism* (2nd ed.). Austin, TX: Pro-Ed.

Smith, T., Eikeseth, S., Buch, G., & Lovaas, I. (1995). *Early learning measure.* Unpublished test. (Available from Dr. T. Smith, Department of Psychology, Washington State University, PO Box 644820, Pullman, WA 99164-4820)

Smith, T., & Lovaas, O. I. (1997). The UCLA Young Autism Project: A reply to Gresham and MacMillan. *Behavioral Disorders, 22*, 202–218.

Smith, T., McEachin, J. J., & Lovaas, O. I. (1993). Comments on replication and evaluation of outcome. *American Journal on Mental Retardation, 97*, 385–391.

Sparrow, S. S., Bella, D. A., & Cicchetti, D. V. (1984). *The Vineland Adaptive Behavior Scales.* Circle River, MN: American Guidance Service.

Sparrow, S., Marans, W., Klin, A., Carter, A., Volkmar, F. R., & Cohen, D. J. (1997). Developmentally based assessments. In D. J. Cohen & F. R. Volkmar (Eds.), *Handbook of autism and pervasive developmental disorders* (2nd ed., pp. 411–447). New York: Wiley.

Stutsman, R. (1948). *Guide for administering the Merrill-Palmer Scale of Mental Tests.* New York: Harcourt, Brace & World.

Thorndike, R. L., Hagen, E. P., & Sattler, J. M. (1986). *Stanford-Binet Intelligence Scale* (4th ed.). Chicago: Riverside.

Volkmar, F. R., Klin, A., Siegal, B., Szatmari, P., Lord, C., Campbell, M., Freeman, B. J., Cicchetti, D. V., Rutter, M., Kline, W., Buitelaar, J., Hattab, Y., Fombonne, E., Fuentes, J., Werry, J., Stone, W., Kerbeshian, J., Hoshino, Y., Bregman, J., Loveland, K., Szymanski, L., & Towbin, K. (1994). Field trial for autistic disorder in *DSM-IV*. *American Journal of Psychiatry, 151,* 1361–1367.

Wechsler, D. (1992). *Manual for the Wechsler Individual Achievement Test.* San Antonio, TX: Psychological Corp.

Weinberg, R. A. (1989). Intelligence and IQ: Landmark issues and great debates. *American Psychologist, 44,* 99–104.

White, K. R. (1985–1986). Efficacy of early intervention. *Journal of Special Education, 41,* 401–416.

Home Visiting Programs: Primary and Secondary Prevention in At-risk Children

Introduction to Part IV

Home visiting is the most common form of early intervention, yet numerous early intervention researchers have claimed that such programs (that focus on changing parenting and parent–child interactions) have limited or no effects when compared to out-of-home specialized preschools (Guralnick, chapter 1; Ramey and Ramey, 1998; Scarr and McCartney, 1988; Wasik et al., 1990). This conclusion is based primarily on studies with children at-risk for school failure reporting child IQ as the major outcome measure. More recently, early interventionists have begun to realize that judging a program effectiveness based solely on changes to child IQ ignores other important benefits. Although improving cognitive abilities and preventing school failure are worthy goals for many at-risk children, early intervention also has a place in preventing other long-term negative outcomes such as emotional, behavioral, and psychiatric disorders; out-of-home placement; substance abuse; and criminality. The selections below attest to the power of early home visiting programs to reverse or prevent long-term problems in at-risk children.

References

Ramey, C. T. & Rainey, S. L. (1998). Early intervention and early experience. *American Psychologist, 53*, 109–120.

Scarr, S. & McCartney, K. (1988). Far from home: An evaluation of the mother–child home program in Bermuda. *Child Development, 59*, 531–543.

Wasik, B. H., Ramey, C. T., Bryant, D. G., & Sparling, J. J. (1990). A longitudinal study of two early intervention programs: Project CARE. *Child Development, 61*, 1682–1696.

Children of low-income, low-IQ parents are considered to be most in need, and benefit the most from early intervention (Ramey and Ramey, 1992). It is assumed that children of parents with cognitive limitations should be placed in specialized preschools as soon as possible after birth to make up for the presumed lack of nurturing and stimulation in the home (Garber, 1988). It also is frequently assumed that low-IQ parents are unable to learn to become more nurturing and caring parents, and perhaps it would be best to routinely remove their children from the family home altogether (Hayman, 1990).

Despite the high-risk status of these children, little research has been conducted to determine if the quality of the home environment, parenting, and child outcomes could be improved through home visitation and parent education. In a series of studies, Feldman and his associates developed a skill-based parent education model specifically for low-IQ parents. In two studies using single-case designs, Feldman showed that parents with cognitive limitations could learn to provide more responsive and stimulating interactions (Feldman et al., 1986, 1989), but it was difficult to assess the increased benefits to the children because of potentially confounding maturation effects. In this chapter, Feldman et al. ran a randomized clinical trial of a home-based parent education program that controlled for both child maturation and potential attention-placebo effects.

To teach low-IQ parents to interact with their children in a way that would promote child development, Feldman et al. scoured the developmental literature to identify the specific skills that should be taught. Not surprisingly, numerous studies consistently found significant correlations between a set of general parenting styles (such as sensitivity and responsivity) and child cognitive outcomes (e.g., Clarke-Stewart and Apfel, 1979), but few studies demonstrated a cause-and-effect relationship between specific parenting skills and child development. This was to be expected because most parents provide these interactions naturally. However, the low-IQ parents who participated in this study were not initially providing these interactions, so that it was possible to run a controlled study to test the effects of increasing specific parenting behaviors (related to sensitivity, responsivity, and affection) on specified child outcomes. In this study, Feldman et al. focused on improving child language development because this was identified as a serious deficit in a previous study of infants who had low-IQ parents (Feldman, Case, Towns, and Betel, 1985) and is crucial for further cognitive development. The results suggested that increasing specific parenting behaviors through training provided in the home resulted in corresponding and sustained improvements in child language. Note, however, that while the intervention was associated with significant pre- to post-intervention increases in the language and social items of the Bayley Scales of Infant Development, the overall developmental quotients did not significantly improve. This result may reflect the insensitivity of the overall Bayley Mental Development Index score in detecting specific intervention effects (Siegel, Cooper, Fitzhardinge, and Ash, 1995). It may also mean that to achieve maximum effects on child development it may be necessary to combine parent education with a more intensive (and considerably more expensive) specialized preschool experience that has been shown to increase IQ scores and school achievement in children of parents with intellectual disabilities (Garber, 1988; Ramey and Ramey, 1992).

References

Clarke-Stewart, K. A. & Apfel, N. (1979). Evaluating parental effects on child development. In L. S. Schulman (Ed.), *Review of research in education*. Vol. 6 (pp. 47–119). Itasca, IL: Peacock.

Feldman, M. A., Case, L., Towns, F., & Betel, J. (1985). Parent education project I: The development and nurturance of children of mentally handicapped mothers. *American Journal of Mental Deficiency, 90*, 253–258.

Feldman, M. A., Towns, F., Betel, J., Case, L., Rincover, A., & Rubino, C. A. (1986). Parent education project II: Increasing stimulating interactions of developmentally handicapped mothers. *Journal of Applied Behavior Analysis, 19*, 23–27.

Feldman, M. A., Case, L., Rincover, A., Towns, F., & Betel, J. (1989). Parent education project III: Increasing affection and responsivity in developmentally handicapped mothers: Component analysis, generalization, and effects on child language. *Journal of Applied Behavior Analysis, 22*, 211–222.

Garber, H. L. (1988). *The Milwaukee Project: Preventing mental retardation in children at risk*. Washington, DC: American Association on Mental Retardation.

Ramey, C. T. & Ramey, S. L. (1992). Effective early intervention. *Mental Retardation, 30*, 337–345.

Siegel, L. S., Cooper, D. C., Fitzhardinge, P. M. & Ash, A. J. (1995). The use of the Mental Development Index of the Bayley Scale to diagnose language delay in 2-year-old high risk infants. *Infant Behavior & Development, 18*, 483–486.

SEVEN

Effectiveness of Home-based Early Intervention on the Language Development of Children of Mothers with Mental Retardation

Maurice A. Feldman, Bruce Sparks, and Laurie Case

Children of mothers with mental retardation are at risk for developmental delay, particularly in language (Feldman, Case, Towns, and Betel, 1985; Feldman and Walton-Allen, in press; Garber, 1988). Feldman et al. (1985) found that approximately 50% of 2-year-old children raised by mothers with mental retardation were scoring at least one standard deviation below the mean on the Mental Development Index (MDI) of the Bayley Scales of Infant Development (BSID; Bayley, 1969) and that the primary problem area was language. Furthermore, the children's MDI score was strongly positively correlated to the quality of the home environment and mother–child interactions. Other studies (Crittenden and Bonvillian, 1984; Feldman et al., 1986; Feldman, Case, Rincover, Towns, and Betel, 1989; Peterson, Robinson, and Littman,

Feldman, M. A., Sparks, B., & Case, L. (1993). Effectiveness of home-based early intervention on the language of development of children of parents with mental retardation. *Research in Developmental Disabilities, 14,* 387–408. Includes use of tables 1, 2 & 4 and figure 2. Copyright 1993 Pergamon Press Ltd.

1983; Tymchuk and Andron, 1992) have found that mothers with low IQ are less sensitive, responsive, and reinforcing to their children when compared to mothers of both middle and low socioeconomic status. Because these positive maternal interactions are consistently associated with optimal child development (e.g., Beckwith, 1971; Bee et al., 1982; Clarke-Stewart and Apfel, 1979; Lewis and Goldberg, 1969), interactional deficits seen in mothers with mental retardation may be partly responsible for the language delay observed in their children.

If maternal interactional styles of mothers with low IQ influence their children's language development, then interventions that improve their stimulating interactions with their children should increase their children's language performance. Although several studies (Feldman et al., 1986, 1989; Leifer and Smith, 1990; Peterson, et al., 1983; Slater, 1986; Tymchuk and Andron, 1992) have shown that mothers with low IQ can be taught to increase their positive and stimulating interactions, the impact of parent-focused intervention on the children is not clear. Peterson et al. (1983) did not present any child data of the effects of teaching mothers with low IQ to increase reflective statements and praising and to decrease direct commands on their preschool children. In a case study, Leifer and Smith (1990) reported increased exploration in the therapy room by a young child whose mother had received psychotherapy and parent training. Feldman et al. (1986) found that only two of seven children (age range, 4–22 months) showed consistent pre–post parent training increases in child vocalizations after their mothers were taught to increase their talking, looking, praising, and imitation of child vocalizations.

Feldman et al. (1989) found increases in vocalizations of two children (aged 13 and 21 months) after training mothers to imitate child vocalizations, but ascending (maturational) baselines partially obscured the effects. These two children also showed substantial pre–post parent training increases in percentage correct language items on standardized developmental tests. An examination of the figures of the Tymchuk and Andron (1992) study reveals that only 2 of 11 children (age range, 12–60 months) of mothers with low IQ increased their positive vocalizations. As in Feldman et al. (1986, 1989), these results may be related to maturation. Slater (1986) found significant increases in correct answers, the complexity of child language, and some subscales of the McCarthy Scales of Children's Abilities (McCarthy, 1972) in two groups of preschool children (mean age, 49.5 months) whose mothers received training in asking questions and telling stories based on field trips.

Thus, although several studies have shown that mothers with low IQ can be taught to increase their positive interactions, the effects of parent training on their children have not been well established. Only one study (Slater, 1986) with preschool children used a between-group design with random assignment to training and attention-control groups to evaluate the impact of increased maternal interactions on the child. Although other studies with low income families have shown that home-based intervention can improve the development of at-risk children (Gutelius et al., 1972; Gutelius, Kirsch, MacDonald, Brooks, and McErlean, 1977; Levenstein, 1970; Olds, Henderson, Chamberlin, and Tatelbaum, 1985; Powell and Grantham-McGregor, 1989), no study has yet clearly ascertained that the language performance of infants and toddlers of mothers with low IQ will benefit from parent-focused training.

The purpose of this study, then, was to determine the impact of a home-based parent training program on the language development of children of mothers with mental retardation. The mothers were considered by social service and child protection agencies to be neglecting (but not abusing) their young children, and the children were considered to be at risk for environmentally induced developmental delay. Children and their mothers who received training in positive and stimulating interactions were compared to an attention-control group whose mothers received training in skills unrelated to interactions (e.g., home safety, handling emergencies) and to a comparison group of low and middle socioeconomic status mothers without mental retardation and with children of similar ages.

Method

Subjects

Twenty-eight mothers, independently diagnosed as mentally retarded, voluntarily participated. Although the diagnosis had usually been made when they were in school, the mothers' deficits in community living skills and their updated low WAIS-R IQ scores (although sometimes above 70) maintained their eligibility for programs for persons with mental retardation. Their cognitive limitations could not be traced to any apparent biological problem. Twenty-seven mothers were Caucasian-Canadians, and one was Japanese-Canadian. Nineteen of the 28 mothers were welfare recipients, with no one reporting a family income over C$20,000 (Canadian dollars). All were the primary care providers for their children. The children of these mothers who were observed in this study consisted of 16 boys and 12 girls who ranged in age from 5 to 28 months. None of the children was breast-fed, and none had any known physical contraindications for normal growth and development.

The mothers were referred by advocates, public health nurses, child protection workers, and pediatricians who were concerned that the mothers were not providing a sufficiently stimulating home environment to ensure the normal cognitive development of their children. Indeed, upon entering the program, 16 children were already showing delays (i.e., scoring < 1 SD below the mean on the Bayley Scales of Infant Development, Mental Development Index; BSID-MDI). Before their involvement in this study, seven of nine mothers who had a previous child had that child taken into custody because of documented neglect ($n = 2$), physical abuse ($n = 1$), or workers' concerns about parenting competency ($n = 4$). Moreover, nine mothers were currently under the court-ordered supervision of a child-protection agency. The 28 mothers were randomly assigned to either a training or an attention-control (safety and emergency training) group. Demographic information about each group is provided in table 7.1 (sufficient and reliable information about the fathers was not available).

A mixed comparison group of 38 mothers of low to high socioeconomic status without mental retardation, whose parenting skills were not of concern, was included for social comparison of pre- and post-intervention mother–child interaction and child language scores and to establish realistic training goals. These mothers were either recruited from day-care centers or were acquaintances of colleagues. The mean age of these mothers was 30 years (range, 22–42); 34 were Caucasian-Canadians, 1 was Afro-Canadian, and 3 were Chinese-Canadian. Although IQ scores were not available, the comparison mothers were likely of normal intelligence: 19 had obtained University degrees, 16 others had completed high school, and the remaining 3 had completed at least 10th grade. The comparison children were 24 boys and 18 girls (in four families two children were observed), ranging in age from 4 to 46 months; based upon the reports of the observers and the mothers,

Table 7.1 Comparison of the training and attention-control groups on demographic variables

Demographic Variable	Training (n = 14)	Attention-control (n = 14)
Mean maternal age	25.9	27.9
Mean maternal IQ (WAIS-R)	73.5	69.4
Mean child age	13.3 months	13.7 months
Mean number of services	2.9	2.9
Mean Bayley Mental Developmental Index	86.6	75.8
Child delayed[a]	6	10
Mean HOME total score	30.6	25.5
Moves in last year	0.4	0.9
Crowding ratio[b]	1.0	1.0
Child gender	6/14 boys	10/14 boys
Mother previously in an MR institution	1	1
Previous child removed prior to intervention	2/4	5/5
Court-ordered supervision	4	5
Spouse present	10	8
More than one child living at home	3	1
Mother had special education	6	11
Subsidized housing	7	9
Subsidized income	9	10
Prenatal problems	3	3
Perinatal problems	2	2
Mean total current risk factors[c]	1.1	1.4

Notes: None of the comparisons between the training and attention-control groups on demographic variables were statistically significant ($ps > .05$ on two-tailed dependent t-tests or McNemar tests of differences between correlated proportions). [a]A score of greater than one standard deviation below the mean on the BSID-MDI (Bayley, 1969); based upon independent assessments. [b]Number of people in the home divided by the number of rooms. [c]Current problems include maternal IQ under 60, having a previous child removed, more than one move in the previous year, mother having physical or psychological ailments, abusive or nonsupportive spouse (Tymchuk & Andron, 1992).

all these children were developing normally. The median family income of the comparison group was C$30,000 (range, C$6,500–90,000). Three of the mothers were receiving welfare. None of the comparison mothers had received formal education in child-care, nursing, or early childhood education. For statistical analyses, the comparison group was divided into two subgroups: families with children in the (a) pretest age range (4–28 months, $n = 26$) or (b) posttest age range (14–44 months, $n = 25$).

Measures

Based on a review of the child development literature and our previous work, we selected the following mother and child behaviors to monitor:

1 Mother talks to child. Any verbalization directed at the child (e.g., asking questions, prompting, labelling).
2 Mother imitates/expands child vocalizations. Repeating or elaborating (within 5 s) sounds made by the child during the observation interval.
3 Mother praises child. Comments directed at the child expressing approval or pleasure contingent on appropriate child behavior.
4 Mother provides physical affection. Gently hugging, cuddling, kissing, patting, stroking, or tickling her child (passively holding the child was not considered physical affection).
5 Child vocalization. Any nonverbal sound emanating from the child's vocal cords except a cry, burp, whine, or scream.
6 Child verbalization. Any word or word approximation spoken by the child. Scoring of child verbalizations was only implemented for the last seven pairs of children in the training and control groups to provide more details on child language performance. Posttraining audio and videotapes of mother–child conversations were also available on nine children whose mothers had received interaction training. These tapes allowed for further analysis of the qualitative features of the children's speech into: (a) Positive – any functional verbalization other than whining, crying, yelling, screaming, or imitation of mothers' verbalizations; (b) Negative – any verbalization that includes crying, whining, yelling, or screaming; and (c) Imitative – copying the verbalization just spoken (within 5 s) by the mother.

In addition to the above target behaviors, the BSID was administered to 12 of the 14 pairs of training and control group children by independent and experimentally naive assessors before and after parent training.

The pre- and post-BSIDs were also subjected to the Kent Adaptation (Reuter, Stancin, and Craig, 1981), an item analysis that categorizes BSID items into five developmental domains (language, social, cognitive, fine motor, and gross motor).

Recording procedures and reliability

To make the pre-, post-, and follow-up observations as natural as possible, the mother-child dyad was observed in its home; the play sessions were not formally structured, and the mothers were simply asked to "play with your child the way you usually do." No further instructions or training were provided during these probes, which lasted approximately 10 min; a 10-s observe, 10-s record, partial interval time sampling procedure was employed. The observers, some of whom also served as trainers, had been trained to a criterion of at least 85% agreement with a previously trained observer. Reliability checks were conducted on 30.4% of the tests by another independent observer, who was either another therapist or a naive observer (41% of the reliability sessions involved a second observer who was naive to the experimental hypotheses and conditions). Interobserver agreement was calculated as agreements divided by agreement plus disagreements × 100%; overall agreement equalled 92.5% (range, 75–100%). Interobserver agreement for each behavior was calculated using Kappa, which corrects for chance agreements (Hartmann, 1977). Mean Kappa coefficients were: physical affection −.92; talking to child −.91; imitation of child vocalizations −.94; praise −.96; child vocalizations −.73; and child verbalizations −.95.

In addition, to ascertain the emergence of language during the training phase, the trainers conducted observational probes, using the same method described above, immediately following each training session. Reliability checks were made on 13% of these observations for the last seven children in the training and control groups, and the Kappa coefficient for child verbalizations was .76.

With respect to the audio and video tape posttraining recordings of mother–child conversations on nine trained families, two observers independently transcribed the first 10 min of each tape (one per family), and then they met to create one final transcript by mutually resolving any discrepancies in exact wording. The final transcription was then coded independently by both observers for the occurrence of positive, negative, and imitative verbalizations. Interobserver agreement equalled 93.7% (range, 85.2–100) across the three types of verbalizations. Kappas for each behavior were: (a) positive –.92, (b) negative –1.0, and (c) imitative –.92.

Experimental design

First, the initial differences in maternal interactions and child language performance between the 28 families with mothers with low IQ and the 26 families with non-mentally retarded mothers and their children in the same (pretest) age range were compared. Second, the families with mothers with low IQ were pair-matched on child age (within 1 month), and each pair member was randomly assigned to either an interaction training or attention-control group ($n = 14$ per group). Each mother was seen (and trained) individually in her home. A posttest score was obtained for each pair of families after the training group mother reached criterion on all skills trained and before the attention-control group mother was scheduled to receive training. A posttest BSID was also obtained on 12 of the 14 children in each group. Comparisons (controlling for pretest variability) were made between the training and attention-control groups' posttest maternal interactional and child language scores, BSID, and the Kent Adaptation of the BSID. Subsequently, the posttest scores of these two groups were compared to the performance of the non-mentally retarded mothers comparison group with children in the same (posttest) age-range ($n = 25$).

Participation in the training or attention-control group did not preclude involvement with other social service agencies (e.g., public health nurses, advocates, child welfare workers); after the posttests, attention-control group mothers were offered individual home-based interaction training.

Procedure

Pretest

Before the pretest, one to two visits lasting about 1 h were made with all participants in their homes to develop rapport, obtain consents, and explain the observational procedures. All mothers with and without mental retardation were told that they were participating in a study "looking at the ways mothers interact with their young children." The pretest involved observing each mother–child dyad for 10 min while they were playing in their living room with the child's toys following the request to "play with your child the way you usually do." No training was provided to the mothers during the pretest. The attention-control mothers did not receive feedback regarding their performance on the pretest until they were debriefed after they received (or declined) training.

Interaction training

The trainers were five women (three of whom were mothers) with undergraduate degrees in psychology or early childhood education. Each family had a consistent trainer for the duration of the study. Before their involvement in this study, the parent trainers had received instruction (readings, discussions, modelling, and feedback) over 1 month in the clinical and research skills needed to work with at-risk families, young children, and parents with cognitive limitations. At the time of the study, the actual experience of the trainers working with similar families ranged from 3 to 8 years.

Parent training sessions were scheduled weekly in the family home in the play context and consisted of verbal instruction and discussion, modelling, feedback, and reinforcement. The sequence of training was imitation, then praise, followed by physical affection for eight of the families; two of these families did not complete training in physical affection because they terminated their participation in the program. For the other six families, the sequence of training was praise followed by imitation, but physical affection was neither monitored nor trained. In the context of teaching each interaction skill, the mothers were also encouraged to look at their children, but this skill was not explicitly measured; mother talking to her child was observed, but not specifically trained. The therapists also gave mothers recommendations on play activities that matched the child's developmental level and provided toys on loan if the parents did not own appropriate toys.

The actual training session consisted of the trainer first describing the interactional skill to be taught and why it is important for the mother to learn (e.g., "just like us, children like to be praised when they do something well"). Then the trainer would model the skill several times with the mother's own child (e.g., "see how I gave John a cuddle and how much he liked it"). The trainer then asked the mother to try it, and would: (a) prompt (e.g., "he just said 'book' when you showed it to him, so you should say 'yes,' it's a 'book' back to him right now"), (b) praise (e.g., "that's it, you remembered to repeat ball, just after she said 'ball'!"), and (c) correct (e.g., "sound happier when you praise Mary").

Immediately following the completion of a training session, the therapist gave the general prompt to the mother "play with your child the way you usually do" and observed for the occurrence of the trained skills. Based upon this observation, the mothers received coupons contingent on scoring at least 30% correct on each skill (praise, imitation, physical affection) currently being trained (these were the approximate mean scores of mothers without mental retardation in our previous studies; Feldman et al., 1986, 1989). The coupons were exchangeable for small gift items (e.g., public transit tickets, children's clothing, accessories, and toys). Following completion of the training session, the therapist would also give intermittent verbal feedback to the mother on the skills trained that day if observed to occur spontaneously during the remainder of the visit

As the 30% training criterion was met on each skill, another skill was added to each training session. The training phase lasted as long as it took each mother to reach criterion on all of her target skills over 3 consecutive weekly visits. Across skills, the mean duration of training was 45 weeks (range, 17–89 weeks). The mean duration of training was 8.7 weeks (range, 1–35 weeks) for imitation, 10.3 weeks (range, 1–27 weeks) for praise, and 15.9 weeks (range, 3–25 weeks) for physical affection; training physical affection took significantly longer than training imitation ($t(11) = 3.52$, $p < .01$, 2-tailed test). The training group received a mean of 21.4 visits (range, 7–31). Although a home visit usually lasted 60 min, the amount of time actually spent in interaction training was about 10 min. Training in interactional skills was always considered the priority of each visit and was carried out at the beginning of the visit while, during the remaining time, the trainer offered advice and support on other issues raised by the mother (e.g., housing, financial, and family problems).

Attention-control group

Home visits with the attention-control group members were designed to duplicate in as many ways as possible the experiences of the interactional training group, except that the control group received training in home safety and emergency skills. As with the interaction training group, each visit lasted about 60 min, and training in safety and emergency skills was the priority. This training used the same instructional strategies as interaction training described above (i.e., discussion, modelling, feedback, coupon reinforcement) and also took approximately 10 min to complete. In addition, to control for the occurrence of play sessions and the presence of toys in the interaction training group, the mothers in the attention-control group were also: (a) asked to play with their children, (b) given advice on play activities to match the developmental level of their child, and (c) loaned child age-appropriate toys. No training was provided on any of the interaction skills to the control group during the training phase. The control group received a mean of 23.6 visits (range, 3–58).

Posttest, follow-up, and replication

After completion of interactional training for the training group mothers and before such training commenced with the control mothers, each training group mother and her attention-control partner received one observational probe that served as the posttest. As in the pretest, the mothers were observed playing with their children following being asked to "play with your child the way you usually do." After the posttests, interaction training was offered to the mothers in the attention-control group; eight mothers accepted.

Interaction skills of eight available mothers in the original interaction training group were monitored for 13–82 weeks following the end of training ($M = 55$ weeks). The posttest and follow-up procedures were similar to the pretest in that no training was provided during these observations. No booster training was given during the follow-up period, and the coupon reinforcement was gradually thinned as described in Feldman et al. (1992a). At the time of the follow-up test (i.e., the last observation session for each family), five of the eight follow-up mothers had not been receiving coupons, (mean duration without coupons was 26.8 weeks, range, 4–48 weeks), and the three mothers still receiving coupons had only a 1 in 6 chance of actually, receiving a coupon if they maintained criterion performance on all the trained skills.

Results

Pretraining comparisons

Compared to the non-mentally retarded mothers with children in the same age range, the pretest scores of the 28 mothers with low IQ showed significantly less: (a) total interactions (i.e., sum total occurrence of the four maternal categories per session) ($t(52)$ = 2.18, $p < .02$); (b) imitation of child vocalizations ($t(52)$ = 3.91, $p < .001$); (c) praising ($t(52)$ = 2.81, $p < .005$); and (d) talking ($t(46)$ = 3.88, $p < .002$). Physical affection was not significantly different ($t(47)$ = 1.14, $p > .05$). The children of the mothers with low IQ demonstrated significantly fewer vocalizations ($t(52)$ = 2.66, $p < .005$). Because none of the children of parents with mental retardation verbalized on the pretest, a t-test could not be conducted. Instead, a test of independent proportions (Ferguson, 1966, pp. 177–178) revealed that significantly fewer children of mothers with low IQ demonstrated verbalizations than children of mothers without mental retardation (z = 2.41, $p < .01$) (all tests are one-tailed).

Training versus attention-control groups

Figure 7.1 illustrates the mean percent correct pretest, posttest, and follow-up child behavior scores for the interaction training and attention-control groups (with a comparison to the mean score of the non-mentally retarded mothers group). Although the training and attention-control groups were matched on the child's age at pretest and between-group differences on demographic measures and the mean pretest scores were not significantly different, considerable within-group (error) variance was found in the pretest scores of all dependent variables except child verbalizations (which showed no variation because all children in both groups had pretest scores of zero). It has been recommended that experimental studies with small sample sizes use Analysis of Covariance (ANCOVA) to reduce the influence of within-group variability (Cook and Campbell, 1979; Stevens, 1986); therefore, we used ANCOVA (with the pretest score, serving as the covariate) to measure between-group posttraining differences for all of the maternal measures and child vocalizations; a one-tailed paired t-test was used to

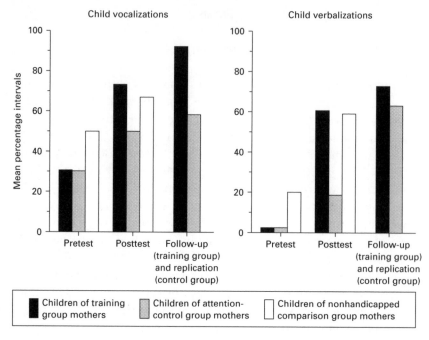

Figure 7.1 Mean percentage observational intervals of child behaviors at pretest, posttest, follow-up, and replication for the 14 children of mothers with low IQ in each of the training and attention-control groups. Pretest and posttest verbalization scores are based on 7 children in each group. Follow-up and replication data for vocalizations are based on 8 and 8 subjects, respectively; follow-up and replication data for verbalizations are based on 4 and 4 subjects, respectively. Also included are the mean percentage child vocalizations and verbalizations for two sets of age-matched children of nonmentally retarded mothers (pretest child age range, 4–28 months, $n = 26$ children; posttest child age range, 14–44 months, $n = 25$ children)

compare between-group posttest child verbalization scores. The findings, which are presented in table 7.2, revealed that both the mothers and the children in the training group scored significantly higher than the attention-control group on all the posttests.

Of the 14 children for whom we have verbalization scores, no children of mothers with low IQ were verbalizing in the pretest. On the posttest, however, twice (6 vs. 3) as many of the seven children in the training group than in the attention-control group were speaking. In addition, based upon data recorded by the therapists on each visit for

Table 7.2 Mean and SD for % correct pretest and posttest scores for training group and attention-control group

Skill	Pretest		Posttest		F^a
	Training	Attention-Control	Training	Attention-Control	
Total maternal interactions	27.8 (12.0)	24.1 (8.6)	47.5 (13.0)	25.0 (6.2)	33.5***
Imitation of child vocalizations	7.6 (20.2)	16.1 (30.4)	55.1 (34.0)	3.4 (6.9)	28.6***
Praise	5.0 (19.9)	3.6 (8.4)	37.9 (15.3)	2.9 (6.1)	64.0***
Physical affection	14.4 (20.7)	10.7 (13.8)	22.2 (15.6)	8.6 (11.0)	5.5*
Talking to child	82.9 (27.6)	78.6 (24.1)	97.1 (7.3)	86.4 (15.5)	5.1*
Child vocalizations	31.4 (25.4)	30.7 (28.9)	73.6 (18.2)	50.7 (19.0)	10.3**
Child verbalizations	0.0 (0.0)	0.0 (0.0)	60.0 (34.6)	18.6 (27.3)	3.6[b]**

Notes: [a] F values were based upon analysis of covariance of posttest scores, with pretest scores serving as the covariates for all maternal skills and child vocalizations. [b] Because there was no variance in the pretest verbalization scores, a one-tailed paired t-test of the posttest scores was used.

*$p < .05$. **$p < .01$. ***$p < .001$.

Table 7.3 Mean and SD for Bayley Scales of Infant Development and Kent Adaptation of Bayley Scales of Infant Development domain scores

	Pretest		Posttest		
	Training	Attention-Control	Training	Attention-Control	F^a
CA (months)	7.3 (5.0)	7.9 (4.9)	22.3 (5.3)	21.0 (3.6)	.03
BSID					
MDI[b]	88.5 (16.4)	82.8 (19.1)	85.3 (17.3)	80.5 (22.6)	.03
MDI DA[c]	6.3 (4.0)	6.3 (2.7)	19.7 (4.1)	17.4 (4.0)	2.38
Kent Adaptation					
Language DA	6.3 (3.6)	6.5 (2.8)	19.4 (4.2)	16.4 (3.8)	3.95**
Cognitive DA	6.5 (4.4)	6.2 (3.0)	20.3 (4.6)	17.7 (4.6)	2.2
Social DA	5.7 (2.8)	5.6 (1.8)	18.9 (4.5)	16.0 (4.3)	3.65*
Fine Motor DA	6.4 (3.7)	6.4 (2.9)	20.2 (4.9)	17.4 (4.6)	2.86
Gross Motor DA	6.9 (4.3)	6.0 (2.6)	18.4 (5.1)	16.8 (3.7)	.67

Notes: [a] F values were based upon Analysis of Covariance of posttest developmental ages with pretest developmental ages serving as the covariates. [b] MDI = Mental Developmental Index of BSID. [c] DA = Mental Developmental Index Developmental Age Equivalent (months). *p = .07. **p = .06.

these same seven pairs of children, the children of the training group mothers began to verbalize at an earlier age (mean age 15.3 months, $SD = 3.8$) than the age matched children of the attention-control group mothers (mean age, 17.7 months $SD = 3.9$, $t(6) = 2.63$, $p < .02$ (one-tailed dependent t-test).

Table 7.3 presents the results of the pretest and posttest scores on the Bayley Scales of Infant Development and each domain on the Kent Adaptation. An ANCOVA (with the pretest score serving as the covariate) was used to measure between-group posttraining differences on the BSID and the domains of the Kent Adaptation. Significant differences between the posttest scores of the two groups were found on the language and social domains of the Kent Adaptation.

Analysis of the posttraining audio and video tapes of nine families who received interaction training (six in the training group and three in the attention-control group following their training in the replication phase) revealed that the children's language was positive a mean of 58.4% (range, 20–95.2) of the time, imitative a mean of 40.8% (range, 2.4–80), and negative a mean of 0.8% (range, 0–5.4); only two children were observed to demonstrate any negative verbalizations. The imitative responses generally occurred in the context of labelling and imitation games, such as saying the alphabet or repeating numbers (98.4% of imitative verbalizations occurred in response to these age-appropriate games).

Training versus attention-control versus posttest comparison group

The mean posttest scores of the training and control groups were compared to the performance of non-mentally retarded mothers and their children age-matched for the posttest age of the children of parents with mental retardation. One-way analyses of variance revealed significant differences among the three groups on all posttest observational measures: (a) total interaction ($F(2, 51) = 8.66$, $p < .001$); (b) imitation ($F(2, 51) = 16.01$, $p < .001$); (c) praise ($F(2, 51) = 18.18$, $p < .001$); (d) physical affection ($F(2, 46) = 3.75$, $p < .05$); (e) talking ($F(2, 44) = 6.24$, $p < .005$); (f) vocalizations ($F(2, 51) = 4.04$, $p < .03$); and (g) verbalizations ($F(2, 30) = 4.52$, $p < .02$).

Pairwise comparisons of the posttest scores using the Tukey method to control for inflating the probability of making a Type I error due to multiple comparisons (significance level set at < .05) showed that: (a) the training group mothers had significantly more total interactions, praise, imitation of vocalizations, physical affection, and talking to their children than the attention-control group mothers; (b) the training group mothers showed significantly more total interactions, imitation, praise, and physical affection with their children than the normative comparison group mothers, but talking was not significantly different; (c) the attention-control group mothers had significantly less imitation, praise, and talking to their children than the normative comparison group mothers, but physical affection and total interactions were not significantly different; (d) the children of the training group mothers vocalized and verbalized significantly more than the children of the attention-control group mothers; (e) there were no significant differences between the children of the training group mothers and the children of the normative group mothers on the occurrence of vocalizations and verbalizations; and (f) the children of the attention-control group mothers verbalized significantly less than the children of the normative comparison group mothers, but there were no significant differences in occurrence of vocalizations.

Follow-up and replication

We were able to conduct follow-up observations ranging from 13 to 82 weeks ($M = 55$ weeks) after training on 8 of the 14 mothers in the original training group. As can be seen in figure 7.1, the remaining members of the interaction training group generally maintained their skills. The difference between the pretest and follow-up scores of the training group was significant on all measures except physical affection and talking to the child: (a) total interaction score ($t(7) = 4.7, p < .005$); (b) imitation ($t(7) = 4.53, p < .005$); (c) praise ($t(7) = 4.25, p < .005$); (d) physical affection ($t(4) = .88, p > .05$); (e) talking ($t(7) = .83, p > .05$); (f) vocalizations ($t(7) = 7.55, p < .001$); (g) verbalizations ($t(3) = 2.98, p < .05$). (all one-tailed dependent t-tests). The training group posttest and follow-up scores were significantly different on only child vocalizations, which continued to increase from the posttest score ($t(7) = 1.99, p < .05$, one-tailed test). As can be seen in figure 7.1, upon their mothers receiving training, the children in the attention-control group replicated the results of the first training group.

Discussion

This study found that home-based parent–child interaction training significantly increased the responsive and reinforcing interactions of mothers with mental retardation, which resulted in significant increases in the emergent language performance of their infants and toddlers. By using a between-group design with age-matching and random assignment to a training or attention-control group, we were able to diminish Hawthorne and maturational effects as alternative explanations. Increased child language development was seen in both direct observational measures of vocalizations and verbalizations and on the language items of the BSID. Children in the training group spoke their first words significantly sooner than children in the control group. Moreover, although the parent training focused on stimulating the child's language, significant increases were also seen on the child's social development scores on the BSID, perhaps reflecting the increased maternal social reinforcement the child received for appropriate social acts during play (note that there is no overlap of items in the language and social development domains of the Kent Adaptation of the BSID).

As in our previous work (Feldman et al., 1986, 1989), we saw that training resulted in qualitative improvements in mother–child interactions. Before training, although the mothers with low IQ would talk to their children, they were rarely contingently responsive to their children (i.e., providing little praise or imitation of child vocalizations); instead the mothers engaged in parallel (rather than interactive) play, or would be highly directive and controlling. After training, mother–child interactions were considerably more pleasant and reciprocating. The mothers with low IQ became more sensitive and responsive, and began acknowledging their children's attempts to communicate; the children in turn would "catch on" that their babbling and words were successful in getting their mothers to respond in desired ways. Analyses of audio and video taped posttraining transcripts of mother–child conversations revealed that the majority of child speech was functionally positive in nature. The qualitative changes in maternal interaction style were reflected in the fact that in the training group talking to the child did not significantly increase from pretest to follow-up, but praising and imitating child vocalizations did. This finding suggests that the improvements in child language were a function of increased quality rather than just quantity of mother–child verbal interactions.

Although previous research teaching interactional skills to mothers with low IQ (Feldman et al., 1986, 1989; Peterson et al., 1983; Tymchuk and Andron, 1992) reported inconsistent maintenance, in this study we found that of the mothers who continued in follow-up, most maintained their skills after training ceased. Perhaps the use of tangible reinforcement contingent on meeting prespecified performance criteria and gradually thinning reinforcement during the follow-up period facilitated maintenance (Feldman et al., 1989, 1992a).

We also examined the number of children removed from the families by child welfare agencies before and after the families' involvement in this study. We were able to monitor 25 of the original 28 families for up to 3 years after their participation. Despite having a variety of other services (e.g., advocate, public health nurse, visiting homemaker) before their involvement in our parent education program, 7 of 9 (78%) of the families with a previous child lost that child. After participating in parent education, only 5 of 25 (20%) had the target child of this study subsequently removed by child protection authorities due to risk or actual incidents of child neglect (3) or abuse (2) (none of these mothers had a previous child removed).

Recently, several authors (Accardo and Whitman, 1990; Tymchuk and Andron, 1992) have suggested that various risk factors may impede responsiveness to the child and to parent-focused intervention. Based on casebook information, many of the 28 mothers with low IQ in our study had one or more risk factors, including an abusive or unsupportive spouse ($n = 14$ mothers), maternal depression ($n = 9$), multiple moves ($n = 8$), and a previous child removed ($n = 7$). We therefore examined the correlations between the total number of risk factors and: (a) pretest maternal total interaction scores, (b) pretest child vocalization and verbalization scores, (c) weeks to reach the training objectives, (d) posttest maternal total interaction scores, (e) posttest child vocalization and verbalization scores, and (f) drop outs (those families in the training group who did not want follow-up visits and those families in the attention-control group who did not want subsequent training). All of these correlations were low (range, .03–.18), and none were statistically significant. Thus, in this study, the accumulation of potentially debilitating conditions did not appear to affect greatly the observed mother–children interactions or responsiveness to our intervention.

Certain limitations of this study should be noted. The results are based on one pretest, posttest, and follow-up observation session; and we did not directly measure generalization. We have, however, previously demonstrated interaction training and generalization effects across sequential observations (Feldman et al., 1986, 1989). Also, significant increases in child language behavior (above what would be expected by maturation) would not likely occur if the training group mothers were only providing stimulating interactions once a week during the trainer's visit.

Furthermore, the Kent Adaptation of the BSID can be considered a generalization test. It was administered under considerably different conditions than the training situation: (a) the naive testers were strangers to the child, (b) the parent trainers were usually absent, (c) the mothers were not interacting with the child, (d) the test settings were not the same as the training situations, and (e) the BSID covered language and other skills not specifically taught to the children during parent interaction training. The significant increase in the language developmental age scores on the Kent Adaptation of the BSID strongly suggests that the training group children did improve their language in a generalized manner.

Another limitation was the variability in the duration of follow-up (13–82 weeks). One training group mother started to receive child behavior management training, thereby making her ineligible for a no (further) training follow-up. Five training families requested no further involvement after "graduating" (i.e., reaching the training objectives). In retrospect, perhaps if we had made the transition from training to follow-up less discriminable, more mothers would have continued in follow-up.

Because of the relatively high drop out in follow-up, we conducted post hoc analyses on possible differences in the dependent measures between the training group families who dropped out and those who stayed. The only mother or child measure that was significantly different was that the mean posttest child vocalization score was lower for the dropouts ($M = 60\%$, $SD = 17.9$) than for the stayers ($M = 83.8\%$, $SD = 10.6$, $t(12) = 3.12$, $p < .01$, two-tailed). It should be noted, however, that the vocalizations of the dropout children did increase significantly from pretest ($M = 31.7\%$, $SD = 27.9$) to posttest ($M = 60\%$, $SD = 17.9$, $t(5) = 2.79$, $p < .04$). Moreover, although the stayers continued to increase their vocalizations between posttest and follow-up, if it is assumed hypothetically that the dropouts had in fact stayed but showed no further increase in child vocalizations (i.e., we assigned each drop out child a follow-up score equal to his or her posttest score), then the pretest to follow-up increase with all the training group children included would still have been significant ($t(13) = 6.21$, $p < .001$, one-tailed). However, given the high drop out rate and the significant difference in posttest child vocalizations between the stayers and drop outs, the follow-up results should be interpreted cautiously.

Six attention-control families were not available for replication because: (a) they did not want training (2), (b) the child was removed by child protection authorities (1), (c) the child was placed in the custody of the (estranged) father (1), (d) they received child behavior management training rather than language stimulation interaction training (1), or (e) they moved out of the catchment area (1).

Although we were able to increase child language behaviors significantly by home-based parent training, it is likely that the combination of home and specialized preschool intervention would result in more extensive effects on the children, such as significant increases in overall DA on standardized developmental tests (Garber, 1988; Martin, Ramey, and Ramey, 1990). Because financial and other resource constraints often limit the availability of such specialized infant/toddler preschool programs, a parent-focused approach that minimizes language delays to some extent may be a more feasible and cost-effective intervention with at-risk young children (Bronfenbrenner, 1974).

Given the chronicity of the mothers' cognitive impairments coupled with the complexity and changing nature of parenting as the child ages, it is likely that a continuum of intervention will be needed for children of mothers with low IQ. In addition to interaction training to promote language and cognitive development, we find that these families often need training in basic child-care, health, and safety (Feldman et al., 1992a; Feldman, Case, and Sparks, 1992b; Tymchuk, Hamada, Andron, and Anderson, 1990), child behavior management (Ducharme and Feldman, 1990; Fantuzzo, Wray, Hall, Goins, and Azar, 1986; Tymchuk, Andron, and Tymchuk, 1990), and toilet training (Feldman et al. 1992a, 1992b). Recent evidence suggests that school-age children of mothers with low IQ may show a variety of intellectual, academic, and behavior problems (Feldman and Walton-Allen, in press); therefore, continued support – such as academic remediation, social skills training, and counselling – for these children may be needed during the school years. In addition to the focus on the child, multiple interventions for the mothers, themselves, may benefit the entire family. These include individual and marital therapy, substance abuse program, stress management, social skills training, academic and vocational upgrading.

In conclusion, this study demonstrated that increasing positive interactions of mothers with mental retardation toward their young children resulted in faster emergence and improved child language performance over that expected by maturation alone. As recommended by Warren and Kaiser (1988), we attempted to provide converging evidence of the impact of parent interactional training on the children's acquisition, quantity, quality, functionality, and generalizability of language (percent intervals of vocalizations and verbalizations during mother–child play, item analysis of standardized developmental test performance, the child's use of language during mother–child conversation). The findings suggest that home-based interaction training for parents with mental retardation may help to decrease language and other delays typically seen in many of these children (Feldman et al., 1985; Feldman and Walton-Allen, in press; Garber, 1988; Martin et al., 1990).

References

Accardo, P. J., & Whitman, B. Y. (1990). Children of mentally retarded parents. *American Journal of Diseases in Children, 144*, 69–70.

Bayley, N. (1969). *Bayley scales of infant development: Birth to two years.* New York: Psychological Corporation.

Beckwith, L. (1971). Relationship between attributes of mothers and their infants' IQ scores. *Child Development, 42*, 1083–1097.

Bee, H. C., Barnard, K. E., Eyres, S. J., Gray, C. L., Hammond, M. A., Spietz, A. L., Snyder, C., & Clark, B. (1982). Predictions of IQ and language skill from perinatal status, child performance, family characteristics, and mother–infant interaction. *Child Development, 53*, 1134–1156.

Bronfenbrenner, U. (1974). Is early intervention effective? *Columbia Teachers College Record, 76*, 279–303.

Clarke-Stewart, K. A., & Apfel, N. (1979). Evaluating parental effects on child development. In L. S. Schulman (Ed.), *Review of research in education.* Vol. 6 (pp. 47–119). Itasca, IL: Peacock.

Cook, T. D., & Campbell, D. T. (1979). *Quasi-experimentation design and analysis for field settings.* Boston: Houghton Mifflin.

Crittenden, P. M., & Bonvillian, J. D. (1994). The relationship between maternal risk status and maternal sensitivity. *American Journal of Orthopsychiatry, 54,* 250–262.

Ducharme, J. M., & Feldman, M. A. (1990, September). *A multimodal approach to mitigate the risk of child abuse by parents with cognitive limitations.* Paper presented at the Eighth International Congress on Child Abuse and Neglect, Hamburg.

Fantuzzo, J. W., Wray, L., Hall, R., Goins, C., & Azar, S. (1986). Parent and social-skills training for mentally retarded mothers identified as child maltreaters. *American Journal of Mental Deficiency, 91,* 135–140.

Feldman, M. A., Case, L., Garrick, M., MacIntyre-Grande, W., Carnwell, J., & Sparks, B. (1992a). Teaching child-care skills to parents with developmental disabilities. *Journal of Applied Behavior Analysis, 25,* 205–215.

Feldman, M. A., Case, L., Rincover, A., Towns, F., & Betel, J. (1989). Parent education project III. Increasing affection and responsivity in developmentally handicapped mothers: Component analysis, generalization, and effects on child language. *Journal of Applied Behavior Analysis, 22,* 211–222.

Feldman, M. A., Case, L., & Sparks, B. (1992b). Effectiveness of a child-care training program for parents at risk for child neglect. *Canadian Journal of Behavioural Science, 24,* 14–28.

Feldman, M. A., Case, L., Towns, F., & Betel, J. (1985). Parent education project I: The development and nurturance of children of mentally retarded parents. *American Journal of Mental Deficiency, 90,* 253–258.

Feldman, M. A., Towns, F., Betel, J., Case, L., Rincover, A., & Rubino, C. A. (1986). Parent education project II: Increasing stimulating interactions of developmentally handicapped mothers. *Journal of Applied Behavior Analysis, 19,* 23–37.

Feldman, M. A., & Walton-Allen, N. (in press). *Intellectual, academic, and behavioral status of school-age children: Maternal mental retardation and poverty.* Manuscript submitted for publication.

Ferguson, G. A. (1966). *Statistical analysis in psychology and education* (2nd ed.). New York: McGraw-Hill.

Garber, H. L. (1988). *The Milwaukee project: Preventing mental retardation in children at risk.* Washington, DC: American Association on Mental Retardation.

Gutelius, M. F., Kirsch, A. D., MacDonald, S., Brooks, M. R., & McErlean, T. (1977). Controlled study of child health supervision: Behavioral results. *Pediatrics, 60,* 294–304.

Gutelius, M. F., Kirsch, A. D., MacDonald, S., Brooks, M. R., McErlean, T., & Newcomb, C. (1972). Promising results from a cognitive stimulation program in infancy. *Clinical Pediatrics, 11,* 585–593.

Hartmann, D. P. (1977). Considerations in the choice of interobserver reliability estimates. *Journal of Applied Behavior Analysis, 10,* 103–116.

Leifer, M., & Smith, S. (1990). Preventive intervention with a depressed mother with mental retardation and her infant: A quantitative case study. *Infant Mental Health Journal, 11*, 301–314.

Levenstein, P. (1970). Cognitive growth in preschoolers through verbal interaction with mothers. *American Journal of Orthopsychiatry, 40*, 426–432.

Lewis, M., & Goldberg, S. (1969). Perceptual–cognitive development in infancy: A generalized expectancy model as a function of the mother–infant interaction. *Merrill-Palmer Quarterly, 15*, 81–100.

Martin, S. M., Ramey, C. T., & Ramey, S. (1990). The prevention of intellectual impairment in children of impoverished families: Findings of a randomized trial of educational day care. *American Journal of Public Health, 80*, 884–847.

McCarthy, D. (1972). *McCarthy Scales of Children's Abilities.* New York: Psychological Corp.

Olds, D. L., Henderson, C. R., Chamberlin, R., & Tatelbaum, R. (1985). Preventing child abuse and neglect: A randomized trial of nurse home visitation. *Pediatrics, 78*, 65–78.

Peterson, S., Robinson, E., & Littman, I. (1983). Parent–child interaction training for parents with a history of mental retardation. *Applied Research in Mental Retardation, 4*, 329–342.

Powell, C., & Grantham-McGregor, S. (1989). Home visiting of varying frequency and child development. *Pediatrics, 84*, 157–164.

Reuter, J., Stancin, T., & Craig, P. (1981). *The Kent scoring adaptation of the Bayley Scales of Infant Development.* Kent, OH: Developmental Metrics.

Slater, M. A. (1986). Modification of mother–child interaction processes in families with children at risk for mental retardation. *American Journal of Mental Deficiency, 91*, 257–267.

Stevens, J. (1986). *Applied multivariate statistics for the social sciences.* Hillsdale, NJ: Lawrence Erlbaum Associates, Inc.

Tymchuk, A. J., & Andron, L. (1992). Project parenting: Child interactional training with mothers who are mentally handicapped. *Mental Handicap Research, 5*, 4–32.

Tymchuk, A. J., Andron, L., & Tymchuk, M. (1990). Training mothers with mental handicaps to understand developmental and behavioural principles. *Mental Handicap Research, 3*, 51–59.

Tymchuk, A., Hamada, D., Andron, L., & Anderson, S. (1990). Home safety training with mothers who are mentally retarded. *Education and Training in Mental Retardation, 25*, 142–149.

Warren, S. F., & Kaiser, A. P. (1988). Research in early language intervention. In S. L. Odom & M. B. Karnes (Eds.), *Early intervention for infants and children with handicaps* (pp. 89–108). Baltimore: Paul H. Brookes.

Introduction to Chapter 8

This chapter describes one of the few controlled long-term studies of the effects of EI on the prevention of behavioral, emotional, and psychiatric disorders. The EI program started at 6 months of age, lasted 5 years and consisted of about 10 home visits per year in which counseling was provided by a psychiatric nurse. Follow-up psychiatric services were provided as needed. The intervention focused on parent–child interactions, and parenting attitudes and practices. The case notes presented give a flavor of what was covered in the counseling sessions. Although the authors say that the theoretical model was psychodynamic, they also recognized the role of biological, psychological, and sociological variables in influencing parenting and child outcomes. Therefore, their model is consistent with Guralnick's developmental model described in Chapter 1, which was derived from Bronfenbrenner's (1986) ecological model. The authors also recognized the crucial mediational role of parent–child interactions, and the practical advice provided to parents regarding a positive approach to handling child problem behavior are consistent with a variety of models, including social learning theory (Patterson, 1982).

Follow-up results are reported when children were 20–21 years old. The statistically small effect sizes belie the significant cost-benefits and clinical significance of this study. The 5 years of in-home counseling appeared to mitigate the effects of cumulative risk and worked better with high-risk versus low-risk children. It also was more effective in preventing internalizing versus externalizing behaviors. The authors highlight some of the methodological limitations such as alternating rather than random assignment, unvalidated risk assessment tool, reliance on self-report inventories, and greater attrition in the high-risk versus low-risk groups. Self-report measures may introduce response bias, because the raters are not "blind." That is, the treated participants may be prone to say they are doing well. However, the authors cite their earlier evaluations in which they used clinical interviews and found similar effects when the participants were younger. Also, the 31 percent attrition rate, while not unreasonably high compared to similar long-term studies, still may introduce a bias because the high-risk program participants who were doing well may be more likely to respond to the researchers' request for continued participation. Despite these concerns, given the dearth of long-term follow-up studies of home visiting programs on future psychiatric outcomes in at-risk families, this study provides promising evidence that these programs can have meaningful and persistent outcomes.

References

Bronfenbrenner, U. (1986). Ecology of the family as a context for human development. *Developmental Psychology, 22,* 723–742.

Patterson, G. R. (1982). *Coercive family process.* Eugene, OR: Castalia.

EIGHT

Effects of Early Intervention on Psychiatric Symptoms of Young Adults in Low-risk and High-risk Families

Eeva T. Aronen and Terttu Arajärvi

Long-term follow-up studies are needed in order to evaluate the effects of risk and protective factors on the mental health of developing children. However, many prospective longitudinal studies assessing the relevance of early risk and protective factors for later development have follow-up periods of no longer than one to three years (Beardslee, Wright, Clarke-Rothberg, Salt, and Versage, 1996; Brooks-Gunn, Klebanov, Liaw, and Spiker, 1993; Brooks-Gunn et al., 1994; Oberklaid, Sanson, Pedlow, and Prior, 1993). Very few studies have evaluated the extended effects of the childhood variables into adulthood (Farrington, 1991; Harrington, Fudge, Rutter, Pickles, and Hill, 1990; Harrington et al., 1994; Thomas and Chess, 1984), and few long-term studies of such protective factors as early preventive interventions have been carried out (Johnson and Walker, 1987; Lally, Mangione, and Honig, 1988). Hardly any studies of intervention effects extending into young adulthood can be found, despite the fact that the final outcome of the

Aronen, E. T., & Arajärvi, T. (2000). Effects of early intervention on psychiatric symptoms of young adults in low-risk and high-risk families. *American Journal of Orthopsychiatry*, *70*, 223–232. Includes use of tables 1–4. Copyright American Orthopsychiatric Association Inc.

preventive interventions of childhood can be determined only when the subjects are adults.

Predicting future mental health has been considered a difficult task. Multiple factors must be considered in order to make more appropriate predictions, since single-risk factors generally represent no more than 10%–20% of the total risk (Kashani, Ezpeleta, Dandoy, Doi, and Reid, 1991; Rutter, 1994; Sanson, Oberkleid, Pedlow, and Prior, 1991; Seifer, Samerof, Anagnostopolou, and Elias, 1992). Primary preventive interventions, which are usually undertaken during early childhood, may have potential to diminish the effects of risk factors on the child's development. The effects of early traumatic experiences on later development have been found to be devastating and difficult to treat (Farrington, 1991). Early primary interventions that have been reported to reduce the amount of childhood physical abuse and neglect in families at increased risk (Gray, Cutler, Dean, and Kempe, 1979; Larson, 1980; Olds, Henderson, Chamberlin, and Tatelbaum, 1986; Olds, Henderson, and Kitzman, 1994) may have long-term benefits for the child's behavioral and emotional development into adulthood.

The present study is a long-term follow-up of the effects of early risk factors and preventive intervention on psychiatric symptoms of children from infancy to early adulthood. Children selected from the well-baby clinics in the area of Helsinki city were followed from the time of their mothers' pregnancy until they were 20–21 years old. In the initial phase of the study, counseling was provided to the families in their homes during the first six months of the child's life, and family-risk status was assessed. By the time the children were 5–6 years old, the families were subjected to a comprehensive examination to evaluate the effects of counseling at that point (Aronen, Arajärvi, and Linnansaari, 1987). A second follow-up study was conducted when the children were 10–11 years old (Aronen, 1993), and a 15-year follow-up was done when the children were adolescents (Aronen and Kurkela, 1996; Teerikangas, Aronen, Martin, and Huttunen, 1998). The aim of the present 20-year follow-up study was to evaluate the effects of early risk factors and an early protective intervention on psychiatric symptoms in young adulthood, specifically: 1) the effects of the intervention on the quantity and quality of the psychiatric symptoms of young adults; 2) the predictive effect of early family risk status on the psychiatric symptoms of young adults; and 3) the interaction between family risk status and counseling.

Method

Subjects

The basic population of this follow-up study comprised all those Helsinki families into which a child was born between July 1, 1975, and June 30, 1976 (5,500 families). Initially, eight maternity clinic districts were chosen, representing different socioeconomic areas of the city. Of the total cohort, 1,600 families lived in these eight districts. Of these, every eighth family was picked, yielding 196 families, each of which was contacted and asked to participate in an interview. Twenty-three families refused, two children had been admitted to a children's home, and one child had died. Thus, 170 families agreed to take part in the initial (six-month family evaluation) phase of the study. After this first phase, six more families refused to continue and four families had moved. This reduced the sample to 160 families, three of which included twins. Thus, the total number of children in these families was 163 (79 boys and 84 girls, all white and of Finnish nationality, living in the city of Helsinki). Subjects for the present study were those 136 young adults for whom complete data were available in infancy (six months) and in young adulthood (20–21 years).

Procedure

Assignment to risk groups

The 170 families who agreed to take part in the initial phase of the study were visited 3–6 times during the first six months of the child's life by one of four psychiatric nurses, who used clinical interviews and observations in the home to evaluate the childhood of both parents, the psychological and physical illnesses of the child and the parents, the parents' relationship with each other and with their child, and the family's social and economic circumstances. These data were collected by the nurses on a form that contained 63 specific items describing the family situation.

Data relating to the children and their families during the first six months were also compiled from records kept by district nurses at well-baby clinics (e.g., illness of the newborn; health of other family members). If the child had remained in hospital after birth, data on illness of the newborn were obtained from the hospital, as well.

When the child was six months old, these data were used to categorize each family into groups considered to be at either low or high risk with respect to the child's future mental development. Since no relevant risk evaluations were found in the literature at that time, a risk index was created for this study, based on risk factors identified in the literature at the time (Alanen, 1966; Anthony and Koupernik, 1974; Bentovim, 1976; Bolman, 1968; Caplan, 1961). The domains of risk were grouped under three main headings – family relationships (psychological factors), family health (biological factors), and family socioeconomic status (sociological factors) – all of which were seen as contributing to the child's future mental development. These three domains were further divided into subfactors, which were identified as being both relevant with respect to the study's purpose and feasible with respect to the adequacy of the data available.

The risk factors and the scoring assigned to each are presented in table 8.1. In keeping with the work of Anthony and Koupernik (1974), a cumulative risk index was used: the score increased according to the severity of a risk factor and the presence of multiple risk factors. Risk categories were also weighted according to their influence on the mental development of children. This was done on this basis of information from the earlier studies, cited above, as well as the clinical judgment of the research team. Factors considered by Anthony and Koupernik to be definite risk factors were assigned high scores (5–10); these included: mental illness of a parent (e.g., depressive disorders, personality disorders, psychosis), deviant mother/father-child relationships (e.g., parents unable to respond to the baby's needs, absent father), deviant relationship between adult family members (e.g., difficulties between parents and live-in grandparents).

Factors for which there was less definite evidence in regard to degree of risk were assigned moderate scores (3–4); these included: problems in mother's/father's childhood homes (e.g., alcoholism, divorce), deviant relationship between parents (e.g., abuse, fighting), illness of the newborn (e.g., hypoxia, hypoglycemia), psychological problems of a parent (e.g., mild anxiety, depressive symptoms), severe mental illness of a sibling, and severe housing and financial problems.

Factors considered to have only a cumulative effect were assigned low scores (1–2); these included: deviant relationship with a sibling

Table 8.1 Risk factor scoring table

	Degree of severity	
Risk factor	*Mild*	*Severe*
Family relationships		
Deviant mother–child relationship	5 (9)[a]	8 (5)
Deviant father–child/no father	5 (11)	8 (6)
Deviant sibling–newborn relationship	–	2 (0)
Initial mental problems of mother	–	1 (14)
Initial mental problems of father	–	1 (8)
Problems in mother's childhood home	2 (9)	4 (31)
Problems in father's childhood home	2 (12)	4 (25)
Deviant parental relationship	2 (4)	3 (11)
Deviance between other adults in family	3 (0)	5 (2)
Family health		
Illness of newborn	1 (12)	3 (12)
Somatic illness of mother	–	2 (10)
Somatic illness of father	–	2 (11)
Somatic illness of sibling	1 (0)	2 (6)
Mental problems of mother	4 (7)	–
Mental illness of mother	7 (2)	10 (3)
Mental problems of father	4 (13)	–
Mental illness of father	7 (6)	10 (0)
Mental problems of sibling	1 (5)	–
Mental illness of sibling	2 (2)	4 (1)
Severe illness/death of close relative	–	1 (14)
Family socioeconomic status		
Change in child-minder/daycare center	–	2 (0)
Housing problems	1 (4)	3 (8)
Financial problems	–	3 (13)

Note: [a]Figures in parentheses are number of families in initial phase of study who presented problem during the first six months ($N = 170$).

(e.g., extreme jealousy), early psychological problems of parents (e.g., transient anxiety about breast-feeding, coping with the introduction of a baby into the home), physical illnesses of parents or siblings (e.g., asthma, heart disease) or death of a close relative, emotional problems or mild illness of a sibling, change of child-minder (In the risk assessment, the term "deviant" was used to denote disturbed relationships in the family; "problem" was used to describe mental symptoms not reaching the diagnostic level and reported problems in the parents' childhood homes, as well as family financial and housing difficulties).

In this way, a quantitative measurement of family risk was created: risk increased as the sum of the scores of the specific risk factors grew higher. When a family did not have a specific risk factor, the item was scored zero. The range of the total risk-factor score, arrived at by means of simple addition, was 0–78. The determination of the cut-off point between low-risk and high-risk families took place in two phases. In the first phase, 20 families were randomly chosen; their circumstances were evaluated from psychological, biological, and sociological points of view; and a clinical decision was made as to whether or not the family circumstances put the child's future mental health at high risk. When risk scores were tabulated, all the families that had been clinically judged as constituting an increased risk were found to have amassed more than 13 points. The second phase operated in the reverse order. Another 20 randomly chosen families formed a test sample to check the cut-off point. After their individual risk scores were calculated, the research team determined whether the families that had scored more than 13 points did in fact present a risk to the mental development of the child. The cut-off of 13 was deemed to be valid, and was used to assign families into high-risk and low-risk groups. According to these criteria, there were 29 (17%) high-risk and 141 (83%) low-risk families in the initial six-month phase of this study (Aronen and Kurkela, 1996).

Counseling and control groups

When the children were six months old, half of the 160 families that continued to be followed were assigned to a five-year family counseling intervention program; the other half served as a control group. Low-risk families were assigned, alternately, to the counseling and the control groups. The same procedure was followed with the high-risk families. Following attrition at the six-month point, when ten families dropped out of the study, 26 high-risk families (10% attrition) and 134 low-risk families (5% attrition) remained.

Three of the four psychiatric nurses who had conducted the home visits during the child's first six months continued into the counseling phase of the program; one worked full-time, with responsibility for 40 of the 80 families assigned to counseling; the other two nurses worked part-time, each with 20 families in counseling. The control group families, who had also had home visits in the initial phase, were sent a follow-up questionnaire when their child was 2–3 years old. After that, there were no contacts with the control families until the time of the five- and ten-year follow-ups.

The conceptual framework of the counseling was based on the psychodynamic theory of development, and the aim of the counseling was to prevent mental disturbances in children by improving family interaction and influencing parents' childrearing attitudes and practices. The availability of information regarding children's normal development and needs during their first five years was expected to increase parents' understanding of their children and thus promote better relationships. During counseling, the parents' homes of origin and their childhood experiences were also discussed in an attempt to help them examine their own attitudes toward the child and to modify attitudes that might be harmful.

It was assumed that the provision of counseling over the course of the child's first five years would be sufficient to enhance parental attitudes toward child rearing. Each year of counseling had specific aims that were planned according to the child's developmental needs: 0–1 years, the aim was to establish a trusting relationship between the counselor and the family; 1–2 years, the importance of and the approach to setting normal limits for the child were discussed; 2–3 years, the counseling concentrated on the children learning to be more independent, developing their own wills, and making choices; 3–5 years, problems related to the growth of the child's will and its expression, such as temper tantrums, were discussed, and the importance of the father was emphasized.

Home visits with the counseling families took place every 4–6 weeks, i.e., about ten times a year, and covered various aspects of the child's upbringing and family problems (e.g., marital conflicts). The counselors talked with the parents (mother, father, or both) about the child's development, but did not work directly with the child, since the aim was to modify parental attitudes and practices. If therapy or more intensive psychiatric treatment was needed, the family was referred to a community mental health facility.

The counselors, who kept a written record of each visit, were supervised weekly by child psychiatrists belonging to the research team. The home visits continued until the children were five years old. An attempt was made to provide counseling that met the specific needs of each family. At the weekly meeting, the supervisory group discussed the families, examined all attempts to improve family interaction, and provided guidance for the counselors.

Altogether, 76 families continued in counseling for the full five-year period (four families moved away from the Helsinki area during that time). The children were followed up at ages 5–6, 10–11, and 14–15 years to study the effect of early risk factors and counseling on psychiatric outcomes. The results of these follow-ups have been reported elsewhere (Aronen, 1993; Aronen and Kurkela, 1996).

Counseling intervention excerpts

Low-risk family

Following are brief descriptive excerpts (edited slightly for presentation here), drawn from the counselor's notes on five home visits to a low-risk family with two children. The children were born in 1974 and 1976, and the family was seen for a total of 53 visits over the five years during which counseling was in progress.

Counseling visit during the child's first year. The sleep-wake schedule of the child was discussed. The mother complained of having no time for herself, as the child (age 8 months) fell asleep so late in the evenings. It was determined that the child took two long naps during the day; the counselor mentioned that it was no wonder the child did not fall asleep earlier, and she asked the parents to move the naps to earlier times and shorten them. At the same counseling visit, the annoying behavior of the older sibling (age 2 years) was discussed. The counselor pointed out that this may be due partly to normative jealousy toward the baby, and that perhaps more attention should be given to the elder sibling. At the next visit, the parents told the counselor that their life had taken a turn for the better; they had modified the sleep-wake schedule of the children, both children now went to bed much earlier, and the parents had some time of their own in the evenings.

Counseling visit during the second year. How to toilet train the child (age 20 months) was discussed, and the counselor helped the mother to be consistent and rewarding in teaching the child. This subject came up again during a visit three months later, and it turned out that the child had learned bowel and bladder control without problems.

Counseling visit during the third year. The mother wanted to discuss how to set limits for the children, how to teach them good manners, and how to deal with temper tantrums. The parents were encouraged in the setting of limits, especially with the younger child, who had started to resist going to bed in the evening. During the following visits, the limit-setting theme was discussed again and the parents were pleased that they were counseled in this matter.

Counseling visits during the fourth and fifth year. Jealousy between the siblings and their developing their own will at age 4–5 years were discussed. At the final visit, the parents stated that the family as a whole and each individual family member had benefited from the counseling. The children's development during the course of the five years was normal, as observed by the counselor.

High-risk family

A high-risk family with one child, born in 1975, was seen for a total of 58 counseling visits. Following are excerpts from the counselor's notes on visits during each of the five years.

Counseling visit during the first year of the child's lift (age 12 months). The parents talked about the family's financial and housing problems. The mother wanted to know how the fights between the parents would affect the child, as the child already seemed to be scared of loud voices. The counselor told the parents that overhearing parental arguments can make the child frightened and timid and cause sleep problems, and that the child may later experience problems due to not knowing with whom to side when the parents fight. The parents also wanted to know how to deal with the child's possible temper tantrums: do they have to give in, and give the child what he wants? The parents were advised to be consistent, and not give in after first saying no to the child. The parents said that they would try to agree with each other when saying no to the child.

Counseling visit during the second year (child aged 18 months). The child was cranky while eating; the counselor pointed out that there was no use in trying to force the child to eat. Also, toilet training the child was difficult and the mother was using physical punishment (slapping) when the child did not obey. The counselor informed her that it was normal for the child to be negative at that age, and that the child needed more positive attention rather than physical punishment. The counselor noted that there was evidently a lot of tension between the parents. The mother said that the father was a heavy user of alcohol, and that he became aggressive when drunk. During a counseling visit a few months later, the mother mentioned that the child was less cranky and demanding than earlier, as she had tried to spend "positive time" with the child instead of disciplining him all the time. Also, the parents had had fewer fights because the father was drinking less. The counselor told them that it was likely that the child was easier to manage because the relationship between the parents was calmer and the mother was more positive in her behavior toward the child. The mother seemed to be pleased at hearing this.

Counseling visits during the third year. The parents' difficult relationship and the father's alcoholism were discussed with both parents present. The counselor asked the parents to try to talk about their relationship, so that the father could participate at a time when he was not drunk. During the following visits, it was evident that the father's alcohol use had increased (father was drunk during the counselling visit), and the counselor asked the father to contact the treatment facility. The mother was trying to find a new flat for herself and the child. However, the parents remained together, and the father was again able to diminish his alcohol consumption.

Counseling visits during the fourth and fifth year. The father's periodic alcohol use continued; he sought his own treatment during the fourth year and went to group and individual therapy. The counsellor supported the parents in attending to the child's needs in spite of the difficult situation in the family. At the time of the final visit, the family was experiencing a calm period, during which the father was not using alcohol. The mother wanted to talk about the parents' relationship, the father's problems, the child's development, and how the child was dealing with his father's alcoholism. She said that the counsellor was the only person she was able to talk to during these years. It seemed that she had benefited from the counselling and that, through her, the child benefited as well. The child's development, as observed by the counsellor, seemed to be in the normative range, although at times he was cranky and oppositional, most likely reflecting the difficult situation in the home.

Twenty-year Follow-up

When the subjects were 20–21 years old, they were sent a mailing that included the Achenbach Young Adult Self-Report Questionnaire (YASR)

(Achenbach, 1997) and the Beck Depression Inventory (BDI) (Richter, Werner, Heerlein, Kraus, and Sauer, 1998), along with a prepaid return envelope. Two reminders were sent subsequently to those who had not returned the initial mailing. Overall, of the 163 children in the study, 136 (83%) responded as young adults. Of the 26 families in the high-risk group, 20 young adults (77%) participated at this stage, 11 from the counseling and 9 from the control group. From the 134 low-risk families, 116 young adults (87%) responded, 62 from the counseling and 54 from the control group.

The 136 young adults surveyed at the 20-year follow-up did not differ significantly from the 27 who failed to respond, with respect either to initial risk status (low/high-risk, Pearson $X^2 = 0.949$, $df = 1$, $p = 0.33$) or the counseling/control status of the family (Pearson $X^2 = 0.03$, $df = 1$, $p = 0.862$). Information on family composition and the number of moves was collected when the children were 10–11 years old: in 27 of the 136 families, the parents were divorced; 26 families had one child, 74 were two-child families, 28 had three children, and 8 had four children. Fifteen families had not moved at all, 43 had moved once, 32 twice, 25 three times, 10 four times, 7 five times, 2 six times, and 2 seven times.

The symptom checklist of the YASR, consisting of 116 items, and the sum score of the BDI (available for 134 cases) were used as quantitative and qualitative measurements of the young adults' psychiatric symptoms. Respondents to items on the YASR are asked to circle 0 = not true for the subject, 1 = somewhat/sometimes true, 2 = very/often true. The measure yields total problem scores, scores for internalizing and externalizing (broadband) symptoms, and scores for eight separate (narrow-band) syndrome scales: withdrawn, somatic complaints, anxious/depressed, intrusive, thought problems, attention problems, aggressive behavior, delinquent behavior. The withdrawn and anxious/depressed syndrome scales form the internalizing symptom subscale; the delinquent behavior, intrusive, and aggressive behavior symptom scales form the externalizing symptom subscale (Achenbach, 1997). The reports were scored with the Achenbach scoring programs. In the present study, the total problem scores and the internalizing and externalizing symptom scales, as well as the eight narrow-band symptom scores of the YASR, were used as the outcome variables. A cutoff point of 60T on the YASR was used as a mark for possible psychiatric disturbance at age 20–21 years, as suggested by Achenbach.

Statistical analyses

The Systat software program for Macintosh computer was used for analyzing the data. Fisher's exact test (two-tail) was used to compare the frequencies of disturbed adolescents in the counseling and control groups, based on the cut-off point of 60T. Student's *t*-test measured the differences in problem scores between the counseling and the control families. Multiple regression analysis was used in assessing the relative contributions of counseling and initial family risk to the young adults' mental state. In the final analysis, the total score of the YASR served as the outcome variable. The independent variables were the initial family risk and the counseling. For the multiple regression analysis, dummy variables of the independent variables were created (Zar, 1984). To assess the interaction between initial family risk status and counseling, the General Linear Model was used.

Results

Effects of counseling

The young adults in the control families received significantly higher total scores on the YASR and the BDI than did those from the counseling families. YASR mean scores were 36.13 (SD = 21.06) in the control and 29.08 (SD = 17.17) in the counseling group (df = 134, t = 2.148, p = 0.033). On the BDI, means were 4.68 (SD = 5.22) and 3.00 (SD = 3.77), respectively (df = 132, t = 2.154, p = 0.033). As shown in table 8.2, when the YASR cutoff point of 60T was used, there were more disturbed adolescents in the control group than in the counseling group (Pearson X^2 = 4.95, df = 1).

On the 20-year follow-up questionnaires, the 9 high-risk control group subjects had significantly higher YASR total symptom scores than did the 11 high-risk youngsters whose families received counseling (M = 50.67, 23.27, SD = 21.62, 10.05, respectively; Student's t = 3.75, p = 0.001, df = 18). In the low-risk group, the 54 control family subjects also had higher YASR total symptom scores than did their 62 counseling family counterparts, but the difference remained insignificant (M = 33.7, 30.11, SD = 20.16, 18.01, respectively; Student's t = 1.02,

Table 8.2 Frequencies of disturbed young adults in counseling and control groups

Status	Counseling	Control	Total
Normal	69 (58/11)	52 (48/4)	121 (106/15)
Disturbed	4 (4/0)	11 (6/5)	15 (10/5)
Total	73 (62/11)	63 (54/9)	136 (116/20)

Notes: Values in parentheses represent frequencies of low/high-risk families. Fisher's Exact Test, $p = 0.030$.

$p = 0.313$, $df = 114$). There were no young adults scoring 60T or higher on the YASR in the counseled high-risk families. Of the nine high-risk controls, five (56%) scored above the cut-off point at this follow-up (Fishers Exact Test, two-tailed, $p = 0.008$).

Quality of symptoms

The young adults from the control group families had more internalizing symptoms than did those from the counseled families. Total scores for internalizing symptoms were significantly higher in the control than in the counseling group on both the YASR and the BDI. In the narrowband classification of the YASR, the greatest difference between the two groups was on anxiety/depression (see table 8.3). No significant difference was found between groups in the externalizing symptom sum score of the YASR. However, the young adults from the counseling group families had fewer attention problems than did those from control families (table 8.3).

Interaction of family risk and counseling

The initial family risk did not predict psychiatric symptoms in the whole sample. However, when the counseling and the control groups were studied separately, it was found that risk status of the families did have predictive value in the control families but not in the counseling families. For control families, risk status was a significant predictor of

Table 8.3 Quality of YASR symptoms (mean scores): counseling and control groups (*N* = 136)

Symptom	Counseling	Control	t	p
Broad-band				
Internal symptoms	8.19	10.71	2.11	0.037
External symptoms	6.30	7.06	0.87	0.381
Narrow-band				
Withdrawn	2.17	2.73	1.43	0.154
Somatic complaints	1.97	2.54	1.35	0.177
Anxious/depressed	6.01	7.94	2.19	0.030
Intrusive	2.04	2.31	0.89	0.374
Thought problems	0.16	0.35	1.42	0.157
Attention problems	2.85	3.54	1.99	0.048
Delinquent behavior	0.96	1.22	0.78	0.436
Aggressive behavior	3.30	3.52	0.49	0.624

psychiatric symptoms (YASR total score) for young adults (regression coefficient = 16.96; *SE* = 7.33; *p* = 0.0240); risk status most significantly predicted the externalizing symptoms (regression coefficient = 4.46; *SE* = 1.83; *p* = 0.0178) and, to a lesser degree, the internalizing symptoms (regression coefficient = 5.52; *SE* = 2.73; *p* = 0.0478). In the counseling families, the predictive value of the family risk status remained insignificant.

Multiple regression analysis was used to examine concurrently the effects of initial family risk and counseling on YASR total problem scores. Counseling was found to be a significant predictor of better mental health in these young adults. Initial family risk status did not have a significant effect on YASR total score in the overall sample (see table 8.4). These findings suggest an interaction between counseling and initial family risk status. When this was examined by means of the General Linear Model, a significant interaction was found (regression coefficient = 23.8, *SE* = 9.09, *p* = 0.0098), with the interaction term counseling/initial risk being a stronger predictor for the externalizing (regression coefficient = 5.78, *SE* = 2.41, *p* = 0.0179) than the internalizing symptoms (regression coefficient = 6.92, *SE* = 3.34, *p* = 0.0402).

Table 8.4 Effects of counseling and initial family risk on psychiatric symptoms of young adults

Factor	Regression coefficient	SE	p
Counseling[a]	7.001	3.279	0.035
Risk[b]	2.029	3.279	0.315
Constant	25.357		

Notes: Multiple regression analysis: outcome variable is total YASR score; multiple $R = 0.202$, $N = 136$. [a]0 = counseling; 1 = control. [b]0 = low risk; 1 = high risk.

Discussion

The present study suggests that early preventive intervention, based on a psychodynamic theoretical formulation (i.e., modifying relationships), can diminish psychiatric symptoms in young adulthood. The internalizing symptoms, such as depression and anxiety, were most likely to be affected by this type of intervention. These results also suggest that a home-based risk assessment of family relationships, health, and socioeconomic status at age six months may have predictive value for psychiatric symptoms in young adulthood. A significant interaction was found between initial family risk status and the home-based preventive intervention. In particular, the counseling intervention seemed to be more effective for the group of young adults from high-risk families than for those from low-risk families. In the high-risk group, significantly more young adults from control families were judged to be disturbed than were those from families who received counseling. On the other hand, the counseling seemed to diminish the predictive power of the early risk factors: among counseling families, risk status did not predict the later symptoms, whereas, in the control families, early risk had predictive power, especially for the externalizing symptoms. It seems that counseling lessened the risk in the high-risk counseling families and, in so doing, may also have diminished the externalizing symptoms at age 20–21 years.

The present findings are in accord with earlier reports from this longitudinal intervention study, in which results of the five, ten, and fifteen-year follow-ups showed favorable outcomes for the counseling group children. The five-year follow-up, which included psychological testing of the child and a clinical interview of the parents, found more disturbed children in control (10%) than in counseling (5%) group families (Aronen et al., 1987). In the 10-year follow-up study (Aronen, 1993), there was general agreement on the degree of disturbance between child psychiatric assessment based on clinical interviews and a parent questionnaire. Both counseling and initial family risk had significant effects on total score and on the child's mental state, although no significant interaction was found between counseling and initial risk. The 15-year follow-up found more disturbed adolescents in the control than the counseling group (Aronen and Kurkela, 1996). In addition, it was noted that counseling was more effective in reducing internalizing than externalizing symptoms. No significant interaction was found between counseling and initial risk. The difference between these earlier results and the present findings lies in the interaction between initial family risk and counseling. In this study, the effect of counseling on the high-risk group was highly significant, and the counseling seemed to diminish the adverse effects of the early risk factors.

The aim of counseling in this study was to promote the relationship between the child and the caregiver by helping the parents to understand more about their child's developmental as well as individual needs. Thomas and Chess's (1984) goodness-of-fit theory was used here, and parents were made aware of the differences in the child's temperamental structure and the possibilities of better parental management of children with difficult temperament (Teerikangas et al., 1998). The counseling was rooted in a relationship-based approach; parents were considered to be individuals having the responsibility to promote the development of their child. Considerable effort was made to establish good rapport between the counselor and the parents, a process that was found to take from six months to a year and in which it was important that same counselor be assigned to the family for the whole time (Aronen et al., 1987).

The focus of the present study is similar to that of two earlier intervention studies that followed up on efforts at improving parent-child communication and strengthening parent-child relationships. These studies also reported a reduction in child behavior problems, one at ages 7–12 (Johnson and Walker, 1987), the other at age 15 (Lally et al., 1988). Significant positive effects on infant development have been found in other research focused on improving the mother-infant relationship (Lojkasek, Cohen, and Muir, 1994). Not many primary prevention intervention studies with a follow-up into young adulthood were found, making it difficult to compare these results with others. However, in a Perry Preschool Project, which included an important home-visit component, a detectable effect on educational and behavioral outcomes was noted at age 27 (Weikart, 1998).

The current investigation differs from many earlier preventive studies in its focus on the interaction between initial family risk and the intervention. Most earlier studies have involved high-risk populations with one or more assumed risk factors, such as single parenthood, teen-age motherhood, or poverty. In most such research, the families were not thoroughly evaluated and assessed with respect to multiple risk factors (Farran, 1990). However, some research has assessed the effects of multiple risk factors and preventive interventions on aspects of adolescent problem behavior, such as drug abuse, and found that intervention effects were either comparable across all risk subgroups or stronger among families at moderate-to-high risk (MacKinnon, Weber, and Pentz, 1988). In a study of the effects of family-based competence training on parenting behavior and adolescent peer refusal, Spoth et al. (1998) found that intervention efficacy was largely unrelated to cumulative family risk. By contrast, the present findings suggest that counseling worked as a protective factor in the manner described by Rutter (1985), who defined a true protective factor as one that is more powerful in preventing emotional and behavioral symptoms or psychiatric disturbances in a high-risk than in a low-risk population.

Several methodological limitations of the present study should be noted. First, as was discussed in detail in an earlier report of this longitudinal study (Aronen and Kurkela, 1996), the validity of the risk index used is open to question. However, as noted above, every family was evaluated initially in the same way, and families showing multiple problems in health of family members, family relationships, or family socioeconomic status were considered to be high-risk families. The second factor limiting the generalization of these findings is the higher attrition rate among high-risk than among low-risk families. Of the 29 high-risk families recruited at the outset, three dropped out after the initial phase and six of the remaining 26 young adults failed to respond at the 20-year follow-up, an overall attrition rate of 31%. Still, that rate is much lower than has been reported in many other studies, where attrition rates have exceeded 50% (Halpern, 1984; Johnson, 1990;

Johnson and Walker, 1987). A third limitation is that the families were allocated to counseling versus control groups on an alternating basis instead of being randomly assigned. This was done to ensure that an equal number of low- and high-risk families would be allocated to each group.

Both of the outcome measures used here – Achenbach's Young Adult Self-Report and the Beck Depression Inventory – showed the effect of counseling on emotional and, to a lesser extent, behavioral symptoms in young adulthood. It should be noted in this regard that the cut-off point used to designate possible disturbance was not based on any clinical evaluation. Rather, it was felt to be a useful demarcation for presentation of the data, since subjects who scored higher on the symptom scale were more often found in the control rather than the counseling group. Further, all the outcome data were based on self-reports, which are not as valid as is clinical psychiatric status. However, in studying psychiatric symptoms, self-report instruments are the most widely used in both empirical and clinical research.

At an earlier stage of this follow-up study, both the parents and the child were used as informants and the results were concordant. It should also be noted that a small difference in the amount of depressive symptoms (sum of the BDI) between groups may not be seen in the functioning of the young adults. It is, however, interesting that the presence of an environmental factor in the early years of the child's life can be shown to have at least some effect so far into the future (i.e., 15 years after the intervention).

This study thus supports a body of developmental theory stressing the importance of the early years and the impact of the child-caregiver relationship on the child's development (Emde, Bingham, and Harmon, 1993; Stern, 1985; Thomas and Chess, 1984; Zeanah, Boris, and Larrieu, 1997). The findings also imply that adversities present in the early years of life can be modified by a home-based intervention program centered around relationships. The positive effect of counseling in this study can be attributed to the improved quality of the child-caregiver relationship, which served to buffer the child's development even in the presence of multiple risk factors.

Results of this study suggest that some high-risk families can be reached by means of home-based family-counseling programs focused on improving the relationship between child and caregiver. The findings have implications for the time frame of preventive interventions; they help to identify a window of opportunity, and highlight three reasons that an early start is essential. First, it takes time to establish the trusting relationship between counselor and parent that becomes the foundation for effective counseling. Indeed, Larson (1980) demonstrated that preventive intervention produces the best results if started during pregnancy. Second, an early start makes it possible to intervene at a point where parental behavior or attitudes may be easier to modify, before difficult relational problems have emerged and solidified. Third, early intervention can protect and support the child's development, and lead to long-lasting positive effects on behavior and emotional well-being.

For clinicians working with parents and young children, a focus on improving the child-parent relationship should be a treatment option even in families with multiple risk factors. Earlier research has indicated that many aspects of risk are mediated by the low quality of mother-infant interaction (Dodge, Pettit, and Bates, 1994). The present study extends these findings. In particular, it suggests that the effects of early intervention in infancy are sustained over a long period – i.e., into young adulthood – and may be more powerful in high-risk than in low-risk families.

References

Achenbach, T. M. (1997). *Manual for the Young Adult Self-Report and Young Adult Behavior Checklist.* Burlington: Department of Psychiatry, University of Vermont.

Alanen, Y. (1966). The family in the pathogenesis of schizophrenic and neurotic disorders. *Acta Psychiatrica Scandinavica* (Suppl. 189).

Anthony, E. J., & Koupernik, C. (1974). *The child in his family* (Vol. 3). New York: John Wiley.

Aronen, E. T. (1993). The effect of family counseling on the mental health of 10–11-year-old children in low- and high-risk families: A longitudinal approach. *Journal of Child Psychology and Psychiatry, 34*, 155–165.

Aronen, E. T., Arajärvi, T., & Linnansaari, H. (1987). Family counseling in the prevention of mental disturbances in children: A five-year follow-up study. *Nordisk Psykiatrisk Tidsskrift, 41*, 121–127.

Aronen, E. T., & Kurkela, S. A. (1996). Long-term effects of an early home-based intervention. *Journal of the American Academy of Child and Adolescent Psychiatry, 35*, 1665–1672.

Beardslee, W. R., Wright, E., Clarke-Rothberg, P., Salt, P., & Versage, E. (1996). Response of families to two preventive intervention strategies: Long-term differences in behavior and attitude change. *Journal of the American Academy of Child and Adolescent Psychiatry, 35,* 774–782.

Bentovim, A. (1976). Disobedience and violent behaviour in children: Family pathology and family treatment, II. *British Journal of Medicine, 1,* 1004–1006.

Bolman, W. M. (1968). Preventive psychiatry for the family: Theory, approaches, and programs. *American Journal of Psychiatry, 125,* 458–472.

Brooks-Gunn, J., Klebanov, P. K., Liaw, F. R., & Spiker, D. (1993). Enhancing the development of low-birthweight, premature infants: Changes in cognition and behavior over the first three years. *Child Development, 64,* 736–753.

Brooks-Gunn, J., McCarton, C. M., Casey, P. H., McCormic, M. C., Bauer, C. R., Bernbaum, J. C., Tyson, J., Swanson, M., Bennett, F. C., Scott, D. T., Tonascia, J., & Meinert, C. L. (1994). Early intervention in low-birth-weight premature infants: Results through age 5 years from the Infant Health and Development Program. *Journal of American Medical Association, 272,* 1257–1262.

Caplan, C. (1961). *Prevention of mental disorders in children.* New York: Basic Books.

Dodge, K. A., Pettit, G. S., & Bates, J. E. (1994). Socialization mediators of the relation between socioeconomic status and child conduct problems. *Child Development, 65,* 649–665.

Emde, R. N., Bingham, R. D., & Harmon, R. J. (1993). Classification and the diagnostic process in infancy. In C. H. Zeanah (Ed.), *Handbook of infant mental health* (pp. 225–235). New York: Guilford Press.

Farran, D. C. (1990). Effects of intervention with disadvantaged and disabled children: A decade review. In S. J. Meisels & J. P. Shonkoff (Eds.), *Handbook of early intervention* (pp. 501–539). New York: Cambridge University Press.

Farrington, D. P. (1991). Childhood aggression and adult violence: Early precursors and life outcomes. In D. J. Pepler & K. H. Rubin (Eds.), *The development and treatment of childhood aggression* (pp. 5–29). Hillsdale, NJ: Lawrence Erlbaum.

Gray, J. D., Cutler, C. A., Dean, J. G., & Kempe, C. H. (1979). Prediction and prevention of child abuse and neglect. *Journal of Social Issues, 35,* 127–139.

Halpern, R. (1984). Lack of effects of home-based early intervention: Some possible explanations. *American Journal of Orthopsychiatry, 54,* 33–42.

Harrington, R., Fudge, H., Rutter, M., Pickles, A., & Hill, J. (1990). Adult outcomes of childhood and adolescent depression. *Archives of General Psychiatry, 47,* 465–473.

Harrington, R., Bredenkamp, D., Groothues, C., Rutter, M., Fudge, H., & Pickles, A. (1994). Adult outcomes of childhood and adolescent depression: III. Links with suicidal behaviors. *Journal of Child Psychology and Psychiatry, 35,* 1309–1319.

Johnson, D. L. (1990). The Houston Parent-Child Development Center Project: Disseminating a viable program for enhancing at-risk families. *Prevention in Human Services, 7,* 89–108.

Johnson, D. L., & Walker, T. (1987). Primary prevention of behavior problems in Mexican-American children. *American Journal of Community Psychology, 15,* 375–385.

Kashani, J. H., Ezpeleta, L., Dandoy, A. C., Doi, S., & Reid, J. C. (1991). Psychiatric disorders in children and adolescents: The contribution of the child's temperament and the parents' psychopathology and attitudes. *Canadian Journal of Psychiatry, 36,* 569–573.

Lally, J. R., Mangione, P. L., & Honig, A. S. (1988). The Syracuse University Family Development Research Program: Long-range impact of an early intervention with low-income children and their families. In D. Powell (Ed.), *Parent education as early childhood intervention: Emerging directions in theory, research and practice* (pp. 79–104). Norwood, NJ: Ablex.

Larson, C. P. (1980). Efficacy of prenatal and postpartum home visits on child health and development. *Pediatrics, 66,* 191–197.

Lojkasek, M., Cohen, N. J., & Muir, E. (1994). Where is the infant in infant intervention? A review of the literature on changing troubled mother-infant relationships. *Psychotherapy, 31,* 208–220.

MacKinnon, D. P., Weber, M. D., & Pentz, M. A. (1988). How do school-based drug prevention programs work and for whom? *Drug and Society, 3,* 125–143.

Oberklaid, F., Sanson, A., Pedlow, R., & Prior, M. (1993). Predicting preschool behavior problems from temperament and other variables in infancy. *Pediatrics, 91,* 113–120.

Olds, D. L., Henderson, C. R., Chamberlin, R., & Tatelbaum, H. (1986). Does prematal and infancy nurse home visitation have enduring effects on qualities of parental care giving and child health at 25 to 50 months of life? *Pediatrics, 93,* 89–93.

Richter, P., Werner, J., Heerlein, A., Kraus, A., & Sauer, H. (1998). On the validity of the Beck Depression Inventory. A review. *Psychopathology, 31,* 160–168.

Rutter, M. (1985). Resilience in the face of adversity: Protective factors and resilience to psychiatric disorders. *British Journal of Psychiatry, 147,* 598–611.

Rutter, M. (1994). Beyond longitudinal data: Causes, consequences, changes, and continuity. *Journal of Consulting and Clinical Psychology, 62,* 928–940.

Sanson, A., Oberklaid, F., Pedlow, R., & Prior, M. (1991). Risk indicators: Assessment of infancy predictors of preschool behavioral maladjustment. *Journal of Child Psychology and Psychiatry, 32,* 609–626.

Seifer, R., Samerof, A. J., Anagnostopolou, R., & Elias, P. K. (1992). Child and family factors that ameliorate risk between 4 and 14 years of age. *Journal of the American Academy of Child and Adolescent Psychiatry, 31*, 893–903.

Spoth, R., Redmond, C., Shin, C., Lepper, H., Haggerty, K., & Wall M. (1998). Risk moderation of parent and child outcomes in a preventive intervention: A test and replication. *American Journal of Orthopsychiatry, 68*, 565–579.

Stern, D. (1985). *The interpersonal world of the infant.* New York: Basic Books.

Teerikangas, O. M., Aronen, E. T., Martin, R. P., & Huttunen, M. O. (1998). Effects of infant temperament and early intervention on the psychiatric symptoms of adolescents. *Journal of the American Academy of Child and Adolescent Psychiatry, 37*, 1070–1076.

Thomas, A., & Chess, S. (1984). Genesis and evolution of behavioral disorders: From infancy to early adult life. *American Journal of Psychiatry, 141*, 1–9.

Weikart, D. P. (1998). Changing early childhood development through educational intervention. *Preventive Medicine, 27*, 233–237.

Zar, J. H. (1984). *Biostatistical analysis.* Upper Saddle River, NJ: Prentice Hall.

Zeanah, C. H., Boris, N. W., & Larrieu, J. A. (1997). Infant development and developmental risk: A review of the past 10 years. *Journal of the American Academy of Child and Adolescent Psychiatry, 36*, 165–178.

Introduction to Chapter 9

Although crime is a major societal concern, few EI studies have examined long-term prevention of future criminal behavior. In the Elmira Prenatal and Early Infancy Project, Olds and his associates have conducted one of the most comprehensive and rigorous studies in this area. They maintain that there are at least three early causes of anti-social behavior: (a) neurological deficits, (b) abusive, negligent, or overly punitive parenting, and (c) parental criminality and substance abuse. Their preventive EI program focused on these potential contributors; their previous report documented intervention-related changes in these risk factors, with the greatest benefit to mothers who had low psycho-logical resources – e.g., low IQ and sense of mastery, mental health issues (Olds et al., 1998).

They compared three randomly assigned groups of 400 first time mothers, most of who were young, single, and poor (an at-risk group for child abuse and negative child outcomes). The control groups (T1 and T2) received standard postpartum services; one intervention group (T3) received supplemental prenatal nurse home visits, while the second intervention group (T4) received the supplemental prenatal and postnatal nurse home visiting (until the child was 2 years old). The latter intervention focused on prenatal and postnatal care, health and safety, social support, maternal counselling, educational and vocational upgrading. The mothers in the intervention groups were encouraged to reduce cigarette smoking and other substance use during pregnancy and use birth control to increase spacing between births. The intervention mothers also were shown how to be more positive and sensitive parents. Measures included adolescent self-report, parent and teacher report on child behavior, and school and police records (when available). Table 11.3 presents the core findings.

Interestingly, based on self-report, children had fewer arrests and convictions than control group children whether their mothers had received prenatal and postnatal visits or prenatal only. The authors try to account for this unexpected finding by highlighting the possible long-term developmental benefits of reduced maternal smoking during pregnancy in the intervention groups. If this is true, then the adverse consequences of prenatal smoking on child development may be far worse than realized. The positive intervention results on self- and parent-reports are corroborated by the PINS reports, but not by actual arrest records. Overall, however, the findings suggest that this relatively low-cost home visiting program can have a major long-term impact in the reduction in antisocial behavior and criminality, especially in children from at-risk families.

Reference

Olds, D., Henderson, C., Kitzman, H., Eckenrode, J., Cole, R., Tatelbaum, R., Robinson, J., Pettitt, L., O'Brien, R., & Hill, P. (1998). Prenatal and infancy home visitation by nurses. In C. Roe-Collier, L. P. Lipsitt, & H. Hayne (Eds), *Advances in infancy research*. Vol. 12 (pp. 79–130). Stamford, CT: Ablex.

NINE

Long-term Effects of Nurse Home Visitation on Children's Criminal and Antisocial Behavior: Fifteen-year Follow-up of a Randomized Controlled Trial

David Olds, Charles R. Henderson, Jr, Robert Cole, John Eckenrode, Harriet Kitzman, Dennis Luckey, Lisa Pettitt, Kimberly Sidora, Pamela Morris, and Jane Powers

Juvenile crime is a significant problem in the United States. In 1996, law enforcement agencies made 2.9 million arrests of juveniles (children <18 years). Moreover, 19% of all arrests and 19% of all violent crime arrests were accounted for by juveniles. Although the number

Olds, D., Henderson, C. R. Jr., Cole, R., Eckenrode, J., Kitzman, H., Luckey, D., Pettitt, L., Sidora, K., Morris, P., & Powers, J. (1998). Long-term effects of nurse home visitation on children's criminal and antisocial behavior: 15-year follow-up of a randomised controlled trial. *Journal of the American Medical Association, 280*, 1238–1244. Reprinted by permission of the American Medical Association.

of juvenile Violent Crime Index arrests (ie, for murder, forcible rape, robbery, and aggravated assault) declined in both 1995 and 1996, the rate in 1996 was still 60% higher than the 1987 level.[1]

Antisocial behavior can be classified according to its time of onset: prior to puberty (childhood onset) vs after puberty (adolescent onset).[2,3] Childhood onset is characterized by more serious behavioral disruption, such as violent behavior toward classmates and cruelty toward animals beginning as early as age 3 years, but occurs less frequently. The adolescent-onset variety, although sometimes expressed as aggression toward peers, is generally less serious (eg, shoplifting, lying to teachers and parents) and occurs so frequently that some consider it normative.[3] Childhood-onset antisocial behavior is associated with neuropsychological deficits (eg, impaired language and intellectual functioning, attention-deficit/hyperactivity disorder) and harsh, rejecting parenting early in the child's life.[4,5] The adolescent-onset type has been hypothesized to be a reaction to the limited number of responsible roles for adolescents in Western societies.[3]

In earlier articles, we have shown that a program of prenatal and infancy home visitation by nurses improved women's prenatal health-related behavior[6] and reduced the rates of child abuse and neglect,[7,8] maternal welfare dependence, closely spaced successive pregnancies, maternal criminal behavior and behavioral problems due to use of alcohol and other drugs,[8] and children's intellectual impairment associated with prenatal exposure to tobacco.[9,10] These aspects of maternal and child functioning represent significant risks for early-onset antisocial behavior.[11]

This article examines the extent to which this program produced a reduction in children's criminal and antisocial behavior. We expected that the program would reduce antisocial behaviors indicative of the early-onset type but did not expect it to have as dramatic an effect on adolescent-onset antisocial behavior.[11] We expected that program effects would be concentrated on children born to women who were unmarried and from low-income families at registration during pregnancy. One of the treatment conditions used in this study consisted of prenatal home visitation with no post-partum follow-up. We expected that the group receiving only prenatal home visitation would function better than the comparison group but not as well as the group that received prenatal and postnatal home visitation.

Methods

The details of this study's design can be found in an earlier article.[8] A summary of the design is given herein.

Setting, participants, and randomization

Pregnant women were recruited from a free antepartum clinic sponsored by the Chemung County, New York, health department and the offices of private obstetricians in Elmira, NY. We actively recruited women with no previous live births who were less than 25 weeks pregnant and who were young (aged <19 years at registration), unmarried, or of low socioeconomic status (SES). Women without these sociodemographic risk characteristics were permitted to enroll if they had no previous live births. From April 1978 through September 1980, 500 women were invited to participate and 400 enrolled. Eighty-five percent were young, unmarried, or from low-SES households (August Hollingshead, PhD, unpublished manuscript, 1976). After completing informed consent and baseline interviews, women were stratified by sociodemographic characteristics and randomized to 1 of 4 treatment conditions. Persons involved in data gathering were blinded to the women's treatment conditions.

Treatment conditions

Families in treatment group 1 (n = 94) were provided sensory and developmental screening for the child at 12 and 24 months of age. Based on these screenings, the children were referred for further clinical evaluation and treatment when needed. Families in treatment group 2 (n = 90) were provided the screening services offered those in treatment group 1 in addition to free transportation (using a taxicab voucher system) for prenatal and well-child care through the child's second birthday. There were no differences between treatment groups 1 and 2 in their use of prenatal and well-child care (both groups had high rates of completed appointments). Therefore, these 2 groups were combined to form a single comparison group as in earlier articles. Families in treatment group 3 (n = 100) were provided the screening and transportation services offered to treatment group 2 and in addition were provided a nurse who visited them at home during pregnancy. Families in treatment group 4 (n = 116) were provided the same services as those in treatment group 3 except that the nurse continued to visit through the child's second birthday.

Program plan and implementation

In the home visits, the nurses promoted 3 aspects of maternal functioning: (1) positive health-related behaviors during pregnancy and the early years of the child's life, (2) competent care of their children, and (3) maternal personal development (family planning, educational achievement, and participation in the workforce). In the service of these 3 goals, the nurses linked families with needed health care and human services and attempted to involve other family members and friends in the pregnancy, birth, and early care of the child. The nurses completed an average of 9 visits during pregnancy (range, 0–16) and 23 visits from birth to the child's second birthday (range, 0–59). Details of the program can be found elsewhere.[12,13]

Overview of follow-up study

The current phase of the study consists of a longitudinal follow-up of the 400 families who were randomized to treatment and control conditions and in which the mother and child were still alive and the family had not refused participation at earlier phases. The flow of patients from recruitment through the 15-year follow-up is presented in table 9.1. Interviews were conducted with the adolescents, their biological mothers, and their custodial parents if the biological mother no longer had custody. Assessments using parent reports used interview data from the parent who was judged to have had the greatest amount of recent experience with the child.

Assessments and definitions of variables

Assessments conducted at earlier phases are specified in previous articles.[7,8] At the 15-year follow-up assessment, adolescents completed interviews that measured whether they had been adjudicated a person

Table 9.1   Flow of patients from recruitment during pregnancy until 15 years after delivery of first child

	Treatment groups[a]		
	1 and 2 (n = 184)	3 (n = 100)	4 (n = 116)
Program implementation			
No. of completed prenatal home visits, average (range)	—[b]	8.6 (0–16)	8.6 (0–16)
No. of completed postnatal home visits, average (range)	—	—	22.8 (0–59)
Intervening years			
No. of fetal, infant, or child deaths	10	7	9
No. of children adopted[c]	7	6	2
No. of maternal deaths[d]	1	1	0
15-Year follow-up study			
No. of missing biological mothers	12	1	4
No. who refused to participate[e]			
Mothers	6	5	4
Adolescents	10	8	7
No. of completed interviews			
Parents (biological or custodial)	152	81	97
Adolescents	144	77	94
No. of cases with school data (grades 7–9)	139	68	84
No. of cases with teacher report data[f]	117	66	79
No. of cases with probation or family court data[g]	60	27	29

Notes: [a]Treatment groups 1 and 2 are the comparison; treatment group 3 was nurse-visited during pregnancy; and treatment group 4 was nurse-visited during pregnancy and infancy. Of 500 eligible persons invited to participate, 100 refused and 400 were randomized to the various treatment groups. [b]Ellipses indicate data not available. [c]There were 2 adoptions in which interviews were conducted with the child but not the mother. They are not shown. [d]For both cases in which the mother died, the adolescents were interviewed. [e]Refusals include 8 mothers who refused to participate during earlier phases and were not approached for the 15-year follow-up. [f]Data are for cases with at least 1 mathematics or English teacher report of classroom behavior. [g]Data are for subsample of children who resided in original community for their entire lives.

in need of supervision (PINS) resulting from incorrigible behavior such as recurrent truancy or destroying parents' property; their frequency of running away from home; and the number of times they had been stopped by the police, arrested, convicted of a crime or of probation violations, and sent to youth correctional facilities.[14] They also reported on their disruptive behavior in school; number of school suspensions; delinquent and aggressive behavior outside school; experience of sexual intercourse; rates of pregnancy; lifetime number of sexual partners; and frequency of using cigarettes, alcohol, and illegal drugs during the 6-month period prior to the 15-year interview.[15]

Variables were created to summarize the number of occurrences of being stopped by the police, arrested, convicted (adjudicated) of the original crime or of probation violations, and sent to a youth correctional facility. Although we asked the children to report their number of school suspensions and disruptive behaviors in school, we used archived school data and teacher reports to measure these outcomes because they are less subject to reporting bias than are self-report data.

A variable was constructed to characterize the total number of cigarettes currently smoked per day. Separate variables were constructed to count the number of days the children had consumed alcohol or used illegal drugs during the 6-month period prior to the interview. The adolescents were asked questions regarding the effect of alcohol on 5 domains of their lives (trouble with parents, trouble at school, problems with friends, problems with someone they were dating, trouble with police).[16] These data were summarized in an alcohol-use behavioral problem scale (range, 0–5). Corresponding questions regarding use of illegal drugs were omitted because of clerical error.

The self-reports of antisocial and delinquent acts were factor analyzed and found to produce 2 factors, major delinquent acts and minor antisocial acts, with Cronbach α coefficients of .82 and .68, respectively. The adolescents also completed the Achenbach Youth Self-Report of Problem Behaviors, which produces 2 broadband scales: internalizing (anxiety/depression, social withdrawal, and somatic complaints) and externalizing (delinquency and aggression) behavior problems.[17]

Parents were asked questions about their children's behavioral problems (the Achenbach scale); school suspensions; arrests; and use of cigarettes, alcohol, and illegal drugs, including the effect of alcohol and other drugs on their children's lives. Variables were constructed to coincide with those based on the child's self-report of behavior. Parents' reports of their children's behavioral problems caused by substance use included children's use of illegal drugs (range, 0–10).

The number of short-term and long-term suspensions were counted from an abstraction of the children's school records for grades 7 through

9. In New York State, long-term suspensions require a hearing and usually are for serious infractions such as assaulting a student or teacher. Records were analyzed when there were complete school data for 2 of the 3 years. The students' current teachers in English and mathematics completed an "acting out" scale that rated children's disruptive behavior in the classroom (eg, disruptive in class, defiant, obstinate, stubborn).

Finally, the records of 116 children who lived in Chemung County for their entire lives were reviewed by the Chemung County Probation Department and the Chemung County Family Court. Identifying information on the adolescents (name, birth date, sex, Social Security number) was provided to these departments for purposes of matching their records with the participants in this study. The department staff summarized the counts of arrest and PINS records within treatment and risk-status groups. Individual identifiers were not returned in the abstraction of these data, although the children's treatment group, sex, and risk status (ie, whether they were born to an unmarried mother from low SES) were returned.

Results

Equivalence of treatment groups on background characteristics

As indicated in table 9.2, for those families for which 15-year assessments were completed, the treatment groups were essentially equivalent on background characteristics for both the sample as a whole and for women who were unmarried and from low-SES households. Small differences on some background variables (such as paternal receipt of public assistance) led us to include them as covariates.

Encounters with the criminal justice system

Table 9.3 shows that adolescents born to nurse-visited women (treatment group 4) reported more frequent stops by police ($P < .001$) but fewer arrests and convictions and violations of probation ($P = .005$ and .001, respectively); the arrest and convictions and probation violation effects were concentrated among children born to women who were

Table 9.2 Equivalence of treatment conditions on maternal background characteristics measured at registration for children assessed at 15-year follow-up

Dependent variables	Total sample of treatment groups[a]			Low SES, unmarried sample of treatment groups		
	1 and 2 (n = 148)	3 (n = 79)	4 (n = 97)	1 and 2 (n = 62)	3 (n = 30)	4 (n = 38)
Unmarried (%)	62	59	64	100	100	100
Low-SES household (%)	64	70	61	100	100	100
White (%)	90	91	86	87	87	77
Smoker (>4 cigarettes/day)	47	46	58	51	60	59
Male children (%)	55	44	55	44	53	49
Mother working (%)	39	36	31	24	20	20
Mother receiving public assistance (%)	9	10	13	23	29	20
Father working (%)	70	70	67	42	50	52
Father receiving public assistance (%)	4	3	3	10	6	2
Husband or boyfriend in house (%)	58	76	60	21	47	22
Maternal age, mean (SD), y	19.3 (2.9)	19.5 (3.1)	19.4 (3.7)	18.6 (2.5)	19.0 (2.8)	18.2 (3.3)
Maternal education, mean (SD), y completed	11.2 (1.5)	11.6 (1.5)	11.1 (1.6)	10.7 (1.4)	10.9 (1.4)	10.3 (1.5)
Husband or boyfriend education completed, mean (SD), y	11.4 (1.4)	11.7 (1.7)	11.5 (1.6)	11.1 (1.4)	11.0 (1.8)	10.8 (1.5)
Grandmother support, mean (SD)[b,c]	100.4 (10.1)	97.7 (9.2)	101.3 (10.3)	101.6 (10.9)	98.1 (10.3)	104.1 (11.2)
Husband or boyfriend support[b,c]	99.6 (10.5)	102.0 (9.0)	99.0 (9.9)	94.2 (10.6)	98.6 (9.4)	96.8 (9.3)
Locus of control, mean (SD)[b]	99.3 (10.1)	100.6 (9.5)	100.6 (10.2)	97.5 (10.2)	99.2 (10.3)	99.1 (9.9)
Incidence of maternal arrests in New York State prior to randomization[d]	0.09	0.13	0.06	0.13	0.13	0.18

Notes: [a]Treatment groups 1 and 2 are the comparison; treatment group 3 was nurse-visited during pregnancy and infancy; and treatment group 4 was nurse-visited during pregnancy and infancy. SES indicates socioeconomic status. [b]Standardized to mean (100) and SD (10). [c]Locally developed scale that assesses degree to which individual provides emotional and material support to mother. [d]Incidence indicates the mean number of infrequently occurring events within the stated period. Individual cases may have values greater than 1.

Table 9.3 Adjusted rates of children's encounters with criminal justice system from birth to 15 years of age[a]

Dependent variables	Total sample					Low-SES, unmarried sample				
	Treatment group			P value[b]		Treatment group			P value[b]	
	1 and 2	3	4	T1 and T2 vs T3	T1 and T2 vs T4	1 and 2	3	4	T1 and T2 vs T3	T1 and T2 vs T4
Ever PINS (%)	13	11	8	0.75	0.33	14	10	5	0.63	0.14
Incidence of times ran away[c]	0.29	0.23	0.34	0.83	0.07	0.60	0.14	0.24	<0.002	0.003
Incidence of times stopped by police	0.80	0.53	2.25	0.24	<0.001	1.16	0.78	1.46	0.34	0.46
Incidence of arrests	0.36	0.16	0.17	0.005[d]	0.005[d]	0.45	0.15	0.20	0.02	0.03
Incidence of convictions and probation violations	0.27	0.06	0.10	<0.001[d]	<0.001[d]	0.47	0.07	0.09	<0.001	<0.001
Incidence of times sent to youth corrections	0.05	0.05	0.04	0.98	0.98	0.06	0.03	0.02	0.32	0.12
Incidence of arrests (mother report)	0.12	0.11	0.08	0.73	0.37	0.19	0.16	0.04	0.79	0.05
Incidence of PINS records (subsample, archived data)[e]	0.31	0.17	0.03	0.06	0.007	0.35	0.33	0.00	0.94	0.07
Incidence of arrests (subsample, archived data)[e]	0.35	0.14	0.32	0.15	0.94	0.55	0.22	0.44	0.24	0.74

Notes: [a] Treatment group 1 and 2 (T1 and T2) are the comparison; treatment group 3 (T3) was nurse-visited during pregnancy; and treatment group 4 (T4) was nurse-visited during pregnancy and infancy. Data are adjusted for socioeconomic status (SES), maternal marital status, age, education, locus of control, support from husband or boyfriend, and working status; husband or boyfriend use of public assistance at registration; and sex of child. PINS indicates parson in need of supervision. [b] Test of treatment effect performed on odds ratios for percentage outcomes and difference of logs of incidence for Incidence outcomes. [c] Incidence indicates the mean number of infrequently occurring events within the stated period. Individual cases may have values greater than1. [d] Test conducted without interactions for SES and marital status. [e] No covariates were included in the analysis of the outcome.

unmarried and from low-SES families ($P = .03$ and $<.001$, respectively). For the subsample of children who lived in Chemung County for their entire lives, nurse-visited children (treatment group 4) had fewer official PINS records ($P = .007$). Nurse-visited children whose mothers were unmarried and from low-SES families were reported by their parents to have been arrested less frequently than were their counterparts in the comparison group ($P = .05$). In addition, among adolescents born to unmarried women from low-SES households, those in treatment group 4 reported fewer instances of running away ($P = .003$). As indicated in table 9.3, with the exception of parent report of child arrests, most of these effects were present for children whose mothers were visited only during pregnancy (treatment group 3).

The effect of the treatment group 4 program on the children's reports of running away was concentrated in girls, whereas the effect on parents' reports of the children's arrests and children's reports of convictions and probation violations was greater for boys (data not shown). The effect of the program on arrests was not limited to any specific type of crime, although property crimes were more frequent and, therefore, accounted for a larger portion of the program effect on arrests overall.

School suspensions, behavior problems, and use of substances

Table 9.4 shows that children born to nurse-visited (treatment group 4) women who were unmarried and from low-SES households reported having fewer sexual partners ($P = .003$), smoking fewer cigarettes per day ($P = .10$), and consuming alcohol fewer days during the 6-month period prior to the 15-year interview ($P = .03$). Parents of children born to nurse-visited, unmarried women from low-SES families reported that their children had fewer behavioral problems related to their use of alcohol and other drugs ($P = .08$). For these outcomes, there was some indication that the group visited by nurses only during pregnancy (treatment group 3) did not do as well. Although adolescents in the unmarried, low-SES group reported smoking fewer cigarettes, they also reported higher levels of illegal drug use and their parents reported more behavioral problems due to the use of alcohol and other drugs than did their counterparts in the comparison group. There were no

Table 9.4. Adjusted reports of problem behavior, sexual activity, pregnancy, and use of substances at 15-year follow-up[a]

Dependent variables	Total sample					Low-SES, unmarried sample				
	Treatment groups			P value[b]		Treatment groups			P value[b]	
	1 and 2	3	4	T1 and T2 vs T3	T1 and T2 vs T4	1 and 2	3	4	T1 and T2 vs T3	T1 and T2 vs T4
No. of minor antisocial acts, mean[c]	2.99	2.54	2.88	0.50	0.86	4.06	3.25	3.38	0.42	0.47
No. of major delinquent acts, mean[d]	3.02	2.79	3.57	0.93	0.48	4.09	3.45	3.99	0.60	0.77
No. of externalizing problems, mean[e]	13.73	13.65	13.88	0.95	0.89	14.18	15.63	11.85	0.42	0.17
No. of internalizing problems, mean[e]	10.58	11.19	11.66	0.46	0.19	10.82	11.15	9.85	0.80	0.44
No. of acting out problems, mean[f]	9.61	8.97	9.47	0.41	0.85	10.36	9.79	10.58	0.62	0.85
Ever had sexual intercourse (%)	35	35	42	1.00	0.32	45	55	46	0.44	1.00
Ever pregnant or made someone pregnant (%)	3	2	4	0.97	1.00	8	9	7	0.90	0.74
Incidence of sex partners[g]	1.56	1.10	1.16	0.48	0.90	2.48	2.23	0.92	0.73	0.003

Incidence of short-term school suspensions	0.28	0.11	0.27	0.96	0.97	0.32	0.16	0.38	0.11	0.63
Incidence of long-term school suspensions	0.04	0.00	0.01	1.00	1.00	0.15	0.01	0.04	0.97	0.25
Incidence of cigarettes smoked per day	1.30	0.91	1.28	0.49	0.76	2.50	1.32	1.50	0.07	0.10
Incidence of days drank alcohol	1.57	1.81	1.87	0.97	0.96	2.49	1.84	1.09	0.41	0.03
Incidence of days used drugs	2.28	3.55	2.04	0.49	0.54	4.04	9.38	2.50	0.01	0.24
Alcohol impairment, self-report	0.52	0.50	0.47	0.95	0.35	0.49	0.38	0.55	0.36	0.60
Alcohol and drug impairment, parent's report	0.18	0.20	0.28	0.96	0.68	0.34	0.62	0.15	0.05	0.08

Notes: [a]Treatment groups 1 and 2 (T1 and T2) are the comparison; treatment group 3 (T3) was nurse-visited during pregnancy; and treatment group 4 (T4) was nurse-visited during pregnancy and infancy. Data are adjusted for maternal socioeconomic status, marital status, education, locus of control, support from husband/boyfriend, and working status; husband/boyfriend use of public assistance at registration; and sex of child. [b]Test of treatment effect based on mean differences for means, odds ratios for percentages, and difference of logs of incidence for count data outcomes. [c]Minor antisocial acts included lied to parents, lied to teacher, took car without permission, stayed out all night without permission, been passenger in car where driven drunk, and used fake identification to enter bar. [d]Major delinquent acts included hurt someone who needed bandages, stole something worth more than $50, stole something worth less than $50, trespassed, damaged property on purpose, hit someone because did not like what he or she said, carried weapon, set fire on purpose, and been in fight with gang members. [e]Average of parent and child reports of behavioral problem (analyzed with repeated measures). [f]Average of mathematics and English teachers' reports of students' disruptive behavior in school (analyzed with repeated measures). [g]Incidence indicates mean number of infrequently occurring events within the stated period. Individual cases may have values greater than 1.

treatment differences in teachers' reports of the adolescents' acting out in school; short-term or long-term suspensions; the adolescents' initiation of sexual intercourse; or the parents' or children's reports of major delinquent acts, minor antisocial acts, or other behavioral problems.

Comment

Adolescents born to nurse-visited (treatment group 4) women who were unmarried and from low-SES families had fewer episodes of running away from home, arrests, and convictions and violations of probation than did their counterparts in the comparison group. They also had fewer sexual partners and engaged in cigarette smoking and alcohol consumption less frequently. Their parents reported that they had fewer behavioral problems related to their use of drugs and alcohol. There were no program effects on less serious forms of antisocial behavior, initiation of sexual intercourse, or use of illegal drugs Children in treatment group 4, irrespective of risk, reported being stopped by police more frequently, but they reported fewer arrests and convictions and violations of probation, and the official PINS records corroborated this pattern. The higher rates of being stopped by police is an anomalous finding that has no coherence with any other effects and is likely to be either a sampling or reporting artifact.

The concentration of beneficial effects among children born to unmarried women of low SES is consistent with the results of other preventive interventions that have shown greater effects for children of families at greater social risk.[18] This suggests that these kinds of services ought to be focused on families in greater need by virtue of the mothers' being unmarried and poor.

In general, these findings are consistent with program effects on early-onset antisocial behavior rather than on the more common and less serious antisocial behavior that emerges with puberty.[3] The mere presence of arrests, convictions, and probation violations by the time the children were 15 years old suggests that these children started offending early and that they may be on life-course trajectories that portend recurrent and more serious offenses in the future. Given that early-onset antisocial behavior is associated with (1) subtle neurological impairment, (2) harsh, punitive, and neglectful parenting, and (3) family contexts characterized by substance abuse and criminal behavior,[2–5] it is important to note that this program has affected these aspects of maternal, child, and family functioning at earlier phases in the child's development.[6-11] Moreover, genetic vulnerability to impulsivity and aggression is expressed much more frequently when vulnerable rhesus monkeys experience aberrant rearing[19] (also Allyson J. Bennett, K. Peter Lesch, Armin Heils, et al., unpublished data, 1998), adding to the plausibility of the findings reported here.

The prenatal phase of the program reduced fetal exposure to tobacco, improved the qualities of women's prenatal diets, reduced rates of pyelonephritis, improved levels of informal social support, and reduced intellectual impairment and irritable behavioral styles associated with fetal exposure to tobacco.[6,10,11,21] Prenatal exposure to tobacco is a risk factor for early behavioral dysregulation, problems with attention, and later crime and delinquency.[20] Moreover, the combination of birth complications (and, by implication, neurological impairment) and rejecting parenting substantially increases the likelihood of violent offenses by the time children are 18 years old.[5]

We did not expect prenatal home visitation (treatment group 3) by itself to be as effective as it was in preventing criminal behavior among children born to low-SES, unmarried women. This occurred even though these children's mothers showed almost none of the postnatal benefits observed for those visited during pregnancy and infancy (such as reduced welfare dependence, substance abuse, criminal behavior, and child abuse and neglect).[8] The mechanisms through which these beneficial effects occurred will be examined in future reports, with a focus on the alteration of maternal prenatal health and the children's corresponding neuropsychological functioning,[20,21] as well as prenatal stress, given that stress during pregnancy affects the social and neuro-motor development of nonhuman primates.[22,23]

The impact of the full program (prenatal and infancy home visitation) on children's use of alcohol and number of sexual partners is important because recent evidence indicates that alcohol use prior to age 15 years multiplies the risk of alcoholism in adulthood[24] and multiple partners increase the risk for sexually transmitted diseases, including human immunodeficiency virus infection.[25,26] The effect of the program on alcohol use is consistent with greater alcohol consumption observed among adult rhesus monkeys who experienced aberrant rearing.[27] These findings must be tempered, however, with an acknowledgment of their limitations.

The first limitation is that most of the positive results were concentrated among children born to women who were unmarried and from low-SES households. Although we hypothesized originally that the effects would be greater for women who experienced higher levels of stress and who had fewer personal resources, we did not fully operationalize the stress and resource variables prior to the beginning of the trial. We chose to use characteristics used for sample recruitment as indicators of long-term stress (eg, coming from a low-SES household) and having few personal resources (eg, being unmarried), 2 factors associated with a host of adverse outcomes. However, positive early results from a large urban replication of this study focusing almost exclusively on unmarried, low-income women support our interpretation that the effects observed in the current study are due to the program.[28]

The second limitation is that the arrest and conviction data were based primarily on the children's and parents' reports, which may be subject to treatment-related reporting bias. To validate the children's and parents' reports of undesirable behavior, we compared the rates of school suspensions derived from the school records with the parents' and children's reports of suspensions and found no treatment differences in accuracy. We also regressed the English and mathematics teachers' averaged reports of the adolescents' acting out in school on the adolescents' self-reports of their acting out in school separately for the nurse-visited and comparison group children and found no treatment differences in the slopes of these regressions.

Importantly, the pattern of mean differences for treatment groups 1 and 2 vs treatment group 4 for PINS records on the subsample of children who lived in Chemung County for their entire lives corroborated the pattern of the children's reported arrests. The PINS finding increases our confidence that the treatment differences in the adolescents' reported involvement with the criminal justice system are not the result of the nurse-visited children and their parents simply underreporting their actual levels of involvement. The absence of program effect with the official arrest data may be explained by a significant, 9-fold higher rate of official arrest records prior to randomization (0.44 vs 0.05) found for treatment group 4 mothers who were unmarried and of low SES and whose children remained in Chemung County compared with their treatment group 1 and 2 counterparts.

Finally, we note that the adolescents self-reports of delinquent and antisocia behavior are not completely consistent with the data on reports of arrests and convictions. A survey that used follow-up questions to the assault questions asked in the current study showed that the answers to the questions we used produced responses that frequently were trivial (eg, 33% of the serious violent responses and 64% of the self-reported minor assaults were too insignificant to lead to arrests).[29] This suggests that the particular questions used in this study regarding delinquent behavior did not adequately assess the severity of delinquency. Thus, the treatment differences found in reports of arrests and convictions are likely to be indications of underlying treatment differences in the severity of antisocial behavior that were not assessed adequately by the set of questions asked about particular antisocial behaviors.

This program prevented only the more serious forms of antisocial behavior leading to arrests and convictions. Other types of prevention programs may be necessary to reduce more normative types of disruptive behavior among young adolescents.[30] In light of the impact of this program on maternal and youth crime and corresponding government expenditures,[8,31] the US Department of Justice is now supporting an effort to make this program available to a larger number of high-crime communities.[34]

References

1   Snyder H. *Juvenile Arrests 1996*. Washington, DC: US Dept of Justice; 1997:1–12. Office of Juvenile Justice and Delinquency Prevention Juvenile Justice Bulletin.

2   Patterson GR, DeBaryshe BD, Ramsey E. A developmental perspective on antisocial behavior. *Am Psychol*. 1989;44:329–334.

3   Moffitt TE. Adolescence-limited and life-course-persistent antisocial behavior: a developmental taxonomy. *Psychol Rev*. 1993;100:674–701.

4   Moffitt TE. The neuropsychology of conduct disorder. *Dev Psychopathol*. 1993;5:135–151.

5   Raine A, Brennan P, Mednick SA. Birth complications combined with maternal rejection at age 1 year predispose to violent crime at age 18 years. *Arch Gen Psychiatry*. 1994;51:984–988.

6   Olds D, Henderson C, Tatelbaum R, Chamberlin R. Improving the delivery of prenatal care and outcomes of pregnancy: a randomized trial of nurse home visitation. *Pediatrics*. 1986;77:16–28.

7   Olds D, Henderson C, Chamberlin R, Tatelbaum R. Preventing child abuse and neglect: a randomized trial of nurse home visitation. *Pediatrics*. 1986;78:65–78.

8   Olds D, Eckenrode J, Henderson C, et al. Long-term effects of home visitation on maternal life course and child abuse and neglect: 15-year follow-up of a randomized trial. *J AMA*. 1997;278:637–643.

9   Olds D, Henderson C, Tatelbaum R. Intellectual impairment in children of women who smoke cigarettes during pregnancy. *Pediatrics*. 1994;93:221–227.

10 Olds D, Henderson C, Tatelbaum R. Prevention of intellectual impairment in children of women who smoke cigarettes during pregnancy. *Pediatrics*. 1994;93:228–233.

11 Olds D, Pettitt LM, Robinson J, et al. Reducing risks for antisocial behavior with a program of prenatal and early childhood home visitation. *J Community Psychol*. 1998;26:65–83.

12 Olds D, Kitzman H, Cole R, Robinson J. Theoretical and empirical foundations of a program of home visitation for pregnant women and parents of young children. *J Community Psychol*. 1997;25:9–25.

13 Olds D, Korfmacher J. *Journal of Community Psychology Special Issue: Home Visitation I*. 1997;25.

14 Baker P, Mott F. *NLSY Youth Handbook 1989*. Columbus: Center for Human Resources Research, Ohio State University; 1989.

15 Jessor R, Donovan J, Costa F. *Health Behavior Questionnaire*. Denver: Institute of Behavioral Science, University of Colorado; 1992.

16 Kessler R. The National Comorbidity Survey: preliminary results and future directions. *Int Rev Psychiatry*. 1994;6:365–376.

17 Achenbach TM, Edelbrock CS. Behavioral problems and competencies reported by parents of normal and disturbed children aged 4–16. *Monogr Soc Res Child Dev*. 1981;46. Serial No. 188.

18 Brooks-Gunn J, Gross RT, Kraemer H, Spiker D, Shapiro S. Enhancing the cognitive outcomes of low birth weight, premature infants: for whom is the intervention most effective? *Pediatrics*. 1992;89:1209–1215.

19 Higley J, King S Jr, Hasert M, Champoux M, Suomi S, Linnoila M. Stability of interindividual differences in serotonin function and its relationship to severe aggression and competent social behavior in rhesus macaque females. *Neuropsychopharmacology*. 1996;14:67–76.

20 Olds D. Tobacco exposure and impaired development: a review of the evidence. *Ment Retard Dev Disabilities Res Rev*. 1997;3:257–269.

21 Pennington B, Bennetto L. Main effects or transactions in the neuropsychology of conduct disorder? commentary on "the neuropsychology of conduct disorder." *Dev Psychopathol*. 1993;5:153–164.

22 Clarke AS, Soto A, Bergholz T, Schneider M. Maternal gestational stress alters adaptive and social behavior in adolescent rhesus monkey offspring. *Infant Behav Dev*. 1996;19:453–463.

23 Schneider ML, Coe CL. Repeated social stress during pregnancy impairs neuromotor development of the primate infant. *J Dev Behav Pediatr.* 1993;14:81–87.

24 Grant B, Dawson D. Age at onset of alcohol use and its association with *DSM-IV* alcohol abuse and dependence: results from the National Longitudinal Alcohol Epidemiologic Survey. *Natl J Subst Abuse.* 1998;9:103–110.

25 Shafer MA, Hilton JF, Ekstrand M, et al. Relationship between drug use and sexual behaviors and the occurrence of sexually transmitted diseases among high-risk male youth. *Sex Transm Dis.* 1993;20:307–313.

26 Joffe GP, Foxman B, Schmidt AJ, et al. Multiple partners and partner choice as risk factors for sexually transmitted disease among female college students. *Sex Transm Dis.* 1992;19:22–278.

27 Higley JD, Hasert MF, Soumi, SJ, Linnoila M. Nonhuman primate model of alcohol abuse: effects of early experience, personality, and stress on alcohol consumption. *Proc Natl Acad Sci .*1991;88:7261–7265.

28 Kitzman H, Olds D, Henderson C, et al. Effects of home visitation by nurses on pregnancy outcomes, childhood injuries, and repeated childbearing: a randomized controlled trial. *JAMA.* 1997;278:644–652.

29 Huizinga D. Assessing violent behavior with self reports. In. Milner JS, ed. *Neuropsychology of Aggression.* Boston, Mass: Kluwer Academic Publishers; 1991.

30 Hawkins JD, Von Cleve E, Catalano RF. Reducing early childhood aggression: results of a primary prevention program. *J Am Acad Child Adolesc Psychiatry.* 1991;30:208–217.

31 Karoly LA, Greenwood PW, Everingham SS, et al. *Investing in Our Children: What We Know and Don't Know About the Costs and Benefits of Early Childhood Interventions.* Santa Monica, Calif: RAND; 1998.

32 Elliott DS. *Blueprints for Violence Prevention.* Boulder: Center for the Study and Prevention of Violence, Institute of Behavioral Science, University of Colorado at Boulder; 1997.

Part V

Family Aspects

Introduction to Part V

As explicated by Guralnick in chapter 1, child developmental outcomes may be mediated by parenting behavior and attitudes that in turn may be influenced by many variables (e.g., life stressors and hassles, parental physical and mental health, financial resources, social and spousal support, child characteristics). EI programs (particularly those that increase family social support and empowerment) also may have direct benefits on parents and other family members (Dunst et al., 1994). Although the first generation of EI programs emphasized child-focused interventions and outcomes, more recently EI services have become more family-centered and researchers have turned their attention to a broader range of family process and outcome variables (Guralnick, 1997).

It is generally up to the parents to pick and choose from a variety of EI program options available in many communities. Most EI programs require some degree of parental participation that can range from simply giving consent and being kept up-to-date on their child's progress, to attending parent support and education groups, to active and intensive involvement as their child's therapist. The impact of parent involvement in EI programs for children with or at-risk for developmental problems remain unclear (Casto and Mastropieri, 1986), but many programs are based on the belief that the more parental involvement the better (chapters 1 and 2). Indeed, some EI researchers have argued that improvements in parent–child interactions must occur for EI to be effective (Mahoney, Boyce, Fewell, Spiker, and Wheeden, 1998). Chapter 10 provides an overview of the evolution of the family-centered approach by one of its leading proponents. Chapter 11 reports on the effects of three EI program variables on several parent/family outcomes and chapter 12 examines family variables that predict parental involvement in EI programs.

References

Casto, G. C. & Mastropieri, M. A. (1986). The efficacy of early intervention programs: A meta-analysis. *Exceptional Children, 52,* 417–424.

Dunst, C. J., Trivette, C. M., & Thompson, R. B. (1994). Supporting and strengthening family functioning: Toward a congruence between principles and practice. In C. J. Dunst & C. M. Trivette (Eds), *Supporting & strengthening families, Vol. 1: Methods, strategies and practices* (pp. 49–59). Cambridge, MA: Brookline Books.

Guralnick, M. J. (1997). Second generation research in the field of early intervention. In M. J. Guralnick (Ed.), *The effectiveness of early intervention: Directions for second generation research* (pp. 3–20). Baltimore: Paul H. Brookes.

Mahoney, G., Boyce, G., Fewell, R. R., Spiker, D., & Wheeden, C. A. (1998). The relationship of parent–child interaction to the effectiveness of early intervention services for at-risk children and children with disabilities. *Topics in Early Childhood Special Education, 18,* 5–17.

Introduction to Chapter 10

Carl Dunst is a leader in the promotion of family empowerment and family-centered EI. He has developed and researched a model of EI that emphasizes social support as a key element in achieving positive child and family outcomes. He maintains that all forms of social support – both formal (i.e., services) and informal (e.g., family, friends) need to be part of an EI model. He maintains that informal support systems are more effective than professionally driven approaches, and that parents need to be in charge of the support process. In this chapter, Dunst updates his original theory based on an additional 15 years of research. His research is exemplary in taking "feel-good" philosophical principles – e.g., empowerment, promotion, family-based – and operationally defining them. He then empirically tests these practices on an array of family, parent, and child outcomes. His work has highlighted the crucial role of *how* (in addition to what) interventions are provided. Support and services can be either competency-enhancing or competency-inhibiting. Ironically, Dunst's research indicates that the more effective professional services emulate informal support help-giving. In this chapter, Dunst outlines a "third generation" of EI research that will aim to eliminate distinctions between child- and family-focused services and meld competency-enhancing everyday experiences with planned interventions.

TEN

Revisiting "Rethinking Early Intervention"

Carl J. Dunst

A confluence of theory and research in diverse but compatible fields of inquiry was used some fifteen years ago as a framework for proposing a social systems approach to early intervention (Dunst, 1985). "Rethinking Early Intervention" included a social support definition of early intervention, a set of principles for structuring the provision of social support, and a social systems framework for understanding the influences of social support (as well as other factors) on child, parent, and family functioning.

The conceptual and theoretical formulations described in "Rethinking Early Intervention" proved useful for guiding both research and practice, informing better operationalization of key concepts, and developing models and approaches to early intervention and family support. Key concepts have continually been revised and updated based on findings from our own research and practice, as well as that of others. In retrospect, the model building I attempted was somewhat crude, but it nonetheless stimulated a number of lines of research and practice, shedding light on the kinds of environmental experiences supporting and strengthening child, parent, and family functioning. The purposes of this article are threefold: (a) Summarize and comment on the content of "Rethinking Early Intervention," (b) revisit major theses in terms of changes and advances in model development, and (c) describe a third

Dunst, Carl J. (2000). Revisiting "rethinking early intervention." *Topics in Early Childhood Special Education, 20*, 95–104. Copyright © 2000 by PRO-ED, Inc, reprinted with permission.

generation model incorporating new knowledge into a framework for designing and implementing early intervention and family support.

Rethinking Early Intervention

Woven throughout "Rethinking Early Intervention" was an assertion that early intervention is an environmental variable and that children and their parents and families are the recipients of many different kinds of social support that can and often do function as a form of early intervention. Stated differently, social support was viewed as an important source of environmental opportunities and experiences contributing to variations in human development and functioning.

Social support definition of early intervention

Early intervention was defined as the "provision of support to families of infants and young children from members of informal and formal social support network members that impact both directly and indirectly upon parent, family, and child functioning" (Dunst, 1985, p. 179). Social support provided by informal and formal social support network members was viewed as the source of information, guidance, advice, and so on needed by parents for carrying out childrearing responsibilities and for promoting child learning and development (Bronfenbrenner, 1979). The time and energy and knowledge and skills gained by provision of support and the resources, experiences, opportunities, and so forth emanating from the support were viewed as necessary but not sufficient conditions for positively influencing child, parent, and family functioning.

The most radical feature of the definition was the contention that interventions should emphasize mobilization of supports from informal network members rather than relying solely or primarily on formal supports from professionals and professional help-giving agencies (Hobbs, 1975; Hobbs et al., 1984). At the time I attempted to draw implications of this assertion for practice, research was being conducted demonstrating the influences of social support from family members, friends, neighbors, and others on different aspects of personal and family well-being, parenting attitudes, parenting interactional styles, and parent attributions about various aspects of child behavior and competence (see Dunst, 1985). In addition to this research, "Rethinking Early Intervention" included preliminary data indicating that informal support (but not formal support) was positively related to different aspects of child, parent, and family functioning. This finding was somewhat puzzling and stimulated the conduct of several studies attempting to understand this perplexing result. What we found was both interesting and intriguing. Support provided by early intervention practitioners was judged as most helpful and beneficial when the practitioners were identified as members of a family's informal social support network. The opposite was the case when the practitioners were identified as members of the family's formal support network.

Proactive empowerment through partnerships

"Rethinking Early Intervention" proposed adoption of three principles as guiding beliefs for working with families. The Proactive Empowerment through Partnerships (PEP) principles were proposed as a way of reversing pathologic thinking about families and intervention practices. The first principle emphasized strengths rather than weaknesses or deficits as the focus of intervention practices (Hobbs, 1975; Zigler and Berman, 1983). The empowerment principle emphasized family control over and access to desired resources rather than provision of supports that were dependency-forming and competency-impeding (Rappaport, 1981). The partnership principle emphasized collaboration between families and practitioners, rather than the use of professionally centered approaches to intervention, as a primary means for supporting and strengthening family functioning (National Center for Clinical Infant Programs, 1985).

The PEP principles were viewed as a particular way of conceptualizing and structuring early intervention practices, and especially for altering attitudes toward family competence and practitioner's roles when interacting with families. As pointed out later, the PEP principles became the foundation of a new paradigm for conceptualizing and structuring different kinds of interventions building on the thoughtful work of many other individuals interested in similar issues (e.g., Foster, Berger, and McLean, 1981; Hobbs et al., 1984; Katz, 1984; Rappaport, 1981; Stoneman, 1985; Zigler and Berman, 1983).

Social systems theory

"Rethinking Early Intervention" included an integration of theoretical formulations and empirical evidence from social network theory (Mitchell and Trickett, 1980; Unger and Powell, 1980), ecological psychology (Bronfenbrenner, 1979; Cochran and Brassard, 1979), help seeking theory (Gourash, 1978), and adaptational theory (Crnic, Friedrich, and Greenberg, 1983). Social network theory is concerned with the properties of social support networks and how social network members are sources of support and resources nurturing and sustaining supportive relationships and exchanges among network members. Ecological psychology is concerned with the nature of relationships among people, groups, organizations, and such in different socioecological niches and how these relationships and events influence, both directly and indirectly, family functioning, parenting attitudes and competence, child behavior and development, and other aspects of human functioning. Help-seeking theory posits an inverse relationship between the provision of support from informal social network members and the need for professional services. Adaptational theory provides a framework for explaining reaction and adaptation to adverse life events, including the birth and rearing of a child with a disability. Collectively, these four frameworks formed the foundation for understanding how different personal and environmental factors contribute to variations in child, parent, and family functioning. The social systems model suggested by these separate but highly compatible theoretical orientations was systematically examined as part of a line of research studying the intrafamily and extrafamily factors associated with variations in different aspects of child, parent, and family functioning (e.g., Dunst and Trivette, 1988; Dunst, Trivette, and Cross, 1986; Dunst, Trivette, Hamby, and Pollock, 1990; Trivette, Dunst, and Hamby, 1996c).

Reflections and Revisions

Over time, my interest in family-centered practices has become primarily conceptual and empirical (Dunst, 1997; Dunst and Trivette, 1996) rather than philosophical. Philosophically, family-centered practices grounded in reasoning about what is the right thing to do without explicit regard to the characteristics and consequences of family-centered practices has always seemed to me shortsighted. I believe that a philosophically based, family-centered approach is likely to run its course as a fad and is open to all kinds of criticism, as has recently occurred (Feldman, Ploof, and Cohen, 1999; Mahoney et al., 1999). Furthermore, a philosophically based approach makes it too easy to make claims like, "We have always been family-centered" and not be held accountable for such claims.

In contrast to a philosophical orientation, studying family-centered principles and practices conceptually and empirically has permitted advances in our understanding of the construct "family-centeredness," its operational features, and the relationship between adoption and adherence to family-centered practices and their influence on people who are treated in this way. Conceptually, the practices which operationally define a family-centered approach, and which differentiate it from other ways of working with families (Dunst, Johanson, Trivette, and Hamby, 1991), are now known to be part of a new paradigm (see below) for conceptualizing and implementing environmental interventions (Dunst, 1997). Empirically, evidence is accumulating about the kinds of family-centered practices most important in terms of their positive consequences (Trivette and Dunst, 1998) and how interventions done in a family-centered manner are related to improved functioning in a number of life domains (Dunst, 1999b; Dunst and Trivette, 1996).

Paradigms and models

In addition to influencing thinking about family-centered practices, the PEP principles were the impetus for several lines of inquiry and research on different models for structuring and implementing intervention practices. This included efforts to understand the operational characteristics of promotion (Dunst, Trivette, and Thompson, 1990), strengths- and asset-based (Dunst, 1998), empowerment (Dunst, Trivette, and LaPointe, 1992), resource-based (Trivette, Dunst, and Deal, 1997), and partnership (Dunst, Johanson, Rounds, Trivette, and Hamby, 1992; Dunst and Paget, 1991) models.

An extensive review of the human services and health care literature was the foundation for a differentiation between treatment, prevention, and promotion models and the synthesis of relevant research about the consequences of interventions based on each model (Dunst, Trivette, and Thompson, 1990). Findings led us to contend that the absence of problems cannot be taken to mean the presence of positive functioning; therefore, treating or preventing problems or poor functioning was not the same as enhancing or strengthening capacity (see especially Bond, 1982; Cowen, 1994; Seeman, 1989). Strengths- and asset-based models evolved in response to the increased recognition that building on strengths, interests, preferences, and so forth is a more productive approach to affecting behavior change than are efforts directed primarily toward correcting weaknesses or alleviating deficits (Benson, 1997; Kretzmann and McKnight, 1993). The thoughtful work of Rappaport (1981) was used as a basis for investigating the operational features of an empowerment model (Dunst, Trivette, et al., 1992), and the kinds of help-giving practices most likely to have empowering consequences (Dunst and Trivette, 1996; Trivette and Dunst, 1998). Contradictions inherent in professionally centered and service-based approaches and solutions to problems (Sarason, Carroll, Maton, Cohen, and Lorentz, 1977) were used as the foundation for proposing a resource-based approach to intervention where the resources afforded by social support network members, rather than services made available by professional programs and agencies, were viewed as the experiences and opportunities strengthening and promoting competence.

Taken together, the operational characteristics of promotion, strengths-based, resource-based, and empowerment models became part of a new paradigm for conceptualizing, developing, and implementing different kinds of intervention programs and practices (see Dunst and Trivette, 1997). Table 10.1 contrasts the new paradigm characteristics with those of a more traditional approach to human services intervention. Corroborating research now indicates that practices aligned with the new paradigm models (see Dunst and Trivette, 1997) produce more positive benefits than do more traditional practices, at least in certain areas of functioning. Recent evidence indicates that, in some cases, traditional practices are actually associated with negative effects in certain domains of functioning (Dunst, 1999b; Dunst, Hamby, and Brookfield, 1999).

In contrast to the above, conceptualizations and operationalization of the partnership construct have not proved as fruitful. Our own work, as well as that of others (see Dunst, Trivette, and Snyder, 2000), on family/professional partnerships has led us, despite the appeal of the term, to reconsider earlier contentions about the primary importance

Table 10.1 Defining features of contrasting approaches for conceptualizing and implementing Early Intervention

New paradigm	Traditional paradigm
• *Promotion models*: Focus on enhancement and optimization of competence and positive functioning	• *Treatment models*: Focus on remediation of a disorder, problem, or disease, or its consequence
• *Empowerment models*: Create opportunities for people to exercise existing capabilities, as well as develop new competencies	• *Expertise models*: Depend on professional expertise to solve problems for people
• *Strengths-based models*: Recognize the assets and talents of people, and help people use these competencies to strengthen functioning	• *Deficit-based models*: Focus on correcting people's weaknesses or problems
• *Resource-based models*: Define practices in terms of a broad range of community opportunities and experiences	• *Service-based models*: Define practices primarily in terms of professional services
• *Family-centered models*: View professionals as agents of families and responsive	• *Professionally centered models*: View professionals as experts who determine the needs of people from their own as opposed to other people's perspectives

of the partnership construct for intervention (Dunst, 1985; Dunst, Trivette, et al., 1988). A critical review of the partnership literature finds that the term is not well defined, there is little agreement about its operational characteristics, the characteristics identified as the indicators of partnerships are not different from those of other kinds of interpersonal relationships, and the benefits associated with partnership relationships have not been well documented (Dunst et al., 2000). The primacy I (Dunst, 1985) and others have given to family/professional partnerships seems to have diverted attention away from program and practitioner factors that matter more in terms of positive consequences

(Dunst and Trivette, 1997). As part of our critical analysis of the partnership literature, we argued that partnerships are best thought of as a particular kind of participatory helping experience contributing to empowerment-type consequences, rather than as a special kind of practice (Dunst et al., 2000).

Definition of early intervention

The definition of early intervention originally proposed in "Rethinking Early Intervention" has been changed only slightly: Early intervention is the provision of support and resources to families of young children from members of informal and formal social support networks that both directly and indirectly influence child, parent, and family functioning (Dunst, Trivette, and Jodry, 1997). However, our understanding of key features of the definition and its implications for practice have changed. First, it is now generally acknowledged that a family's social network provides support and resources needed for everyday living, carrying out parenting responsibilities, and supporting child learning and development. This often includes support from a mix of intrafamily, informal, community, and formal social network members. Second, the supportive exchanges that occur among social support network members constitute the contexts for a broad range of environmental experiences and opportunities influencing child, parent, and family behavior and development. These experiences and opportunities are now recognized as the kinds of supportive exchanges strengthening existing competence and promoting new capabilities (Bronfenbrenner, 1992). Third, because social support is an environmental variable, it "appears to operate whether or not [it is] deliberately manipulated" (Horowitz, 1994, p. 32). Consequently, any number of supportive experiences and opportunities, besides those associated with more traditional early intervention program practices, can and do operate as early intervention. Fourth, depending on the kind of support provided and the recipient of the support, it can have either direct or indirect influences on a developing child, his or her parents, and the family (see below).

An extensive review of the social support literature (Dunst et al., 1997) with a focus on how and in what manner support functions as early intervention indicated that research findings reinforce the assertion regarding the importance of informal supports from personal network members (Dunst, 1985; Hobbs, 1975). Findings as a whole indicate that informal rather than formal support shows the strongest relationship to any number of child, parent, and family outcomes. Our understanding of why this is true is no longer perplexing. Social support provided in a way that mirrors the characteristics of family-centered help-giving seems to bolster the positive influence of the resources provided by personal network members (Dunst and Trivette, 1997; Dunst et al., 1997).

Social systems theory

Research using social systems theory focused on the direct and indirect influences of social support on child, parent, and family functioning (Dunst et al., 1997). Practice focused on identifying the principles, guidelines, methods, and strategies operationally defining a family systems approach to intervention (Dunst, Trivette, et al., 1988; Dunst, Trivette, and Deal, 1994).

Social Support Research

Figure 10.1 shows the model that evolved from our understanding of the linkages between social support and other domains of functioning with an eye on the influence of social support as a form of early intervention (see Dunst, 1999b; Trivette et al., 1996c). According to this model, social support and resources directly influence the health and

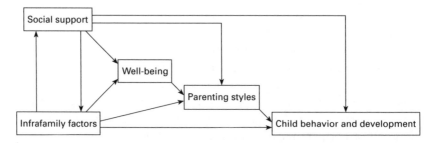

Figure 10.1 Model depicting the direct and indirect influences of social support (environmental variable) and intrafamily factors (person variables) on parent and family well-being, parenting styles, and child behavior and development

well-being of a support recipient; both support and health/well-being influence parenting styles, and support, well-being, and parenting styles directly and indirectly influence child behavior and development. In addition, intrafamily factors, including, but not limited to, family SES, parent coping, and child characteristics (e.g., temperament) were examined in terms of their influence on well-being, parenting styles, and child behavior and development.

Our own research (see Dunst et al., 1997), as well as that of others (e.g., Affleck, Tennen, Rowe, Roscher, and Walker, 1989), indicates that there are complex but nonetheless discernable relationships between social support and different aspects of child, parent, and family functioning. For example, Dunst (1999b) reported findings demonstrating the direct and indirect influences of social support and family SES on parent well-being and parent interactional styles and the influences highly supportive and minimally directive parenting styles have on child development (see also Dunst et al., 1997). On the one hand, this kind of research indicates that social support indeed appears to operate as a form of intervention, and on the other hand helps make clear the linkages and relationships between different aspects of intrafamily and extrafamily factors and their influences on child, parent, and family functioning.

Family systems intervention

Fast forwarding through different attempts to identify and operationalize key components of a family system approach to intervention (Dunst, Trivette, et al., 1988; Dunst, Trivette, and Deal, 1994; Trivette, Deal, and Dunst, 1986), we arrive at the model shown in figure 10.2. The intersecting components of the model (family concerns and priorities, family competence and assets, family/community resources and supports) depict the relationships between family desires, the supports and resources necessary to achieve desired outcomes, and the family's use of individual and collective capabilities for mobilizing its social support network. The family-centered help-giving practices component defines the behaviors used by practitioners for both supporting and strengthening family functioning and for promoting competence for family acquisition of desired resources and outcomes. Viewed somewhat differently, the intersecting components of the model pertain to what is done, and the family-centered help-giving component emphasizes how

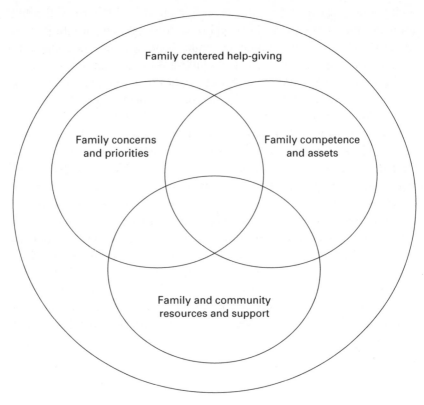

Figure 10.2 Four components of a family system intervention model

interventions are done. This distinction is an important one in light of evidence indicating that how help is provided matters as much, if not more, than what is done if positive consequences are to be realized (e.g., Karuza, Rabinowitz, and Zevon, 1986).

Research and practice on the different components of the model have been a major focus of work during the past 15 years (e.g., Dunst and Leet, 1987; Dunst and Trivette, 1996; Dunst, Trivette, Gordon, and Pletcher, 1989; Dunst, Trivette, and Mott, 1994; Trivette et al., 1997). The outcomes have included a better understanding of the operational features of each component of the model as well as adoption of specific paradigms for structuring interventions in each component. This has included a better understanding of the conditions and processes influencing family desires and concerns (e.g., Dunst, Leet, and Trivette, 1988), the identification and actualization of child, parent, and family assets (Dunst, 1998), and the use of a resource-based model for promoting the flow of resources for achieving desired outcomes (Trivette et al., 1997).

The help-giving practices component of the model has received considerable investigative attention as a result of findings indicating that it matters a great deal in terms of how help is provided if it is to have optimal positive benefits. Based on findings from an ongoing line of help-giving research (see Trivette and Dunst, 1998), we concluded that family-centered practices are a special case of effective help-giving based on the observation that the principles and practices operationally defining a family-centered approach are nearly identical to those identified as the help-giving attitudes, beliefs, and behaviors most associated with competency-enhancing and empowering consequences. This led us to describe these practices as family-centered help-giving (Dunst and Trivette, 1996).

As a result of our research, the key features of the help-giving practices component of our model have become very explicit. We now know that effective family-centered help-giving is comprised of both relational and participatory elements. Relational elements include behavior typically associated with good clinical practice (active listening, empathy, etc.) and positive helpgiver attributions and beliefs about family competence and capability. Participatory elements include family choice and action based on choice, as well as helpgiver responsiveness to and support of family decisions. Whereas relational practices are a necessary condition for effective practitioner/family transactions, they are not sufficient for either strengthening family competence or promoting new capabilities. The latter has been found to be the case only when the family is an active participant in achieving desired outcomes (Dunst, 1997; Trivette, Dunst, Boyd, and Hamby, 1995–1996; Trivette, Dunst, and Hamby, 1996a, 1996b). Placed in a wider web of the direct and indirect social systems influences on child, parent, and family functioning, family-centered help-giving mediates and moderates the influences of other intrafamily and extrafamily factors on various outcomes (Dunst, 1999b; Dunst, Brookfield, and Epstein, 1998; Dunst et al., 1999).

Future Directions

"Rethinking Early Intervention" constituted a first generation model
for describing the principles and elements of a particular approach to
family systems intervention. The Reflections and Revisions section of
this paper included material pertaining to advances in our understanding of the broader-based parameters and characteristics of family systems intervention. The updated model, the new paradigm upon which
it is based (see table 10.1), and research disentangling the characteristics and consequences of various kinds of social support comprises
a second generation model. A third generation model is indicated for
at least two reasons. The first has to do with the need for resolution of
an ongoing misunderstanding about the intervention targets of family
systems intervention. The second has to do with a need to incorporate
further advances into a model that broadens attention to other important aspects of environmental influences and interventions.

As originally envisioned and is still the case, family in our family
systems approach meant the family as a whole, as well as individual
family members, including the child constituting the focus of entry into
early intervention. Somehow the child got lost in the minds of some in
terms of being a family member. This has led to comparisons and contrasts between family-centered/family systems models and other child-
focused, relationship-focused, and parent–child focused models (Kelly
and Barnard, 1999; Mahoney et al., 1999; Weston, Ivins, Heffron, and
Sweet, 1997) that seem to me artificial and divisive (Dunst, 1999b). In
the context of a broader-based social systems model, these other kinds
of interventions are all environmental factors (Bronfenbrenner, 1992)
that function as sources of opportunities (Garbarino and Abramowitz,
1992) to the extent they support and strengthen child, as well as parent and family functioning. Despite this, it now seems to me that any
model that is going to be useful needs to explicitly incorporate parent–
child and child features into it if the debate about family-centered/
family support models versus any other kind of model is to be abated.
This is especially the case in light of convincing evidence about the contextual and sociocultural foundations of child learning and development
and parenting and child rearing roles and styles most conducive to promoting child competence (e.g., Bornstein, 1991; Bronfenbrenner, 1999;
Goncu, 1999; Lancy, 1996; Rogoff, Mistry, Goncu, and Mosier, 1993).

The kind of model that would directly address the above features, as well as retain key features from our family systems model for intervention, has been the focus of my attention for the past several years (Dunst, 1999a). The integrated framework that is emerging is evidence based. Evidence from diverse but compatible lines of research have been synthesized with an emphasis on the social systems and environmental variables that are associated with development-enhancing and family-strengthening consequences. The model is shown in figure 10.3. Early intervention conceptualized in this way includes children's learning opportunities (Dunst and Bruder, 1999), parenting supports (Cowan, Powell, and Cowan, 1998), and family/community supports (Trivette et al., 1997) provided in a family-centered manner (Trivette and Dunst, 1998). Development-enhancing child learning opportunities are ones that are interesting, engaging, and competency producing and result in a child's sense of mastery about his or her capabilities. Parenting supports include the information, advice, and guidance that both strengthen existing parenting knowledge and skills and promote acquisition of new competencies necessary to carry out childrearing responsibilities and provide development-enhancing learning opportunities. Family and community supports include any number and type of intrafamily, informal, community, and formal resources needed by parents to have the time and energy to engage in parenting and childrearing activities. Family-centered practices place families in central and pivotal roles in decisions and actions involving child, parent, and family priorities and preferences. The provision and mobilization of child learning opportunities, parenting supports, and family/community resources strengthen existing capabilities and promote child, parent, and family competence.

In addition to the key elements of each dimension of the model, the intersections of the overlapping dimensions operationally define additional elements of effective practices (see Figure 10.3). The intersection of children's learning opportunities and family/community supports defines the activity settings serving as the sources and contexts of natural learning opportunities as part of family and community life (Dunst and Bruder, 1999). Activity settings include the many different experiences and opportunities afforded children as part of daily living, child and family routines, family rituals, special occasions and events, family and community celebrations and traditions, and so forth that are either planned or happen serendipitously and which across time and in their aggregate constitute the life experiences of a developing

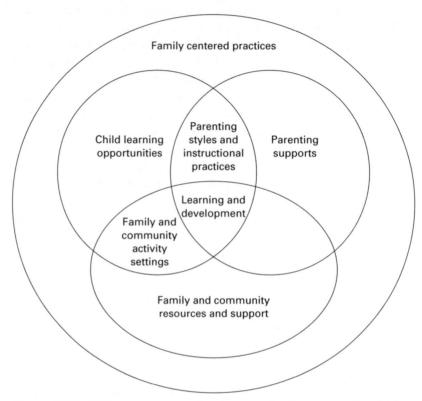

Figure 10.3 Major components of an integrated evidence-based model for early intervention and family support

child (Bronfenbrenner, 1992). The intersection of children's learning opportunities and parenting supports define the parenting styles and instructional practices most likely to have development-enhancing consequences. The research literature on the characteristics and consequences of different kinds of parenting styles (e.g., Mahoney, 1988; Schaffer, 1977) and instructional practices (see Wolery, 1994; Wolery and Sainato, 1996) is extensive and directly informs practice about the social environmental conditions best suited for promoting child competence. Parenting styles and instructional practices characterized by contingent responsiveness to child-initiated and -directed behavior, and caregiver behavior that provides children opportunities for practicing emerging skills and elaborating on existing capabilities, are ones most likely to have competency-enhancing effects. The intersection of parenting and family/community supports defines the kinds of participatory and interactional opportunities parents have with personal social support network members influencing parenting attitudes and behaviors. According to Cochran (1990, 1993), parents' support networks influence parenting by providing emotional and instrumental support, encouraging or discouraging specific parenting attitudes and behaviors, and providing models and opportunities to learn alternative or new parenting and childrearing interactional styles.

The third generation model briefly described here is currently being used for guiding research that is investigating different environmental factors functioning as interventions – both intentionally planned and as part of naturally occurring life experiences and opportunities. The model is also being used as a framework for conceptualizing and structuring early intervention and family support. Inasmuch as the knowledge base about the environmental factors associated with positive child, parent, and family outcomes directly informs practice by specifying the conditions that ought to be emulated and mirrored, the implications and usefulness of the model become apparent. As has been the case with the first and second generation models, the third generation model, and lessons learned from research and practice using it, ought to inform further advances in our understanding of effective, evidence-based approaches to early intervention.

References

Affleck, G., Tennen, H., Rowe, J., Roscher, B., & Walker, L. (1989). Effects of formal supports on mothers' adaptation to the hospital-to-home transition of high risk infants: The benefits and costs of helping. *Child Development, 60,* 488–501.

Benson, R. (1997). *All kids are our kids.* San Francisco: Jossey-Bass.

Bond, L. (1982). From prevention to promotion: Optimizing infant development. In L. Bond & J. Joffe (Eds.), *Facilitating infant and early childhood development* (pp. 5–39). Hanover, NH: University Press of New England.

Bornstein, M. H. (Ed.). (1991). *Cultural approaches to parenting.* Hillsdale, NJ: Erlbaum.

Bronfenbrenner, U. (1979). *The ecology of human development: Experiments by nature and design.* Cambridge, MA: Harvard University Press.

Bronfenbrenner, U. (1992). Ecological systems theory. In R. Vasta (Ed.), *Six theories of child development: Revised formulations and current issues* (pp. 187–248). Philadelphia: Jessica Kingsley.

Bronfenbrenner, U. (1999). Environments in developmental perspective: Theoretical and operational models. In S. L. Friedman & T. D. Wachs (Eds.), *Measuring environment across the life span: Emerging methods and concepts* (pp. 3–28). Washington, DC: American Psychological Association.

Cochran, M. (1990). Personal networks in the ecology of human development. In M. Cochran, M. Larner, D. Riley, L. Gunnarson, & C. Henderson (Eds.), *Extending families: The social networks of parents and their children* (pp. 3–33). New York: Cambridge University Press.

Cochran, M. (1993). Parenting and personal social networks. In T. Luster & L. Okagaki (Eds.), *Parenting: An ecological perspective* (pp. 149–178). Hillsdale, NJ: Erlbaum.

Cochran, M., & Brassard, J. (1979). Child development and personal social networks. *Child Development, 50*, 601–616.

Cowan, P., Powell, D., & Cowan, C. (1998). Parenting interventions: A family systems perspective. In W. Damon (Series Ed.), I. E. Sigel, & K. A. Renninger (Vol. Eds.), *Handbook of child psychology: Vol. 4. Child psychology in practice* (5th ed., pp. 3–72). New York: Wiley.

Cowen, E. L. (1994). The enhancement of psychological wellness: Challenges and opportunities. *American Journal of Community Psychology, 22*, 149–179.

Crnic, K., Friedrich, W., & Greenberg, M. (1983). Adaptation of families with mentally retarded children: A model of stress, coping and family ecology. *American Journal of Mental Deficiency, 88*, 125–138.

Dokecki, P. R. (1983). The place of values in the world of psychology and public policy. *Peabody Journal of Education, 60*, 108–125.

Dokecki, P. R., & Heflinger, C. A. (1989). Strengthening families of young children with handicapping conditions: Mapping backward from the "street level." In J. J. Gallagher, P. L. Trohanis, & R. M. Clifford (Eds.), *Policy implementation and PL 99-457: Planning for young children with special needs* (pp. 59–84). Baltimore: Brookes.

Dunst, C. J. (1985). Rethinking early intervention. *Analysis and Intervention in Developmental Disabilities, 5*, 165–201.

Dunst, C. J. (1990). Family support principles: Checklists for program builders and practitioners. *Family Systems Intervention Monograph Series, 2*, Number 5. Morganton, NC: Western Carolina Center, Family, Infant and Preschool Program.

Dunst, C. J. (1995). *Key characteristics and features of community-based family support programs.* Chicago: Family Resource Coalition.

Dunst, C. J. (1997). Conceptual and empirical foundations of family-centered practice. In R. Illback, C. Cobb, & H. Joseph, Jr. (Eds.), *Integrated services for children and families: Opportunities for psychological practice* (pp. 75–91). Washington, DC: American Psychological Association.

Dunst, C. J. (1998, July). Identifying and building on child, family and community assets. Paper presented at the Hilton Head Summer Institute, Hilton Head, SC.

Dunst, C. J. (1999a). An integrated framework for studying the influences of environmental factors on child, parent and family functioning: Implications for investigating and practicing early intervention and family support. Manuscript in preparation.

Dunst, C. J. (1999b). Placing parent education in conceptual and empirical context. *Topics in Early Childhood Special Education, 19,* 141–147.

Dunst, C. J., Brookfield, J., & Epstein, J. (1998, December). *Family-centered early intervention and child, parent and family benefits: Final report.* Asheville, NC: Orelena Hawks Pucker Institute.

Dunst, C. J., & Bruder, M. B. (1999). Family and community activity settings, natural learning environments, and children's learning opportunities. *Children's Learning Opportunities Report, 1*(2).

Dunst, C. J., Hamby, D., & Brookfield, J. (1999). Modeling the effects of early intervention variables on parent and family well-being. Manuscript in preparation.

Dunst, C. J., Johanson, C., Rounds, T., Trivette, C. M., & Hamby, D. (1992). Characteristics of parent–professional partnership. In S. Christenson & J. C. Conoley (Eds.), *Home–school collaboration: Building a fundamental educational resource* (pp. 157–174). Washington, DC: National Association of School Psychologists.

Dunst, C. J., Johanson, C., Trivette, C. M., & Hamby, D. (1991). Family-oriented early intervention policies and practices: Family-centered or not? *Exceptional Children, 58,* 115–126.

Dunst, C. J., & Leer, H. E. (1987). Measuring the adequacy of resources in households with young children. *Child: Care, Health and Development, 13,* 111–125.

Dunst, C. J., Leet, H. E., & Trivette, C. M. (1988). Family resources, personal well-being, and early intervention. *Journal of Special Education, 22,* 108–116.

Dunst, C. J., & Paget, K. (1991). Parent–professional partnerships and family empowerment. In M. Fine (Ed.), *Collaboration with parents of exceptional children* (pp. 25–44). Brandon, VT: Clinical Psychology.

Dunst, C. J., & Trivette, C. M. (1988). Determinants of parent and child interactive behavior. In K. Marfo (Ed.), *Parent-child interaction and development disabilities* (pp. 3–31). New York: Praeger.

Dunst, C. J., & Trivette, C. M. (1996). Empowerment, effective help-giving practices and family-centered care. *Pediatric Nursing, 22,* 334–337, 343.

Dunst, C. J., & Trivette, C. M. (1997). Early intervention with young at-risk children and their families. In R. Ammerman & M. Hersen (Eds.), *Handbook of prevention and treatment with children and adolescents: Intervention in the real world* (pp. 157–180). New York: Wiley.

Dunst, C. J., Trivette, C. M., & Cross, A. H. (1986). Mediating influences of social support: Personal, family, and child outcomes. *American Journal of Mental Deficiency, 90*, 403–417.

Dunst, C. J., Trivette, C. M., & Deal, A. G. (1988). *Enabling and empowering families: Principles and guidelines for practice.* Cambridge, MA: Brookline Books.

Dunst, C. J., Trivette, C. M., & Deal, A. G. (Eds.). (1994). *Supporting and strengthening families: Methods, strategies and practices.* Cambridge, MA: Brookline Books.

Dunst, C. J., Trivette, C. M., Gordon, N. J., & Pletcher, L. L. (1989). Building and mobilizing informal family support networks. In G. H. Singer & L. Irvin (Eds.), *Support for caregiving families* (pp. 121–141). Baltimore: Brookes.

Dunst, C. J., Trivette, C. M., Gordon, N. J., & Starnes, A. L. (1993). Family-centered case management practices: Characteristics and consequences. In G. H. Singer & L. L. Powers (Eds.), *Families, disability, and empowerment: Active coping skills and strategies for family interventions* (pp. 89–118). Baltimore: Brookes.

Dunst, C. J., Trivette, C. M., Hamby, D., & Pollock, B. (1990). Family systems correlates of the behavior of young children with handicaps. *Journal of Early Intervention, 14*, 204–218.

Dunst, C. J., Trivette, C. M., & Jodry, W. (1997). Influences of social support on children with disabilities and their families. In M. Guralnick (Ed.), *The effectiveness of early intervention* (pp. 499–522). Baltimore: Brookes.

Dunst, C. J., Trivette, C. M., & LaPointe, N. (1992). Toward clarification of the meaning and key elements of empowerment. *Family Science Review, 5*(1/2), 111–130.

Dunst, C. J., Trivette, C. M., & Mort, D. W. (1994). Strengths-based family-centered intervention practices. In C. J. Dunst, C. M. Trivette, & A. G. Deal (Eds.), *Supporting and strengthening families: Methods, strategies and practices* (pp. 115–131). Cambridge, MA: Brookline Books.

Dunst, C. J., Trivette, C. M., & Snyder, D. (2000). Family–professional partnerships: A behavioral science perspective. In M. Fine & L. Sherrod (Eds.), *Collaboration with parents and families of children and youth with exceptionalities* (2nd edn, pp. 27–48). Austin, TX: PRO-ED.

Dunst, C. J., Trivette, C. M., & Thompson, R. B. (1990). Supporting and strengthening family functioning: Toward a congruence between principles and practice. *Prevention in Human Services, 9*(1), 19–43.

Family Resource Coalition. (1987). *What are the assumptions of the Family Resource Movement?* Chicago: Family Resource Coalition.

Feldman, H. M., Ploof, D., & Cohen, W. I. (1999). Physician–family partnerships: The adaptive practice model. *Developmental and Behavioral Pediatrics, 20*, 111–116.

Foster, M., Berger, M., & McLean, M. (1981). Rethinking a good idea: A reassessment of parent involvement. *Topics in Early Childhood Special Education,* *1*(3), 55–65.

Garbarino, J. (1983). Social support networks: RX for the helping professionals. In J. Whittaker & J. Garbarino (Eds.), *Social support networks: Informal helping in the human services* (pp. 3–28). New York: Aldine.

Garbarino, J., & Abramowitz, R. (1992). The ecology of human development. In J. Garbarino (Ed.), *Children and families in the social environment* (2nd edn, pp. 11–33). New York: de Gruyter.

Goncu, A. (Ed.). (1999). *Children's engagement in the world: Socio-cultural perspectives.* Cambridge, England: Cambridge University Press.

Gourash, N. (1978). Help seeking: A review of the literature. *American Journal of Community Psychology, 6,* 413–423.

Hobbs, N. (1975). *The future of children.* San Francisco: Jossey-Bass.

Hobbs, N., Dokecki, R, Hoover-Dempsey, K., Moroney, R., Shayne, M., & Weeks, K. (1984). *Strengthening families.* San Francisco: Jossey-Bass.

Horowitz, F. D. (1994). Developmental theory, prediction, and the developmental equation in follow-up research: Introduction. In S. L. Friedman & H. C. Haywood (Eds.), *Developmental follow-up: Concepts, domains, and methods* (pp. 27–44). San Diego: Academic Press.

Kaiser, A. P., & Hemmeter, M. L. (1989). Value-based approaches to family intervention. *Topics in Early Childhood Special Education, 8*(4), 72–86.

Karuza, J., Rabinowitz, V., & Zevon, M. (1986). Implications of control and responsibility on helping the aged. In M. Baltes & P. Bakes (Eds.), *The psychology of control and aging* (pp. 373–396). Hillside, NJ: Erlbaum.

Katz, R. (1984). Empowerment and synergy: Expanding the community's healing process. In J. Rappaport, C. Swift, & R. Hess (Eds.), *Studies in empowerment: Steps toward understanding and action* (pp. 201–226). New York: Haworth.

Kelly, J. F., & Barnard, K. E. (1999). Parent education within a relationship-focused model. *Topics in Early Childhood Special Education, 19,* 151–157.

Kretzmann, J., & McKnight, J. (1993). *Building community from the inside out.* Evanston, IL: Northwestern University, Center for Urban Affairs and Policy Research.

Lancy, D. R. (1996). *Playing on the mother ground: Cultural routines for children development.* New York: Guilford Press.

Mahoney, G. (1988). Enhancing the developmental competence of handicapped infants. In K. Marfo (Ed.), *Parent–child interaction and developmental disabilities: Theory, research, and intervention* (pp. 203–219). New York: Praeger.

Mahoney, G., Kaiser, A., Girolametto, L., MacDonald, J., Robinson, C., Safford, P., & Spiker, D. (1999). Parent education in early intervention: A call for a renewed focus. *Topics in Early Childhood Special Education, 19,* 131–140.

Mitchell, R. E., & Trickett, E. J. (1980). Task force report: Social networks as mediators of social support. *Community Mental Health Journal, 16,* 27–43.

National Center for Clinical Infant Programs. (1985). *Equals in this partnership: Parents of disabled and at-risk infants and toddlers speak to professionals.* Washington, DC: National Centre for Clinical Infant Programs.

Rappaport, J. (1981). In praise of paradox: A social policy of empowerment over prevention. *American Journal of Community Psychology, 9,* 1–25.

Rogoff, B., Mistry, J., Goncu, A., & Mosier, C. (1993). Guided participation in cultural activities by toddlers and caregivers. *Monographs of the Society for Research in Child Development, 58*(8, Serial No. 236).

Sarason, S. B., Carroll, C., Maton, K., Cohen, S., & Lorentz, E. (1977). Human services and resources networks: Rationale, possibilities, and public policy. Cambridge, MA: Brookline Books.

Schaffer, R. (1977). *Mothering.* Cambridge, MA: Harvard University Press.

Seeman, J. (1989). Toward a model of positive health. *American Psychologist, 44,* 1099–1109.

Shelton, T. L., Jeppson, E. S., & Johnson, B. H. (1987). *Family-centered care for children with special health care needs.* Bethesda, MD: Association for the Care of Children's Health.

Stoneman, Z. (1985). Family involvement in early childhood special education programs. In N. Fallen & W. Umansky (Eds.), *Young children with special needs* (2nd edn, pp. 442–469). Columbus, OH: Merrill.

Trivette, C. M., Deal, A., & Dunst, C. J. (1986). Family needs, sources of support, and professional roles: Critical elements of family systems assessment and intervention. *Diagnostique, 11,* 246–267.

Trivette, C. M., & Dunst, C. J. (1998, December). Family-centered helpgiving practices. Paper presented at the 14th Annual Division for Early Childhood International Conference on Children with Special Needs, Chicago.

Trivette, C. M., Dunst, C. J., Boyd, K., & Hamby, D. W. (1995–1996). Family-oriented program models, helpgiving practices, and parental control appraisals. *Exceptional Children, 62,* 237–248.

Trivette, C. M., Dunst, C. J., & Deal, A. G. (1997). Resource-based approach to early intervention. In S. K. Thurman, J. R. Cornwell, & S. R. Gottwald (Eds.), *Contexts of early intervention: Systems and settings* (pp. 73–92). Baltimore: Brookes.

Trivette, C. M., Dunst, C. J., & Hamby, D. W. (1996a). Characteristics and consequences of help-giving practices in contrasting human services programs. *American Journal of Community Psychology, 24,* 273–293.

Trivette, C. M., Dunst, C. J., & Hamby, D. W. (1996b). Factors associated with perceived control appraisals in a family-centered early intervention program. *Journal of Early Intervention, 20,* 165–178.

Trivette, C. M., Dunst, C. J., & Hamby, D. W. (1996c). Social support and coping in families of children at risk for developmental disabilities. In M. Brambring, H. Rauh, & A. Beelmann (Eds.), *Early childhood intervention: Theory, evaluation and practice* (pp. 234–264). Berlin, Germany: de Gruyter.

Unger, D. G., & Powell, D. R. C. (1980). Supporting families under stress: The role of social networks. *Family Relations: Journal of Applied Family and Child Studies, 29,* 566–574.

Weston, D. R., Ivins, B., Heffron, M. C., & Sweet, N. (1997). Formulating the centrality of relationships in early intervention: An organizational perspective. *Infants and Young Children, 9*(3), 1–12.

Wolery, M. (1994). Instructional strategies for teaching young children with special needs. In M. Wolery & J. Wilbers (Eds.), *Including children with special needs in early childhood programs* (pp. 119–140). Washington, DC: National Association for the Education of Young Children.

Wolery, M., & Sainato, D. M. (1996). General curriculum and intervention strategies. In S. L. Odom & M. E. McLean (Eds.), *Early intervention/early childhood special education: Recommended practices* (pp. 125–158). Austin, TX: PRO-ED.

Zigler, E., & Berman, W. (1983). Discerning the future of early childhood intervention. *American Psychologist, 38,* 894–906.

Introduction to Chapter 11

Despite the strong philosophical support for a family-centered model of EI and the proliferation of such services, little research exists showing that the other family members benefit directly from participation in these programs. In this longitudinal study, three parent/family outcomes – parent stress, perception of the helpfulness of social support, and family cohesion – were investigated before and after intervention. Service variables were summarized into intensity, duration, and comprehensiveness. The different EI service variables had differential effects on the three parent/family outcome measures. The study would have been strengthened by controlled comparisons and presentation of possible developmental functions arising from their findings. The authors highlight both the strengths and limitations of their study, and suggest avenues of future research (one of which – factors influencing parent participation – is addressed in the next chapter).

ELEVEN

The Effect of Early Intervention Services on Maternal Well-being

Marji Erickson Warfield, Penny
Hauser-Cram, Marty Wyngaarden
Krauss, Jack P. Shonkoff,
and Carole C. Upshur

The Effect of Early Intervention Services on Maternal Well-being

The effectiveness of early intervention services for young children with disabilities has been a critical area of inquiry for the last 25 years. Recent reviews (e.g., Guralnick, 1998) as well as past meta-analyses (Casto and Mastropieri, 1986; Shonkoff and Hauser-Cram, 1987) indicate that children with disabilities who participate in early intervention services have developmental advantages over comparison groups. Most studies on the effectiveness of early intervention (EI), however, have focused on child outcomes (Bailey, et al., 1998), especially cognitive performance (e.g., Dunst and Trivette, 1994).

Although EI services aim to prevent or minimize children's developmental problems, such services do not focus exclusively on children's cognitive growth (Guralnick, 1997). Since the passage of Part H of the Education of the Handicapped Act Amendments of 1986 (PL 99-457),

Erickson Warfield, M., Hauser-Cram, P., Wyngaarden Krauss, M., Shonkoff, J.P., Upshur, C.C. (2000). The effect of early intervention services on maternal well-being. *Early Education and Development, 11*, 499–517.

which was renamed Part C of the reauthorized Individuals with Disabilities Education Act (IDEA) (PL 105-17) in 1997, EI services have evolved from a primary focus on the child to an emphasis on the family system in which the child is nurtured. According to Part H (now Part C), the primary goal of EI is "to enhance the capacity of families to meet the special needs of their infants and toddlers with disabilities" (Education of the Handicapped Act Amendments of 1986, Pub. L. No. 99-457, 100 Stat. 1145). Indeed, the requirement that EI programs develop an Individualized Family Service Plan (IFSP) illustrates the acknowledgment by both policy makers and service providers that families are central to the development of children with special needs (Krauss, 1990). From this perspective, children with disabilities, like typically developing children, are viewed as being embedded within an ecological network of systems where the family is the core and where services like EI have impacts on both the family and the child (Bronfenbrenner, 1986; Lerner, 1998). Thus, rather than being primarily child-focused, EI programs for children with disabilities tend to function more broadly as family support services (Dunst, Trivette, and Jodry, 1997).

What can be said, however, about the extent to which and the ways in which EI services affect families? Stated differently, how much, if any, of the observed changes in parental well-being and family functioning that occur during the early childhood period can be attributed to the provision of early intervention services? This is a thorny and largely unanswered question, but one that is asked repeatedly by researchers, service providers, and policy analysts.

The importance of family functioning and parenting skills for children's development has received considerable theoretical and empirical support. Most recently, Guralnick (1998) presented a developmental approach for the study of child outcomes and reviewed the empirical evidence regarding the importance of experiential factors governing the course of a child's cognitive development, including the quality of parent-child interactions, family-orchestrated child experiences, and attention to health and safety provided by the family. He notes further that these three general proximal patterns of family interaction are in turn the products of an array of family characteristics, including the psychological well-being of the parents, the types and levels of supports available and utilized, and family interaction patterns. His emphasis on the importance of studying what parents as individuals and as "heads" of the family bring to their parenting challenge is consistent with a broad literature that recommends a multidimensional approach to the study of program effectiveness and parenting outcomes (Hauser-Cram, Warfield, Upshur, and Weisner, 2000; Krauss, 2000). It also suggests that an important role for EI programs is to enhance, if not maintain, parental equilibrium in the face of learning how to care for a young child with a disability. To the extent, then, that EI programs positively affect parental management of stress, nurture the activation of appropriate levels of social support, and promote family cohesion, EI programs may both help to shore up the quality of the family as a caregiving environment, and enhance the psychological well-being of parents.

Despite the family-focus of EI programs, family-centered outcomes have been a relatively neglected aspect of efficacy studies both historically and currently. This paucity of family outcomes was highlighted in the findings of a meta-analysis of EI studies conducted over a decade ago (Shonkoff and Hauser-Cram, 1987). For this meta-analysis, 31 studies were selected representing the best available data on the impact of early intervention services for biologically vulnerable children younger than three years of age. Only seven of these studies included any parent-related outcomes other than measures of program satisfaction, and no study used measures of maternal well-being or family functioning. Given that those data were collected before the passage of PL 99-457, such neglect is instructive but not surprising. During the last decade, however, few investigations have filled that void (Bailey, et al., 1998; Guralnick, 1998; Krauss, 1997). The lack of family-focused outcomes research stems from several issues: the difficulty of defining appropriate family level outcomes; the reluctance of researchers and program staff to judge how families as units, and parents as individuals function; and the emphasis within programs to monitor what they do for families, rather than assess the effects of their programs on families (Krauss, 2000).

Notwithstanding the technical dilemmas involved in investigating parent outcomes, researchers continue to argue for the inclusion of parental and family outcomes in studies of EI impacts. Bailey and his colleagues (Bailey et al., 1998) contend that discussion about the relation between families and EI programs has been focused primarily on rationale and processes, rather than on outcomes. Alternatively, they propose a framework for assessing family outcomes based on two broad concerns: the family's perception of the EI experience (e.g., McBride, Brotherson, Joanning, Whiddon, and Demmitt, 1993; Upshur, 1991) and the impact of services on the family. They outline several areas of family life where the impact of EI services may be assessed. One of these domains is the family's perceived quality of life. While noting that quality of life is a complex construct with multiple dimensions, they pinpoint specific dimensions that are relevant for efficacy studies of early intervention, such as enhancement of social support and amelioration of parenting stress. Krauss (1990) reviewed the literature on the range of potential impacts on the family accruing from their participation in early intervention programs and noted that reduction of parenting stress, strengthening of parental and familial social support networks, and promotion of healthy family functioning were among the most commonly recommended areas for investigation. The present study focuses on these three outcomes (parenting stress, social support, and family functioning) in recognition of the need to expand the scope of efficacy research to include consideration of the effect of services on multidimensional aspects of parental and familial well-being.

Stress associated with parenting is ubiquitous as mothers and fathers make adjustments to the parenting role. Such adaptations typically include changes in the relationship with one's spouse and friends, and the increased need for time and fatigue management. Although much research has focused on stress and coping in families raising children with disabilities, there is considerable evidence that parenting stress is not invariably elevated in families of young children with disabilities (Gallimore, Bernheimer, and Weisner, 1999; Scott, Atkinson, Minton, and Bowman, 1997). We have found that parenting stress was more highly related to other factors affecting the family, such as divorce and debt, than to children's cognitive impairment (Warfield, Krauss, Hauser-Cram, Upshur, and Shonkoff, 1999). There is little empirical research, however, on whether service interventions are associated with changes in parenting stress over time.

Social support for parents of children with disabilities is widely viewed as a buffer, or a set of resources that can blunt the potentially deleterious effects of normative and non-normative stress (Dunst and Trivette, 1990). Although social support networks are often characterized by their size, function and helpfulness, the helpfulness dimension has proven most salient in empirical work (Dunst, Trivette, and Cross, 1986). Increasing the helpfulness of social networks makes it possible for families to mobilize resources to meet their needs (Dunst and Trivette, 1990). Consequently, many early intervention programs explicitly seek to enhance the sources of social support available to participating families, either through the use of parent support groups, or through providing linkages between parents and other community resources (Sloper, 1999).

Finally, among the many dimensions and qualities that characterize family functioning, the core issues identified most frequently are adaptability, cohesiveness, and communication (Olson, Russell, and Sprenkle, 1983). These qualities share an emphasis on relational dimensions and suggest that families in which members are cohesive – that is, are connected and enjoy being together – have the potential of providing optimal growth opportunities for their children.

Among the relatively few studies that have looked at family dynamics, investigations of children with developmental disabilities indicate that family cohesiveness is an important predictor of child outcomes. In a study of 115 families of children with mental retardation, Mink, Nihira, and Meyers (1983) found that more cohesive, harmonious families had children with more positive socioemotional functioning. Mink and Nihira (1986) further found that family cohesiveness influenced the psychological adjustment of adolescents with learning problems. In an investigation of 34 preschool children with Down syndrome, Hauser-Cram (1993) reported that children from families with higher levels of cohesiveness demonstrated higher levels of mastery motivation on cognitively challenging tasks. Hauser-Cram and colleagues (Hauser-Cram, Warfield, Shonkoff, Krauss, Upshur, and Sayer, 1999) also have found that children with Down syndrome from families with more positive and cohesive relationships demonstrated significantly greater growth in communication, socialization, and daily living skills over the first five years of life. Taken together, these studies underscore the importance of family cohesiveness as a predictor of later development in young children with developmental disabilities. Therefore, one implication of these findings is that EI programs should aim to support, or enhance, the connectedness of family members.

In order to assess the effectiveness of EI services on parenting stress, social support, and family cohesion, however, the services themselves must be quantified in some way. The measurement of intervention services varies greatly. Guralnick (1998) delineates three aspects of service provision that are critical to understanding its efficacy: density, duration, and comprehensiveness. Density, also known more commonly as intensity, refers to the level of intervention occurring within a specified time period; duration refers to the length of time services are delivered; and comprehensiveness refers to the range of different service components that are provided. No investigators have studied the relation between these three aspects of service provision and maternal well-being or family functioning.

In this analysis we investigate the relation between the intensity, duration, and comprehensiveness of early intervention services and changes in parental stress, levels of social support, and family cohesiveness. We reported elsewhere that there is tremendous variability in the intensity of services (as measured by service hours) provided to families during their first year in early intervention programs (Shonkoff, Hauser-Cram, Krauss, and Upshur, 1992). The present analysis builds on our earlier findings by including data from the full "career" of families in early intervention programs, including information on the three outcomes as measured upon entry into the service system, and again at the conclusion of early intervention services.

Method

Sample

The subjects were participants in the Early Intervention Collaborative Study (EICS), which is a longitudinal investigation of the predictors of resilience and vulnerability in the emerging competencies of young children with disabilities, and the adaptive capacities of their families (Shonkoff, et al., 1992). All families were recruited to the study at the time of their enrollment in one of 29 EI programs in Massachusetts and New Hampshire. Families with a child who met specific criteria in one of the following three groups were eligible to participate in the research: (1) children with Down syndrome (confirmed through medical record review); (2) children with motor impairments defined as evidence of abnormal muscle tone (hypotonia or hypertonia) or coordination deficit, along with delayed or deviant motor development, with or without other areas of delay; and (3) children who demonstrated evidence of delays in two or more areas of development, with no established diagnosis or etiology that implied a specific prognosis. In addition, all children had to be 27 months of age or younger when they enrolled in EI. A total of 190 families were recruited into the study.

The sample for the present analysis consists of 133 children and families for whom complete data were available on all the variables used in the analysis. Comparisons made between the 133 cases in the sample and those eliminated due to incomplete data ($n = 57$) revealed statistically significant differences in mothers' marital status, employment status, and years of education and family income. The analysis sample included families with higher annual incomes, mothers with more years of education, more married mothers, and more mothers who were employed. There were no statistically significant differences between the groups in terms of child diagnostic category, child gender, or child cognitive performance.

In the analysis sample, slightly more than one-half of the children was male (56.4%), but the children were evenly distributed across the three diagnostic groups: Down syndrome (31.6%), motor impairment (37.6%), and developmental delay (30.8%). Mean age at study entry was 10.0 months (standard deviation [SD] = 6.5) and the initial mean Mental Developmental Index (MDI) measured using the Mental Scale of the Bayley Scales of Infant Development (Bayley, 1969), was 62.8 ($SD = 24.9$). The majority (77.4%) were full-term births.

The mothers were 29.8 ($SD = 4.8$) years of age on average when their children entered EI. The vast majority were married (85.0%) and Euro-American (93.2%). On average, they had completed 14.2 ($SD = 2.4$) years of schooling, and 58.0% were not employed outside the home upon entry into the study. The families varied in terms of economic status, with one-third (33.1%) reporting an income of less than $20,000 annually while two-fifths (40.0%) reported an income of $30,000 or more (1985–1987 dollars).

Procedure

The data were gathered from two sources. First, home visits were conducted by our project staff with each family within one month of their enrollment in an EI program and again within one month of the child's third birthday (i.e., age of exit from EI). An in-depth interview was conducted with the mother and a standardized cognitive and functional assessment was conducted with the child. After each home visit, packets of self-administered questionnaires were completed by the mothers and returned to the study office.

Second, EI providers completed monthly service forms for each child and family by recording the number of hours of service received from the program in each of seven defined categories: (1) home visits; (2) center-based individual child-only services; (3) center-based individual parent only services; (4) center-based individual parent-child services; (5) center-based child only group services; (6) center-based parent and child group services; and (7) center-based parent group sessions, attended by mothers and fathers, both together and separately. A new form was completed each month from the point of entry into EI to the point of discharge at age three. A family's participation in the EICS study did not influence the amount or type of services received. Services were individualized in accordance with the needs identified jointly by family members and EI staff. Over the course of their EI experience, most families received an array of services, with each type of service represented. A prior analysis of the variation in service formats revealed substantial differences in both the intensity and the combinations of services received by a given child and family on a month-to-month basis (Erickson, 1991).

Measures

Parenting stress

The Parenting Stress Index (PSI) was completed by mothers after each home visit by our project staff (Abidin, 1995). The PSI is a measure of the magnitude of stress in the parent-child system that consists of 101 items with primarily 5-point Likert scale responses. The Parenting Domain score was used in the analysis. The Parenting Domain score is composed of seven subscales that measure parent attachment to the child, sense of competence in the parenting role, parental depression, parent health, social isolation, restrictions in role, and relations with spouse. Higher scores indicate greater parenting stress. Cronbach's alpha reliability coefficient for the Parenting Domain score was .92 at entry to EI and .93 at discharge from EI at age three years. The PSI has been used extensively in research and clinical settings to determine parental adaptation patterns (Goldberg, Morris, Simmons, Fowler, and Levison, 1990; McKinney and Peterson, 1987; Noh, Dumas, Wolf, and Fisman, 1989; Shonkoff, et al., 1992). Cutoff points have been established to identify individuals with elevated stress who should be referred for mental health services.

Family cohesiveness

At entry to EI, family cohesiveness was measured using the Family Adaptability and Cohesion Evaluation Scale (FACES II), which is a 30-item self-report form that each mother completed (Olson, Bell, and Portner, 1982). Sixteen of the items form a family cohesiveness subscale which measures the degree to which family members are emotionally disengaged from each other (lower scores on the scale) or are emotionally connected (higher scores on the scale). The Cronbach's alpha reliability coefficient for the EICS sample was .88 for the cohesiveness subscale. At age 3, the study's measure of family cohesiveness was changed to a shorter instrument, a nine-item subscale of the Family Environment Scale (FES) (Moos, 1974), to reduce respondent burden. Similar to FACES II, the FES cohesiveness subscale assesses the degree of commitment, help, and support family members provide to one another. The reliability of this subscale was .61.

Social support helpfulness

Social support helpfulness was measured based on a scale adapted from the Family Support Scale developed by Dunst, Jenkins, and Trivette (1984). The scale used in this study consisted of 15 items and tapped a variety of sources of formal and informal support such as spouse, relatives, friends, neighbors, service providers and parent groups. After each home visit by our project staff, mothers were asked to complete the scale by rating the helpfulness of each source of support using a five-point Likert scale. A total helpfulness score was computed by summing the responses. Cronbach's alpha reliability coefficient was .64 at entry to EI, and .72 at discharge from EI at age three years.

Intensity of services

Service intensity was defined as the average total hours of service received per month and was calculated by dividing the total number of service hours received by the total number of months each child and family participated in an EI program. On average, children and families received 8.7 hours of service per month ($SD = 5.1$, range $= .12$ to 29.6). As shown in table 11.1, the total hours per month were most likely to consist of home visits and child group services, followed by parent

Table 11.1 Means and *SDs* of service intensity variables

Variable	Mean	SD
Average hours per month		
Home visits	3.1	1.8
Individual child only	0.2	0.4
Individual parent only	0.0[a]	0.1
Individual parent and child	0.6	0.9
Child group	2.6	2.9
Parent and child group	1.1	1.8
Parent support group	1.2	1.6

Note: [a]The actual value is 0.02.

support group services and parent and child group services. Individualized center-based services were provided less often.

Service duration

EI provides services to families with children between birth and three years of age. Sample children and their families participated in EI for different lengths of time depending on the age of the child at program entry. On average, children and families participated for 26.1 months (*SD* = 7.1, range = 11.0 to 39.0 months).

Comprehensiveness of services

Comprehensiveness was defined as the number of different types of services received over the course of a family's participation in EI. Of the seven different types of services available, families received an average of 4.5 services (*SD* = 1.4, range = 1 to 7).

Child characteristics

The Mental Scale of the Bayley Scales of Infant Development, measured at entry to EI, was used to assess cognitive performance (Bayley, 1969). The Mental Developmental Index was adjusted for gestational age for children born prematurely. Type of diagnosis was analyzed as a dummy variable comparing the motor impaired group to the other two groups (i.e., Down syndrome and developmental delay) since being in the motor impaired group was significantly correlated with higher stress ($r = .20$, $p < .05$), lower family cohesion ($r = -.25$, $p < .01$), and lower social support ($r = -.24$, $p < .01$) at age three years. Age of the child at entry to EI was also analyzed due to its relation to service duration.

Mother characteristics

Years of education, marital status (i.e., married versus not married), and employment status (i.e., employed versus not employed), measured at entry to EI, were assessed as potential correlates of maternal well-being.

Statistical analysis

Several analytic procedures were conducted to test the hypothesized relations between service dimensions and changes in maternal well-being. First, correlations were computed between the score at entry to EI and the score at discharge from EI for each of the three outcome measures. Second, paired *t*-tests were conducted to examine change in each of the three outcome measures. Third, correlations were conducted to assess the relation between the child and mother characteristics and the three service intervention variables and to identify the significant correlates of maternal well-being. Fourth, based on the results of these correlation analyses, hierarchical regression models were tested to examine the extent to which service intensity, duration, or comprehensiveness, over and above child and mother characteristics, predicts changes in parenting stress, family cohesion, and social support between entry to and exit from EI. Interactions between the service variables and both the child and mother characteristics variables and the score for each dependent variable measured at entry to EI, were also computed. The interaction terms were created by centering the variables prior to multiplication, as recommended by Aiken and West (1991). The interaction terms were entered last into the regression models to see if they explained a significant portion of the remaining variance. The final models reported here contain only those interaction terms that were statistically significant.

Table 11.2   Descriptive and correlational statistics for measures of
maternal well-being at entry and discharge from EI

| | *Entry to EI* | | *Discharge from EI* | | |
Variable	M	SD	M	SD	r
Parenting stress	119.0	24.9	122.1	25.5	0.74*
Family cohesion	65.6	9.4	7.4	1.7	0.36*
Social support	23.8	7.8	27.7	9.3	0.52*

Notes: The measure of family cohesion used at entry to EI (i.e., FACES II) was different
from that used at discharge from EI (i.e., FES). * $p < 0.001$.

Results

Table 11.2 shows the statistically significant associations between the
score at entry to EI and the score at discharge from EI for each of the
three outcome measures. The results of the paired t-tests indicated that
the greatest change between the two time points was in social support.
Social support helpfulness increased significantly from 23.8 to 27.7
($t = 5.3$, $p < .001$). Parenting stress increased only slightly ($t = 2.0$,
$p = .05$). In general, the mothers in the sample did not report excessive
parenting stress. Less than 12% of the sample reported scores in the
clinical range at either time point. Finally, although the family cohesion
scores at the two time points were significantly correlated, any increase
or decrease in cohesion cannot be assessed since different scales were
used.

Correlations between the child and mother characteristics and the
three measures of service intervention were computed to identify patterns of service provision (see table 11.3).

Cognitive performance was significantly and negatively associated
with service intensity. Thus, children with lower cognitive abilities
received more hours of EI services per month. As expected, children
who entered EI at younger ages received services for more months than
children who entered EI at older ages. Finally, mothers with more years
of education received more hours of EI services per month and a more
comprehensive set of services.

Table 11.3 Correlations between child and mother characteristics and service intensity, duration, and comprehensiveness

Variable	Intensity	Duration	Comprehensiveness
Child			
Cognitive performance	−0.36**	0.06	−0.13
Motor impaired	−0.06	−0.13	0.01
Age at entry to EI	0.14	−0.84**	−0.07
Mother			
Years of education	0.31**	0.06	0.18*
Employed	−0.04	−0.08	−0.14
Married	0.04	0.02	0.06

Notes: All distributions were examined for normality and log transformations were performed where necessary. * $p < 0.05$. ** $p < 0.001$.

Correlations between each of the three dependent variables and the variables measuring child and mother characteristics and service intensity, duration, and comprehensiveness were also conducted to identify significant correlates to be entered into the hierarchical regression models (see table 11.4).

Among the child characteristics examined, only diagnostic group was significantly correlated with the outcomes at age three. Children with motor impairments, as compared to those with Down syndrome or developmental delay, had mothers who reported less cohesion and support and more parenting stress at age three years. Similarly, only one of the mother characteristics variables was a significant correlate of the age three outcomes. Mothers with more years of education reported greater family cohesion and support and less parenting stress at age three years.

Different service variables were correlated with the different outcome measures. Greater service intensity was significantly and positively correlated with increased family cohesion.

Neither intensity, duration, nor comprehensiveness was significantly associated with changes in parenting stress and thus no hierarchical regression analyses were conducted on this outcome. In contrast, all three service variables were significantly associated with changes in the helpfulness of social support.

Table 11.4   Correlations between child, mother, and service characteristics and measures of maternal well-being at age three years

Variable	Parenting stress	Family cohesion	Social support
Child			
Cognitive performance	−0.03	0.05	−0.15
Motor impaired	0.20*	−0.25**	−0.24**
Age at entry to EI	−0.04	0.01	−0.11
Mother			
Years of education	−0.21*	0.27**	0.17*
Employed	−0.10	0.10	0.12
Married	−0.16	0.15	0.16
Service			
Intensity	−0.04	0.20*	0.26*
Duration	0.05	0.03	0.19*
Comprehensiveness	0.05	0.06	0.18*

Notes: All distributions were examined for normality and log transformations were performed where necessary. * $p < 0.05$. ** $p < 0.01$.

Hierarchical regression analyses were conducted on family cohesion in order to determine whether overall service intensity remained as a significant predictor of change in maternal well-being once the other correlates were controlled for. The regression model entered the significant correlates of service provision and family cohesion into the model first, followed by the level of family cohesion measured at entry to EI, service intensity and the significant interaction terms. Table 11.5 presents the results of the hierarchical regression analysis for family cohesion.

Diagnostic group, years of maternal education, family cohesion at entry to EI, and overall service intensity were significant predictors of cohesion. After controlling for these variables, however, an interaction between diagnostic group and service intensity was also a significant predictor of change in family cohesion. Although greater service intensity improved family cohesion for all diagnostic groups, mothers of children without motor impairment (i.e., children with either Down syndrome or developmental delay) experienced greater increases than mothers of children with motor impairment.

Table 11.5   Predictors of change in family cohesion

		Family cohesion	
Independent variables		beta	R^2 change
1	Cognitive performance	0.05	0.3
2	Motor impaired	−0.26	6.1**
3	Mother's years of education	0.25	6.3**
4	Family cohesion at entry to EI	0.29	7.8**
5	Overall service intensity	0.17	2.3*
6	Intensity* Motor Impaired	0.48	2.5*
Adjusted R^2			0.22

Notes: * $p < 0.05$. ** $p < 0.01$.

Additional analyses were conducted to identify whether the intensity of any particular type of service (e.g., home visits, child groups, etc.) was a predictor of change in cohesion. None of the separately considered service intensity variables was significant.

Hierarchical regressions were also analyzed for the support outcome in order to identify which of the three service variables were significant predictors of change in support, over and above child and mother characteristics. The regression models entered the significant correlates of service provision and social support into the model first, followed by the level of support reported at entry to EI and the service variables. None of the tested interaction terms between the independent variables and the service variables was significant (see table 11.6).

Diagnostic group and social support at entry to EI were significant predictors of support. After controlling for these variables, service intensity was also found to be a significant predictor of change in support helpfulness. More intensive services predicted greater increases in support helpfulness. Additional analyses revealed that specific types of services were responsible for this increase. More intensive parent support group services (R^2 change = 2.0, $p < .05$) and more intensive child group services (R^2 change = 1.9, $p < .05$) were each significant predictors of increases in social support when entered into the equation separately in place of overall intensity. Interactions between these two intensity variables and the child and mother characteristics variables and the

Table 11.6 Service intensity as a predictor of change in social support

| | | Social support | |
Independent variables	beta	R² change
1 Cognitive performance	−0.15	2.2
2 Motor impaired	−0.31	8.8***
3 Mother's years of education	0.14	1.8
4 Social support at entry to EI	0.48	22.2***
5 Service intensity	0.23	3.9**
Adjusted R²		0.37

Notes: ** p < 0.01. *** p < 0.001.

Table 11.7 Service comprehensiveness as a predictor of change in social support

| | | Social support | |
Independent variables	beta	R² change
1 Motor impaired	−0.24	5.7**
2 Mother's years of education	0.15	2.4
3 Social support at entry to EI	0.50	24.9***
4 Service comprehensiveness	0.15	2.1*
Adjusted R²		0.33

Notes: * p < 0.05. ** p < 0.01. *** p < 0.001.

prior level of support variable were also entered into the equation but none was found to be significant.

Further, as shown in table 11.7, service comprehensiveness was also a significant predictor of change in social support.

The receipt of a greater number of different services produced greater gains in support helpfulness. Interaction terms were also entered into this equation but were not found to be significant.

Finally, duration was not found to be a significant predictor of change in support (R^2 change = 0.4, $p > .05$). No analysis was conducted entering combinations of the overall intensity, intensity of parent support group services, intensity of child group services, and service comprehensiveness variables in the same model since they are highly intercorrelated with one another (r ranges from .58 to .68).

Discussion

Despite the emphasis in EI on enhancing the capacity of the family system to meet children's special needs, few investigations have focused on family outcomes. The analyses presented in this investigation were designed to determine the extent to which the intensity, duration, and comprehensiveness of early intervention services received "explain" positive changes in family-related outcomes reported by mothers of young children with disabilities as they are discharged from EI services. Three aspects of maternal well-being were considered, including parenting stress, social support helpfulness, and family cohesiveness.

Several important findings emerge from these analyses. First, the overall intensity of EI services, the intensity of parent support group services, the intensity of child group services, and the number of different types of services received each predicted positive and significant change in social support helpfulness between entry to and exit from EI. These results expand upon our previous findings which showed that intensity of parent group participation was related to increases in both the helpfulness and size of social support networks after one year of EI services (Krauss, Upshur, Shonkoff, and Hauser-Cram, 1993).

Given the high level of intercorrelation between the four significant measures of EI intervention in our current analysis, it appears that families who become more engaged in the program report larger increases in the helpfulness of the maternal support network. Thus, these mothers, in comparison to those who were less engaged (e.g., those who chose not to participate in the support groups as much or who were offered a more restrictive set of services), reported being better able to engender help from supportive others, both inside and outside the family. As a result, these mothers were able to blend their young child with a disability into the family by building a helpful network of support that extends beyond the immediate family.

Unfortunately our data are not able to explain why some mothers became more engaged in the EI program than others. Given the variables that were controlled for in the analysis (e.g., cognitive performance, years of education) factors other than individual characteristics may play a role such as the organization and resources of the different EI programs and the training and experience of EI staff members. Future research is needed on the system level factors influencing EI service participation.

It is noteworthy, however, that we found positive and significant relations between maternal education and the intensity and comprehensiveness of services. Mothers with higher levels of education received more hours of service per month and a greater range of services. This may be because they advocated for more services, took greater advantage of the services available, or the service system itself was biased toward more educated families in service distribution. Families with fewer resources and lower education face multiple barriers to service utilization such as transportation difficulties and the need to manage other pressing family problems. Given their needs, however, one might expect the bias to be in the opposite direction. Our study is not the first to find this positive relation between service utilization and maternal education (e.g., Kochanek and Buka, 1998a), and future investigations should focus on understanding this relation.

Further, we note that most families received a modest level of EI services. An average of 8.7 hours of service per month (or roughly 2 hours per week) is equivalent to the time many parents spend taking a child to a grocery store once a week. Given such a low intensity of service, it is remarkable that EI produces measurable effects on family life. We speculate that the impact of EI occurs both through direct means from service provider to parent and through indirect means from parents linking with other parents to share adaptive strategies and provide mutual support. Mahoney, O'Sullivan, and Dennebaum (1990) assessed the extent to which the services received by 503 families of young children with disabilities who were enrolled in EI programs throughout the United States were family-focused. They found that the greater the tendency of programs to work directly with families, the more likely mothers were to perceive service benefits. Programs rated as more family-focused provided more direct family instructional activities (e.g., showing parents a range of games to play with their child), linked families with other helpful services and other parents, and encouraged parents to share their experiences with other parents. These varied ways of working with families point to the benefits of more comprehensive interventions.

Second, an interaction effect between diagnostic group and over-all service intensity predicted significant change in family cohesion. Although greater service intensity improved family cohesion for all diagnostic groups, mothers of children without motor impairments (i.e., children with Down syndrome or developmental delay) experienced greater increases than mothers of children with motor impairments. EI is known to be a highly individualized, multidisciplinary, multi-service program (Guralnick, 1997). Families vary widely in the exact arrangement of services provided to them, but most receive a combination of home-based and center-based, individualized and group services (Erickson, 1991; 1992). The data collected for this study indicate that the intensity of this constellation of services supports families (some more than others) in building cohesive relationships within the family unit. Unfortunately, our data do not determine *how* this occurs. It appears that beliefs about the importance of the principles of family-centered services are strong among EI service providers (Kochanek and Buka, 1998b; McBride, Brotherson, Joanning, Whiddon, and Demmitt, 1993). We speculate that the individualized nature of services, guided by family-centered principles of practice, lend support to the family, and that such support, if of sufficient intensity, serves families in their optimization of cohesive functioning. Future research needs to specify those discrete program mechanisms that interact with child and family characteristics to influence these outcomes (Guralnick, 1997; Hauser-Cram, Warfield, and Krauss, 1997).

Future research also needs to examine why greater service intensity benefits certain families more than others. In addition to poorer family cohesion, the correlation analyses also revealed that mothers of children with motor impairment reported higher levels of parenting stress and lower levels of helpful social support. The pervasiveness of these findings suggests that the accommodations to family life required of parents of children with motor impairment are more extensive than those required of other families. The nature of these accommodations may make it difficult for others to step in and provide support and respite. Gallimore, Weisner, Bernheimer, Guthrie, and Nihira (1993) have examined the ways in which families of children with disabilities create daily routines in response to their child's needs. These special accommodations may include allowing extra time for caregiving activities (e.g., dressing, bathing, etc.), as well as scheduling participation in EI services. While many families make such accommodations in stride, and others "make meaning" out of these changes, some families find that such accommodations take a toll on family life. Further research should explore how EI services can better assist parents of children with motor impairment to make accommodations that respect and enhance the family's internal and external support structure.

Third, no effects of EI services were found for reducing maternal parenting stress. Perhaps that is because the mothers in this study did not report excessively high levels of parenting stress either at entry to EI or at discharge when children turned three years of age. Although a small but marginally significant increase in parenting stress occurred for the sample as a whole, the mean parenting stress for the EICS sample at age three was nearly identical to that of the norming sample composed of mothers of typically developing three-year-olds (Abidin, 1995). Indeed, very few families in this sample were in the clinical stress range at either time point, and the correlation between parenting stress at entry and exit from EI was substantial ($r = .74, p < .001$), indicating that little change existed for the group as a whole. Thus, it is not surprising that hours of EI service do not relate to changes in stress levels in this sample where stress remains relatively stable and within the normative range. It is possible that participation in EI provides the general support that allows mothers to continue to function with normative, rather than greatly accelerating, levels of parenting stress. It is also possible, however, that given relatively modest hours of service and the array of services generally provided, EI is not well positioned to provide the types of clinical interventions needed by those few mothers who are highly stressed.

Our findings of a positive relation between different aspects of EI service intervention and both family cohesiveness and maternal social support suggest there may be other family outcomes that are influenced significantly by EI services. Thus, future research needs to examine whether EI affects other aspects of family functioning and adaptation, and the extent to which these effects are related to the intensity, duration, and comprehensiveness of services. Outcomes such as greater life satisfaction, enhanced parenting competence, and improved sibling relationships, among others, warrant careful examination (Bailey, et al., 1998; Krauss, 2000). Family perceptions of the EI experience (e.g., appropriateness, responsiveness, helpfulness, etc.) also deserve increased investigation (Bailey, et al., 1998; Upshur, 1991).

This investigation has several limitations. First, outcome measures were based on maternal report. Thus, the findings are susceptible to shared variance issues and, even more importantly, to restricted inter-pretation, as other family members may view the family differently. Fathers in particular are often neglected in research on families of children with disabilities (Hornby, 1995; Lamb and Billings, 1997) and their perspectives have been found to differ in several important ways from those of mothers (Krauss, 1993).

Further, although the sample included families who varied in their ethnic status, the vast majority are Euro-American. Views of the meaning of both disability and family cohesiveness, as well as feelings regarding the receipt of formal intervention services, vary for different cultural groups (Hanson, 1992; Skinner, Bailey, Correa, and Rodriguez, 1999). Thus, the relation found between service intensity and compre-hensiveness and family outcomes is not necessarily generalizable to all families.

Despite these limitations, the results of this investigation point to the value of EI services for families of children with disabilities. Specifically, our analysis is the first to identify different aspects of EI service inter-vention as significant predictors of two core aspects of maternal well-being, improved family cohesion and extended networks of helpful social support.

References

Abidin, R. (1995). *Parenting stress index: Manual* (3rd ed.). Odessa, FL: Psycho-logical Assessment Resources.

Aiken, L. S., & West, S. G. (1991). *Multiple regression: Testing and interpreting interactions*. Newbury Park, CA: Sage.

Bailey, D. B., McWilliam, R. A., Darkes, L. A., Hebbeler, K., Simeonsson, R. J., Spiker, D., & Wagner, M. (1998). Family outcomes in early intervention: A framework for program evaluation and efficacy research. *Exceptional Children, 64*, 313–328.

Bayley, N. (1969). *The scales of infant development*. New York: Psychological Corp.

Bronfenbrenner, U. (1986). Ecology of the family as a context for human development: Research perspectives. *Developmental Psychology, 22*, 723–742.

Casto, G., & Mastropieri, M. A. (1986). The efficacy of early intervention pro-grams: A meta-analysis. *Exceptional Children, 52*, 417–424.

Dunst, C., Jenkins, V., & Trivette, C. (1984). The Family Support Scale: Reli-ability and validity. *Journal of Individual, Family, and Community Wellness, 1*, 45–52.

Dunst, C. J., & Trivette, C. M. (1990). Assessment of social support in early intervention programs. In S. J. Meisels & J. P. Shonkoff (Eds.), *Handbook of early childhood intervention* (pp. 326–349). New York: Cambridge University Press.

Dunst, C. J., & Trivette, C. M. (1994). Methodological considerations and strategies for studying the long-term effects of early intervention. In S. L. Friedman & H. C. Haywood (Eds.), *Developmental follow-up: Concepts, domains, and methods* (pp. 277–313). San Diego, CA: Academic Press.

Dunst, C., Trivette, C., & Cross, A. (1986). Mediating influences of social support: Personal, family, and child outcomes. *American Journal of Mental Deficiency, 90*, 403–417.

Dunst, C. J., Trivette, C. M., & Jodry, W. (1997). Influences of social support on children with disabilities and their families. In M. J. Guralnick (Ed.), *The effectiveness of early intervention* (pp. 499–522). Baltimore: Brookes.

Education of the Handicapped Act Amendments of 1986, Pub. L. No. 99–457, 100 Stat. 1145, (1987).

Erickson, M. (1991). Evaluating early intervention services: A cost-effectiveness analysis. Unpublished doctoral dissertation, Brandeis University.

Erickson, M. (1992). An analysis of early intervention expenditures in Massachusetts. *American Journal on Mental Retardation, 96*, 617–629.

Gallimore, R., Bernheimer, L. P., & Weisner, T. S. (1999). Family life is more than managing crisis: Broadening the agenda of research on families adapting to childhood disability. In R. Gallimore, L. P. Bernhemier, D. L. MacMillan, D. L. Speece, & S. Vaughn (Eds.), *Developmental perspectives on children with high-incidence disabilities* (pp. 55–80). Mahwah, NJ: Erlbaum.

Gallimore, R., Weisner, T. S., Bernheimer, L. P., Guthrie, D., & Nihira, K. (1993). Family responses to young children with developmental delays: Accommodation activity in ecological and cultural context. *American Journal on Mental Retardation, 98*, 185–206.

Goldberg, S., Morris, P., Simmons, R., Fowler, R., & Levison, H. (1990). Chronic illness in infancy and parenting stress: A comparison of three groups of parents. *Journal of Pediatric Psychology, 15*, 347–358.

Guralnick, M. J. (1997). Second generation research in the field of early intervention. In M. J. Guralnick (Ed.), *The effectiveness of early intervention* (pp. 3–20). Baltimore: Brookes.

Guralnick, M. J. (1998). Effectiveness of early intervention for vulnerable children: A developmental perspective. *American Journal on Mental Retardation, 102*, 319–345.

Hanson, M. J. (1992). Ethnic, cultural, and language diversity in intervention settings. In E. W. Lynch & M. J. Hanson (Eds.), *Developing cross-cultural competence* (pp. 3–18). Baltimore: Brookes.

Hauser-Cram, P. (1993). Mastery motivation in three-year-old children with Down syndrome. In D. J. Messer (Ed.), *Mastery motivation: Children's investigation, persistence, and development* (pp. 230–250). London: Routledge.

Hauser-Cram, P., Warfield, M. E., & Krauss, M. W. (1997). An examination of parent support groups: A range of purposes, theories, and effects. In T. I. K. Youn & W. R. Freudenburg (Eds.), *Research in social problems and public policy* (pp. 99–124). Greenwich, CT: JAI Press.

Hauser-Cram, P., Warfield, M. E., Shonkoff, J. P., Krauss, M. W., Upshur, C. C., & Sayer, A. (1999). Family influences on adaptive development in young children with Down syndrome. *Child Development, 70,* 979–989.

Hauser-Cram, P., Warfield, M. E., Upshur, C. C., & Weisner, T. S. (2000). An expanded view of program evaluation in early childhood intervention. In J. P. Shonkoff & S. J. Meisels (Eds.), *Handbook of early childhood intervention.* (2nd ed., pp. 487–509). New York: Cambridge University Press.

Hornby, G. (1995). Fathers' views of the effects on their families of children with Down syndrome. *Journal of Child and Family Studies, 4,* 103–117.

Individuals with Disabilities Education Act Amendments of 1997, 20 U.S.C. 1401 *et seq.*

Kochanek, T. T., & Buka, S. L. (1998a). Patterns of service utilization: Child, maternal, and service provider factors. *Journal of Early Intervention, 21,* 217–231.

Kochanek, T. T., & Buka, S. L. (1998b). Influential factors in the utilization of early intervention services. *Journal of Early Intervention, 21,* 323–338.

Krauss, M. W. (1990). New precedent in family policy: Individualized family service plan. *Exceptional Children, 56,* 388–395.

Krauss, M. W. (1993). Child-related and parenting stress: Similarities and differences between mothers and fathers of children with disabilities. *American Journal on Mental Retardation, 97,* 393–404.

Krauss, M. W. (1997). Two generations of family research in early intervention. In M. J. Guralnick (Ed.), *The effectiveness of early intervention* (pp. 611–624). Baltimore: Brookes.

Krauss, M. W. (2000). Family assessment within early intervention programs. In J. P. Shonkoff & S. M. Meisels (Eds.), *Handbook of early childhood intervention.* (2nd ed., pp. 290–308). New York: Cambridge University Press.

Krauss, M. W., Upshur, C. C., Shonkoff, J. P., & Hauser-Cram, P. (1993). The impact of parent groups on mothers of infants with disabilities. *Journal of Early Intervention, 17,* 8–20.

Lamb, M. E., & Billings, L. A. L. (1997). Fathers of children with special needs. In M. E. Lamb (Ed.), *The role of the father in development* (3rd ed., pp. 179–190). New York: Wiley.

Lerner, R. M. (1998). Theories of human development: Contemporary perspectives. In W. Damon (Series Ed.) & R. M. Lerner (Vol. Ed.), *Handbook of child psychology: Vol. 1. Theoretical models of human development* (5th ed., pp. 1–24). New York: Wiley.

Mahoney, G., O'Sullivan, P., & Dennenbaum, J. (1990). A national study of mothers' perceptions of family-focused early intervention. *Journal of Early Intervention, 14,* 133–146.

McBride. S. L., Brotherson, M. J., Joanning, H., Whiddon, D., & Demmitt, A. (1993). Implementation of family-centered services: Perceptions of families and professionals. *Journal of Early Intervention, 17,* 414–430.

McKinney, B., & Peterson, R. (1987). Predictors of stress in parents of developmentally disabled children. *Journal of Pediatric Psychology, 12,* 133–150.

Mink, I. T., & Nihira, K. (1986). Family life-styles and child behaviors: A study of direction of effects. *Developmental Psychology, 22,* 610–616.

Mink, I. T., Nihira, K., & Meyers, C. E. (1983). Taxonomy of family lifestyles: I. Homes with TMR children. *American Journal of Mental Deficiency, 87,* 484–497.

Moos, R. H. (1974). *Family environment scale.* Palo Alto, CA: Consulting Psychologists Press.

Noh, S., Dumas, J. E., Wolf, L. C., & Fisman, S. D. (1989). Delineating sources of stress in parents of exceptional children. *Family Relations, 38,* 456–461.

Olson, D., Bell, R., & Portner, J. (1982). *Family adaptability and cohesion evaluation scales (FACES II).* St. Paul, MN: Family Social Science.

Olson, D., Russell, C., & Sprenkle, D. (1983). Circumplex model of marital and family systems: 6. Theoretical update. *Family Process, 22,* 69–83.

Scott, B. S., Atkinson, L., Minton, H. L., & Bowman, T. (1997). Psychological distress of parents of infants with Down syndrome. *American Journal on Mental Retardation, 102,* 161–171.

Shonkoff, J. P., & Hauser-Cram, P. (1987). Early intervention for disabled infants and their families: A quantitative analysis. *Pediatrics, 80,* 650–658.

Shonkoff, J. P., Hauser-Cram, P., Krauss, M. W., & Upshur, C. C. (1992). Development of infants with disabilities and their families: Implications for theory and service delivery. *Monographs of the Society for Research in Child Development, 57* (6, Serial No. 230).

Skinner, D., Bailey, D. B., Correa, V., & Rodriguez, P. (1999). Narrating self and disability: Latino mothers' construction of identities vis-a-vis their child with special needs. *Exceptional Children, 65,* 481–495.

Sloper, P. (1999). Models of service support for parents of disabled children. What do we know? What do we need to know? *Child: Care, Health and Development, 25,* 85–99.

Upshur, C. C. (1991). Mothers' and fathers' ratings of the benefits of early intervention services. *Journal of Early Intervention, 15,* 345–357.

Warfield, M. E., Krauss, M. W., Hauser-Cram, P., Upshur, C. C., & Shonkoff, J. P. (1999). Adaptation during early childhood among mothers of children with disabilities. *Developmental and Behavioral Pediatrics, 29,* 9–16.

Introduction to Chapter 12

EI researchers now consider parent participation vital (e.g., Chapters 1 and 2). The home visiting programs described in part IV require substantial parental involvement in carrying out the recommendations of the home visitor on a regular basis. Indeed, parental participation was related to program success in Chapters 5 and 12. Yet, little is known about variables affecting parents' willingness to participate in EI programs. This well-constructed study examined factors affecting parental involvement in EI programs. It is one of the few studies to present data on fathers as well as mothers. As seen in figure 12.1, the authors used an ecological-interactional framework, similar to that described in chapter 1. In this case, the model was being used to generate hypotheses about variables affecting parental involvement rather than child outcomes. The authors included several commonly researched factors such as parental distress, social support, marital satisfaction, and family demographics. However, they also measured (infrequently-researched) parental coping strategies and hypothesized that they have both direct and indirect effects on parental participation.

The results provided partial support for their hypothetical model and suggested that different models are needed to explain maternal and paternal involvement. Indeed, as hypothesized, positive coping strategies directly influenced parental involvement. One important change the data bring to their original model is the role of family functioning. Instead of it being directly related to parental involvement, its effects were mediated through stress and coping strategies.

The results also suggest one reason why biologically vulnerable children in less-resourced families do not do as well as similar children from relatively well-resourced families (Sameroff and Chandler, 1975). If the latter families tend to access more programs and maintain higher levels of involvement in effective interventions, then their children with disabilities may have better developmental outcomes than those of lower-income, less-educated parents who do not get as involved. If this is the case, then the system may not be reaching families most in need. Novel strategies, such as payment for participation, may be necessary to motivate increased parental participation in needed EI programs (Feldman, 1998).

References

Feldman, M. A. (1998). Preventing child neglect: Child-care training for parents with intellectual disabilities. *Infants & Young Children, 11*, 1–11.

Sameroff, A. J., & Chandler, M. J. (1975). Reproductive risk and the continuum of caretaking causality. In F. D. Horowitz, M. Hetherington, S. Scarr-Salapatek, & G. Siegel (Eds), *Review of child development research*. Vol. 4 (pp. 187–243). Chicago: University of Chicago Press.

TWELVE

Family Predictors of Maternal and Paternal Involvement in Programs for Young Children with Disabilities

Susana Gavidia-Payne and
Zolinda Stoneman

Introduction

Child developmentalists have long been interested in understanding the links between children's home and family life and their success at school (Adams, 1976; Bronfenbrenner, 1974; Gordon, 1977, National Education Association, 1972, Radin, 1972; Wallat and Goldman, 1979). One area that has received substantial research attention is the degree to which parents, particularly mothers, become involved in their children's school programs and activities. Studies have consistently found that parents who are more involved in their children's education have sons and daughters who experience greater social success (Epstein, 1990; Fehrman, Keith, and Reimers, 1987; Grolnick and Slowiaczek, 1994; Olmsted and Rubin, 1983; Reynolds, 1989; Stevenson and Baker, 1987; Zigler and Muenchow, 1992). Although the importance of parental involvement is generally acknowledged, there is relatively little information about what factors cause some parents to be actively involved in

Gavidia-Payne, S. and Stoneman, Z. (1997). Family predictors of maternal and paternal involvement in programs for young children with disabilities. *Child Development, 68*, 701–717. Includes use of tables 1–3, and figures 1–3. Copyright the Society for Research in Child Development Inc.

their children's educational programs, whereas other parents are less involved or not involved at all.

Interest has been particularly high in parent involvement during the early childhood period (Cordon, 1977; Langenbrunner and Thornburg, 1980; Radin, 1972; Wardle, 1982; Zigler and Muenchow, 1992). Parents are young children's primary teachers, highlighting the importance of close links between the home environment and the child's participation in preschool and day-care programs (Brody and Stoneman, 1982; Laosa and Sigel, 1982). The emphasis on parent involvement has been continuous in programs serving young children with developmental delays and disabilities, where family participation is considered to be an indispensable element of sound early intervention practices (Dunst, Trivette, and Deal, 1988; Fewell, 1986; Slentz, Walker, and Bricker, 1989). Family characteristics, needs, and resources have emerged as major imperatives in the implementation of educational and developmental goals (Turnbull and Turnbull, 1986; Wikler, 1986). Examples of the involvement frequently offered to parents have included participation and observation in the classroom, parent-child instruction, home visits, parent education groups, parent support groups, and counseling (Deberry, Ristau, and Galland, 1984).

Theoretically, the study of parent involvement has also received some attention. Bronfenbrenner's ecological approach to human development is a highly recognized framework that conceptualizes parent involvement as one variable influenced by a variety of systems (Bronfenbrenner, 1974). In the area of developmental disabilities, the most recently articulated theoretical perspective regards parent involvement processes within an ecological context to include a variety of social systems that may have an impact on the child's development and family adjustment (Dunst, 1985). Despite such theoretical efforts, there is a dearth of empirical evidence that addresses the constructs and models proposed (Turnbull, Summers, and Brotherson, 1986). Furthermore, it has been suggested that the study of parental involvement is plagued with inconsistencies and controversy as to its meaning and place within the broader spectrum of child and family variables (Casto and Lewis, 1984; Guralnick, 1989; Turnbull and Winton, 1984; White, Taylor, and Moss, 1992). With a few exceptions (Early Intervention Research Institute, 1990; Lowitzer, 1989), research about the identification of the factors, especially family factors, influencing parent involvement for the 0–5 years of age population with developmental disabilities is generally lacking. Indeed, parent involvement has been conceptualized as either an outcome of early intervention programs or as an independent variable affecting child and family outcomes (Innocenti, Hollinger, Escobar, and White, 1993). Whereas consideration of the effects of parental involvement efforts on family-related outcomes is critical, the understanding of the variables contributing to lesser or greater involvement is equally essential in the development of sensitive and effective early intervention initiatives. As Guralnick (1993) suggests, to arrive at a complete understanding of the effectiveness of early intervention, an explicit consideration of mediating, moderating, and reciprocal influences among critical variables is required. Given what we know about the significant and complex role of family processes (Walsh, 1982) and the increasing recognition of the pivotal role of family strengths and needs in intervention (Paget, 1992), it is imperative to examine the factors explaining the parent involvement construct.

Thus, the purpose of this study was to investigate how select family characteristics relate to the involvement of mothers and fathers in early intervention programs. Of particular interest was to determine the extent to which these characteristics predict maternal and paternal involvement in early intervention programs. Family demographic factors (income and education), social support, emotional well-being (stress and depression), marital adjustment, family functioning, and coping were the family variables included in this study.

Model

Figure 12.1 illustrates the theoretical model tested. It depicts the interrelationships among the constructs included in the hypotheses. The model specifies three theoretical constructs: Family demographics, family characteristics, and parent involvement in early intervention programs. Family demographic factors included parental level of education and income level. Family characteristics were defined by parents' family functioning, marital adjustment, social supports, stress, and coping.

In developing our hypothetical model we were guided by two theoretical perspectives, the ecological process model of parenting posited by Belsky (1984) and the theoretical work on coping done by Folkman and Lazarus (Folkman, Schaefer, and Lazarus, 1979; Lazarus and Folkman, 1984). In using the approach proposed by Belsky, we considered active

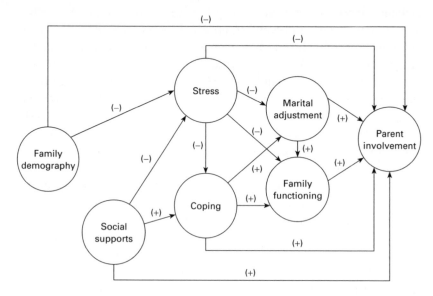

Figure 12.1   Theoretical model for predictors of parental involvement

involvement in children's intervention programs to be one component of parenting influenced by contextual factors similar to those influencing other, more commonly studied, parenting indices. As such, social support (with particular emphasis on support derived from the marital relationship) and the psychological well-being of the parent (the absence of stress or depression) were posited as important direct and indirect determinants of parental involvement. Cognitive coping (Folkman et al., 1979; Lazarus and Folkman, 1984) is added to this conceptualization because of the importance of coping strategies in determining whether stressful events (such as those surrounding a child with disabilities) result in adaptational or maladaptational outcomes. In this case, the adaptational outcome is considered to be the active involvement of parents in their children's intervention programs. Positive coping is considered to be the use of active, problem-focused coping strategies when faced with the problems and challenges related to their son or daughter with a disability. These coping strategies are posited to be determined, in part, by the same contextual factors delineated by Belsky (1984) as affecting positive parenting.

Specifically, it was expected that low income and less parent education would be associated with increased stress and decreased parent involvement (Baker, 1989; Lowitzer, 1989). Service providers' reports were used for the outcome measurement of parent involvement to minimize single-rater bias. After these characteristics were accounted for, we expected that parents who reported higher marital adjustment, healthy family functioning, and strong social supports would experience less stress and utilize more effective, problem-focused coping strategies than families with less positive marital, family, and social supports. Availability of social supports to parents has been linked to decreased levels of stress and depression (Bristol, 1979, 1984). Similarly, healthy family functioning and strong marital supports serve as resources to decrease depression and stress (Belsky, 1984; Frey, Greenberg, and Fewell, 1989; McKinney and Peterson, 1987).

Researchers have found positive relations between family functioning, marital adjustment, and parental participation in training or intervention programs for parents of children with disabilities (Baker, Landen, and Kashima, 1991) and with conduct disorders (Griest and Forehand, 1982; Griest and Wells, 1983). Similarly, adaptable families have been found to be more involved with their children's programs than less adaptable families (Early Intervention Research Institute, 1988). Based on these studies, we hypothesized both a direct relation between marital/family adjustment and parent involvement, and an indirect path mediated by stress and coping variables. Finally, we anticipated that parents experiencing high stress would be less likely to mobilize active, problem-focused coping strategies in dealing with problems related to their child with a disability (Frey et al., 1989; Knussen, Sloper, Cunningham, and Turner, 1992), resulting in reduced parent involvement in their child's early intervention program. We also expected a direct path between high stress and diminished parent involvement. The literature provided little guidance in predicting different pathways for mothers and fathers, so identical hypothetical models were posed for parents of both genders.

Method

Participants

The sample comprised 80 two-parent families of 0- to 5-year-old children who had an identified developmental disability and who were receiving early intervention services at the point of data collection (sample data were collected in categories). Of these 80 families, 73 couples completed questionnaires. Mothers (85%) and fathers (77.5%) were predominantly European American. The average age for mothers and fathers was 32.7 and 35.9 years, respectively. Approximately 86% of mothers and 84% of fathers had completed a high school education. Average annual family income for this sample was $35,000. These families had an average of 2.24 children at home including their child with disabilities.

The ages of the children with disabilities ranged between 10 and 72 months: From 0 to 10 months old (1%), 25–36 months old (25%), 37–48 months old (25%), 49–60 months old (17%), and 61–72 months old (25%). Of these children, 44 (55%) were male and 36 (45%) were female. Disabilities of children of participating families included physical disabilities (25%), Down Syndrome (22%), cerebral palsy (20%), mental retardation (9%), visual impairment (5%), hearing impairment (5%), autism (4%), and fragile X (1%). About half (45%) of these children experienced a mild form of disability.

Forty public and private agencies in charge of delivering early intervention and preschool special education services in the state of Georgia were contacted to assist with the recruitment of families. Twenty-five of those agencies, with approximately 30 individual early intervention staff, participated in the study. Participating early intervention services were located throughout rural and urban Georgia. Approximately 48% of the agencies provided services to infants and toddlers, 29% to preschoolers, and 18% to both groups. The types of early intervention/ preschool special education service provided to these children were home-based (35%), center-based (40%), and a combination of both (19%). These children also received a variety of therapies. Nearly 50% of children received between 30 and 60 min of physical therapy a week. About 44% of children received occupational therapy, and approximately 70% received at least 20 min of speech therapy.

Procedure

Questionnaires were prepared and distributed to early intervention and preschool special education agencies, which distributed them among those families eligible for the study. Upon receipt of returned parental questionnaires, early intervention staff provided ratings on the involvement of participating mothers and fathers. Families received $10 for both mothers' and fathers' returns, and service agencies received $5 per each family recruited for the study.

Measures

Responses provided by mothers and fathers constituted the largest source of information on which the constructs of interest were based. The instruments used in this study are a combination of both established and relatively new measures. Most of the instruments have been widely used in the study of individuals and typical families, with reported acceptable reliability and validity indices. However, the use of these measures with families of children with disabilities has been limited, providing scarce information about their psychometric properties. The approach used to develop construct measures followed a strategy implemented by Dishion, Patterson, Stoolmiller, and Skinner (1991). Each scale was developed based on previous definitions of already established scales. The resulting scales were then tested for internal consistency using the reliability procedure stipulated in the SPSS statistical package (SPSS Inc., 1990) Items with an item-total correlation of less than .20 were discarded. Principal components analysis was then used to evaluate the scales that were expected to measure the same construct. A single-factor solution was used to ascertain the composition of the latent variables and their respective manifest indicators. Manifest indicators with loadings of less than .30 were eliminated.

Family demographics

Demographic information was collected through the family demographic data sheet. For both mothers' and fathers' models, two indicators of family demographic characteristics were included: maternal education and mothers' reports of total family income, and paternal education and fathers' reports of total income.

Social supports

The social supports construct was measured by the Family Support Scale (FSS; Dunst et al., 1988). This scale includes 18 items rated on a

5 point Likert scale, ranging from "Not at all helpful" (1) to "Extremely helpful" (5).

Marital adjustment

Marital adjustment of mothers and fathers was measured by the Dyadic Adjustment Scale (DAS; Spanier, 1976). Spanier reported an overall scale reliability of .96 and a high correlation (.88) with the Locke-Wallace Marital Adjustment Scale.

Family functioning

The McMaster Family Assessment Device (FAD; Miller, Bishop, Epstein, and Keitner, 1985) was used to assess family functioning. The FAD is a 60-item multidimensional measure, based on the McMaster Model of Family Functioning (MMFF). The FAD scales included in this study were problem solving, communication, roles, affective involvement, and general functioning.

Stress

Stress of mothers and fathers was assessed by two measures, namely, the Hassles and Uplifts Scale (DeLongis, Folkman, and Lazarus, 1988) and the Center for Epidemiologic Studies Depression Scale (CES-D; Radloff, 1977). The Hassles and Uplifts Scale consists of 53 items which participants rate on how much of a hassle and/or uplift they were for them that day on a 4 point scale ranging from "None or not applicable" (0) to "A great deal" (0). The CES-D is a 20-item scale used to assess depressed mood, feelings of guilt and worthlessness, feelings of help-lessness and hopelessness, psychomotor retardation, loss of appetite, and sleep disturbance. This scale was designed for use in studies of the epidemiology of demographic symptomatology in the general popula-tion. The symptoms assessed are those that may be associated with clinical diagnosis of depression but which may also accompany other diagnoses, such as "normal" (Radloff, 1977, p. 385). The possible range of scores is zero to 60, with the higher scores indicating more symp-toms, weighed by frequency of occurrence during the past week.

Coping

Coping, or response to stress, of mothers and fathers was assessed through the Coping Orientations to Problems Experienced Scale (COPE;

Carver, Scheier, and Weintraub, 1989). This instrument assesses people's active coping efforts as well as serving to distinguish among several distinct aspects of active coping. The COPE also was developed to measure a set of coping responses that may potentially impede or interfere with active coping (Carver et al., 1989). In our study, all COPE items were introduced except the suppression of competing activities and restraint coping scale items.

Parent involvement

Parent involvement was measured by using service providers' ratings of parent involvement in a revised version of the Parent Involvement Index (PII; Lowitzer, 1989). Service agency staff were asked to rate parents as low, average, or high on three aspects of involvement: (1) parental attendance, that is, attending Individual Educational Program (IEP) and Individual Family Service Plans (IFSP) meetings, nonrequired activities such as workshops, scheduled appointments, and so on; (2) parental knowledge, that is, knowledgeable about their child's disability, his or her right to education, and so on; (3) parental cooperation, that is, parental assistance in projects, providing carryover of the child's goals into the home. Scores in the three areas were aggregated to create an overall index of parental involvement.

The parent involvement measure used in this study underwent face and content validity work as part of a pilot study conducted prior to this investigation (Gavidia-Payne, 1992). Three judges were asked to comment on the presentation, wording, and actual content of the items. As a result of this process, some wording of the items was modified. In addition, service providers' ratings of maternal and paternal involvement were correlated with mothers' and fathers' ratings of their own involvement in early intervention programs. Service providers' ratings and fathers' ratings correlated highly in total paternal involvement, $r(67) = .39, p < .001$, attendance, $r(67) = .48, p < .001$, and knowledge, $r(67) = .44, p < .001$. Service providers' ratings and mothers' ratings correlated significantly in the cooperation scale, $r(75) = .23, p < .04$, only. The moderate correlations between mothers' and service providers' ratings may be an indication of the various groups' differing perceptions of the same events. The strong internal consistency indices, on the other hand, are clear evidence of the reliability of the parent involvement measure.

Results

Findings are presented in four steps: (1) a report of the descriptive characteristics and differences of the measurement (manifest) variables, which constitute the latent constructs separately for mothers and fathers; (2) examination of the correlations among latent variables separately for mothers and fathers; (3) report of the measurement model via the examination of the adequacy of manifest variables as indicators of their respective latent constructs for both groups of mothers and fathers; and (4) presentation of separate models for mothers and fathers, testing for the adequacy of the model in predicting paternal and maternal involvement.

Descriptive characteristics of measurement variables

The means, standard deviations, and t tests for differences between mothers and fathers for all the measurement variables are displayed in table 12.1. The means for maternal and paternal involvement indicate high involvement in their children's early intervention programs. These mothers and fathers also experience about average marital adjustment, average family functioning, and relatively low levels of depression. The standard deviations in the CES-D indicate considerable variability. The t tests indicate significant differences between various maternal and paternal constructs.

Relations among latent variables

Latent variables included in these correlations were those generated by the exploratory factor analysis described earlier. Correlations are presented in table 12.2, part A, for mothers and table 12.2, part B, for fathers. Maternal education and income levels were positively associated with maternal involvement, problem-focused coping, and family functioning, and negatively correlated with maternal stress. Increased maternal social supports were linked to healthier family functioning and marital adjustment, increased levels of problem-focused coping, and higher involvement. Maternal perceptions of marital adjustment were correlated strongly with family functioning, stress, and problem-focused

Table 12.1 Results of *t* tests for differences between mothers and fathers in all manifest variables

Variables	Mothers (N = 75) M	SD	Fathers (N = 67) M	SD	t
Demographics:					
Education	2.86	1.20	2.91	1.34	0.93
Total income	4.04	2.14	4.14	2.26	1.51
Parental involvement:					
Attendance	7.96	1.35	5.21	2.16	11.13***
Knowledge	10.26	2.13	7.81	2.97	8.52***
Cooperation	12.68	2.76	8.67	3.36	10.90***
Marital adjustment:					
Consensus	49.28	7.58	47.26	8.79	2.16*
Satisfaction	38.58	5.29	38.50	5.50	0.15
Cohesion	13.58	3.48	13.26	3.25	0.36
Affection	8.92	2.49	8.92	2.40	1.21
Family functioning:					
Problem solving	3.07	0.39	3.07	0.37	0.05
Communication	2.95	0.35	2.90	0.33	0.92
Roles	2.63	0.45	2.76	0.34	−2.97**
Affective involvement	3.06	0.43	3.02	0.45	0.66
General functioning	2.96	0.29	2.91	0.25	1.34
Family social supports:					
Informal kin	9.05	5.05	8.01	2.12	1.90
Formal kin	6.58	4.21	5.58	3.78	2.45**
Cope:					
Active coping	8.51	2.13	7.98	2.12	1.62
Planning	9.14	2.42	7.98	2.42	1.28
Seeking social supports/instrumental	12.37	3.29	9.72	3.09	5.58***
Seeking social supports/emotional	11.92	3.24	8.33	2.96	7.28***
Positive reinterpretation and growth	9.17	1.95	8.88	2.00	1.01
Acceptance	8.92	2.05	8.64	2.02	0.85
Turning to religion	11.64	3.86	10.57	4.03	2.95**
Focus on and venting of emotions	10.55	2.86	8.72	3.11	3.81***
Denial	14.91	1.73	14.56	1.83	1.38
Stress:					
Household	5.52	3.97	2.14	2.76	6.64**
Financial	3.78	3.57	3.80	3.77	−0.03
Work	2.66	2.50	4.66	4.01	−3.88***
Home management	3.28	3.14	2.38	3.02	1.92
Health	2.04	2.53	1.25	1.80	2.10*
Personal life	1.71	2.28	1.45	1.96	0.72
Family and friends	2.95	2.76	2.38	2.87	1.37
CES-D depression	6.60	8.32	4.27	6.56	2.02*

Notes: * $p < 0.05$. ** $p < 0.01$. *** $p < 0.001$.

Table 12.2 Correlation matrix for latent variables

A. Mothers	1	2	3	4	5	6	7	8	9
1 Family demographics	1.00								
2 Social supports	0.15	1.00							
3 Hassles at work	-0.11	-0.09	1.00						
4 Family functioning	0.25*	0.28**	0.00	1.00					
5 Marital adjustment	-0.06	0.29**	0.00	0.59***	1.00				
6 Stress	-0.38***	-0.04	0.35**	-0.34**	-0.22*	1.00			
7 Problem-focused coping	0.28**	0.38***	-0.03	0.22**	0.17	-0.21*	1.00		
8 Coping by turning to religion/denial	0.20*	0.18*	-0.07	0.26*	0.07	-0.26**	0.14	1.00	
9 Maternal involvement	0.40***	0.27*	-0.04	0.21*	0.12	-0.26**	0.38***	0.32**	1.00

B. Fathers	1	2	3	4	5	6	7	8	9
1 Family demographics	1.00								
2 Social supports	0.09	1.00							
3 Family functioning	-0.08	0.11	1.00						
4 Marital adjustment	-0.21*	0.07	0.71***	1.00					
5 Stress	0.03	-0.18	-0.47***	0.44***	1.00				
6 Coping by seeking social support	0.09	0.21*	0.41***	0.25*	0.15	1.00			
7 Coping by turning to religion/denial	0.17	0.47***	0.29**	0.28**	-0.25*	0.28**	1.00		
8 Problem-focused coping	0.35***	0.13	0.36***	0.28**	-0.27**	0.48***	0.42***	1.00	
9 Paternal involvement	0.49***	0.26*	0.16	0.11	-0.17	0.38**	0.31**	0.27**	1.00

Notes: * $p < 0.05$. ** $p < 0.01$. *** $p < 0.001$.

coping and moderately with maternal involvement. Higher maternal stress was linked to lower family functioning, marital adjustment, coping, and maternal involvement. Mothers' problem-focused coping was positively related to maternal involvement.

For fathers, the demographic composite (i.e., level of education and family income) was significantly linked with marital adjustment, problem-focused coping, and paternal involvement. Increased perceptions of paternal social supports were related to increased levels of coping by seeking social support, turning to religion, and absence of denial. A pattern of negative correlations was found between stress and family functioning, marital adjustment, and coping. Finally, coping by seeking social support, turning to religion, and problem-focused coping were positively related to paternal involvement.

Measurement models

Model testing of maternal and paternal involvement in early intervention programs implementing structural equation modeling (SEM) constituted the core of the analyses. Latent variable path analysis with partial least squares (LVPLS), a data analysis package developed by Lohmoeller (1984), was used to calculate the measurement models and, subsequently, the full models separately for mothers and fathers.

The basic rationale for the use of LVPLS is that it provides the user with an indication of how well a structural model fits the data. Also, it allows for the consideration of the direct and indirect influences among latent constructs, all of which are included in the present study's hypotheses. More important, SEM with partial least squares was initially developed by Wold (1975) for situations in which data do not meet the highly restrictive assumptions (e.g., sample size, the need for inclusion of all relevant variables, assumption of multivariate normality of distribution of variables) that underlie maximum likelihood techniques such as LISREL (Falk and Miller, 1992).

Structural model analyses

The results of the models for mothers and fathers are presented in Table 12.3. Regression path coefficients, correlations between predictor and predicted latent constructs (i.e., amount of variance in the outcome

Table 12.3 Results for mothers' and fathers' models

Variables	Mothers		Fathers	
	Beta	r	Beta	r
Hassles at work:[a]				
Family demographics	−0.10	−0.11	—	—
Social supports	−0.08	−0.09	—	—
Family functioning:				
Family demographics	0.18*	0.22	−0.09	−0.08
Social supports	0.30*	0.32	0.12	0.11
Hassles at work	0.05	0.00	—	—
Stress:				
Family demographics	−0.35*	−0.38	0.01	0.03
Social supports	0.06	−0.04	0.00	−0.18
Hassles at work	0.35*	0.35	—	—
Family functioning	−0.31*	0.31	−0.47*	0.47
Problem-focused coping:				
Social supports	−0.33*	0.38	0.09	0.13
Hassles at work	0.06	−0.03	—	—
Family functioning	0.15*	0.31	0.35*	0.36
Stress	−0.18*	−0.21	0.13*	−0.28
Coping by turning to religion/denial:				
Social supports	0.13	0.18	0.44*	0.47
Family functioning	0.13*	0.24	0.20*	0.29
Stress	−0.22*	−0.26	−0.08	−0.25
Parental involvement:				
Family demographics	0.26*	0.40	0.49*	0.49
Social supports	0.11*	0.27	0.09	0.26
Hassles at work	0.05	−0.04	—	—
Stress	−0.07	−0.26	−0.13	−0.17
Problem-focused coping	0.22*	−0.38	−0.17	0.27
Coping by seeking social supports	—	—	0.34*	0.38
Coping by turning to religion/denial	0.20*	0.32	0.13*	0.31
Coping by seeking social supports:[b]				
Social supports	—	—	0.16*	0.21
Family functioning	—	—	0.39*	0.41
Stress	—	—	0.20	−0.02

Notes: [a]Variable included in mothers' model only. [b]Variable included in fathers' model only.

variables accounted for by the paths coefficients), are indicated. Falk and Miller (1992) assert that the path coefficient multiplied by its corresponding correlation provides an estimate of the percentage of the variance explained. A predictor variable should account for at least 1.5% of the variance in a predicted variable.

Path coefficients that account for sufficient variance (i.e., above 2%) are signaled with an asterisk in Table 12.3. Another set of statistics included in the analysis and reported in this study is the coefficient RMS COV (E,U), which stands for the root mean square of the covariance between the residuals of the manifest and latent variables. This is an index of how well the model as a whole fits the variance of the data, and it represents the correlation between the variance of the manifest and latent variables not accounted for by the model relations (Falk and Miller, 1992). This coefficient is zero in a model that perfectly describes the relations between all the variables, whereas a coefficient above .20 is evidence of an inadequate model. Finally reported are the squared multiple correlations of latent variables (arithmetic average of the multiple R squares for all the endogenous variables), and the communality index (h^2). A value below .30 in the latter also indicates a poor fit of the model to the data.

Mothers' model

Figure 12.2 illustrates those coefficient paths accounting for sufficient variance in their respective endogenous variables. Several paths were not sufficiently strong to warrant inclusion in the presentation of the model in figure 12.2. Higher income and level of education were related to lower maternal stress ($\beta = -.35$), healthier perceptions of family functioning ($\beta = .18$), and higher maternal involvement ($\beta = .40$). Increased levels of maternal social supports were associated with healthier family functioning ($\beta = .30$), and increased problem-focused coping ($\beta = .33$). Mothers' healthier perceptions of family functioning contributed to lower levels of stress ($\beta = -.31$) and increased problem-focused coping ($\beta = .15$). Lower levels of hassles at work are associated with lower maternal stress ($\beta = .35$), which in turn lead to increased problem-focused coping ($\beta = -.18$) and coping by turning to religion and less denial ($\beta = -.22$).

Of particular importance are the direct paths between the various coping strategies and maternal involvement. Increased problem-focused

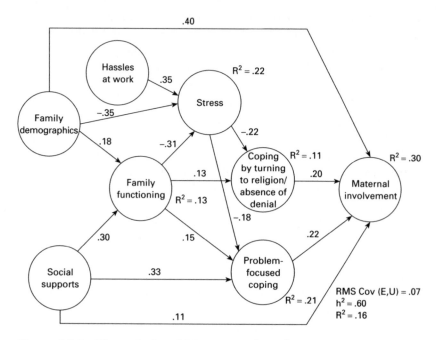

Figure 12.2　Theoretical model for maternal involvement

coping ($\beta = .22$) and coping by turning to religion, and less denial ($\beta = .20$) were associated with higher levels of maternal involvement. The mothers' model yielded an RMS Coy (E,U) = .07, a mean communality coefficient of $h = .60$, and a mean $R = .16$. These figures indicate a moderately strong fit of the model to the data.

Fathers' model

Figure 12.3 presents the predominant path coefficients in the fathers' model. Family demographics accounts for a considerable amount of variance in paternal involvement ($\beta = .49$). Similarly, a reasonably strong path between family functioning and stress ($\beta = -.47$) indicates that fathers' healthier perceptions of family functioning were associated with less stress, which in turn contributes to increased levels of problem-focused coping ($\beta = -.13$). Healthier paternal perceptions of family functioning were also directly associated with increased levels of problem-focused coping ($\beta = .35$), increased coping by seeking social

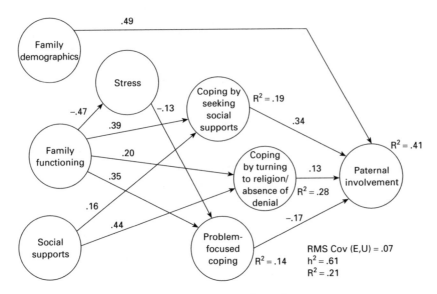

Figure 12.3 Theoretical model for paternal involvement

supports (β = .39), increased coping by turning to religion and less denial (β = .20). The latter coping strategies were in turn positively related to paternal involvement (coping by seeking social supports, β = .34; coping by turning to religion and absence of denial, β = .13). Last, the fathers' model provides strong evidence of a good fit to the data: RMS Cov (E,U) = .07, h^2 = .61, R^2 = .21.

The relations between stress and coping by seeking social supports and between problem-focused coping and paternal involvement deserve further analysis. As indicated earlier, the signs for the path coefficients and correlation coefficients for both of these associations were opposite. As Falk and Miller (1992) suggest, this scenario may be indicative of the existence of a suppressor effect. In such cases, if a large amount of variance in one construct is accounted for by the other constructs in the model, this may considerably alter the path coefficients between that variable and the other constructs it predicts. To test this possibility, the path coefficient from family functioning to coping by seeking social supports was eliminated from the fathers' model. As a result of this modification, the path coefficient between coping by seeking social supports and stress dropped significantly, confirming the existence of a suppressor effect between these two variables. A similar phenomenon occurred in the relation between problem-focused coping and, paternal involvement. In this case, the "suppressing variable" (i.e., family demographics) was not directly linked with problem-focused coping; however, it masked the relation between problem-focused coping and paternal involvement. By eliminating the path between family demographics and paternal involvement, the sign of the path coefficient between problem-focused coping and paternal involvement changed to a positive value. This modification in the model not only made the path coefficient between problem-focused and parental involvement significant, but it also decreased the amount of variance accounted for by the model. In view of this scenario, it was feasible to consider the existence of an interaction between family demographics and problem-focused coping in relation to paternal involvement. This possibility was tested by performing a 2×2 ANOVA. The results disclosed significant interactions between family demographic levels and problem-focused coping levels on paternal involvement, $F(3, 67) = 4.19$, $p < .05$. Tests of simple main effects were conducted through a one-way ANOVA to determine differences between group levels. This analysis yielded significant differences on paternal involvement between the low family demographic–low coping group ($x = 17.1$) and the high family demographic–low coping group of fathers ($x = 25.7$).

Discussion

The purpose of this study was to explore the ability of family characteristics to predict maternal and paternal involvement in early intervention programs. Our findings support the contention that maternal and paternal perceptions of family processes, dyadic relationships, and well-being influence the extent to which mothers and fathers become involved in their children's early intervention programs.

Relations formulated in the hypothesis in regard to maternal involvement were supported. Mothers who enjoyed greater financial security and who were more educated tended to become more involved in their children's programs. This finding is consistent with previous research conducted in the area (Lowitzer, 1989). Also, mothers who experienced less stress and who consistently employed a variety of coping strategies tended to be more involved. Through the use of problem-focused strategies, in particular, these mothers initiate and plan direct actions that eventually lead them to take an active role in their children's programs. Furthermore, mothers' experience of fewer hassles enhances their capacity to handle demands through active planning and seeking instrumental and emotional support with friends, relatives, and through their religious affiliations. Other studies have also found that mothers in families of children with disabilities tend to employ problem-focused coping strategies (Frey et al., 1989) and rely on religious supports (Fewell and Vadasy, 1986; Friedrich, Cohen, and Wilturner, 1988) in dealing with stress. Also, mothers' assessments of their family functioning influence maternal involvement indirectly through coping. It is likely that mothers' perceptions of their family interactions as being more healthy enhance their coping abilities, which in turn mobilize their involvement.

As for paternal involvement, findings partially support the proposed hypotheses with the emergence of somewhat more complex relations among variables. Fathers who actively employed coping strategies, such as seeking instrumental and social supports and who also coped by turning to religion/absence of denial, become more involved in their children's programs. This is consistent with the notion suggested by other authors (Markowitz, 1984) who report that fathers participate in their children's programs indirectly. It is likely that fathers in this sample become involved by seeking services for their children, even though they may not attend meetings or actively communicate with service providers. The more educated and more financially secure fathers were more involved in their children's programs. Furthermore, low problem-solving coping fathers who reported greater financial resources and education were the most involved. This finding highlights the notion that the usefulness of problem-focused coping (i.e., taking action, planning, positive reinterpretation) may not be in itself of great significance to paternal involvement unless fathers are educated and financially secure. It is also important to note that paternal problem-focused coping is the only strategy associated with family demographics. Thus, it is possible that fathers utilize other coping mechanisms independently from environmental influences.

Another set of hypotheses, which predicted a positive relation between maternal social supports and coping either directly or through family functioning were also confirmed. This is not surprising because previous research suggests that mothers with strong social supports cope better than mothers with diminished levels of support (Friedrich, Cohen, and Wilturner, 1985). The indirect path between maternal social supports and coping by turning to religion/absence of denial through family functioning indicates that mothers' healthy family relationships strengthen their capacity to use a wider range of coping strategies, including both problem-focused and spiritual orientations. These findings are consistent with previous research (Friedrich, 1979; Friedrich et al., 1985) indicating that marital satisfaction is a strong predictor of how well mothers of children with disabilities cope with stress.

Family functioning also mediates the relation between maternal social supports and stress. It has been found that the instrumental and expressive role of partners, in particular, is critical in determining mothers' perceptions of their families and experience of stress (Bristol, Gallagher, and Schopler, 1988). Mothers' access to significant others is likely to enhance healthy interactions within their immediate family environment (Bristol, 1987; Fewell and Vadasy, 1986) and assist them in their daily caregiving roles. In addition, mothers' perceptions of work hassles are positively linked to their perceptions of stress. Indeed, previous findings suggest that the inadequate distribution of roles in the family, with mothers carrying the weight of daily caregiving, is associated with greater maternal stress (Beckman, 1991; Gallagher, Beckman, and Cross, 1983; Gowen, Johnson-Martin, Goldman, and Appelbaum, 1986; Harris and McHale, 1991). Overall, the relations between social supports, family functioning, and stress are consistent with those in previous research (Crnic, Greenberg, Ragozin, Robinson, and Bashan, 1983; Dunst and Trivette, 1986; Dunst, Trivette, and Cross, 1986) that shows positive associations between social supports and other variables, including family integrity, parenting, and attitudes about family life.

The relation between social supports and family functioning for fathers is less clear. It can be speculated that either lack or availability of social supports is not as critical for fathers, given that their partners are likely to be the major point of contact between their families and their network of resources. Social supports as perceived by fathers, however, are positively and directly linked to two coping constructs (i.e., seeking social supports and turning to religion/absence of denial), and unrelated to the third coping construct (i.e., problem focused). It is possible that the helpfulness of supports perceived by fathers activates more emotional/spiritual rather than problem-focused coping strategies. This assertion is tenable given that fathers may not need to mobilize problem-focused strategies to start with, because they do not tend to experience the consistent and ongoing daily demands that mothers do. Yet fathers' stress, which is most significant in the work domain, is negatively associated with problem-focused coping. These findings suggest that, when compared to mothers, fathers are faced with different stressors and therefore may be using different resources and coping orientations. Research findings about gender differences in cognitive coping with stress (Miller and Kirsch, 1987) are not conclusive. It has been found that men and women do not differ in their use of problem-focused coping, although women tend also to use other strategies such as emotion-focused coping (Billings and Moos, 1981). Other research suggests that men use more problem-focused coping strategies (Folkman and Lazarus, 1980).

The role of family functioning in fathers' stress and coping experiences is also critical. When fathers rate their family environment as more harmonious, cohesive, and orderly, they experience less stress and are able to cope more effectively by taking action, seeking social and instrumental support, and turning to religion. This finding is consistent with previous research about fathers (Frey et al., 1989) indicating that less psychological stress and better family adjustment are associated with a higher proportion of problem-focused coping. Overall, particular dynamics of families may be responsible for mediating stress for its members (Shapiro, 1983), whether this stress arises from financial duress or from within the family itself. Indeed, family resources such as cohesiveness, flexibility, and support may be acting as stress mediators (Hobfoll and Spielberger, 1992).

Finally, support emerged for family demographics as predictors of family functioning and stress for mothers only. It is likely that mothers who enjoy financial security are able to have greater material resources, which in turn enhance satisfaction with and positive interactions within their families. Equally, more educated mothers tend to place more value on issues such as information sharing and problem-solving as ways of engaging in more organized and harmonious relationships within their families. Similar findings are reported elsewhere (Dunst and Trivette, 1986). As for the links between maternal levels of income and education and stress, our findings are consistent with previous research that indicates that resources available to caregivers influence caregivers' subsequent level of stress (Baker, 1989; Brinker, Baxter, and Frazier, 1992).

In sum, findings in the present study underscore the paramount importance of family variables in predicting processes that typically have been conceptualized as program driven. Conceptual frameworks that promote a more ecological approach to guiding empirical studies in the area have been lacking. Fortunately, Bronfenbrenner's theoretical framework (Bronfenbrenner, 1979) among others (Gallimore, Weisner, Kaufman, and Bernheimer, 1989) has been and continues to be employed in research of families of members with disabilities (Dunst et al., 1988). More efforts in this direction are needed as researchers are consistently faced with the challenge to find theoretical referents to guide their work. Thus, the study of parental involvement from perspectives that examine the comparable predicting ability of both family and program variables seem worth pursuing. In addition, with the current emphasis on family-centered approaches in early intervention practice, it may be useful to conceptualize parental involvement as a variable influenced by factors similar to those affecting parenting outcomes.

Theoretically, these findings corroborate typical family models that encompass a variety of family variables to explain particular family and individual outcomes such as parenting, stress, adjustment, and coping (Belsky, 1984; McCubbin, 1979; McCubbin and Patterson, 1983). The predictive strength of coping strategies for both maternal and paternal involvement indicates that cognitive coping is playing a much more important role than previously acknowledged; this type of coping is currently the focus of much attention (Turnbull et al., 1993). Similarly, family functioning, including dyadic and system relationships, should be acknowledged as a significant contributing factor to the understanding of parental involvement.

The generalizability of the present study is limited given the sampling utilized. Also, given the cross-sectional nature of this study, it is not possible to determine causality. Many of the relations between variables posed in the model are reciprocal in nature, exerting mutual interactive influences. In the current model, paths consistent with the guiding conceptual framework were posited and tested.

References

Adams, D. (1976). *Parent involvement: Parent development.* Berkeley, CA: Center for the Study of Parent Involvement.

Baker, B. L. (1989). *Parent training and developmental disabilities* (Monograph of the American Association on Mental Retardation, 13). Washington, DC: American Association on Mental Retardation.

Baker, B. L., Landen, S. J., & Kashima, K. J. (1991). Effects of parent training on families of children with mental retardation: Increased burden or generalized benefit? *American journal on Mental Retardation, 96,* 127–136.

Beckman, P. J. (1991). Comparison of mothers' and fathers' perceptions of the effect of young children with and without disabilities. *American journal on Mental Retardation, 95,* 585–595.

Belsky, J. (1984). The determinants of parenting: A process model. *Child Development, 55,* 83–96.

Billings, A. G., & Moos, R. H. (1981). The role of coping resources and social resources in attenuating the stress of life events. *Journal of Behavioral Medicine, 4,* 139–157.

Brinker, R. P., Baxter, A., & Frazier, W. (1992). *Socio-economic status modulates the effects of family stress and early intervention participation upon subsequent development of infants.* Paper presented at the twenty-fifth annual Gatlinburg Conference on Research and Theory on Mental Retardation and Developmental Disabilities, TN, March 19–21,1992.

Bristol, M. M. (1979). *Maternal coping with autistic children: The effect of child characteristics and interpersonal support.* Unpublished doctoral dissertation, University of North Carolina at Chapel Hill.

Bristol, M. M. (1984). Family resources and successful adaptation to autistic children. In E. Schopler & G. Mesibov (Eds.), *The effects of autism on the family* (pp. 289–311). New York: Plenum.

Bristol, M. M. (1987). Mothers of children with autism or communication disorders: Successful adaptation and the Double ABCX Model. *Journal of Autism and Developmental Disorders, 17,* 469–484.

Bristol, M., Gallagher, J. J., & Schopler, E. (1988). Mothers and fathers of young and developmentally disabled and non-disabled boys: Adaptation and spousal support. *Developmental Psychology, 24,* 441–451.

Brody, G. H., & Stoneman, Z. (1982). Families as teachers of cognitive and language competencies. In J. Worell (Ed.), *Development during the elementary years.* New York: Academic Press.

Bronfenbrenner, U. (1974). *A report on longitudinal evaluations of preschool programs: Vol. 3. Is early intervention effective?* (DHEW publication OHD 76 30025). Washington, DC: U.S. Government Printing Office.

Bronfenbrenner, U. (1979). *The ecology of human development: Experiments by nature and design.* Cambridge, MA: Harvard University Press.

Carver, C. S., Scheier, M. F., & Weintraub, J. K. (1989). Assessing coping strategies: A theoretically based approach. *Journal of Personality and Social Psychology, 56,* 267–283.

Casto, G., & Lewis, A. C. (1984). Parent involvement in infant and preschool programs. *Journal of the Division for Early Childhood, 8,* 49–56.

Crnic, K. A., Greenberg, M. T., Ragozin, A. S., Robinson, N. M., & Bashan, R. B. (1983). Effects of stress and social support on mothers and premature and full-term infants. *Child Development, 54,* 209–217.

Deberry, J. K., Ristau, S. J., & Galland H. C. (1984). Parent involvement programs: Local level status and influences. *Journal of the Division for Early Childhood, 8,* 173–185.

DeLongis, A., Folkman, S., & Lazarus, R. S. (1988). The impact of daily stress on health and mood: Psychological and social resources as mediators. *Journal of Personality and Social Psychology, 54,* 486–495.

Dishion T. J., Patterson, G. R., Stoolmiller, M., & Skinner, M. L. (1991). Family, school, and behavioral antecedents to early adolescent involvement with antisocial peers. *Developmental Psychology, 27,* 172–180.

Dunst, C. J. (1985). Rethinking early intervention. *Analysis and Intervention in Developmental Disabilities, 5,* 165–201.

Dunst, C. J., & Trivette, C. M. (1986). Looking beyond the parent-child dyad for the determinants of maternal styles of interaction. *Infant Maternal Health Journal, 7,* 69–80.

Dunst, C. J., Trivette, C. M., & Cross, A. H. (1986). Mediating influences of family support: Personal, family, and child outcomes. *American Journal of Mental Deficiency, 90,* 403–417.

Dunst, C. J., Trivette, C., & Deal, A. (1988). *Enabling and empowering families: Principles and guidelines for practice.* Cambridge, MA: Brookline.

Early Intervention Research Institute. (1988). *Longitudinal studies of the effects and costs of early intervention for handicapped children* (Annual report, 1987–1988). Logan, UT: Author.

Early Intervention Research Institute. (1990). *Utah parent involvement study* (Report no. 13). Logan, UT: Author.

Epstein, J. I. (1990). School and family connections: Theory, research, and implications for integrating sociologies of education and family. *Marriage and Family Review, 15,* 99–126.

Falk, R. F., & Miller, N. B. (1992). *A primer for soft modeling.* Akron, OH: University of Akron Press.

Fehrman, P. G., Keith, T. Z., & Reimers, T. M. (1987). Home influence on school learning: Direct and indirect effects of parent involvement on high school grades. *Journal of Educational Research, 80,* 330–337.

Fewell. R. R. (1986). The measurement of family functioning. In L. Bickman & D. L. Weatherford (Eds.), *Evaluating early intervention programs for severely handicapped children and their families* (pp. 263–307). Austin, TX: Pro-Ed.

Fewell, R. R., & Vadasy, P. F. (Eds.). (1986). *Families of handicapped children: Needs and supports across the life span.* Austin, TX: PRO-ED.

Folkman, S., & Lazarus, R. S. (1980). An analysis of coping in a middle-age community sample. *Journal of Health and Social Behavior, 21,* 219–239.

Folkman, S., Schatefer, C., & Lazarus, R. S. (1979). Cognitive processes as mediators of stress and coping. In V. Hamilton & D. M. Warburton (Eds.), *Human stress and cognition* (pp. 266–298). New York: Wiley.

Frey, K. S., Greenberg, M. T., & Fewell, R. R. (1989). Stress and coping among parents of handicapped children: A multidimensional approach. *American journal on Mental Retardation, 94,* 240–249.

Friedrich, W. N. (1979). Predictors of the coping behavior of mothers of handicapped children. *Journal of Consulting and Clinical Psychology, 47,*1140–1141.

Friedrich, W. N., Cohen, D. S., & Wilturner, L. T. (1985). Coping resources and parenting mentally retarded children. *American Journal of Mental Deficiency, 90,* 130–139.

Friedrich, W. N., Cohen, D. S., & Wilturner, L. T. (1988). Specific beliefs as moderator variables in maternal coping with mental retardation. *Child Health Care, 17,* 40–44.

Gallagher, J. J., Beckman, P., & Cross, A. H. (1983). Families of handicapped children: Sources of stress and its amelioration. *Exceptional Children, 50,* 10–19.

Gallimore, R., Weisner, T. S., Kaufman, S. Z., & Bernheimer, L. P. (1989). The social construction of ecocultural niches: Family accommodation of developmentally delayed children. *American journal on Mental Retardation, 94,* 216–230.

Gavidia-Payne, S. T. (1992). *The relationship between family functioning and parent involvement in early intervention programs.* Paper presented at the one hundred sixteenth annual meeting of the American Association on Mental Retardation, New Orleans.

Gordon, I. J. (1977). Parent education and parent involvement: Retrospect and prospect. *Childhood Education, 54,* 71–79.

Gowen, J., Johnson-Martin, N., Goldman, B., & Appelbaum, M. (1986). Feelings of depression and parenting competence of mothers of handicapped and nonhandicapped infants: A longitudinal study. *American journal on Mental Retardation, 9,* 259–271.

Griest, D. L., & Forehand, R. (1982). How can I get any parent training done with all these other problems going on: The role of family variables in child behavior therapy. *Child and Family Behavior Therapy, 4,* 73–80.

Griest, D. L., & Wells, K. C. (1983). Behavioral family therapy with conduct disorders in children. *Behavior Therapy, 14,* 37–53.

Grolnick, W. S., & Slowiaczek, M. L. (1994). Parents' involvement in children's schooling: A multidimensional conceptualization and motivational model. *Child Development, 65,* 237–252.

Guralnick, M. J. (1989). Recent developments in early intervention efficacy research: Implications for family involvement in P. L. 99–457. *Topics in Early Childhood Special Education, 9,* 1–17.

Guralnick, M. J. (1993). Second generation research on the effectiveness of early intervention. *Early Education and Development, 4,* 366–378.

Harris, V. S., & McHale, S. M. (1991). Family life problems, daily caregiving activities, and the psychological well-being of mothers of mentally retarded children. *American Journal on Mental Retardation, 94,* 231–239.

Hobfoll, S. E., & Spielberger, C. D. (1992). Family stress: Integrating theory and measurement. *Journal of Family Psychology, 6,* 99–112.

Innocenti, M. S., Hollinger, P. D., Escobar, C. M., & White, K. R. (1993). The cost-effectiveness of adding one type of parent involvement to an early intervention program. *Early Education and Development, 4,* 306–326.

Knussen, C., Sloper, P., Cunningham, C. C., & Turner, S. (1992). The use of the Ways of Coping (Revised) questionnaire with parents of children with Down's Syndrome. *Psychological Medicine, 22,* 775–786.

Langenbrunner, M. R., & Thornburg, K. R. (1980). Attitudes of preschool directors, teachers and parents toward parent involvement in schools. *Reading Improvement, 17,* 286–291.

Laosa, L. M., & Sigel, E. B. (1982). *Families as learning environments for children.* New York: Plenum.

Lazarus, R., & Folkman, S. (1984). *Stress, appraisal, and coping.* New York: Springer.

Lohmoeller, J. (1984). *LVPLS 1.6 program manual: Latent variable path analysis with partial least-squares estimation.* Cologne: Universitaet zu Koehn, Zentralarchiv fuer Empirische Sozialforschung.

Lowitzer, A. (1989). *Family demographics, family functioning, and parent involvement.* Paper presented at the Society for Research in Child Development, Kansas City, MO. (ERIC Document Reproduction Service No. ED 311669)

Markowitz, J. (1984, Summer). Participation of fathers in early childhood special education programs: An exploratory study. *Journal of the Division for Early Childhood, 8,* 119–131.

McCubbin, H. I. (1979). Integrating coping behavior in family stress theory. *Journal of Marriage and the Family, 41,* 237–244.

McCubbin, H. I., & Patterson, J. M. (1983). The family stress process: The double ABCX model of adjustment and adaptation. In H. I. McCubbin, M. B. Sussman, & J. M. Patterson (Eds.), *Social stress and the family: Advances and developments in family stress theory and research* (pp. 7–38). New York: Haworth.

McKinney, B., & Peterson, R. A. (1987). Predictors of stress in parents of developmentally disabled children. *Journal of Pediatric Psychology, 12,* 133–150.

Miller, I. W., Bishop, D. S., Epstein, N. B., & Keitner, G. I. (1985). The McMaster family assessment device: Reliability and validity. *Journal of Marital and Family Therapy, 11,* 345–356.

Miller, S. M., & Kirsch, N. (1987). Sex differences in cognitive coping with stress. In R. C. Barnett, L. Biener, & G. K. Baruch (Eds.), *Gender and stress* (pp. 159–184). New York: Free Press.

National Education Association. (1972). *Parent involvement: A key to better schools.* Washington, DC: National Education Association.

Olmsted, P. P., & Rubin, R. I. (1983). Parent involvement: Perspectives from the Follow Through experience. In R. Haskins & D. Adams (Eds.), *Parent education and public policy.* Norwood, NJ: Ablex.

Paget, K. D. (1992). Parent involvement in early childhood services. In M. Gettinger, S. N. Elliot, & T. R. Kratochwill (Eds.), *Preschool and early childhood treatment directions* (pp. 89–111). Hillsdale, NJ: Erlbaum.

Radin, N. (1972). Three degrees of maternal involvement in a preschool program: Impact on mothers and children. *Child Development, 43,* 1355–1364.

Radloff, L. S. (1977). The CES-D Scale: A self-report depression scale for research in the general population. *Applied Psychological Measurement, 1,* 385–401.

Reynolds, A. J. (1989). A structural model of first-grade outcomes for an urban, two socioeconomic status, minority population. *Journal of Educational Psychology, 81,* 594–603.

Shapiro, J. (1983). Family reactions and coping strategies in response to the physically ill or handicapped child: A review. *Social Sciences and Medicine, 17,* 913–931.

Slentz, K. L., Walker, B., & Bricker, D. (1989). Supporting parent involvement in early intervention. A role-taking model. In G. H. S. Singer & L. K. Irvin (Eds.), *Support for caregiving families* (pp. 221–267). Baltimore: Paul H. Brookes.

Spanier, G. B. (1976, February). Measuring dyadic adjustment: New scales for assessing the quality of marriage and similar dyads. *Journal of Marriage and the Family, 38,* 15–30.

SPSS, Inc. (1990). *SPSS/PC + 4.0 Base Manual.* Chicago: SPSS.

Stevenson, D., & Baker, D. (1987). The family-school relation and child's school performance. *Child Development, 43,*1348–1357.

Turnbull, A. P., Paterson, J. M., Behr, S. K., Murphy, D. L., Marquis, J. G., & Blue-Manning, A. J. (Eds.). (1993). *Cognitive coping: Families and disability.* Baltimore: Paul H. Brookes.

Turnbull, A. P., Summers, J. A., & Brotherson, M. J. (1986). Family life cycle: Theoretical and empirical implications and future directions for families with mentally retarded members. In J. J. Gallagher & P. Vietze (Eds.), *Families of handicapped persons: Research, programs, and policy issues* (pp. 45–77). Baltimore: Paul H. Brookes.

Turnbull, A. P., & Turnbull, H. R. (1986). *Families, professionals, and exceptionality: A special partnership.* New York: Merrill.

Turnbull, A. P., & Winton, P. J. (1984). Parent involvement policy and practice: Current research and implications for families of young, severely handicapped children. In J. Blacher (Ed.), *Severely handicapped young children and their families: Research in review* (pp. 377–395). Orlando, FL: Academic Press.

Wallat, C., & Goldman, R. (1979). *Home/school/community interaction.* Columbus, OH: Merrill.

Walsh, F. (Ed.). (1982). *Normal family processes.* New York: Guilford.

Wardle, P. (1982). Are parents being left out of their children's early care and education? *Day Care and Early Education, 9,* 29–31.

White, K. R., Taylor, M. J., & Moss, V. D. (1992). Does research support claims about the benefits of involving parents in early intervention programs? *Review of Educational Research, 2,* 91–125.

Wikler, L. M. (1986). Family stress theory and research on families of children with mental retardation. In J. J. Gallagher & P. M. Vietze (Eds.), *Families of handicapped persons: Research, programs, and policy issues* (pp. 167–195). Baltimore: Paul H. Brookes.

Wold, H. (1975). Path models with latent variables: The NIPALS approach. In H. Blalock (Ed.), *Qualitative sociology: International perspectives on mathematic and statistical model building* (pp. 307–357). New York: Academic Press.

Zigler, E., & Muenchow, S. (1992). *Head Start: The inside story of America's most successful educational experiment.* New York: Basic Books.

Part VI

Future Directions

THIRTEEN

The Future of Early Intervention Research and Practice

Although we still have much to learn, the field of early intervention has grown enormously over the past thirty years. While the optimistic predictions of the late 1960s about ending poverty and mental retardation has given away to cautious realism, indeed, there have been great accomplishments. This book highlights but a few of the programs that have demonstrated important and durable effects in improving the lives of at-risk children and their families.

Where do we go from here? As Carl Dunst described in chapter 10, sensitive family-centered programs will continue to evolve and be the primary venue of EI services, especially for children with established disabilities. Nonetheless, specific, intensive child-focused interventions (typically provided within a family-centered context) tend to demonstrate the most powerful results (e.g., chapters 2, 3, 5, and 6) and will continue to be to offered. In this chapter, I highlight some recent events, technological and research advances, and new models that may impact on the EI field in the near future.

Early Detection and Prevention

Virtually everyday brings new discoveries of the genetic mechanisms related to an increasing number of disorders associated with developmental, learning, motor, sensory, and behavioral problems. For example, a recent study has implicated maternal excess production of dopamine during pregnancy coupled with fetal susceptibility as a possible mechanism of some forms of autism (Robinson, Schutz, Macciardi, White, and Holden, 2001). These discoveries have major implications for early detection, prevention, and intervention. Like Down syndrome, many more genetic diseases will be detectable during fetal development, and many parents-to-be will be faced with difficult decisions. With other conditions that do not manifest at birth, genetic testing (along with family histories and other information) could give accurate information about susceptibility (i.e., the probability of acquiring the condition). Under these circumstances, high-risk infants can be targeted for close monitoring and preventative interventions. Using the autism example above, if it is possible to identify newborns at higher risk for becoming autistic, then the infants could be followed very closely. If the child begins to show incipient autistic symptoms (e.g., lack of social responsiveness, stereotypic behaviors), then the parents could be offered strategies to reroute aberrant behavior and promote more typical development by, for example, creating a special early learning home environment.

Of course, at this point this type of preventative EI is conjecture, and even if biological mechanisms can be identified, much more research is required to ascertain the developmental processes and validate early screening instruments and prevention strategies. Further in the future lies the possibility of gene therapy where genes related to particular disorders could be fixed or replaced by genes associated with healthy development. It is important to remember, however, that most genetic conditions are not the result of one defective gene and that for most diseases the biological links are extremely complex.

Best-fit and Practice Models

Another recent technological advance has been in the survival of very low birth-weight newborns (<2,000g.). These children are at-risk for developmental and medical problems. As was seen in chapter 5, intensive EI offered through the IHDP in the US was not effective for these children (although it was for heavier low birth-weight children). These findings highlight the need for more focused forms of EI research and intervention. Typically, parents are offered an array of services and children with different problems are enrolled together in the same type of EI program. The ecological-interactional developmental model stressed throughout this book serves to encourage research that identifies service variables that produce maximum benefits, given a particular set of biological and environmental factors. This research should enhance the provision of tailor-made programs for specific disorders. What may be appropriate and effective for a child with Down syndrome, for example, may be quite different than for a child with Fragile X syndrome.

To carry this approach one-step further, research will begin to identify best-fit models that not only tailor programs to specific child characteristics, but also take into account parent, family, and neighborhood factors. Thus, a EI program for Down syndrome offered to a low-income, socially isolated, single parent may have shared and different features to a program offered to a two- parent, well-resourced family. Families most in need often are not receptive to EI services because they do not see them as being relevant or sensitive to their own situation. Recent "two-generation" (St Pierre et al., 1995) and cultural-specific programs (Bruder, Anderson, Schultz, and Caldera, 1991) are consistent with a best-fit approach that addresses the entire family context, but more process and evaluative studies are needed.

The implementation of effective comprehensive EI models will require close attention to quality control. Chapter 2 described how empirically supported interventions get watered down when they are implemented on a large scale. Research is needed on effective dissemination strategies to efficiently move knowledge from research to practice (Odom and Kaiser, 1997). New implementation research could examine effective methods to promote and ensure culturally sensitive (Wayman, Lynch, and Hanson, 1990) and inclusive practices (Buell and Minnes, 1994).

Early Parenting Education and Health Promotion

Through epidemiological research and studies of resilient children, we now have considerable evidence-based knowledge of which prenatal and postnatal experiences, and parenting styles lead to optimal developmental outcomes in at-risk children (J. Robinson, 2000). Parents are assumed to know how to do it naturally (parental instinct theory) or have obtained this knowledge through parent role models and personal experience with children (osmosis theory). However, there are far too many children at-risk for poor outcomes that are preventable (e.g., smoking during pregnancy, see chapter 9; lack of parenting skills, see chapter 7). There is increasing recognition of the value of a primary prevention and health promotion approach (Dunst et al., 1994; Odom and Kaiser, 1997), but more perspective parents need to be reached. Healthy life-style, sexual, prenatal and parenting practices as well as information about child development could be efficiently disseminated to a large number of future parents in high school courses. Also, agencies and research centers should continue to set up websites that provide accessible and useful evidence-based information and advice related to parenting and child development. In many countries there is an incredible need to teach adolescents safe-sex practices to reduce the incidence of sexually transmitted diseases, especially HIV/AIDS.

Expansion of EI

Recent EI studies, with a variety of at-risk conditions, have suggested that current EI program durations need to be expanded both downwards and upwards. Impressive long-term longitudinal data from programs that started in infancy (see chapters 3, 5, 8, 9, 11) have resulted in increased funding for EI programs for at-risk infants (e.g., Early Head Start). At the same time, well-controlled studies have indicated that for maximum and sustained benefits, EI may need to continue into the primary school years (chapter 3; Reynolds and Temple, 1998). In the near future in many jurisdictions, it may become routine for school boards to be responsible for infant and preschool EI services, in order to promote a seamless transition of specialized programs into the school years.

There also is need for extension of developmental goals of many EI programs. Most programs for children at-risk for school failure have focused on improving cognitive development (usually measured by IQ tests). However, programs that also emphasize the development of social competence may generate a broader range of long-term benefits in healthy adult adjustment (Weikart, 1998). For example, it is well-known that children with developmental delay are at increased risk for serious, life-long behavioral and psychiatric disorders, yet few infant development and preschool programs for these children address the prevention of these problems. As we learn more about the genesis of behavior disorders in children with developmental delay (Feldman, Hancock, Rielly,

Minnes, and Cairns, 2000), future research could identify effective prevention strategies (e.g., creating natural and specialized learning environments that promote communicative and social competence and discourage aberrant behavior) that could be incorporated into existing EI programs.

Conclusion

This chapter highlighted but a few of the upcoming trends and developments in EI research and practice. The new millennium has heralded a renewed interest in prevention and EI. Funding for EI research and programs has increased dramatically and programs are adopting more evidence-supported interventions. At the same time, in the US and other developed countries, there are now a greater proportion of at-risk children (especially those living in poverty) than ever before. Many developing countries lack even rudimentary EI services that could be very effective in improving childhood health and development. Thus, despite tremendous gains, considerable work remains to reach as many at-risk children as possible to help them overcome early adversities.

References

Bruder, M. B., Anderson, R., Schultz, G., & Caldera, M. (1991). Project profile: Ninos Especiales Program, a culturally sensitive early intervention model. *Journal of Early Intervention, 15*, 268–277.

Buell, M. K. & Minnes, P. M. (1994). An acculturation perspective on deinstitutionalization and service delivery. *Journal on Developmental Disabilities, 3*, 94–107.

Dunst, C. J., Trivette, C. M., & Thompson, R. B. (1994). Supporting and strengthening family functioning: Toward a congruence between principles and practice. In C. J. Dunst & C. M. Trivette (Eds), *Supporting & strengthening families, Vol. 1: Methods, strategies and practices* (pp. 49–59). Cambridge, MA: Brookline Books.

Feldman, M. A., Hancock, C. L., Rielly, N., Minnes, P., & Cairns, C. (2000). Behavior problems in young children with or at risk for developmental delay. *Journal of Child and Family Studies, 9*, 247–261.

Odom, S. L. & Kaiser, A. P. (1997). Prevention and early intervention during early childhood: Theoretical and empirical bases for practice. In W. E. McLean Jr. (Ed.), *Ellis' handbook of mental deficiency, psychological theory and research.* Third Edition (pp. 137–172). Mahwah, NJ: Lawrence Erlbaum Associates.

Reynolds, A. J. & Temple, J. A. (1998). Extended early childhood intervention and school achievement: Age thirteen findings from the Chicago Longitudinal Study. *Child Development, 69,* 231–246.

Robinson, J. L. (2000). Are there implications for prevention research from studies of resilience? *Child Development, 71,* 570–572.

Robinson, P. D., Schutz, C. K., Macciardi, F., White, B. N., & Holden, J. J. (2001). Genetically determined low maternal serum dopamine beta-hydroxylase levels and the etiology of autism spectrum disorders. *American Journal of Medical Genetics, 100,* 30–36.

St. Pierre, R., Layzer, J., & Barnes, H. (1995). Two-generation programs: Design, cost, and shared-term effectiveness, *The Future of Children, 5,* 76–93.

Wayman, K. I, Lynch, E. W., & Hanson, M. J. (1990). Home-based early childhood services: Cultural sensitivity in a family systems approach. *Topics in Early Childhood Special Education, 10*(4), 56–75.

Weikart, D. P. (1998). Changing early childhood development through educational intervention. *Preventive Medicine, 27,* 233–237.

Index